D1446646

# PORTENTS
# OF
# REBELLION

# PORTENTS
# OF
# REBELLION

RHETORIC AND REVOLUTION IN
PHILADELPHIA, 1765–76

# STEPHEN E. LUCAS

TEMPLE UNIVERSITY
PRESS
PHILADELPHIA

Temple University Press, Philadelphia 19122
© 1976 by Temple University. All rights reserved
Published 1976
Printed in the United States of America

International Standard Book Number: 0-87722-087-5
Library of Congress Catalog Card Number: 75-30281

TO MY MOTHER

# CONTENTS

# FOREWORD

"THE real American Revolution," John Adams wrote in 1818, was the "radical change in the principles, opinions, sentiments, and affections of the people" which took place during the eleven years preceding the Declaration of Independence. Primarily a psychological and spiritual phenomenon, this Revolution occurred "in the minds and hearts of the people" and was guided by the rhetoric of Whig writers and speakers.[1] Samuel and John Adams, Josiah Quincy, Jr., Thomas Jefferson, Arthur Lee, James Otis, William Livingston, Patrick Henry, John Dickinson, and many others wrote and distributed hundreds of pamphlets, essays, and broadsides, organized carefully planned demonstrations, composed persuasive songs, plays, and poems, and delivered countless speeches and sermons designed to increase discontent with British rule. When the conflict between England and the colonies began in the 1760s, few Americans seriously anticipated independence. Moreover, the probability of the thirteen colonies' acting together on anything appeared remote; they seemed more likely to war with one another than with England. It was partly through the rhetoric of colonial protesters that Americans reached a level of focused dissatisfaction which ultimately impelled them to seek independence from British rule.

This was the belief of many Americans who lived through the dramatic 1760s and 1770s. To Loyalist commentators and historians the Revolution was, in the words of Peter Oliver of Massachusetts, "the most wanton and unnatural rebellion that ever existed." "The whole story of empire," said Daniel Leonard, could not "furnish another instance of a forcible opposition to government with so much apparent and little real cause." Joseph Galloway contended that, at the time the Revolution broke out, "the people in the colonies were more free, unencumbered, and happy than any others on earth."[2] To men like Oliver, Leonard, and Galloway, the onset of revolutionary turmoil resulted from "the pride, ambition, and resentment of a few abandoned demagogues, who were lost to all sense of shame and of humanity." Leonard put the Loyalists' interpretation trenchantly in his "Massachusettensis" letters. From the very beginning of the imperial controversy, he explained, the agitation against England was directed by a handful of firebrands who sought to enhance their own political ambitions by creating "an American commonwealth, upon the ruin of the British constitution." But knowing there was "no oppression which could be either seen or felt," these schemers set out to inflame the public temper "by publications charged with falsehood and scurrility." By their "perpetual incantation[s]" Whig incendiaries infused "the subtle poison" of disaffection "into the body of the people," where it "stole through all the veins and arteries, contaminated the blood, and destroyed the very stamina of the constitution." In this fashion, Leonard believed, fundamentally decent and loyal citizens were duped into sanctioning civil war and rebellion.[3]

Americans who supported the Revolution naturally interpreted its ultimate causes and the motives of the men who directed it much differently than did the Loyalists. Yet Whigs and Loyalists were in substantial agreement that anti-British writers and speakers played vital roles in shaping public opinion against the mother country. William Gordon, the first participant in the Revolution to publish a history of it, stressed the significance of the Whigs' "command of the press," which gave them "the superiority in point of influence, over their antagonists in the periodical publications of the day." David Ramsay, another participant-historian, believed that "in establishing American independence, the pen and the press had merit equal to that of the sword." He thought the Revolution would never have come about "unless the great body of the people had been prepared for it" by Whig writers and orators who "labored in enlightening their countrymen on the subject of their political interests, and in animating them to a proper line of conduct in defense of their liberties." John Adams often noted the persuasive efforts of those, like himself, who labored to alter the colonists' political allegiance. "Thirteen clocks were made to strike together," he marveled, "a perfection of mechanism which no artist had ever before effected." Adams warned that to write a correct account of the Revolution students would have to search all the records, handbills, speeches, pamphlets, and newspapers to discover "by what means this great and important alteration in the religious, moral, political, and social character of the people of the thirteen colonies . . . was begun, pursued, and accomplished."[4]

The testimony of Adams and his contemporaries has special salience in light of what we know today about the nature of revolution and the power of language to evoke social change. Discontent is a psychological phenomenon. Revolutions are rooted less in actual social conditions than in the ways people perceive and respond to those conditions. We live—and eighteenth-century Americans lived—in a symbolically constructed perceptual world in which our sense data "are mediated through a highly learned process of interpretation and acceptance." One of our most important ways of mediating experience—of giving it order, meaning, and evaluative shadings—is through the use of language. As Murray Edelman explains, language does not mirror "reality," but "creates it by organizing meaningful perceptions abstracted from a complex, bewildering world." "The terms in which we name or speak of anything do more than designate it; they place it in a class of objects, thereby suggest with what it is to be judged and compared, and define the perspective from which it will be viewed and evaluated." The linguistic symbols we assign to things, events, and people are not neutral; they are, in Kenneth Burke's words, "loaded with judgments" and thereby "prepare us *for* some functions and *against* others, *for* or *against* the people representing these functions." The verbal symbols we use to make sense of the world coerce our perceptions in ways which invite some types of behavioral responses and deter others: "Call a man a villain, and you have the choice of either attacking or cringing. Call him mistaken and you invite yourself to attempt setting him right."[5]

In short, a choice of words is also a choice of worlds.[6] Language plays a ubiquitous and powerful role in shaping political perceptions, values, and behaviors. For the most part, however, scholarly studies have not assessed the rhetoric of the American Revolution as a means of inducing beliefs that became bases for revolutionary action. Existing accounts of the Revolution are not prominently concerned with explaining the processes of communication by which revolutionary ideas were disseminated, fostered, and intensified. Few have attempted to demonstrate how or why colonial protesters were able through their rhetoric to secure the support of enough Americans to make independence possible.

Consider Moses Coit Tyler's pathbreaking, two-volume *Literary History of the American Revolution.* Surveying the enormous literary output of Whigs and Tories during the years 1763–83, Tyler maintained that the epoch of revolutionary conflict "was a strife of ideas: a long warfare of political logic; a succession of annual campaigns in which the marshalling of arguments not only preceded the marshalling of armies, but often exceeded them in impression upon the final result." By arguing that the Revolution was preeminently "caused by ideas, and pivoted on ideas," Tyler reinforced John Adams's contention that the break from England could not be satisfactorily explained without examining the succession of thoughts and beliefs impressed upon American consciousness during the years preceding the Declaration of Independence. But it was not Tyler's aim to determine how the Whigs' rhetoric contributed to the growth of public support for independence. Rather, he sought to explicate the "inward history" of the Revolution as revealed in the public writings of its participants. His work was essentially a literary history with controlling emphasis upon the artistic and ideological merit rather than upon the persuasive force of colonial discourse.[7]

Since publication of Tyler's work the most noteworthy books on the rhetoric of the Revolution have been written, not by literary or rhetorical critics, but by historians. Yet even the so-called propaganda studies of the Revolution which were prominent in historical scholarship during the middle decades of this century say little of the processes of communicational influence. Philip Davidson's *Propaganda and the American Revolution* is a fair example of this collection of studies. Firmly grounded in the rich store of primary materials, Davidson's work presents an inclusive survey of the propaganda campaigns of Whigs and Loyalists from the Peace of Paris in 1763 to the close of the American struggle for independence in 1783. According to Davidson, the Revolution was "at best but the work of an aggressive minority" who "consciously and systematically" worked to gain public support for their programs. He concluded that without the work of Whig agitators "independence would not have been declared in 1776 nor recognized in 1783." The great value of Davidson's work lies in its comprehensiveness. But therein also lies its major shortcoming. Although he recounts who the propagandists were, what they did, and how they went about it, Davidson does not explain why their varied efforts were successful or unsuccessful. He tells us much about the Whigs' rhetorical techniques, but little about the interactive processes through which those techniques may have influenced colonial opinion. Nor does he provide theoretical grounds for inferring that Whig rhetoric could actually have exerted determinative impact upon the ways Americans thought and acted during the revolutionary era.[8]

In recent years most historians have eschewed the perspectives of the propaganda studies, and no one has done so more emphatically than Bernard Bailyn, in whose writings the "neo-Whig" interpretation of the Revolution has reached its fullest and most succinct expression. The Revolution, Bailyn argues, "was above all else an ideological, constitutional, political struggle and not primarily a controversy between social groups undertaken to force changes in the organization of the society or the economy." Bailyn admits that the Whigs' pamphlets "aim to persuade," but he insistently rejects the notion that the polemical literature of the revolutionary period represented "merely the desire to influence by rhetoric and propaganda the inert minds of an otherwise passive populace." Rather, that literature may be most profitably read as a key to the thoughts, motivations, and actions of the revolutionary leaders. Like most neo-Whig historians, Bailyn is interested less in the ways Whig rhetoric may have influenced popular opinion than in the extent to which it reveals the revolutionaries' "assumptions, beliefs, and ideas—the articulated world view—that lay behind the manifest events of the time."[9]

There can be no gainsaying Bailyn's achievement in explicating the ideas contained in Whig rhetoric and pointing up the salience of those ideas to the revolutionary movement. But by arguing that the Revolution can best be explained by reference to ideological currents, Bailyn, and other neo-Whigs, inevitably invite inquiry concerning how the revolutionary Whig ideology spread and acquired sufficient popular acceptance to trigger the quest for American political autonomy. Neo-Whig historians have emphasized the importance of ideas and perceptions in creating a spirit of independence in colonial America. What has not been adequately explained are the processes of persuasion and reinforcement by which seminal ideas and perceptions were articulated, fostered, promulgated, and intensified. We need to know, as Professor Jack Greene has noted, not only how Whig discourse reflected the revolutionaries' goals, values, and attitudes, but also how that discourse contributed to the development of a revolutionary mentality within "a significant or strategic segment of the politically relevant population."[10] And to know this, we must understand Whig rhetoric as rhetoric has traditionally been conceived and as colonial spokesmen practiced it—as communication designed to influence particular audiences at particular times and places, as strategic means of "adjusting ideas to people and people to ideas" through suasory discourse, as "the use of words by human agents to form attitudes or to induce actions in other human agents."[11]

In short, vital questions about the rhetoric of the Revolution as a mode of social influence have yet to be properly explored. This book seeks answers to those questions. I elected to focus on one center of political and rhetorical activity because throughout the British-American quarrel the conditions which most vitally affected the audiences Whig spokesmen addressed were local rather than intercolonial. Much more than geography separated Americans in one colony from Americans in another. Quaker merchants in Philadelphia, for example, saw themselves as having little in common with Anglican planters in the Virginia tidewater region or with Presbyterian farmers in the Massachusetts backcountry. Nor was there homogeneity of background, outlook, and interest among residents of individual colonies. The march of the Paxton Boys in Pennsylvania, the maraudings of Regulators in South Carolina and North Carolina, and the uprisings of tenant farmers in New York dramatically testify to the presence of diversity. Colonial society was significantly fragmented, and the dispute with England was seldom divorced from economic, political, social, religious, and ethnic squabbles at the local level.[12] To explore the persuasive potential of Whig rhetoric, therefore, it is necessary to consider that rhetoric in relation to local conditions and audiences.

Philadelphia offers an especially interesting locale upon which to concentrate. The colonial cities were entrepôts for radical political philosophy as well as for people, leadership, and events out of which revolutionary activity could arise. No city was more vital than Philadelphia, the cultural and economic hub of the colonies, "the capital of the new world." In size and prosperity it was among the leading cities in the British empire. By influence or experience it was probably known to more Americans than any other colonial city.[13] Although other cities—most notably Boston—have received more attention from historians, Philadelphia with its mix of English, Welsh, German, and Scotch-Irish inhabitants better represented the heterogeneity of the general American population than did Boston. Moreover, Boston was for many reasons atypical in the intensity of its opposition to British rule after 1765. Deep divisions over resistance and rebellion emerged in most parts of America and those divisions were accurately reflected in Philadelphia. As Carl Bridenbaugh, the foremost student of urban life in colonial America, observes, "Not until Americans had learned to think like Americans, and not like transplanted Englishmen, were they ready to sever the ties, sentimental and political, which bound them to the Old World. In Philadelphia, rapidly growing, economically prosperous, secular, democratic and cosmopolitan, that process—in microcosm—is best seen at work."[14]

For historians who may read this book I wish to stress that to evaluate the rhetoric of the Revolution as a mode of social influence does not require one to adopt the view of the propaganda studies that the revolutionary leaders were disingenuous propagandists who cleverly exploited high-sounding political and philosophical principles to beguile an unsuspecting populace into rebellion. It is both possible and desirable to reconcile significant aspects of the propaganda studies with the neo-Whig position that the revolutionaries were sincerely attached to the ideals expressed in their discourse and were motivated by the fear that American rights and liberties were being systematically destroyed by the British government.

For instance, there can be no doubt that the vast majority of the speeches and publications by Whig spokesmen during the years 1765–76 were designed to shape, to guide, to manipulate the perceptions, attitudes, and actions of various segments of the colonial populace. Works of rhetoric are invariably pragmatic;

they seek to perform some task; they function ultimately to produce action or change in the world.[15] So it was with the rhetoric of American revolutionaries. But this does not mean that the revolutionaries did not believe what they said and wrote. Doubtless their claims were at times shrill, hyperbolic, and illogical; the polemical literature of Whig protesters is the last place one should look for an evenhanded consideration of the motives of British leaders or the causes of the Revolution. This is somewhat beside the point, however, for there is no substantive evidence to indicate that Whig publicists were not convinced of the truth of their major assertions. Indeed, it was the very depth and strength of their conviction that American economic interests and political liberties were under deliberate assault from ambitious British politicians that impelled the Whigs to seek to arouse their countrymen. Whig spokesmen consciously and avowedly endeavored to mold and direct public opinion at every stage of the imperial controversy, but they did so in the service of the truth as they saw it.

As the propaganda studies emphasize, however, that truth was not constant across the prerevolutionary decade. Whig leaders necessarily modulated their arguments in response to shifting situations and evolving problems. Consider, for example, the progression of Whig argumentation regarding the proper limits of British authority in America. At the time of the Stamp Act protesters denied the right of Parliament to tax the colonies internally or externally, but they granted that Parliament could superintend the economic activities of Americans for the benefit of the empire as a whole. This position was refined at the time of the Townshend Acts, but it remained the generally accepted Whig view until introduction of the Coercive Acts in 1774. Then, faced with a series of statutes that seemed to imperil the very existence of American freedom, Whigs contended that Parliament possessed no legislative authority whatsoever over the colonies. By July of 1776 the Whigs had renounced British sovereignty altogether.

To acknowledge this strategic evolution of Whig political thought impugns neither the relevance of that thought to the revolutionary movement nor the motives of Whig spokesmen. The Whigs' aim, in the broadest sense, was to defend American property and liberty against the intrusions of Parliament and the ministry. But of what practical value would it have been to insist

strictly upon the right of self-taxation as a defense against the
Coercive Acts? If Parliament could legally alter colonial charters,
tamper with the right of trial by jury, and shut down colonial
ports, there seemed nothing it could not and might not do. By
denying Parliament any right to legislative sovereignty in the
colonies, Whigs formulated creditable grounds for renouncing
the Coercive Acts as illegitimate and erected a theoretical barrier
against further parliamentary encroachments upon American
rights and interests. The claims to exemption from parliamentary interference advanced in 1774 were undeniably much
broader than those advanced in previous years, but Whig
spokesmen are not by this fact indictable as Proteus-like
schemers who shifted argumentative positions whenever they
found it convenient. The premises which underlay their arguments in 1774 were remarkably consonant with the premises
which underlay their demands in 1765. In fact, repudiating
the legislative authority of Parliament actually required little
more than the drawing out to their full, logical extension
premises which had been standard in Whig rhetoric from the
very beginning of the British-American dispute.[16]

Finally, as misleading as it would be to stereotype Whig
leaders as ideological chameleons, it would be no less erroneous
to conceive of the colonial audience as a passive, inert, unsuspecting mass that clever agitators could manipulate at will. Rhetorical transactions are best understood as dynamic interactions
in which rhetors and audiences condition the behaviors of each
other. Whig spokesmen influenced the perceptions and beliefs
of the general citizenry, but the citizenry also exercised important sway over Whig spokesmen. Sometimes the public
lagged behind the Whigs and forced them to moderate their
resistance programs; sometimes the public was in advance of the
Whigs and forced them to accelerate the pace of opposition. In
any case, it is inconceivable that Whig leaders could have mobi-
lized a significant portion of the population against the mother
country unless there had existed clear evidence of injustice or
apparent injustice which Americans perceived as threatening
their well-being. One Philadelphian explained to a correspondent in London late in 1774, "There cannot be a greater
error than to suppose that the present commotions in *America*
are owing to the arts of demagogues; every man thinks and acts
for himself in a country where there is an equal distribution of

property and knowledge." John Adams likewise disparaged any notion that the rift between England and America was ultimately due to anything but the folly and duplicity of the British government. No rhetorician, he stated, could "persuade a large people, for any length of time together, to think themselves wronged, injured, and oppressed unless they . . . saw and felt it to be so."[17] Adams's observation has been confirmed time and again in studies of revolution.[18] Revolutions do not take place unless there is sufficient dysfunction in the existing social system to produce a profound sense of discontent among puissant segments of the society. Nor do revolutions occur without the activities of agitators who cultivate and nurture the seeds of discontent. Whig publicists proved themselves skilled "gardeners," but they could not have brought the seeds of discontent to full bloom without the proper soil and climate.

It should be stressed that I am not particularly concerned with cataloging the rhetorical techniques employed by Philadelphia Whigs. Techniques do not themselves persuade. The ways Whig rhetoricians influenced public opinion and behavior can best be explicated by analysis of the substantive qualities of their discourse—its manifest ideological claims, its latent assertions and meanings, its argumentative methods, its figurative and connotative language, the kinds of perceptions and beliefs it encouraged on the part of listeners and readers. This is not a study of "propaganda" as that term is generally, and pejoratively, used. My focus is not upon the integuments of manipulation, but upon the processes of symbolic influence.

I have tried to sustain two analytical perspectives. One perspective accepts the classical characterization of rhetoric as fundamentally situational in nature. The other is informed by the belief that public discourse operates most powerfully as a mode of social influence, not in its capacity to resolve discrete situations, but in its cumulative impact across time. These perspectives are often portrayed as conflicting. In fact, they are complementary—which is readily apparent when one determines to assess the *functional* attributes of the rhetoric of social and political movements. This book is thus structured at once topically and chronologically. It identifies the controlling motifs of Whig discourse in Philadelphia, traces the development of those motifs in response to emerging situations and problems across the years 1765–76, and judges how those motifs induced Philadelphians to adopt certain perceptions, beliefs, and actions.

The first part of the book sketches the communicational environment in which Philadelphia Whigs operated across the years 1765–76. The second part interprets and evaluates the ways Whig rhetoric contributed to the development of a potentially revolutionary mentality from the time of the Stamp Act in 1765 to the battles of Lexington and Concord in April 1775. During these years protesters sought to mobilize Philadelphians against British colonial policies, but they did not seek to foment a revolution. Nonetheless, the most portentous feature of their rhetoric was its progressively impelling divisiveness. As Whig publicists responded to the progression of British legislation, regulation, and enforcement, they portrayed events, presented issues, and prescribed actions in ways that consistently narrowed and ultimately precluded grounds for compromise with England. The third part of the book treats the public debate over independence in Philadelphia during the first six months of 1776. During these months proponents of leaving the empire competed rhetorically with proponents of continued union. The outcome of this contest is obvious, but the rhetorical and political processes by which the outcome was decided illumine one of the most remarkable periods in American history and provide a fascinating study in communicational influence.

The issues raised in this book bear upon prevailing interpretations of the origins, nature, and meaning of the revolutionary movement—at least as it developed in Philadelphia and Pennsylvania.[19] My inquiry is intended to be more, however, than an excursion into history. At bottom, it is an investigation of human communicative behavior which focuses upon men attempting to persuade their fellows to protest against and eventually to reconstitute their political system. I concentrate upon one complex of communicational phenomena that occurred in one historical context, but the questions I ask about those phenomena are not themselves timebound. They could be asked about any situation in which people seek support for protest or revolutionary activities.

This book began as a case study in the rhetoric of protest and revolution. It exists in part because I was dissatisfied with the efforts of rhetorical analysts to explicate the functions of public discourse in the birth, maturation, and demise of social and political movements. One particularly notable deficiency that still exists is a paucity of works dealing holistically with the rhetoric of individual movements from inception through consummation, a deficiency that grew out of and has in turn reinforced a myopic view of the nature of "social movement" and the role of rhetoric therein.[20] I hope at a later time to explore this subject in full. Here it is sufficient to note that too often analysts fail to come to grips with the intrinsically kinetic nature of movement rhetoric. A social or political movement is not a material object that exists only in a given place and at a given time, but is a progression of human behavior which takes place across time and which must be understood in temporal as well as in spatial terms.[21] Neither a movement nor its discourse is static—both are dynamic, fluid, and mutable. My point is not that the discourse of a movement unfolds chronologically; this has long been acknowledged at a theoretical level.[22] Nor is my contention that movements proceed through various stages and that these stages are accompanied by permutations in rhetoric; this too has long been recognized.[23] The temporal progression of discourse is not as vital to understanding the rhetoric of movements as is the cumulative metamorphosis of discourse in response to emerging exigencies. The development of a movement from the stage of inception to the stage of crisis to the stage of consummation is less important than the ways rhetoric helps to propel the movement from stage to stage, or to retard its development. To demonstrate that the rhetoric of a movement is different at moment C from what it was at moment B, and different at moment B from what it was at moment A, is only propaedeutic to the really crucial tasks of explaining *why* the discourse evolved as it did and of assessing *how* that evolution influenced the nature, direction, intensity, and outcome of the movement. If I have succeeded in this study, it should become apparent that rhetoric may function in social and political movements in ways vastly more complex than is usually recognized.

A few mechanical points require comment. In all quotations from eighteenth-century writings I have modernized spelling, capitalization, and punctuation, but I have retained original italics as indicators of rhetorical emphasis. In ascribing authorship of pamphlets I have followed Thomas R. Adams's authori-

tative bibliographic study of American political pamphlets of the
revolutionary era.[24]

Many people contributed to the preparation of this book.
Lloyd Bitzer, Edwin Black, Frederick Haberman, and Eugene
White read portions of the manuscript. I am appreciative to
each for his suggestions. I am particularly obliged to Carroll Arnold, who lent his talents to this study at every stage of its
development. It has also been my good fortune to receive the
counsel of several historians of the Revolution: Joseph Ernst,
John Frantz, Merrill Jensen, and Richard Ryerson, whose close
critique of an early draft of the study improved the final version
considerably. I also wish to thank Kathy Teitz, who typed most
of the manuscript; Nancy Monahan, who aided in many ways;
Steve Ruben, who rechecked the footnotes; the staffs of Pattee
Library, Pennsylvania State University, and of the Pennsylvania
and Wisconsin Historical Societies, who extended many kind-
nesses; and the Graduate School of the University of Wisconsin–
Madison, which provided financial support. Above all, I am
thankful to my wife, Patty, for her assistance and for her understanding.

*Madison, Wisconsin*
*January 1976*

# PART I

# THE COMMUNICATIONAL ENVIRONMENT

# 1

## THE CITY AND ITS PEOPLE

By 1765 Philadelphia bore little resemblance to the "greene countrie towne" envisioned by William Penn when he founded the city in 1682. Stretching two to three miles along the Delaware River and extending about one and one-half miles inland, it boasted a permanent population of some thirty thousand inhabitants. Although young in comparison with its major rivals, New York and Boston, it exceeded both in population, economic development, and cultural attainments. It was the foremost commercial center in North America, and its size, prosperity, and cosmopolitanism made it one of the leading cities in the British empire. Despite suffering the problems of crime, poor sanitation, and disease that plagued other urban centers of the age, it was thought by many Americans to be an ideal city and it was often praised by foreign visitors such as Lord Adam Gordon.

The city of Philadelphia is perhaps one of the wonders of the world, if you consider its size, the number of inhabitants, the regularity of its streets, their great breadth and length, their cutting one another all at right angles, their spacious public and private buildings, quays and docks, the magnificence and diversity of places of worship, . . . the plenty of provisions brought to market, and the industry of all its inhabitants, one will not hesitate to call it the first town in America, but one that bids fair to rival almost any in Europe.[1]

As might be surmised of a city of such diversity, Philadelphia political opinion was pluralistic from 1765 to the declaration of American independence in 1776, a fact which precluded unanimous opposition to the mother country. Although Philadelphia hosted both continental congresses and was home to some of the most powerful and popular political figures of the age, serious divisions over protest and revolution existed among factions of its large and dynamic population. The success of Whig publicists would depend upon how they used the available channels of communication to bridge those divisions and unite a significant portion of the city's politically relevant citizens behind their programs.[2]

Philadelphia had the most highly developed communications network in the colonies. At the center of this network were the city's English-language newspapers, of which there were five by the time of the Revolution.[3] The *Pennsylvania Gazette* was Philadelphia's oldest established newspaper. Published by Benjamin Franklin and David Hall until 1766, and then by Hall and William Sellers, the *Gazette* maintained a moderate though consistent opposition to British policies through most of the years before the Revolution. The *Pennsylvania Journal,* published by William Bradford, was more outspoken in support of the Whig cause. Bradford was a major figure in the city's resistance movement from the time of the Stamp Act onward. His paper was the most prominent outlet for Whig writers in Philadelphia throughout the prerevolutionary period. The *Journal* and *Gazette* occupied the field until Thomas Wharton and Joseph Galloway set up William Goddard as publisher of the *Pennsylvania Chronicle* in January 1767. Goddard's personal, political, and entrepreneurial relationships with his backers were anything but cordial, however, and in May 1769 Wharton and Galloway withdrew from management of the *Chronicle.* An ardent Whig and imaginative printer, Goddard turned the *Chronicle* into Philadelphia's most popular paper before he closed his presses early in 1774 to organize an intercolonial mail establishment.[4]

Philadelphia gained yet another newspaper in the fall of 1771 when John Dunlap established the *Pennsylvania Packet.* Although Dunlap ran few controversial political pieces during his first two years as printer of the *Packet,* he opened its pages thereafter to a wide range of polemicists. Three new papers were founded in the city during the first four months of 1775. On 24 January Benjamin Towne began publishing the *Pennsylvania Evening Post* and by 1776 had committed his paper firmly to the cause of American independence. In 1783 it became the first American daily. Three days after the first issue of the *Evening Post* appeared, James Humphreys, Jr., began publishing the *Pennsyl-*

*vania Ledger,* which he tried to keep politically impartial. This proved to be impossible in such troubled times, however, and Humphreys's practice of opening his paper to writers of all views earned him the wrath of ardent revolutionaries. In November 1776 he fled to the countryside, but he returned to Philadelphia a year later to print a decidedly Tory *Ledger* during the British occupation of the city. The third new paper begun in 1775 was the *Pennsylvania Mercury,* which was introduced early in April. Published by Enoch Story and Daniel Humphreys, the *Mercury* was funded by Galloway and Wharton to provide a vehicle for pro-British opinion. It operated with modest success until destroyed by fire on the last day of 1775.[5]

With the exception of the triweekly *Evening Post,* Philadelphia newspapers appeared weekly, with occasional supplements and semiweekly issues in times of emergency. A year's subscription cost ten shillings until 1776, when some printers raised the price to fifteen shillings. A typical issue was composed of four compactly printed pages roughly ten by fifteen inches; about one-fourth of these pages was devoted to advertising, one-fourth to foreign news, and the rest to domestic news, poems, essays on political and social themes, and commercial and navigational news. Despite improvements in intercolonial and transatlantic transportation, most news stories were from two to eight weeks old by the time they were printed.

The average circulation of individual newspapers in the major colonial cities was about 1,500 per week from the time of the Stamp Act until the dramatic years 1774–76, when the number rose to a little over 2,500 per week. Only the *Gazette,* the *Journal,* and the *Chronicle* attained these levels of circulation in Philadelphia, but the actual number of readers for every paper far surpassed the number of subscribers inasmuch as copies passed from hand-to-hand and the papers were always available at taverns. It is striking that in 1776 there were five newspapers published in Philadelphia—one for every 6,000 inhabitants. In 1970 the average for the United States was one daily or Sunday paper for every 115,000 people.[6]

In comparison with their modern offspring, colonial newspapers were no doubt "petty, dingy, languid, inadequate affairs," as one critic has characterized them. They contained neither editorials nor commanding headlines. A striking essay or major news item was likely to be hidden on an inside page. All this was common practice in the eighteenth century, however, and since the subscriber had a week to pore over his paper, the lack of visual appeal or dramatic placing of materials was not really a problem. In the hands of enterprising publishers colonial newspapers were exceedingly competent engines for the dissemination of information and opinion. An especially important feature was the contributed political essay. These essays usually appeared over a pseudonym—"Cato," "Pacificus," "A Freeborn American," "Philadelphus," and the like—partly to hide the author's identity, partly to create the impression that many persons were writing in support of a cause. Most political essays were serious and argumentative, although a few were humorous, satirical, or allegorical. Most were short, direct appeals which, unlike pamphlets, relied more upon forceful expression and repetition of ideas than upon detailed unfolding of arguments.[7] Since the vast majority of newspaper essays were written expressly to influence local readers, it is through these essays that we can chart most carefully the interplay of local and imperial issues that was so crucial an aspect of public discourse in Philadelphia during the revolutionary period.

Another commonly employed means of propagating opinion was the publication in newspapers of private letters and extracts thereof. These letters were printed without signature under such headings as "Extract of a Letter from a Gentleman in London" or "Correspondence from a Resident of Boston to His Friend in Philadelphia." Most were genuine personal letters contributed by their recipients, but some were deliberate pieces of propaganda written to influence colonial opinion. Whatever the intentions of their authors, these letters were among the most telling sources of intelligence for colonial Philadelphians. They possessed special credibility with the reading public and exerted considerable impact upon opinion in the city. One Philadelphia printer told a London correspondent in 1764, "Your letters are oracles here."[8]

Few observers, Tory or Whig, doubted the influence of colonial newspapers in the British-American controversy. Joseph Galloway, Philadelphia's most skillful apologist for British policy during the prerevolutionary decade, complained during the Stamp Act crisis that the city's printers had combined "to print everything inflammatory and nothing that is rational and cool. By which means everything that is published is ex parte, the people are taught to believe the greatest absurdities, and their passions are excited to a degree of resentment against the mother country beyond all description." John Holt, Whig printer of the *New York Journal,* boasted to Samuel Adams in 1776, "It was by means of newspapers that we received and spread the notice of the tyrannical designs formed against America, and kindled a spirit that has been sufficient to repel them." As Benjamin Franklin pointed out, the press could present the "same truths" time and again in "different lights," not only striking "while the iron is hot" but heating it "continually by striking." William Smith, provost of the College of Philadelphia and a frequent participant in Philadelphia's paper wars, estimated that while a pamphlet might be read or a speech heard "by a few hundred people," the same ideas presented in a newspaper might "be read perhaps by thirty thousand." Similar testimony came from John Witherspoon, who regretted that Thomas Paine's monumentally popular pamphlet, *Common Sense,* had not been first published as a series of newspaper essays. "Common Sense has been read by many," Witherspoon acknowledged, "yet the newspapers are read by many more."[9] Reaching more people on a more consistent basis than either pamphlets or speeches, newspapers constituted the most influential public medium of colonial Philadelphia.

Pamphlets were an important complement to newspapers. Most pamphlets published in Philadelphia presented original discourses, but some—such as John Dickinson's *Letters from a Farmer in Pennsylvania* or Richard Wells's *A Few Political Reflections*—were reprints of notable newspaper essays; others were public speeches or sermons revised and printed for wider distribution. Although some critics hold that there was only a "mechanical distinction" between the newspaper essay and the pamphlet, pamphleteers confronted disadvantages not faced by newspaper essayists. As one Philadelphia author explained in 1776, "If you begin a series of letters in a newspaper you are at full liberty to say as much or as little as you please, to suspend your operations for a time and strike in again when occasion serves." But, he continued, "when you write a pamphlet you are expected to say the best, if not all that can be said on the subject, and if it contains few weighty arguments the author is despised and the subject suffers. There you are obliged to come to a period, but you may write a twelve-month in a newspaper and yet make the public believe that your main argument has not yet appeared." Pamphlets also had special advantages, the most important of which was flexibility in length: they could contain only a few pages of brief, pointed rebuttals, but they could also accommodate longer, fully developed arguments. Pamphlets ran normally from 5,000 to 25,000 words.[10]

The political pamphlet was peculiarly and vitally the form in which was developed the solid framework of constitutional and philosophical thought which colonial protesters used to legitimize their rejection of British authority. At every stage of the imperial controversy the basic elements of Whig political ideology appeared first in pamphlets and then were popularized in the newspapers. With certain exceptions such as *Common Sense,* pamphlets were directed primarily to the politically informed and served especially to unify the thinking of Whig leaders in the various colonies.[11]

Broadsides were another printed means of arousing the populace. They were unique. Confined to a single sheet, they offered less elaborate argumentation than pamphlets and many newspaper essays. They summarized leading points of contention on major issues and provided quick notices of meetings, demonstrations, or other important events. They were printed anonymously and without clues to the identity of their authors. "Tacked at night on the door of town house or tavern, on trees or posts, left on the doorsteps or handed out secretly, the broadsides were read to the groups who gathered around them next day, and thus their influence spread far beyond the confines of the literate public."[12]

Perhaps more than any other colonial city Philadelphia had facilities to publish and distribute a large volume of literature, and its citizens were prepared to consume much of that volume. Printing shops kept pace with the city's growth. The eight shops of 1740 multiplied to twenty-three by the time of the Revolution. Pamphlets and inexpensive editions of European books could be purchased in any of the seventy-seven bookshops which existed in the city between 1761 and 1776.[13] The latest works were also available in the Library Company of Philadelphia. Founded by Benjamin Franklin in 1731, the Library Company was one of the most highly developed subscription libraries in America and was used by a wide range of the city's residents. One librarian was sure that "for every person of distinction and fortune there were twenty tradesmen that frequented the library." In fact, the high literacy rate of middle-class Philadelphians and their eagerness for self-improvement were among their most frequently noted characteristics. "Such is the prevailing taste for books of every kind," wrote Jacob Duché in 1772, "that almost every man is a reader; and by pronouncing sentence, right or wrong, upon the various publications that come in his way, puts himself upon a level, in point of knowledge, with their several authors."[14]

Written communication was not the sole vehicle for rhetorical influence. There was rarely a public meeting or demonstration that did not include at least one speech; some included several. Throughout the controversy with England orators spoke to their fellow Philadelphians at the State House, in Carpenters' Hall, in public taverns, and on street corners. A few of these speeches remain, generally because they were printed in the newspapers or as pamphlets, but most did not survive the occasions that called them forth. Sermons were another mode of oral communication. The Philadelphia clergy, unlike their counterparts in New England, remained aloof from the controversy with England until 1775, perhaps because they agreed with William Tennent that "political subjects do not belong to the pulpit." After the battles of Lexington and Concord, however, Anglican and Presbyterian ministers alike spoke out more frequently on American relations with England, especially because they were called upon to deliver eulogies, fast-day sermons, and invocations to the city militia.[15]

Informal talk was an especially important means of communication in colonial Philadelphia. All parts of the city were within easy walking distance. Merchants, artisans, shopkeepers, and tradesmen lived close together and mixed freely through the city. Everyday life was less like that of a modern urban center than like that of a large village, and conditions were naturally conducive to rumor.[16] Taverns were particularly vital centers of communication; they were places to discuss business, to read the newspapers, and to exchange opinions and gossip. In 1774 there were ninety-three licensed taverns and seventy-two inns doing business in the city; there was one neighborhood drinking place for approximately every 180 persons in Philadelphia. Daniel Smith's elegant City Tavern and William Bradford's bustling London Coffee House are the most famous, but all of Philadelphia's taverns constituted informal community cells.

The importance of this small-group communication to the coming of the Revolution in Philadelphia is impossible to determine, but one student of urban life in colonial America has observed, "If the American Revolution was 'cradled' in any place, it was in the urban public houses."[17]

There was considerable potential for influencing opinion in Philadelphia through formal and informal means. This did not, however, give an inherent advantage to those who sought to increase discontent with British policy. The avenues of communication were open to groups of all political persuasions. Nor were critics of England given many ready-made advantages by the general attitudes of most Philadelphians.

One of the greatest barriers Whig publicists faced was the cautious, moderate, and deferential temper of most Philadelphians. Although suffrage was widely held among taxable males, political power was consistently exercised by the same families and individuals from decade to decade.[18] Except in extraordinary years, few people voted, and the same candidates were elected to the Pennsylvania Assembly time after time, often without opposition. The Assembly was invariably controlled by the Quaker party—also known as the Old Ticket—one of the two great Philadelphia-centered factions that controlled the political order in Pennsylvania. The Old Ticket had originally been the secular arm of the Society of Friends, but a combination of forces had compelled the party to broaden both its base and its leadership. By the mid-1760s it cut across occupational, religious, and ethnic lines, and was guided by Benjamin Franklin and Joseph Galloway, neither of whom was a Quaker. In opposition to the Old Ticket stood the Proprietary faction, which was led by a number of independent gentlemen who normally supported the Penn family in its battles with the Assembly. Whereas the primary strength of the Quaker party was its electoral superiority, the major resource of the Proprietary faction was the governor's patronage powers. Although the Old Ticket was far more cohesive and disciplined than the Proprietary faction, neither was a political party in the modern sense, but a group of men brought together by mutual social, political, religious, and economic preferences. Each was directed by powerful members of the Philadelphia aristocracy.[19] As in most parts of America, rule by the elite was the accepted mode of political life in colonial Philadelphia.[20] The average citizen believed that power emanated from tl. people, who had an inherent right to exercise a close check over the actions of their representatives, but he was usually willing to let the Quaker and Proprietary oligarchies govern the city and colony on a day-to-day basis.[21]

The same was true of imperial matters. As long as times were good and the average citizen remained relatively untouched by parliamentary legislation, he was content to allow his representatives to deal with the mother country. During the dispute with England, Philadelphians confirmed Charles Thomson's judgment that Pennsylvanians in general were "cautious and backward in entering into measures," and Whig leaders from more radical cities such as Boston frequently complained of the "supine and lethargic city of Philadelphia." Even in 1775 a visitor found that in contrast to New York, where "nothing is heard but politics," Philadelphia was a city where "people only minded their business."[22] Rhetoricians of all convictions confronted the task of arousing Philadelphia's politically passive citizens.

Nor did the religious attitudes of most Philadelphians provide predispositions strongly favorable to revolutionary publicists. The principles of religious toleration embodied in the Charter of Privileges had made Pennsylvania a haven for Europeans seeking to escape religious persecution in their homelands. In combination with cheap and fertile land, religious tolerance produced a province with religious and ethnic diversity unknown elsewhere in the eighteenth century. This diversity was strikingly evident in Philadelphia, where Quakers, Anglicans, Jews, Scottish and Scotch-Irish Presbyterians, German Lutherans, German Reformed, Dutch Baptists, German Moravians, and German Roman Catholics mingled freely and worshipped peacefully. Religious freedom gave a strongly secular cast to the city. With the right to worship removed as a central concern of daily life, Philadelphians attended to other matters. Indeed, some residents feared that the religious impulse was very much in decline. Benjamin Rush lamented in 1764 that "religion is at a low ebb among us. . . . Vice and profanity openly prevail in our city. Our Sabbaths are boldly profaned by the most open and flagitious enormities. Our young men in general (who should be the prop of sinking religion) are wholly devoted to pleasure and sensuality, and very few are solicitous about the one thing needful."[23]

Despite the lack of publicly intense religious fervor, religion played a significant role in Philadelphia politics throughout the revolutionary era. Religious preference and political partisanship interacted in powerful ways and often posed formidable obstacles for Whig organizers.[24] Pennsylvania had been founded by a religious sect, and from the beginning Quakers had perceived challenges to their political hegemony as threats to their religious principles. The Holy Experiment, they felt, was safe only in the hands of Friends. Although the Old Ticket maintained control of the Pennsylvania Assembly, a number of forces had eroded Quaker political domination through the 1740s and 1750s. By the 1760s Quaker leaders feared the rising power of the Presbyterians above all else. This fear had deep historical roots and stemmed from a potent blend of religious and political considerations. John Reynell expressed the forebodings of many Friends when he wrote in 1765 that a "Presbyterian government will if possible be intruded upon us." The Presbyterians, he warned, "are grown numberous, have joined in with the proprietary party to strengthen themselves, have been continually abusing and calumniating the Quakers in order to weaken their interest here with the people and represent them odious to the government at home." Should this "imprudent" and "violent" sect take over the reins of power, Quakers would not only forfeit political power but might also suffer the same religious persecution as "some of our brethren in New England." Reynell's concern was unusually strong, but an abiding distrust of the Presbyterians' political strength and religious insularity was endemic among Philadelphia Quakers across the years 1765–76.[25]

Quakers were not alone in suspecting the Presbyterians, most of whom were Scottish or Scotch-Irish. Benjamin Rush noted that Presbyterians incurred "the jealousy, or hatred," of both the Quakers and Anglicans, "who possessed between them the greatest part of the wealth and influence of the city." Alexander Mackraby made a similar observation. "The zealous members of the Church of England," he wrote in 1768, "are full of apprehensions at the great and growing power of the Presbyterians."[26] Not surprisingly, many Presbyterians were uneasy about the designs of Quaker and Anglican leaders. The Presbyterians were the first group to resist the Quaker party's plan for switching Pennsylvania from proprietary to royal government, because they believed the plan to be little more than a ruse invented by the Quakers to continue their own political domination. Presbyterians were also the most zealous opponents of proposals to establish an Anglican bishop in America. An intense paper war over the matter broke out in Philadelphia in the spring of 1768 and continued for more than a year. According to writers for the Presbyterian interest, the campaign for an American bishophric was the work of "ambitious, worldly-minded men" who hoped to "prepare the way for Episcopal domination" of "all posts and places—civil, ecclesiastical, and military." Anglican spokesmen countered by charging that Presbyterians were a self-righteous, intolerant lot who hoped to destroy the American arm of the Church of England because it presented "the greatest check to their *political* designs."[27]

Certainly not all Philadelphia Presbyterians mistrusted the religio-political motives of Anglicans and Quakers, any more than did all Anglicans and Quakers believe in the existence of a Presbyterian plot to gain political control of Pennsylvania and press religious conformity upon its residents. Still, such suspicions were widely enough held to present serious problems to Whig leaders who sought to unite Philadelphians in opposition to English colonial policy.

Another barrier facing Whig protesters was the general fondness most Philadelphians had for England and for all things British. Most residents felt they lived under the most enlightened form of government the world had yet seen. They delighted in British achievements in Europe, idealized the constitution, and were proud to be members of the empire. To be sure, during the years preceding the Stamp Act repeated transportations of British convicts to Pennsylvania, limitations placed upon the colonial iron industry, constraints imposed on trade by the Sugar Act, and the suspension of colonial paper money as legal tender all aroused discontent and tempered somewhat Philadelphians' satisfaction with British rule. In addition, many of the city's German and Scotch-Irish inhabitants, who together comprised about 50 percent of the population, felt little intrinsic identity with or loyalty to England.[28] Nevertheless, Philadelphians were by and large contented with their position in the empire. Joseph Reed recalled in 1774 that "no King ever had more loyal subjects; or any country more affectionate colonists" than Philadelphians were before 1765. In those "happy days," Reed remembered, the king "was always mentioned with a respect approaching to adoration, and to be an *Englishman* was alone a sufficient recommendation for any office of friendship and civility." Charles Thomson thought there had never in history been "a people so numerous, so far removed from the seat of royalty, who were so loyal, so attached to their king, and who at the same time had such true sentiments of liberty" as the people in Philadelphia and throughout the American colonies.[29]

Thomson understood, however, that Philadelphians' respect and affection for the mother country could not be taken for granted. Philadelphians expected England to treat the colonies in accordance with certain fundamental beliefs about the limits of legitimate political authority and the nature of a just relationship with the parent state. They expected that the imperial government would not violate the sanctity of the colonists' elected lower houses of assembly upon which the colonists depended for the immediate protection of their personal property and political liberty; that British leaders would impede the colonists' pursuit of their own social and economic interests as little as possible given the demands of a mercantile economy of empire; that British leaders would not interfere with the right of colonists as individuals to exercise their personal initiative and autonomy; and that England would treat the colonies in accordance with those fundamental postulates of Anglo-American political and social life upon whose observance freedom and liberty ultimately depended.[30] As long as British colonial policy operated within the bounds of these expectations, it was not likely that Philadelphians would become sufficiently disaffected to favor secession from the empire. But if British colonial policy ever contravened these expectations, they would provide a strong foundation upon which Philadelphia Whigs could justify public protest against the mother country and ultimately separation from her.

Among the most important determinants of political behavior in Philadelphia was the antipathy of many citizens toward external control of the colony. This concern had for years induced the Assembly to seize every opportunity to enhance its authority and to restrict that of the Penn family. Ironically, the same concern contributed to the failure of the Quaker party's plan to eliminate the influence of the Penns by changing Pennsylvania from proprietary to royal government. In the

1764 Assembly elections the people of Philadelphia registered their disapproval of the plan by rejecting the Quaker party candidates, Benjamin Franklin and Samuel Rhoads, and filling the city's two Assembly seats with John Dickinson and George Bryan, both of the Proprietary faction. Although the contest was close, its results are significant because Philadelphia had long been a stronghold of the Quaker party and a center of anti-proprietary sentiment. In 1764 over half of the city's voters affirmed not only their traditional opposition to external control of the colony, but also their specific dislike of control by the crown. They preferred to take their chances with an unpopular and discredited proprietor rather than with George III. On the eve of the Stamp Act crisis, a majority of the Philadelphia electorate revealed fears, suspicions, or hatreds of royal government strong enough to compel them to forsake the Quaker party in order to render their reservations publicly.[31]

At the beginning of 1765 the residents of colonial America's largest city were loyal citizens of the British empire and were far from ready to jump headlong into rebellion against a system that, on balance, had treated them rather well. At the same time, an undercurrent of disenchantment with British policy and government was beginning to gather power. There was an ambivalence toward imperial affairs that reinforces our perception of Philadelphians as a people who held many views of the empire. That perception is strengthened by examination of the major publics whom the city's protesters had greatest need of persuading—Quakers, merchants, and mechanics.

Although Pennsylvania was established by Quakers as a "holy experiment," it is anachronistic to describe Philadelphia in 1765 as the "Quaker city." As early as 1735 the strength of the Society of Friends had passed to its rural Meetings, especially in Philadelphia, Chester, and Bucks counties. By 1750 Quakers numbered only about eight hundred families in the city of Philadelphia or about one-fourth of the population. By 1770 they comprised only one-seventh of the population. As a result of large-scale Quaker removals to rural areas, expulsions of members from Meeting, failure to proselytize on any but a minor scale, and conflict between spiritual and temporal values which led some Quakers to disavow the Society of Friends in

favor of the more fashionable Anglican establishment, the religious loyalties of most Philadelphians came to be divided
among the Society and the Anglican, Presbyterian, and German
Lutheran churches.[32] Nonetheless, Quakers still composed an
influential force in Philadelphia because of their prominence in
trade, their moral leadership, and their political leverage.[33]

The veneer of solidarity the Society of Friends generally
presented to outsiders masked a variety of outlooks and orienta-
tions. Through most of the eighteenth century severe tension
existed between the "reformers," who sought to uphold the
Quaker testimony in its pure form and to induce their brethren
to repudiate their preoccupation with worldly things, and the
"politicians," who tended to view the Society as a political
pressure group and to fasten their attention almost solely upon
secular issues. Between these two factions stood the "politiques,"
men who shared the reformers' devout allegiance to the Society's traditional religious principles as well as the politicians'
penchant for partisan secular activity. The politiques were especially influential inasmuch as they had access to positions of
authority within both the provincial government and the
administrative structure of the Society. Consequently, they
played pivotal roles in determining the official response of
Philadelphia Quakers to the revolutionary movement.[34]

The reformers remained aloof from the British-American
dispute and urged their fellow Quakers to do likewise.
Politicians and politiques, on the other hand, split into militant
and nonmilitant factions. During the Stamp Act crisis they
joined in denouncing England's unconstitutional taxes while si-
multaneously seeking to prevent the occurrence in Philadelphia
of the mob violence which accompanied protest in some other
colonies. Politically minded Friends also played a conspicuous
role in the campaign against the Townshend duties. William
Allen noted in 1768 that "in their own way" Quakers were "as
zealous . . . as their neighbors" in opposing parliamentary
taxation. In 1769 eight Quakers were named to the committee
whose responsibility it was to enforce the boycott on British imports. John Reynell, a leading Quaker politique, chaired the
committee. At the same time, however, the committee's coercive
and extralegal methods deeply distressed other powerful politiques—most notably James and Israel Pemberton—who
counseled Friends to stay clear of measures that might vitiate the

Society's religious scruples or corrode its political influence with the home government.[35]

For the most part, politically minded Quakers were willing to support the Philadelphia resistance movement as long as it remained nonviolent. To the extent that "petitions, remonstrances and joint associations not to import dutied items could prevail," Quakers "cheerfully lent their aid." But their principles did not allow them to "resist unto blood," and as protest gradually escalated toward rebellion, more and more Quakers grew cool toward the Whig cause. Few participated openly in the demonstrations against the Tea and Coercive acts; those who did were almost exclusively Quaker politicians. By mid-1774 leading politiques saw the storm gathering and, wishing to avert war, lent their support to moderate forces in an attempt to discourage radicalism and to restore tranquil relations between England and the colonies. Eventually, the Society of Friends adopted an officially neutral stance toward the conflict, but its members could not escape the opprobrium of being labeled Loyalists once the war began. On the other hand, some notable figures of the Revolution in Philadelphia came from the ranks of Quaker politicians—among them Clement and Owen Biddle, Timothy Matlack, Christopher Marshall, Richard Humphreys, and Thomas Mifflin. Most of the 25,000 Quakers in Pennsylvania at the time of the Revolution remained neutral; four or five hundred "Free Quakers" actively aided the American cause.[36] While a large number of Quakers provided a receptive audience for Whig rhetoric before the 1770s, far fewer provided such an audience after 1773.

A British visitor was not far from the truth when he remarked in 1765 that "everybody in Philadelphia deals more or less in trade." Not only was Philadelphia the busiest port in America, but by 1768 the tonnage of ships which entered and cleared its harbor exceeded that of all British ports except those of London and Liverpool.[37] In the preindustrial age of the eighteenth century, virtually every aspect of Philadelphia's economic life had its roots in commerce. Consequently, as in most northern cities, Philadelphia's merchant aristocracy constituted the dominant element in economic and social affairs. Mostly Quaker or Anglican and comprising but a fraction of the city's population, the merchants controlled most of its wealth and provided many of the leaders of the revolutionary movement until its later stages. But while merchants were often drawn together by similar economic interests, there was among them the same diversity of opinion about the dispute with England that characterized other groups in the city.

In the eighteenth century, the term "merchant" was applied to one who regularly engaged in maritime commerce. The man who bought and sold his goods within the province and sold them at retail was generally known as a shopkeeper or storekeeper. The man who imported his goods and sold them at wholesale was considered a merchant. Merchants ranged from poor to rich, but the annual income of the average established trader was about £500 sterling, sufficient to place him near the top of the economic class structure. The most prosperous merchants were typically those engaged in the dry goods trade. Cloth and other varieties of dry goods accounted for more than one-half the total value of imports from the mother country; the most valuable items were British woolens. A gross profit of 25 percent was not unusual for merchants trading in dry goods; net profit normally ran about 10–13 percent, lucrative by any standards. In combination with investments in land and other speculative ventures, this high profit margin made the dry goods dealers, a great many of whom were Quakers, the aristocrats of Philadelphia's mercantile community.[38]

Philadelphia merchants were forced into the middle of the British-American controversy in 1765 when the city's Whig leaders decided on a policy of economic coercion to force England to rescind the Stamp Act. By refusing to import British goods, the Whigs contended, colonists could exert pressure on British merchants, who would thereupon urge Parliament to repeal the detested stamp tax. The strategy worked, and thereafter the almost instantaneous response of Philadelphia Whigs to any "unconstitutional" act of Parliament was to readopt nonimportation. But while the city's merchants were more or less united in support of suspending trade in 1765–66, they divided into moderate and radical camps during the period of the Townshend Acts. The radical merchants, led by Charles Thomson, favored an immediate boycott of British imports. The moderates, many of whom were in the dry goods trade, were determined not to suspend trade until all other means of securing redress had failed. By March 1769 it was clear that repeal of the Townshend duties was not imminent; then the moderates agreed to nonimportation. But when word arrived in May 1770 that Parliament had rescinded all of the Townshend duties save that on tea, moderate merchants, again led by the traders of dry goods, campaigned to abolish the nonimportation agreement. They were again opposed by the more radical merchants, who wanted to maintain the boycott until the duty on tea was rescinded. Finally, in September 1770, the moderates prevailed, and the merchants' committee voted by a margin of almost two to one to reopen the port to British shipping.[39]

The divisions among traders which opened in 1768–70 were occasioned by a mixture of religious, political, and economic motives and widened as the protest movement escalated in succeeding years. Distressed by the Boston radicals' "wanton" attack upon private property in the Tea Party of December 1773, alarmed by the growing power of "the people" in Philadelphia's resistance movement, and unhappy with the shift in protest from reform to rebellion, many moderate and some heretofore radical merchants became increasingly disaffected with the Whig cause. At the time of the Coercive Acts, Whig tacticians began to establish committees of correspondence throughout the province to "put it out of the power of the merchants . . . to drop the opposition when interest dictated the measure." After November 1774 fewer and fewer moderate merchants could be counted among the Whig inner circle or among the members of Philadelphia's Whig committees. By 1776 a sizeable portion of the city's mercantile community had joined the ranks of those who sought to prevent divorce from the mother country. Still, there was no uniformity among the merchants on the question of independence. Many merchants—among them George Bryan, Daniel Roberdeau, Thomas Mifflin, John Dixon, Robert Morris, and George Clymer—sided with the revolutionaries and lent strong assistance to the American cause. The split between revolutionary and anti-revolutionary merchants was influenced by a combination of factors, including age, wealth, and religion. Younger, less affluent, Anglican or Presbyterian merchants supported independence more than did their older, wealthier, or Quaker colleagues.[40]

The most important audience for Philadelphia protesters was the city's large and aggressive middle class. It was this group that would provide most of the popular support for the resistance movement. But like Quakers and merchants, members of the middle class were far from united. "The spirit of liberty and resistance . . . drew into its vortex the mechanical interest, as well as that numerous portion of the community in republics, styled *The People*," Alexander Graydon recalled, but "notwithstanding this almost unanimous agreement in favor of liberty, neither were all disposed to go to the same lengths for it, nor were they perfectly in unison in the idea annexed to it."[41]

Members of the middle class were generally called "mechanics." The eighteenth-century mechanic was defined broadly by his contemporaries as anyone who worked with his hands, and the term generally referred to all groups below the level of merchants, lawyers, and other professionals, and above the level of indentured servants, slaves, or unskilled laborers. Mechanics included master craftsmen, shopkeepers, carpenters, blacksmiths, hatters, tailors, shoemakers, printers, shipbuilders, and tanners, to name but a few. For the most part, mechanics belonged to the economic category known today as small business, and they are best viewed as independent, self-employed entrepreneurs. The basic industrial unit in colonial urban society was the family, and success or failure in a given trade depended upon the head of the family. He supervised every step in the business process from procurement of raw materials to final sale. Unlike laborers in modern cities, most Philadelphians worked alone or with an apprentice and one or two helpers. Mechanics and their families comprised more than one-half of the city's population.[42]

Pennsylvania may or may not have been the "paradise for artisans" one visitor labeled it in the mid-eighteenth century, but Philadelphia's expanding and diversified economic environment offered abundant opportunities for success. The vagaries of the colonial economic system notwithstanding, most Philadelphia mechanics lived as comfortably as their equals anywhere on earth.[43] As in any society, however, the middle class in Philadelphia was not a homogeneous mass. Where an individual stood in the ill-defined hierarchy among mechanics depended upon his craft, his skill, and, above all, his material success. Well-established men became known as "respectable tradesmen" or "substantial mechanics." Those less successful and those engaged in the waterfront trades were referred to as "inferior mechanics."[44] The mechanics displayed diversity in matters of religion as well. Although most were members of the Presbyterian, Anglican, or German Lutheran churches, many

substantial mechanics were Quakers, and others were Roman
Catholic, Moravian, Baptist, or Methodist.[45]

It is hazardous to generalize about the attitudes of
Philadelphia's middle class. The middle class itself left behind
little in the way of diaries and letters and is most often referred
to in the writings of prominent men and in newspaper accounts
simply as "the people," "the middling sort," or "the mechanics."
It is also imperative to avoid the inclination to perceive the
mechanics in a decentralized, colonial culture as linear
precursors of the Marxist proletariat of nineteenth- and
twentieth-century industrialized societies. There is little to indicate that the attitudes of the modern "Marxist" laborer bear
more than superficial and passing resemblance to those of the
colonial mechanic.

From most indications the middle class of colonial
Philadelphia was not particularly radical either socially or
politically. Most mechanics were self-employed, self-made men
whose single most conspicuous quality was their driving ambition to get ahead in the world. Their goals and attitudes were
most accurately reflected in the pragmatism and material success of Benjamin Franklin, who had risen from the ranks of
"leather aprons" to fame and fortune. Mechanics took seriously
the values of frugality, industry, sobriety, and education
preached in *Poor Richard's Almanac* and aspired to the comforts
and opportunities of prosperity. Their aim was to climb to the
top of the social and economic ladder, not to destroy it.[46]

Mechanics did not seek to destroy existing social structures,
but by the mid-1760s they were demanding greater access to and
influence within those structures. Those engaged in local manufacturing competed with the city's merchants, but generally
under severe handicaps. For one thing, merchants possessed
much more political influence than mechanics—an important
fact inasmuch as the Pennsylvania legislature exercised extensive regulative control over most aspects of economic life. For
another, mechanics occupied an institutionally inferior place in
the mercantile scheme, which placed greatest value upon goods
imported from England and discouraged domestic manufacturing.[47] Philadelphia mechanics thus had reason to resent both the
city's importers, who frequently seemed to profit at their
expense, and the mercantile system, which was strongly rigged
against colonial manufacturers.

Another source of irritation was that mechanics seldom occupied influential offices in either municipal or provincial government. Nor did they have a meaningful voice in the inner councils of the Quaker and Proprietary factions. As one writer complained in 1770, the customary procedure was "for a certain group of gentlemen to nominate persons and settle the ticket . . . without ever permitting the affirmative or negative voice of a mechanic to interfere." Consequently, the Assembly was composed almost exclusively of merchants, lawyers, and well-to-do farmers, and a mechanic was as likely to become a member of that body as was "a Jew or a Turk."[48] For the most part, these political and economic dissatisfactions remained latent until the mid-1760s. Thereafter the active desires of many mechanics to improve their economic opportunities and political influence were powerful forces in the city.

Like other groups in Philadelphia, mechanics did not chart a uniform course during the imperial controversy. In local politics mechanics had long supported the Quaker party and they tended to follow the party's program of nonviolent opposition to the Stamp Act. For example, the White Oaks, an organization of ship's carpenters, opposed the Stamp Act (as did almost all Philadelphians) and took part in the celebrations at its repeal. But they staunchly resisted those who advocated violent resistance and even defended the unpopular stamp distributor, John Hughes, from an angry mob seeking his resignation.[49] But although Quaker party leaders worked hard to prevent violence in Philadelphia, they worked equally hard to evince their dislike of the Stamp Act, and they quickly acceded to popular demands to boycott British imports until Parliament repealed the act. That significant portions of the mechanic community favored the Old Ticket's position is suggested by the Assembly elections of October 1765, just one month before Grenville's legislation was to go into effect. Despite the efforts of the Proprietary faction to discredit Franklin and Galloway as supporters of the Stamp Act, the Old Ticket reversed its defeat of the previous year and captured all the seats in Philadelphia, Bucks, Chester, and Lancaster counties as well as the one seat contested in the city of Philadelphia. The results of the election indicate that most voters preferred nonviolent, constitutional, yet firm resistance to the Stamp Act.[50]

During the early period of protest against the Townshend duties most mechanics continued to adhere to the moderate policies of the Quaker party. But by 1769 many—especially those involved in local manufacturing—had moved to support the Whigs' campaign to use nonimportation to force Parliament to rescind the duties. In the 1770 Assembly elections many mechanics deserted the Old Ticket for the more radical Whig-Presbyterian group headed by Charles Thomson and John Dickinson. Thereafter, Thomson and fellow Whig strategists actively and systematically recruited mechanics to Whig-Presbyterian ranks by convincing them that their political and economic fortunes were closely allied with the aims and methods of the resistance movement.[51] From the time of the Tea Act mechanics were among the Whigs' most strident and influential supporters. That support, however, was never unanimous. Even among Whiggish mechanics there were pronounced radical and moderate divisions; substantial mechanics and those with commercial connections tended to be more cautious in sanctioning radical measures than those who had no commercial connections or who had yet to enjoy much economic success.[52] And while firmly united in opposition to British actions that imperiled American rights or interests, many mechanics were still not prepared to take the final step of revolution as late as May 1776.[53] Like other major publics, Philadelphia mechanics manifested the diversity and pluralism which defined the essential nature of public opinion in the city throughout the years before revolution.

# PART II

# PRELUDE
# TO REVOLUTION

## A DECADE OF PROTEST

# PROLEGOMENON

FOR most of the 150 years preceding the American Revolution, British policy toward the North American colonies was marked by inattention and insouciance. But when England was faced with huge debts accumulated in the Seven Years' War, she turned to the colonies as a source of revenue, and when taxes mild in comparison with those borne in England were resisted by the Americans, she stood ready to defend the principle of parliamentary authority. In Philadelphia the dispute between England and America which eventually led to the Revolution first reached major proportions with the passage of the Stamp Act in 1765 and was rekindled by the Townshend Acts (1767), the Tea Act (1773), and the Coercive Acts (1774). Resistance to each of these measures was fanned and to some extent institutionalized by "patriotic" writers and speakers.

Philadelphia's Whig leaders encouraged united and unyielding opposition to Parliament and the ministry at every stage of the imperial controversy, but they were not seeking to trigger a revolution during the years 1765–75. The subject of independence was seldom broached before the outbreak of war in New England in April 1775 and did not become a topic of intense public debate in Philadelphia until publication of *Common Sense* in January 1776. During the decade of protest before the battles of Lexington and Concord, Philadelphia Whigs shared John Dickinson's belief that, "torn from the body to which we are united by religion, liberty, laws, affections, relation, language and commerce, we must bleed at every vein."[1]

The long-range effects of public discourse, however, are often more profound than the immediate consequences it was designed to produce. As Benjamin Rush later stated, the men whose rhetoric galvanized opposition to British authority in Philadelphia were little more than "blind actors" in a drama whose denouement they could neither foresee nor determine.[2] Sincere as Whig spokesmen were in disavowing independence through the years 1765–75, they nonetheless adopted and argued for public positions which tended consistently and inexorably to preclude the middle ground and to undermine compromise as a tenable option. Often unknowingly and almost always undeliberately, they radicalized opinion in the city to a point where the major issues dividing Philadelphians from the mother country could not be resolved through negotiation and accommodation. In the course of ten years of protest large numbers of Philadelphians came to adopt a system of perceptions, values, and beliefs quite different from that they had held in 1765. Under the pressure of events and the prodding of Whig rhetoricians they had become nascent revolutionaries by the beginning of 1776.

Before turning to the record, it will be useful to introduce the most notable of the men who "by their publications governed the public mind" in Philadelphia and from whom came "nearly all the political information which set Pennsylvania in motion, and united her with her sister colonies."[3] These men included Benjamin Franklin, who, despite his absence from the colonies from 1765 until May 1775, exerted considerable influence in Philadelphia through his many essays and letters published in the city's newspapers; William Bradford, publisher of the *Pennsylvania Journal,* whose staunch support of the Whig cause earned him the title "patriot-printer of the Revolution"; James Wilson, a lawyer of Scottish parentage whose *Considerations on the Nature and the Extent of the Legislative Authority of the British Parliament* (1774) demonstrated the legal and intellectual foundations for denying the sovereignty of Parliament over the colonies; Joseph Reed, lawyer, businessman, patriotic orator and writer, member of the Continental Congress, and military secretary to George Washington; Thomas Mifflin, merchant, member of the Pennsylvania Assembly, aide-de-camp to General Washington, and perhaps the most talented Whig orator; Thomas McKean, delegate to the Stamp Act Congress from Delaware, chairman of the Philadelphia Committee of Inspection and Observation, and inveterate foe of England throughout the British-American dispute; and George Clymer, prosperous merchant, early and ardent Whig, and a signer of both the Declaration of Independence and the federal Constitution.[4] Above all these, however, stand two figures of paramount importance.

A "gentleman by birth, a lawyer by training, and a politician by inclination," John Dickinson is one of the most enigmatic figures of the revolutionary era. Because he opposed the Declaration of Independence and deeply feared social disorder, Dickinson is often portrayed as a profoundly conservative man who backed out of the revolutionary movement when it began to threaten his own privileged social and political position. But conservative as he may have been in his devotion to law and traditional institutions, Dickinson was far from conservative when it came to defending Philadelphians against the encroachments of Parliament and the ministry. In fact, his disapproval of independence in July 1776 was founded on the conviction that the best time for separation had not yet arrived; once independence was declared, he supported his countrymen through military and political activities. His refusal to vote for independence has at times obscured the prominent role he played in developing, leading, and sustaining opposition to the mother country at every stage from 1765 to 1775. During these years he was by far the most influential Whig spokesman in Philadelphia. Although not a gifted orator, Dickinson was a political writer of consummate skill. He composed many of the most important state papers of the age, including the proclamations of the Stamp Act Congress and the Declaration of the Causes of Taking up Arms for the Continental Congress. These along with his numerous essays, broadsides, and pamphlets earned him the sobriquet, "Penman of the Revolution." Through his major works—*The Late Regulations Respecting the British Colonies on the Continent of America* (1765), *An Address to the Committee of Correspondence in Barbados* (1766), *Letters from a Farmer in Pennsylvania* (1768), *An Essay on the Constitutional Power of Great Britain* (1774), and letters "To the Inhabitants of the British Colonies in America" (1774)— we can follow the mainstream of rhetorical protest as it developed in Philadelphia from the time of the Stamp Act through the period of the Coercive Acts.[5]

While every protest movement needs its men of words, it also needs its men of action. If Dickinson was Philadelphia's most conspicuous Whig rhetorician, Charles Thomson was its most important Whig organizer. Actually, Thomson is best known for his services as secretary of both continental congresses. For nearly fifteen years he sat at the secretarial table listening to the debates, recording, in effect, the birth of the nation. As year followed year, delegates came and went, but Thomson, the "per-

petual secretary," remained. His contributions to the Whig cause
before 1774 are less easily documented than those of his fellows,
primarily because he destroyed virtually all his private papers
shortly before his death. Still, it is possible to piece together evidence of his significance in the agitational movement of 1765–
75. Thomson served on the committee that demanded the
resignation of stamp distributor John Hughes in 1765, but he
does not appear to have played a major role in the Stamp Act
controversy. His name does not appear in the correspondence
of the Sons of Liberty, and his surviving private correspondence
reveals an ambivalent attitude toward the protest measures
adopted in 1765–66. It was during the period of the Townshend
Acts, when he and Dickinson were the most outspoken
proponents of boycotting British imports, that Thomson moved
to the front of the resistance movement. From 1768 to 1770 he
organized the radical merchants and mechanics into an effective
political machine which in later years took the dominant part in
moving Philadelphia toward independence. Although we can
identify few of the pseudonymous pieces Thomson wrote during the course of his protest activities, the ones we can distinguish reveal him to have been a capable but hardly outstanding
writer. His talents lay less in public writing and speaking than in
coordinating, directing, and sustaining the protest energies of
Philadelphia's middle class. John Adams aptly dubbed him "the
Sam Adams of Philadelphia, the life and cause of liberty."[6]

The Whig leaders of colonial Philadelphia differed from one
another in religion, occupation, and political background, but
they were remarkably similar in significant respects. As a group
they were successful, well-educated, politically experienced, and
among "the most considerable gentlemen" of Philadelphia,
"both in fortune and ability." As Alexander Graydon recalled,
most of the men who guided Philadelphia's resistance movement from 1765 to 1775 were of "the better sort" and included
some of "the most wealthy and respectable" residents of the
city.[7] They were not, however, united formally. Although
Philadelphians used the term "Whig" to distinguish those
colonists who supported the resistance movement from the
"Tories" who opposed it,[8] there was no such thing as a Whig
party in the city during the decade of protest. Nor can all those
distinguished as Whigs in 1765 be identified as Whigs in 1775.
Some who figured prominently in agitation against the Stamp

Act were repelled by the course of protest thereafter, while others who did not play major roles in the Stamp Act controversy later became eminent Whigs. The leading Whig publicists I have identified were the most prominent members of a shifting alliance of a comparatively small group of men who were in the vanguard of protest during the years 1765–75.

It should also be noted that not all of the anti-British rhetoric issued in Philadelphia during the decade of protest was the work of local writers and speakers. Many newspaper essays were reprinted from English or from other colonial newspapers; about half of the fifty pamphlets dealing with the imperial dispute published in Philadelphia between 1765 and 1776 were written by men who were not directly allied with the city's protest movement. Such "foreign" writings often exerted considerable impact upon opinion in the city, however, and also require our attention.

Philadelphia Whigs encountered two general rhetorical problems during the decade of protest. One was to convince Philadelphians that British colonial policy posed fundamental threats to American rights and interests. The other was to unite Philadelphians behind a firm program of resistance to those policies. In attending to these problems, Whig publicists sometimes tailored their arguments to particular segments of the Philadelphia audience—especially to mechanics, without whose support the movement stood no real chance of success. During the early years of protest, however, such direct adaptation was the exception rather than the rule. Many Whig gentlemen were not strongly inclined to view ordinary citizens as a meaningful audience for political discourse; they often wrote "as if they were dealing with reasonable and cultivated readers like themselves."[9] It was only as Whigs worked to broaden the base of the protest movement from 1768 to 1770 that they began to address "the people" more directly. But Philadelphia was too confined a communicational environment to allow Whigs to cultivate one religious, ethnic, social, or economic faction to the exclusion of others. Consequently, when Philadelphia protesters did modulate their discourse to the demands of a popular audience, they commonly addressed the general community. Their aim was not just to get a specific group of citizens to adopt one or another specific action, but to forge a movement that enjoyed support from all major interest groups in the city.

# 2

# THE ECONOMIC BASIS
# OF PROTEST

THE relationship between economic discontent and revolutionary activity is complex. Most students of the subject readily acknowledge that a relationship, sometimes a strong one, does exist, but that actual economic conditions are less important than how people perceive and react to those conditions. The development of a revolutionary frame of mind is a psychological process in which what men believe to be true is more important than what actually is true.[1] One way to assess the role of economics in the coming of the American Revolution is thus to examine the ideas colonists held about their economic status at home and within the empire. The question to be pursued in this chapter is whether the ideas promulgated by Whig writers and speakers in Philadelphia during the decade of protest encouraged a sufficiently strong sense of economic grievance to help account for the permanent rift which ensued in 1776.

Examination of the pamphlets, newspapers, broadsides, and speeches circulated in Philadelphia from 1765 to the outbreak of war in 1775 reveals that Whig publicists discussed two types of economic matters, which I shall call first-order and second-order economic matters. First-order economic matters relate directly to immediate, day-to-day issues of economic self-interest. Arguments concerning first-order economic matters included complaints about the direct economic consequences of specific acts of Parliament. Such complaints were surprisingly uncommon in Philadelphia throughout the prerevolutionary decade. Another group of first-order economic arguments involved economic advantages or disadvantages which might befall certain groups of colonists as they joined or withdrew from the protest movement. Such arguments were telling to the Whigs' quest for the support of Philadelphia mechanics during the disputes over nonimportation from 1767 to 1770 and constituted a potent weapon in the Whigs' rhetorical arsenal thereafter.

Second-order economic matters relate to broad questions of economic justice or injustice, advantage or disadvantage, and may project economic prospects into the distant future. Arguments concerning second-order economic matters derived from four recurring, interrelated themes of economic distress applied generally to all acts of Parliament from 1765 to 1775: (1) England had no justification for seeking vast amounts of revenue in America; (2) England was economically exploiting America to feed the greedy appetites of West Indian planters and British politicians; (3) by levying individual taxes, Parliament laid the foundation for future tax burdens; (4) by attacking American property, Parliament laid the foundation for more grievous assaults upon American liberty. Whig spokesmen who addressed these themes ignored the immediate economic consequences of parliamentary legislation and directed themselves instead to the moral and fiscal inequity and the potential long-range economic dangers of that legislation. In the process, they welded powerful interconnections between economic interest and ideological principle which were important in shaping the direction and intensity of protest in Philadelphia.

Of the major writings against the Stamp Act in Philadelphia, only John Dickinson's *Late Regulations Respecting the British Colonies on the Continent of America* focused on first-order economic issues. Dickinson pursued two basic arguments. First, he held, the Stamp Act placed an unfair financial burden on Americans already suffering from the currency and trade restrictions imposed by Parliament in 1764. Because of the Revenue and Currency acts, "multitudes" of Pennsylvanians were "already ruined." Trade was decaying and money was so scarce that reputable freeholders were unable to pay their debts; during the last quarter alone thirty-five people had filed for bankruptcy in Philadelphia courts. Now came the Stamp Act, imposing further burdens on the "exhausted colonies" and drawing off "the last drops of their blood." Second, Dickinson attacked the Stamp Act as an unfair law which fell disproportionately and "with the greatest violence" upon those "least able to bear it"—merchants whose profits had already been sharply

curtailed by trade regulations and *"the lower ranks of people"* who
were no longer able to acquire easy credit. Wealthy colonists who
had money to let at interest would thereby profit from the act,
while its "whole weight" would fall "on the necessitous and industrious," who most of all required "relief and encourage-
ment."[2]

Dickinson's arguments seem to have been well adapted to
what Philadelphians were thinking in 1765. Although the Stamp
Act was not burdensome in comparison with its counterpart in
England, it came at a bad time for Philadelphians, who were still
suffering from the depression which followed the Seven Years'
War. Problems caused by the postwar depression had already
been aggravated by the Revenue and Currency acts of 1764. By
the fall of 1765 many Philadelphians believed themselves in an
economic crisis which, while not caused by the Stamp Act, was
bound to be aggravated by it.[3] That strong grounds existed for
objecting to the act as economically inexpedient was affirmed by
Joseph Galloway, leader of the powerful Quaker party.
Galloway urged Philadelphians to admit England's need for
revenue and to plead inability to pay the stamp tax. Repeal of
the tax would more surely follow, he declared, if Americans
abandoned their idle threats regarding constitutional rights and
instead demonstrated to Parliament "the poverty of our circumstances" and "our incapacity to pay the impositions."[4] But
despite Galloway's advice and Dickinson's arguments, and
despite a situation seemingly ripe for assailing the first-order
economic consequences of the Stamp Act, almost all public
protest against the act in Philadelphia objected to its unconstitutionality rather than to its economic inexpediency.

Nor were there many detailed first-order economic protests
against the Townshend Acts. The Townshend Acts were a series
of statutes invoking new regulations designed to curtail colonial
smuggling and imposing import duties on various commodities
shipped from England. Public protest against the acts in
Philadelphia focused almost exclusively upon the new duties,
but not upon their possible economic impact. Inspired by
Dickinson's *Letters from a Farmer in Pennsylvania*, Whig rhetoricians attacked the duties as insidious manifestations of Parliament's unconstitutional quest to tax Americans, but few maintained that the duties harmed commercial interests or imposed
extravagant demands upon the general citizenry. Even though

the new assessments came at a time of tight money and impending recession, Whigs readily conceded that the amount assessed was "not very grievous." Their indictments of the Townshend duties centered, as the Philadelphia Committee recalled in 1774, "not [upon] the value of the tax, but the *indefeasible right of giving and granting our own money* (a RIGHT FROM WHICH WE CAN NEVER RECEDE)."[5]

Arousing discontent with acts of Parliament was the first of several problems facing Whig publicists at the time of the Townshend Acts. A further problem was to implement a plan of resistance that would put sufficient pressure on England to force repeal of the offending legislation. Resolving this problem was sometimes more difficult than inciting disapproval with Parliament. It was often true, as one Whig lamented, that while "all ranks and denominations" opposed the efforts of Parliament to tax Americans, they were not at all united on what would be "the most eligible method to obtain redress."[6] At no time before the debate over independence in 1776 was disagreement regarding the best method of protest more intense in Philadelphia than during the controversy surrounding the Townshend Acts. The Whigs' drive for nonimportation encountered strenuous resistance from Philadelphians who favored less radical modes of dissent. The Whigs' use of first-order economic appeals during the battles over nonimportation had repercussions which affected Philadelphia's resistance movement well after the struggles of 1767–70 had subsided. Thus the subject merits close attention.

The campaign for nonimportation was initiated by Dickinson's *Letters from a Farmer,* which began appearing serially in the city newspapers early in December 1767. For the next three months the "Farmer" argued "with peculiar elegance and perspicuity" that the Townshend Acts posed grave dangers to American liberty. Encouraged by the fact that nonimportation had influenced Parliament to rescind the Stamp Act, Dickinson recommended a similar program of economic coercion to compel British merchants and manufacturers to work for repeal of the Townshend duties.[7]

But Dickinson's eloquence did not move the city's merchants to agree to boycott British goods. Nor were the merchants persuaded by the Whig speakers who addressed them at private meetings in March and April of 1768, even though traders in

New York and Boston had already agreed to nonimportation on condition that merchants in Philadelphia do the same.[8] Faced with the merchants' refusal to stop importing on their own, Whig publicists began an intensive public crusade in May to force them to accept a boycott.

The merchants, however, did not lack advocates. Foremost among them was Joseph Galloway, the Whigs' most persistent and persuasive adversary during the decade of protest. Always deferential to British authority, Galloway did not share the Whigs' outrage over the Townshend Acts. He did not approve of the acts, but neither did he think them sufficiently odious to warrant "drastic" measures of resistance. His opposition to nonimportation was also occasioned by his devotion to advancing the fortunes of the Quaker party. By dampening the fires of protest, he hoped to encourage the British ministry to look with favor upon the party's proposal to convert Pennsylvania from proprietary to royal control. In addition, since the leading protesters were also the chief organizers of the fledgling Presbyterian faction, which was challenging the Quaker party's electoral hegemony in Philadelphia, Galloway instinctively rebuffed the Whigs and their programs as a matter of party policy. Whatever his motives, Galloway was a formidable antagonist. In 1768 he was at the peak of his popularity and influence. As leader of the Quaker party and speaker of the Pennsylvania Assembly, he was the most powerful politician in the colony.[9]

Through the spring and summer of 1768 the battle raged—Dickinson, Charles Thomson, and their fellow Whigs attacking the merchants for "preferring the sale of a few goods" to the restitution of America's rights and privileges; Galloway and his compatriots charging that nonimportation was "premature," "highly imprudent," and potentially destructive of Philadelphia's flourishing commerce.[10] A crucial test of the strength of the opposing factions came in the October elections for the Pennsylvania Assembly. The Quaker party, led by Galloway, assumed a strong position against suspending trade. The party's primary opposition came from the Presbyterian faction, whose leaders, Thomson and Dickinson, were the most visible and influential advocates of boycotting British goods. Nonimportation was not the only issue in the contest, of course, but it was important enough that the election effectively constituted a referendum on the issue. The results showed that the

Whigs had failed to generate widespread public support for a boycott. The city's two Assembly seats were captured by James Pemberton and John Ross, Quaker party stalwarts and staunch foes of nonimportation. Dickinson finished third in the balloting. Most critically, Galloway and his party retained the support of the White Oaks and other mechanic groups. The Old Ticket's victory seemed so complete that Galloway exulted to Benjamin Franklin: "Great pains have been taken in this city by some hot headed, indiscreet men, to raise a spirit of violence against the late act of Parliament, but the design was crushed in its beginning . . . so effectually that, I think, we shall not soon have it renewed."[11]

The Quaker party's triumph was attributable to a number of factors, including the party's political savvy and organization and Galloway's adept attacks upon the Whigs and their schemes. It was also attributable to a crucial miscalculation by Whig rhetoricians. Close analysis reveals that two potentially complementary campaigns emerged in Philadelphia during 1768. One was concerned with domestic issues—Pennsylvania's declining economy and how to rejuvenate it. The other, orchestrated by Dickinson and Thomson, was concerned with imperial questions—the Townshend Acts and what to do about them. Before the October election, however, Whig leaders made no discernable efforts to unite these two movements. They thereby forfeited a golden opportunity to energize support for nonimportation and to solidify the resistance movement at the expense of the Quaker party.

Seventeen sixty-eight was not a good year economically for the large majority of Philadelphians. Beginning in the last two months of 1767 and continuing into 1768 numerous essays, notices, and poems lamenting a lack of circulating currency and complaining of resulting economic hardships appeared in the city's newspapers. "A Tradesman," for instance, noted recent "declensions in our trade, and scarcity of circulating cash." "Another Farmer" pointed out that six or seven years ago the province had been prosperous and money plentiful. But, he added, of the £600,000 in paper money formerly circulating, only about £190,000 were left, and "in a short time the remainder of our paper money will be sunk, whence must follow, barter, trust, declension of trade, and of course bankruptcies, poverty and want." Most writers attributed the lack of circulat-

ing money to one or both of two factors—the Currency Act of
1764 and Pennsylvanians' infatuation with high-priced foreign
luxuries which drew money out of the colony into the tills of
British merchants. For these problems most writers advocated
one or both of two solutions—issuing additional bills of credit
and consuming fewer foreign goods while manufacturing more
at home.[12]

One special characteristic of these laments about the lack of
available currency deserves close notice: the rhetoric was not
directed against the mother country. Writers seemed to accept
the Currency Act and the economic distress of the colony as legitimate and accomplished facts. Their intention was not as
much to stir up opposition to England as to find an efficacious
means of restoring prosperity to Pennsylvania. Complaints
about Pennsylvania's lack of money were voiced prior to and independent of the protests against the Townshend duties.
Indeed, when news of the Townshend Acts reached America,
most Philadelphians seem to have been undisturbed. The
Pennsylvania Assembly was most concerned with the heavy
restrictions placed upon the colony's money supply by the Currency Act of 1764. In a letter to London merchants in October
1767 the legislature thanked them for assistance in repealing the
Stamp Act and identified limitations on the issuance of paper
money as the principal colonial grievance of the moment.[13]

At much the same time that anxiety over the lack of circulating currency peaked in Philadelphia, Thomson and Dickinson
began their campaign for nonimportation, but their campaign
was independent of the drive for economic frugality and
retrenchment. Although unconnected in origin, these two
movements were potentially confluent. Whigs advocated nonimportation as an efficacious means of resisting unconstitutional
taxation, but boycotting British goods would also be an excellent
way to counteract the currency shortage and to restore prosperity. Here was an excellent opportunity to unite behind the
Whig cause those Philadelphians who were distressed about economic conditions and those who were dismayed over the
Townshend Acts.

Inexplicably, Whig publicists did not seek to fuse the two
groups. In fact, it was the preoccupation of Philadelphians with
local economic affairs that prompted Dickinson to write his *Letters from a Farmer*. To Dickinson, the Quartering Act, the suspen-

sion of the New York Assembly, and, above all, the Townshend Acts presented fundamental dangers to the liberties of the colonies. All but ignoring the first-order economic aspects of the acts, Dickinson, Thomson, and other Whig rhetoricians advocated nonimportation, not because it would restore prosperity to Pennsylvania, but because it was the best way to secure repeal of unconstitutional legislation.[14] This error in strategy helped delay the advent of nonimportation by several months.

Happily for the Whigs, the October election did not "crush" the protest movement, as Galloway thought it had. In March 1769 the merchants relented and adopted nonimportation accords.[15] Their change of mind was prompted by several factors, one of which was increased popular pressure for nonimportation from Philadelphia's mechanics, many of whom had voted against the Whigs the previous October.[16] There are a number of explanations for the mechanics' conversion, but to some degree it resulted from important adjustments in the Whigs' rhetorical strategy following the October election. Before October, Whigs had oriented their discourse toward the merchants—cajoling, threatening, flattering, appealing to patriotism and idealism as the occasion seemed to demand. Now they redirected their campaign toward the mechanics and urged them to compel the merchants to institute a boycott. Moreover, the October election showed that arguments regarding the unconstitutionality of the Townshend duties were alone insufficient to solicit ample public support for nonimportation. In the months following the October contest advocates of nonimportation supplemented their familiar constitutional and political arguments with strong entreaties to the economic interests of mechanics.

This shift in strategy was executed most effectually in an essay signed "A Tradesman," which appeared just ten days after the disastrous October poll. Entitled "To the Farmers and Tradesmen of Pennsylvania," the essay appealed brilliantly to "the *laboring* part" of the community. Why, asked its author, were Pennsylvanians "poor and much straitened for cash," despite living in "a most fertile country" peopled by "industrious inhabitants?" The reason was plainly "our destructive importations from *Great Britain*." Not only did British products suck the people's money out of the colony, but worse still, they undermined colonial tradesmen, who too often saw "their

neighbors supplied with imported goods" while their own lay
"dead on their hands, and they and their families suffer[ed] for
want of the proceeds of them." Compounding these problems
were the Townshend Acts, "the snare in which our whole liberty
and property is to be caught, entangled, fettered, limited,
bound, and at last utterly destroyed." The solution to all these
difficulties was not to import any goods from England until the
obnoxious legislation was repealed. Unfortunately, the
merchants could not be trusted "to renounce their own interest
. . . in favor of the public good." Consequently, it was up to the
people themselves not to purchase the traders' wares. General
concurrence to this plan, "A Tradesman" assured, would induce
the merchants to stop importing and thereby restore prosperity
to the farmers and tradesmen, who were, after all, "the most
substantial part of the province."[17]

Arguments such as those advanced by "A Tradesman" constituted only a minor part of the total case for nonimportation, but
they added urgency to the Whigs' constitutional appeals and
helped secure the support of enough mechanics to pressure
recalcitrant merchants into instituting a boycott. The backing of
the mechanics was crucial to Whig leaders for other reasons as
well. No protest movement could long be sustained which did
not include a substantial portion of the Philadelphia middle
class. Nor could the Whig-Presbyterian faction hope to dis-
mantle the Quaker party's domination of provincial politics
without undermining the merchant-mechanic coalition that had
long assured the electoral hegemony of the Old Ticket in the
city. When disputes over nonimportation flared again in 1770,
Whig writers and speakers responded with another masterful
blend of constitutional and economic appeals designed to keep
and enlarge their following among mechanics.

The period of nonimportation hurt many Philadelphia
merchants, especially after the initial phase during which
traders unloaded their surplus inventories of less desirable
goods. Nonimportation proved to be an economic blessing,
however, for many of the city's mechanics. Throughout the
northern and middle colonies nonimportation encouraged
frugality and increased use of domestic manufactures. Without
the normal supply of British goods, there was a great demand
for American-made products, which spurred an economic
upsurge for Philadelphia's mechanics.[18] By the beginning of

1770 the recession that had hung over the city for two years began to disappear. Good times were in the offing.

Then in April 1770 Parliament repealed all of the Townshend duties except that on tea. Merchants, especially those in the dry goods trade, had grown progressively more discontented with nonimportation through 1769 and early 1770. When word of the repeal arrived they began to press for an end to the boycott. Whigs, however, urged that nonimportation be continued until Parliament removed the duty on tea. As we shall see in the next chapter, their major argument was that the boycott should be retained as a matter of principle since the tea tax violated American rights as surely as did the other duties. But having learned well the lessons of 1768–69, and being acutely aware that nonimportation was "extremely suited to the present [economic] circumstances of the colonies, even if" the Townshend Acts were "taken away," they strengthened their argument with first-order economic appeals to Philadelphia mechanics.[19]

The return of prosperity in 1770 was not due to nonimportation alone, but nonimportation was the most visible catalyst for the recovery, a circumstance Whig spokesmen capitalized upon. In the first place, they enumerated the general fiscal advantages created by the ban on British goods. "Amor Patriae" deemed nonimportation "a blessing to all America, by clearing her from an immense debt, and establishing many useful manufactures in her different provinces." Bringing things closer to home, "A Pennsylvanian" exclaimed that during the boycott Pennsylvania had "increased more in wealth than it ever did, in any equal space of time, since its first settlement." In the second place, Whigs amplified upon the ways nonimportation had benefited mechanics in particular. Not all mechanics had profited from the boycott, "A Tradesman" admitted, but those who had suffered were "few when compared to the number who received great benefit from it." Seeking to drive a wedge between mechanics and merchants, Whigs pointed to the rapid growth of domestic manufacturing during the previous year and charged that merchants wanted to resume importing in order to suppress the competition for customers from mechanics "extensively engaged in valuable manufactures." Not only would renewed importation compromise the essential rights of all Americans, Whigs warned, it would also destroy the common man's resurgent "felicity and prosperity."[20]

Partially through appeals such as these, Whig publicists successfully encouraged large numbers of mechanics to pressure
the merchants to continue nonimportation.[21] Nonetheless, the
dry goods merchants engineered repeal of the boycott.[22] In the
October Assembly elections, held less than two weeks after the
repeal, large numbers of Philadelphia's mechanics who believed
they owed their prosperity to the boycott deserted the Quaker
party, which had failed to support extended nonimportation,
and cast their ballots for the Whig-Presbyterian group, which
had strongly advocated continuing the boycott. The desertion of
the mechanics from the Old Ticket was so severe that Joseph
Galloway was forced to seek election from conservative Bucks
County rather than from Philadelphia County, which had
returned him to the Assembly every year since 1765.[23]

To attribute the mechanics' support of nonimportation and
flight from the Quaker party solely to economic self-interest
would oversimplify a complex historical phenomenon. Some
mechanics no doubt supported the protest movement because
they feared that the continued tax on tea severely endangered
American liberty. Others may have changed their traditional
voting patterns because of special dissatisfactions with the
Quaker party.[24] Still others may have been influenced by
William Goddard's sensational pamphlet, *The Partnership,* in
which Goddard accused Galloway and his colleague Thomas
Wharton of denigrating the intelligence and abilities of the
mechanics whose votes they so readily accepted.[25] Nevertheless,
it is clear that many mechanics allied with the Whig-Presbyterian
faction because it championed programs economically beneficial
to Philadelphians engaged in domestic manufacturing.[26]

The change in the mechanics' allegiance had far-reaching
consequences for the resistance movement. Some mechanics
continued to vote for the Quaker party, but the party's hold on
them became ever more insecure after the battles over nonimportation. Whig-Presbyterian leaders, meanwhile, continued in
future years to court the mechanics. Significantly, it is after 1770
that we read most about the important role of Philadelphia
mechanics in the coming of the Revolution. They flocked to the
side of the Whigs in the surge of protest activity in 1773, lent almost united support to the Continental Association in 1774, provided most of the membership in the city militia in 1775, and
lent strong impetus to the drive for independence in 1776.[27] By

adapting their rhetoric to the first-order economic motives of Philadelphia mechanics during the embroilments over nonimportation, Whig leaders helped to create a coalition which would carry the city from protest to revolution.

After the resumption of importation in 1770, no new imperial controversies of significance materialized in Philadelphia until news of the Tea Act arrived late in the summer of 1773. Devised to relieve the East India Company's financial difficulties, this legislation also promised to benefit colonial consumers. The act maintained the import duty on tea established in 1767, but by allowing the East India Company to deal directly with colonial retailers it enabled Philadelphians to buy tea at one-half its former legal price and at a rate competitive with that demanded by colonial smugglers.[28] Nor did it pose an immediate threat to the profits of legitimate traders, who had continued to boycott tea when the duty on it was not rescinded with the rest of the Townshend duties. By 1773 virtually all of the tea coming into Philadelphia was handled by a few enterprising smugglers, and they alone stood to sacrifice business because of the act.[29]

In generating and focusing discontent with the Tea Act, Whig rhetoricians conceded that the threepence duty on tea was "trifling" and that the act as a whole even promised "some pecuniary advantage." They argued that the seemingly innocuous duty had to be opposed because it violated the colonists' right of self-taxation and thus posed "the most dangerous stroke that has ever been meditated against the liberties of America."[30] As with protest against the Townshend Acts, opposition to the level of taxation imposed by the Tea Act was precluded by the priority given the claim that it was the method of raising revenue and not the amount raised that most vitally endangered Philadelphians.

While the tea tax was not vulnerable to attack on first-order economic grounds, other provisions of the Tea Act raised the specter of an eventual East India Company monopoly on all goods imported from the Orient—a monopoly which the Whigs claimed menaced the economic well-being of every Philadelphian. This argument was forwarded most persuasively in two broadsides circulated in the city during the last two months of 1773. "A Mechanic" issued warning that while the East India Company had chartered colonial vessels to bring their tea to America and had appointed local merchants as factors for distributing the tea, the company ultimately planned to use its own ships and its own agents and thereby eliminate any possible colonial profit. "A Mechanic" further alleged that the company also hoped to establish a monopoly on all other Indian goods sold in America. This accomplished, the company would "sell goods at any exorbitant price," ruining colonial merchants, shipbuilders, and artisans—all of whom would "groan under the dire oppression."[31]

A second inflammatory piece of rhetoric came from John Dickinson. Writing as "Rusticus," he urged his fellow citizens to oppose the Tea Act, not only because it was unconstitutional, but also because it marked a new step in the British scheme to strip Americans of their property. By establishing a monopoly for the East India Company, he predicted, "WE, our WIVES and CHILDREN, together with the HARD EARNED FRUITS OF OUR LABOR," would be given over to a "*bankrupt company* to augment [its] stock and to *repair* [its] *ruined fortunes*." In some of the most virulent language he employed at any time during the decade of protest, Dickinson assailed the company for its history of pillage in Asia and forecast dire consequences for Philadelphians should it gain a foothold in America.

[The East India Company] have levied war, excited rebellions, dethroned lawful princes, and sacrificed millions for the sake of gain. The revenues of mighty kingdoms have centered in their coffers. And these not being sufficient to glut their avarice, they have, by the most unparalleled barbarities, extortions and monopolies, stripped the miserable inhabitants of their property and reduced whole provinces to indigence and ruin. Fifteen hundred thousand, it is said, perished by famine in one year, not because the earth denied its fruits, but [because] this company and its servants engrossed all the necessaries of life and set them at so high a rate that the poor could not purchase them. Thus having drained the sources of that immense wealth, which they have for several years past been accustomed to amass and squander away on their lusts and in corrupting their country, they now, it seems, cast their eyes on *America,* as a new theatre, whereon to exercise their talents of rapine, oppression, and cruelty.[32]

In arguing that the Tea Act portended an East India Company monopoly on all Oriental goods, the Whigs raised what on first sight would appear to have been a volatile economic issue for Philadelphia merchants. But despite the fact that Oriental goods composed one-third of Philadelphia's total imports, there is little evidence that the city's importers were unusually concerned with the prospect of monopoly.[33] On the other hand, anti-monopoly arguments may have had an effect upon the general body of citizens, many of whom shared the British tradition of hostility toward monopoly and especially toward that granted by government.[34] Fears of and antipathy toward monopoly and "the narrow-hearted monopolizer" were expressed often during the decade of protest. To colonial Philadelphians, monopoly seemed no less than an "atrocious crime," "one of the greatest abuses to the trade of a free people."[35] But even though the Whigs' injunctions against an East India Company monopoly played skillfully upon well-established public attitudes, the impact of this line of anti–Tea Act rhetoric may still have been relatively minor. Significantly, the resolutions adopted at the public meeting held in October 1773 to protest the act did not mention monopoly or its possible economic consequences.[36] Discontent, and the protesters' rhetoric, focused upon the unconstitutionality of the tax on tea.

Not surprisingly, there were virtually no first-order economic protests in Philadelphia against the Coercive Acts. The first of these acts, passed early in 1774, closed the port of Boston to commerce until the city reimbursed the East India Company for the tea which had been destroyed in the Boston Tea Party. After an interval of two months, Parliament passed two other acts which altered fundamental provisions of the Massachusetts charter. The Coercive Acts did not affect Philadelphia directly, but to many of the city's residents they were tyrannical. Through the summer of 1774 Whig rhetoricians denounced the acts above all else as irrefutable evidence that "a corrupt and prostituted ministry" were "pointing their destructive machines against the sacred liberties of the Americans," conspiring "by every artifice" to "plunder them of their property, and . . . their birthright, *liberty*."[37] Few if any Whigs urged opposition to the Coercive Acts because they presented immediate economic disadvantages to Philadelphians. The very fact that the acts were not aimed at Philadelphia precluded such strategy.

As we have seen, one of the most remarkable features of Whig rhetoric in Philadelphia was the paucity of arguments regarding first-order economic matters. Even when Whigs made im-

portant use of first-order economic arguments—as during the
disputes over nonimportation in 1770—they subordinated those
arguments to broader political appeals. Some reasons for this
can be suggested. One simple explanation is that Whig publicists
committed a crucial error. There are sound strategic explanations, however, for the Whigs' reluctance to assign priority to
first-order economic questions. No act of Parliament or mode of
protest had the same impact upon the first-order economic
interests of all groups in Philadelphia. The Tea Act, for
instance, threatened smugglers but benefited consumers.
Nonimportation aided many mechanics but hurt other
mechanics, especially shopkeepers, and merchants in the dry
goods trade.[38] Whig tacticians may have hoped that by
concentrating upon political issues they could secure the support of a broad cross-section of Philadelphians. In addition, economic self-interest was so subject to the ebb and flow of economic conditions that the level of protest was sure to fluctuate as
the interests of Philadelphians were enhanced or harmed by
parliamentary legislation or by colonial protest measures. A
united campaign of resistance could be better sustained on
political grounds.

Whig spokesmen needed, and sought, a banner under which
merchants and mechanics could band together even as the economic effects of individual statutes or protest activities were
mitigated through time or nullified by repeal. They needed an
appeal so general and yet so succinct as to "coalesce diverse,
often conflicting groups, into one compact mass vibrating to one
hope and to one ideal."[39] The one hope and ideal to which Whig
rhetoricians returned most often was liberty. This is not to say
that there were no economic grounds for uniting Philadelphians
and sustaining a sense of grievance against the mother country.
Such grounds did exist and were employed in the form of
second-order economic arguments.[40] Before turning to the nature and function of these arguments, however, we need to
consider briefly the affinity between economic interest and
ideological principle in the rhetoric of the Revolution.

Underlying much modern scholarship on the Revolution
seems to be an assumption that economic interest and
ideological principle are incompatible or at least highly an-
tagonistic determinants of human behavior. To some historians,
the Revolution grew out of a clash of economic interests between

England and America in which dissenting colonists exploited highly moralistic maxims of philosophy and government to mask more nefarious, mercenary motives.[41] To others, the Revolution was an ideological, constitutional struggle to defend American rights against British encroachments, a struggle which economic interest did not influence in any but the most peripheral fashion.[42]

There are strengths and weaknesses in both of these interpretations. The point to note here is that a bifurcation between ideological principle and economic self-interest is not evident in most revolutionary movements and definitely is not present in the rhetoric of the Revolution in Philadelphia. Passages can be isolated from the literature of protest published in Philadelphia during the prerevolutionary decade to support both interpretations convincingly. But revealing as these passages may be of individual patterns of thought and perception, they are too often considered out of context. When the pamphlets, speeches, broadsides, and essays are read as cohesive, integrated persuasive messages, they quickly disclose that cardinal elements of the revolutionary Whig ideology—preoccupation with American constitutional and natural rights, apprehension about British conspirators, concern about the debilitating effects of luxury and corruption, belief in a special American destiny—are interwoven with examinations of the financial consequences of parliamentary legislation and the proper role of the colonies in the economy of the empire. This interpenetration of economic interest and ideological principle is most evident in the second-order economic arguments employed by Whig writers and speakers during the decade of protest.

At the time of the Stamp Act, Joseph Galloway defended Parliament's attempt to raise revenue in America. It was universally known, he stated, that England struggled under an enormous debt partially incurred by the expense of defending America from "Indian barbarities, popish cruelties, and superstition." It was also well known that during the recently concluded Seven Years' War colonial assemblies had responded to parliamentary requests for funds with stalling, insufficient appropriations, and in some cases, outright refusal. Since England could not gain sufficient revenue by appealing to "the various caprices of our different legislatures," she had no recourse but to compel America to contribute the money which was "so reasonable and necessary for her preservation."[43]

Galloway's rationale could have been written by George Grenville, so accurately did it reflect official British sentiment. Moreover, the feeling that America owed something to England for her protection in the recent war and for the past 150 years was held by many Philadelphians in 1765; and it was the basis of arguments used in the city from 1765 to 1776 by British officials and sympathizers.[44] Whigs opposed the notion that America was indebted to England for past and present aid and advanced cogent second-order economic rationales for resisting parliamentary legislation, especially legislation that taxed Americans.

Of all the arguments advanced by Galloway and others of similar persuasion, the one to which protesting rhetoricians responded least convincingly was the charge that America had failed to donate her fair share to the war effort, perhaps because to a considerable degree Galloway was right. Despite the excellent records of Connecticut, New York, and Massachusetts, most colonies, Pennsylvania included, had met their quotas only partially; others had ignored all of the requisitions.[45] Nonetheless, some Whigs claimed that Americans had done everything in their power to ensure victory against the French and their Indian allies. These writers admitted that some colonies may not have granted all the money requested of them but only because they could not afford to give more. More important, colonial militiamen had shed their blood as freely as British regulars. When one considered the expenditure of both money and lives, explained William Hicks, "the colonists, in proportion to their *real ability,* did more for the general cause than could reasonably be expected, if not more than Great Britain herself." To say that America had reneged on its commitments was "most wretchedly fallacious"—as was also the notion that she should now be burdened with new taxes because she was unable to do even more during the war.[46]

Other Philadelphia Whigs, however, preferred to ignore the Americans' role in the war. They pointed instead to the enormous material advantages England had reaped from the conflict and questioned why the colonists should be forced to pay for them. Dickinson, for example, noted that the late war was of European origin and was fought by England *"solely for her own benefit."* Now Americans were to be taxed for protecting territories from which they could derive no possible benefits. How absurd and unjust for colonists "to be drained of the rewards of their labor to cherish the scorching sands of *Florida,* and the icy rocks of *Canada* and *Nova Scotia,* which never will return to us one farthing that we send to them." In truth England alone benefited from those territories, "and therefore she alone ought to maintain them. . . . Those who feel the benefit, ought to feel the burden."[47]

There were of course inconsistencies among the Whigs' arguments. On one hand, they pleaded America's lack of ability to do more during the Seven Years' War; on the other hand, they pointed with pride to the colonies' economic strength and natural resources.[48] Nor did the protesters' claims always correspond to economic and political realities. The colonies had not lent full assistance to the military effort, but they had profited financially and militarily from the war, which had spurred several years of rapid economic progress and helped secure colonial frontiers from French encroachments and Indian maraudings. But logical consistency and strict conformity to historical fact are less telling in persuasive discourse than psychological validity. Whig rhetoricians and their partisans believed America had been unfairly used during the war for the advantage of England. This belief helps explain their opposition to parliamentary taxation after 1765.

Equally important, in the course of denying that Americans were indebted to England for blood and treasure, Whig publicists began to reexamine the entire system of thought which defined Americans as obligated to England and therefore beholden to her political dictates. That reexamination led Whigs to the conclusion that Americans were in no way financially or morally obligated to their parent state.

No contention advanced by the supporters of Parliament was rejected more emphatically by Philadelphia protesters than the assertion that America was indebted to England for aid received during the early period of settlement and colonization. Time and again Whig spokesmen contended that the colonists were actually outcasts, the orphans and not the children of England. According to "Colonus," for example, the brave men who settled the colonies had been "driven" from their native lands by persecution and had come to America to found a reign of liberty. James Wilson, himself born in Scotland, explained that the colonists came to America, "took possession of it, planted it, [and] cultivated it"—all "at their own expense." Contemporary Americans thus inhabited a glorious continent "settled at the expense of the possessors and sealed with the blood of their ancestors."[49]

These arguments were extended and reinforced by the Whigs' persistent claims that Philadelphians, like other Americans, had toiled mightily to enhance the power and grandeur of England only to be rewarded with oppressive taxes and trade restrictions. It seemed incongruous that loyal subjects who had "extended the dominions of the best of kings over half the globe; enriched his metropolis, supported his manufactures, made his merchants as princes, multiplied his subjects, and dismayed his enemies" were now to be reduced to vassalage and treated as rebels. By colonial industry and trade England "rose to her present eminence," exclaimed John Carmichael, "and now the very power we helped to give her is retorted on us with redoubled vengeance and unheard of cruelty." While the colonies also benefited by the connection with England, said Dickinson, every advantage was already "amply—dearly—paid for" by the restrictions upon American commerce and industry. "Eugenio" estimated those benefits to be £1 million per year, a sum "infinitely too great" considering that each colony had its own government to support. In short, Whigs contended that Americans had supported themselves for more than a century, had greatly enriched the coffers of England, had labored under severe economic restrictions, and were therefore "no more bound in conscience to pay one farthing in discharge of the national debt than . . . to contribute towards lessening the *national debt* of Japan."[50]

According to Whigs, the issue was not whether Philadelphians should pay for their defense and internal government. They should; but they had done so and were doing so. As Richard Wells explained, Philadelphians did not object to assisting Englishmen economically "whenever they stand in need of and convince us of the propriety of the demand."[51] The demands for revenue after 1765 were held by Whigs to be unwarranted in light of history and in view of the amounts of money that already accrued to England through trade duties and restrictions upon

American commerce and manufacturing. Given such views, it
was natural for Whig partisans to entertain a sense of economic
grievance against England, a sense of grievance rooted less in
the feeling that the new taxes were exorbitant than in the belief
that they were unjustified. Adding to and intensifying this sense
of grievance were claims that Americans were being exploited to
gratify the avarice of British merchants, planters, and
politicians.

Before 1765 most Philadelphians granted the legitimacy of
the mercantile system, perhaps because trade regulations were
laxly enforced and easily circumvented. As late as 1773 most
seemed to agree with Dickinson that Parliament possessed the
right to control American trade for the benefit of the whole
empire. Still, when the dispute over taxation flared in 1765 and
again in the years following 1767, some Philadelphia Whigs
began to complain of the "stifling" checks upon colonial commerce and manufacturing. Among the checks to which they objected were the laws against making steel and iron, the restraints
placed upon hatters and the exportation of hats, the prohibition
against carrying woolen goods manufactured in one colony into
another, the ban on directly importing Spanish and Portuguese
wines, the restrictions upon colonial fisheries, the duties laid on
foreign sugar and molasses, and the general practice of shipping
all European and East Indian goods to America by way of England—a practice estimated to increase the cost of such goods by
20 to 40 percent.[52]

It is important to notice that Whigs rarely attacked any of
these statutes and regulations individually and seldom cited
specific amounts of monetary loss. Rather, they grouped the
specifics together as data for their claim that American economic interests were being systematically sacrificed to the
interests of British merchants and West Indian planters. To
Hicks it seemed as if England received nine-tenths of the profit
of even "our most successful commerce" while Americans were
"humbly contented with being well-fed and clothed as the wages
of our labor." Dickinson averred that the colonies were but a
segment of the empire and that the good of the whole was
properly to be considered above the interests of its constituent
parts. But, he charged, the restraints upon American commerce
and manufacturing deprived Philadelphians of the rightful
rewards of their labor, promoted "*partial* [rather] than *general*

interests," and sacrificed "the welfare of millions . . . to the magnificence of a few."[53] The "logic" of this indictment was strengthened by the frequent charges that Americans were being economically exploited by a British government so enervated by luxury and corruption that it could no longer support its own massive weight except by divesting Americans of their hard-earned property.

While British officials and sympathizers attributed most of the country's £140 million national debt to necessary military and political expenditures, Whig protesters in Philadelphia identified the major sources of the debt as governmental corruption, opulence, and mismanagement. When Philadelphians looked to Parliament and the ministry they saw great men such as William Pitt and Edmund Burke. They also saw and were appalled at the seemingly endless creation of new posts and the "great numbers of useless officers" promoted to fill them. They saw frequent changes in the ministry and "ministers retiring with enormous pensions for trifling, if any services." England could control her debt "by abolishing all useless offices and unrighteous pensioners," but she was falling prey to ministerial avarice, "cruelly oppressing an infant country" already deeply in debt because of trade restrictions, contracting currency, and aid extended to England during the war.[54]

Not only was the mother country's debt due to her own lavishness but, the Whigs warned, she was now extending to America the same profligate manner of government which was ruining her at home. With the creation of new American customs posts, the Whigs claimed, England could no longer hide behind the false charge that Americans were being taxed to alleviate legitimate expenses of government. It was now perfectly evident that they were being assessed "for the continuance of the present expensive establishment of commissioners, collectors, etc., with the long train of vermin under them, the better to carry on their long and . . . confirmed plan of corruption and venality." There was no doubt, reported Benjamin Franklin from London, that the post-1764 legislation was all "a piece of ministerial policy" designed to create "an American establishment, whereby they may be able to provide for friends and favorites."[55] According to Whig spokesmen, the question at issue was whether Philadelphians were to be secure in their property, or were to have it "wantonly wrested" from them and "consigned over to a set of greedy harpies." If Americans submitted to Parliament, the government's minions would "multiply and increase in every city and village through the continent," while "swarms of placemen and pensioners" devoured American property "like rapacious locusts."[56]

Arguments that American property was being usurped to satisfy British "extravagance and ambition" were amplified and reinforced by reports from England that the people there were "sunk in luxury" and wished "only to get their hands into the purses of Americans to support them in it." In an especially notable essay, "A Tradesman" portrayed British luxury as "a hungry mischief" which would "assuredly swallow all the wealth and spirits of America." The national debt was already astronomical, and the government's "unbounded luxury and profuseness" would render increased revenues "more and more necessary." Philadelphians might as well think of filling "a bottomless pit" as think of satisfying England's wants when £8,000 sterling was paid for a coach, thousands were given away in pensions, and £10,000 lavished in one night on a ball. Given such excesses, Americans could never get the mother country out of debt short of surrendering everything they owned. England was little more than "a pit that will soon swallow up all the wealth of *America* and, like *Pharaoh's* lean kine, will ne'er be the fatter for it all."[57]

These were arguments the average citizen could easily understand. No doubt some of the dissatisfaction with Parliament after 1765 grew out of general opposition to increased taxes, however small the increases may have been. One Philadelphian explained that it mattered little whether the taxes were called internal or external, trade regulations or revenue duties: "If the money is taken out of my pocket, it is of little importance what epithet is used. I shall not be a farthing the richer or poorer for words and names."[58] But opposition to higher taxes is bound to intensify if those being taxed believe the taxes are going to those who do not deserve or will waste them. The Whigs' essential claim was not just that Philadelphians would eventually be impoverished by parliamentary impositions, but that money was being stolen for illicit purposes by conniving, immoral men. This claim—and the wealth of proof that made it believable—was well calculated to arouse a profound sense of anger and bitterness against not only the inexpediency, but the economic and moral injustice of British policy.

Assertions that England desired an American revenue to feed its "bottomless pit" of corrupt officeholders and luxurious excesses led naturally to the Whigs' third theme of second-order economic grievance: that individual acts of Parliament must be opposed because they established precedents for future tax burdens. This theme was broached as early as 1765, when John Dickinson warned Philadelphians that the Stamp Act should be regarded as an "EXPERIMENT OF YOUR DISPOSITION," shrewdly designed to provide "a detestable precedent" which would justify British politicians when they should "hereafter mediate any other taxation upon you." The theme was voiced again during protest against the Townshend Acts, when Dickinson cautioned that although the duties were not very steep, they established "a PRECEDENT, the force of which shall be established by the tacit submission of the colonies." And the same theme occupied a central position in Whig discourse in 1773, when Thomas Mifflin insisted that the Tea Act provided a warrant for taxation by which "the impositions may be increased at pleasure; and America be subjugated without the possibility of redemption." Whig protesters were asking, Once Parliament is allowed to tax us, where will it end? Most claimed it would end with America "drained of its wealth, and the inhabitants reduced to greater and greater degrees of poverty."[59]

This claim provided an especially compelling reason for sustained opposition to all acts of Parliament that sought to tax Philadelphians. And like other second-order economic arguments, this one too was intimately interwoven with a set of beliefs derived from Whig ideology. One belief was that British leaders harbored conspiratorial designs upon American property, a belief which naturally fostered feelings of political and moral estrangement from the mother country. It also helped deepen the Whigs' sense of economic grievance; for if conspiracy existed, there could be no doubt that Parliament and the ministry would indeed impose further and more stringent taxes when the opportunities arose. As one writer put it, "I know the ministers, or in plain words, their master, Lord Bute, has ordained it shall be."[60]

The Whigs' case against allowing precedents for future taxes also rested upon a set of assumptions regarding the nature of power. It was a widely shared judgment of Philadelphia protesters that power was by nature tenacious, grasping, aspiring, restless, insatiable, and, above all, threatening. "Let power be lodged in the hands of one, or one hundred," proclaimed William Hicks, "it ever was, and ever will be, of an encroaching nature." Philadelphia Whigs drew a clear line between power and right, with the latter always under attack from the former. While not necessarily evil in itself, power was corrupting because of the inability of even good men to resist the temptations of ambition. As one writer explained, "Power is known to be intoxicating in its nature, and in proportion to its extent, is ever prone to wantonness."[61]

Given these views of the dangers of power, we can better understand the fears Whig rhetoricians and their partisans held of the long-range economic consequences of parliamentary taxation. Once Americans granted Parliament the power to tax, it would inevitably exercise that power more and more wantonly and more and more destructively, eventually reducing the once happy colonists to the most deplorable of all conditions, slavery. Dickinson, for example, argued that the time to resist Parliament's insidious scheme to tax America was before the Stamp Act went into effect, not after: "Can we imagine . . . that when so great a point is carried, and *we have tamely submitted,* that any other Ministry will venture to propose, or that the Parliament will consent to pass, an act to renounce this advantage? No! Power is of a tenacious nature: What it seizes it will retain." Hicks made a like connection in his animadversions upon the Townshend duties.

A peaceable submission to the first attacks of encroaching power is altogether incompatible with the genius of liberty. . . . If we exert ourselves in a timely opposition to the first advances of an encroaching power, we may reasonably flatter ourselves with a hope of succeeding; but if we supinely wait 'til this usurped authority is confirmed by time, and strengthened by the common arts of usurpation, we shall vainly endeavor to check its *irresistible progress.* Common sense, and common experience, most incontestably prove that too much caution can not be used in determining the nature and extent of all delegated power.[62]

The Whigs' alarm over the erection of precedents which might institutionalize taxation of the colonies was further intensified and lent especially ominous meaning by the fourth

theme of second-order economic grievance: that by depriving
Americans of their physical property and by assaulting the right
to security of property, parliamentary impositions posed a grave
threat to liberty itself.

Although contemporary American political thought tends to
separate property rights from human or civil rights, no such
dichotomy existed in eighteenth-century American thought.[63]
During the revolutionary era it was widely believed that every
man possessed "a right to anything as to make it [his] own, exclusive of all others' right or claim to it."[64] Taxing Philadelphians
without their consent thus constituted a blatant infringement of
their sacred right to hold and personally divest of their
property. But taxation without expressed consent also presented
an unequivocal threat to liberty itself, for without security of
property there was no guarantee of liberty.[65] This linkage of
liberty to rights of property was not purely theoretical; according to Philadelphia protesters, it was the "rule" governing the
exercise of power and was confirmed by history. "Liberty and
property are necessarily connected," one writer exclaimed. "He
that deprives of the latter without our consent deprives of the
former." Taking a man's property, warned another, was typically the first step in destroying his liberty, for "the same power
that may deprive of the one may also deprive of the other." Yet
another exclaimed, "Our enemies very well know that dominion
and property are closely connected; and that to impoverish us is
the surest way to enslave us.[66]

Whig rhetoricians illustrated the inseparability of political
liberty and economic security by the historical "fact" that no
power was more critical to freedom than the power of the purse.
According to Dickinson, the course of history in such countries
as France, Denmark, Turkey, and Russia proved that "no people
can be *free*, but where taxes are imposed on them *with their own
consent*, given personally, or by their representatives." Another
writer warned that should control of the finances of state be
removed from Americans and lodged in a Parliament guided by
conspirators against American freedom, colonial legislatures
would rapidly disintegrate for want of duties and colonists
would "quickly find that neither the want of laws for internal
police, nor the redress of grievances" would be "deemed a sufficient cause for convening them." As long as Americans com-
manded the pursestrings they would also command the power

to restrain arbitrary rule; "but take that shield from the governed, and governing oppression and tyranny" would "thrive gradually . . . and even rage uncontrollably."[67] Believing that "every other power must follow" the power of the purse, Philadelphia Whigs insisted that while "one law imposing a tax (although small) on America[ns], without their consent," remained in force, the colonists were "in a degree of slavery." Following the same reasoning, the several thousand Philadelphians who gathered at the State House on 20 July 1768 to protest the Townshend duties concluded that any attempt by Parliament to levy taxes on Americans was equally "destructive of property, liberty, and happiness."[68]

The ideational interconnection of property and liberty explains much about the Philadelphia Whigs' neglect of first-order economic questions. To Whig publicists, the primary threat presented by Parliament was not against the economic well-being of individuals or even groups; it was a superordinate threat against the property and liberty of the whole society. Hence while individual acts of Parliament might affect first-order economic concerns differently, protest was always obligatory since all the acts imperiled the entire community's property and liberty. Again, the Whigs derived and moved from an equation within which they interrelated economic interest and ideological principle. While property was the major security of liberty, liberty was also "the great and only security of property." Therefore, any act which abused American liberty menaced American property, and vice versa. On these grounds Whig rhetoricians urged Philadelphians to take care of their property and by extension their liberty; and they urged them equally to "take care of our *rights,* and we *therein* take care of *our prosperity.*"[69]

It is impossible, of course, to measure the impact of the Whigs' second-order economic arguments upon the perceptions and attitudes of the Philadelphia audience to whom they were addressed. Still, we can assess their function and importance by observing their potentially wide popular appeal and the kinds of responses they encouraged.

One of the Philadelphia Whigs' most pressing goals throughout the decade of protest was to maintain as united a resistance movement as possible given the wide and often sharply conflicting political, religious, and economic outlooks among the city's residents. One obvious way to facilitate unity was to place primary emphasis upon broad issues of right and ideological principle. But the nonimportation campaigns of 1768 70 made it clear that protesters could not garner sufficient public support to implement their programs without employing economic as well as political appeals. Unfortunately, not all Philadelphians shared the same immediate financial needs and desires. It would have been impossible therefore to maintain unity had great stress been laid upon first-order economic appeals. Second-order economic appeals were broad enough, however, to command the concern of all groups in the city, for they showed how the property of every one of the city's inhabitants was being immediately exploited and potentially destroyed by the machinations of British politicians. This is not to say that Whig advocates always used second-order economic arguments as deliberate strategy—evidence does not exist to reach any firm conclusion on this matter. But the question of intent is not at issue here. The essential point is that the Whigs' second-order economic appeals allowed the protesters to appeal effectually to what Henry Drinker called "Interest, all powerful Interest," without irrevocably alienating any of Philadelphia's major religious, political, or economic factions.[70]

On balance, the Whigs' second-order economic arguments encouraged two kinds of judgments, one concerning the moral and economic injustice of parliamentary legislation and the other concerning the potential long-range fiscal dangers of Parliament's efforts to tax Americans. Each of these sets of judgments produced a deeper, more severe, less negotiable sense of grievance than that inculcated by first-order economic discontents—by elevating economic questions to the plane of moral questions and by interrelating the security of property with the survival of political liberty. Nor was it necessary for Philadelphians to agree with all of the Whigs' major claims to share this sense of grievance.

By allying questions of economic self-interest with questions of ideological principle, Whig spokesmen made the economic quarrel with England as much moral as mercenary. And they made the political quarrel mercenary as well as moral. For example, while Philadelphia Whigs denied that the doctrine of virtual representation was constitutionally applicable to colonies three thousand miles away from England, they also denounced virtual representation because it authorized Parliament to "give and grant away the goods of colonists at pleasure." Similarly, though Whig spokesmen stated time and again that British leaders were violating the natural rights of Philadelphians to liberty and happiness, they also contended that "there cannot be a stronger natural right than that of a man's making the best profit he can of the natural produce of his lands, provided he does not thereby hurt the state in general." And even slavery, a political condition despised above all else by Whig rhetoricians, was also dreaded as an economic condition that existed when a people "have nothing . . . they can call their own."[71] Throughout the literature of the Revolution in Philadelphia one finds over and over that ideological principle and economic interest energized one another in creating and solidifying a revolutionary set of perceptions and beliefs.

# 3

# THE CASE FOR
# AMERICAN RIGHTS

THE most characteristic strategy of Whig writers and speakers in
Philadelphia throughout the decade of protest was to insist upon
American natural and constitutional rights as the overriding cri-
teria by which all acts of Parliament were to be judged and by
which resistance to those acts was justified.[1] The concern here is
not whether Philadelphia Whigs were successful in the use of
this strategy. They were. By 1776 a majority of Philadelphians
agreed that England had for the past decade violated the most
hallowed constitutional and natural rights of her American subjects. The concern here is how this consensus was created, maintained, and, most critically, intensified as Whig rhetoricians
expanded their definitions of American rights in response to the
progression of British legislation from the Stamp Act crisis to
the beginning of war in 1775.

The ideological tenets enunciated by Whig publicists in 1765
did not remain static during the decade of protest. From the
time of the Stamp Act through the time of the Coercive Acts,
Philadelphia protesters tailored their arguments to changing
conditions and emerging problems. What began as a dispute
over whether Parliament could rightfully tax the colonists
moved to a controversy over whether Parliament could rightfully make any laws at all for the colonies. In asserting and defending the rights of Philadelphians against British encroachments, Whig rhetoricians inexorably diminished the middle
ground of British-American relations and undermined compromise as a conceivable option. This progress toward a
potentially revolutionary frame of mind can be charted not only
in the ideological content of Whig rhetoric regarding matters of
constitutional and natural law, but also in the argumentative
methods characteristically employed by Philadelphia protesters
as they developed and promulgated their case for American
rights.

According to Whig rhetoricians, Philadelphians, like other Americans, were entitled to all the rights and privileges protected by the British constitution, that unwritten but socially accepted body of law and principle according to which the several powers of the state were distributed and by which certain rights were secured to different members of the community. Defined broadly, these fundamental rights were life, liberty, and property. None was forfeited except by consent of the people. Within this general framework there existed other, more specific rights. Among these were the rights of trial by jury and freedom from standing armies in peacetime. Although both of these were important items of contention between protesters and British authorities in various of the thirteen colonies, neither assumed prominence in prerevolutionary rhetoric in Philadelphia.

Whigs in all parts of America reacted negatively to the provisions of the Stamp and Townshend acts which strengthened and extended the jurisdiction of vice-admiralty courts. Indignation was equally evident in Philadelphia, especially in 1765, when the Pennsylvania Assembly deemed the Stamp Act "contrary to *Magna Charta*" and destructive of one of the colonists' "most darling and acknowledged rights, that of trials by juries." But neither in 1765 nor in 1767 did protesters in Philadelphia stress the violation of this right in their animadversions on British legislation. It was not until the first months of 1774 that Whig spokesmen unleashed a campaign against the vice-admiralty courts. This campaign, as Joseph Reed admitted, was designed "to distress and harass" the regional court in Philadelphia and focused more or less equally upon the negative effects of the court upon local trade, the unconstitutional nature of the court, and the obnoxious conduct of its junior officers. Concern over the vice-admiralty courts disappeared quickly and permanently from the city's press when word arrived in May of the Boston Port Act.[2]

Not surprisingly, denunciations of standing armies were most conspicuous and most fervid in the rhetoric of Whig protesters in and around Boston. It was there that relations between British troops and colonial citizens were most strained; it was there that American blood was first drawn by British troops. In marked contrast, military-civilian relations in Philadelphia were placid, even cordial, from 1765, when royal troops were sta-

tioned in the city, until September 1774, when they were with-
drawn. Unlike some legislatures, the Pennsylvania Assembly met
the provisions of the Quartering Act fully and without complaint. To be sure, Philadelphia newspapers occasionally printed
essays claiming that American constitutional rights were being
grievously assaulted by the presence of troops in the colonies,
but very few of these essays were written by Philadelphians. Almost all were reprinted from other tabloids, especially from
ones in New England. While such discourses may certainly have
influenced some Philadelphians, there is little evidence that fear
of a standing army played more than a minor role in the growth
of revolutionary sentiment in the city.[3]

For most of the period preceding the outbreak of war, Whig
publicists in Philadelphia subordinated all other constitutional
considerations to one overriding question: "whether the Parliament of Great Britain has a right to lay taxes on the Americans,
who are not, and cannot, there be represented."[4] The issue of
taxation and representation may not have been the most significant intellectual problem in the British-American controversy.
But it was by far the most important issue in Philadelphia
rhetoric during the years 1765–73. And the private correspondence of Philadelphians of all political persuasions discloses that it was the essential, irreducible issue around which
pivoted opposition to the mother country.[5] The touchstone
argument of Whig publicists in their efforts to unite
Philadelphians against the Stamp, Townshend, and Tea acts was
that all three statutes were unconstitutional encroachments
upon the right of all British citizens to be taxed solely by their
own elected representatives.

The constitutional case against parliamentary taxation was
forged during the Stamp Act crisis. Although the case was complex in its legal details, its basic propositions were clearly summarized by the Pennsylvania Assembly. First, "it is the inherent
right of every *British* subject to be taxed only by his own consent,
or that of his legal representatives." Second, "the only legal
representatives of the inhabitants of this province are the
persons they annually elect to serve as members of Assembly."
Third, "the taxation of the people of this province by any other
persons whatsoever . . . than their representatives in Assembly
is unconstitutional and subversive of their most valuable
rights."[6]

The truth of the first of these propositions, the major premise of the syllogism, was so widely believed in Philadelphia that it operated as a "given," or first principle, in 1765 and throughout the controversy with England. The second proposition, or minor premise, was less readily accepted. Defenders of the Stamp Act in England and America agreed with Whig protesters that "no freeman should be subject to any tax to which he has not given his consent." But, they argued, the act did not violate this right because Americans, like residents of England who did not vote for members of Parliament, were "virtually" represented in the Commons. According to the doctrine of virtual representation, the colonists, as members of the British empire, were subject to the supreme legislative authority of Parliament acting as the representative of all the diverse interests in the empire. Thus Parliament possessed the right to tax Americans, just as it taxed all other members of the British community.[7]

Refuting the notion of virtual representation was the major problem facing protesters who sought to deny the constitutionality of the Stamp Act. In Philadelphia this task was met most persuasively by a newspaper essayist who wrote over the name "Freeman" in the *Pennsylvania Journal* of 13, 20, and 27 June 1765. "Freeman" attacked virtual representation as "a monstrous absurdity" incapable of being logically supported "by any reasonable man." According to "Freeman," it was the very nature of representation that the interest of the representative "be consistent with that of his constituent[s]" and that he "have an exact knowledge" of the circumstances and concerns of his electors. Thus, by definition, the rightful representatives of Philadelphians could not be "persons they never chose nor knew." That virtual representation operated in England did not make the doctrine right, as supporters of Parliament claimed, but proved only that "some of the people in England, as well as those in America," were injured and oppressed. To admit its extension to America would not only sacrifice the constitutional right of self-taxation but would also countenance "an encroachment upon private property" which would allow the enemies of America "to exalt their own interest upon the ruin of ours."[8]

The arguments of "Freeman" were soundly formulated and trenchantly presented, but they were convincing to Philadelphians primarily because the premises upon which they were grounded conformed with and drew upon more than a century of American experience with representative govern-ment. Of course, perfect representation did not exist in Pennsyl-vania any more than it existed anywhere in America. Nonethe-less, many Philadelphians felt, as did James Wilson, that representatives were properly considered the "creatures" of their constituents and were strictly "accountable for the use of that power which is delegated unto them."[9] Within this concep-tion of government, virtual representation seemed little short of an absurdity and an "insult," the "gross falsity" of which was evident to every Philadelphian who knew that he could not "even *huzzah* at a British election."[10]

Later in the Stamp Act controversy, writers on both sides of the Atlantic proposed creating American seats in Parliament as a solution to British-American differences. The proposals were at-tractive at first sight; but they were roundly condemned by Whigs for providing a plausible justification for American taxa-tion without erecting adequate safeguards against it. As one Philadelphia protester explained, to have a few Americans among the more than five hundred members of the lower house would be of no consequence. And as there was no American peerage, colonists could never be represented in the House of Lords. Schemes for colonial representation therefore actually promised Philadelphians only "the shadow of liberty without the substance."[11]

If pursued to their logical conclusion, the Whigs' arguments against virtual representation implied that Parliament had no right to legislate for Americans in any matter, whether it be taxa-tion, defense, or trade regulation. At the time of the Stamp Act, however, Philadelphia Whigs sought only to formulate persua-sive grounds for resisting Grenville's legislation and were not prepared to pursue the ultimate logic of those grounds. "A Friend to the Colony" expressed well the typical attitudes of Whiggish Philadelphians during the turmoil precipitated by the Stamp Act.

I contend not for an equality of the colonies with the mother country; they are, and in the nature of things must be, dependent on it. I only contend for a right in the subjects of this, and every other colony, to the laws of England, and to the undoubted right of Englishmen, that no taxes be imposed upon them but by their respective legislatures.[12]

One particularly interesting and heretofore undiscerned facet of protest against the Stamp Act is that remarkably few of the essays that developed the constitutional case against the stamp tax in Philadelphia were written by Philadelphia Whigs. This was especially evident during the crucial summer months of 1765, when opposition to the Stamp Act emerged and crystallized in the city. The influential "Freeman" essays against virtual representation, for example, appeared first in the *New York Gazette* and were subsequently printed in William Bradford's *Pennsylvania Journal*. In fact, no locally authored discourse about the Stamp Act ran in the Philadelphia press until 29 August, when, over the pseudonym "Americanus," Joseph Galloway urged Philadelphians to moderate their protest by stressing the inexpediency rather than the unconstitutionality of the Stamp Act. The first anti–Stamp Act essay by a Philadelphia writer did not appear for another three weeks, when "A True American" belatedly responded to Galloway. John Dickinson was the only Philadelphia Whig to write any other noteworthy pieces before the end of the year. He wrote two. One addressed the economic impact of the acts of 1764 and 1765; the other appeared in November, well after discontent with the Stamp Act had solidified in the city.[13]

If Whig rhetoricians were not composing essays and pamphlets to arouse dissatisfaction with the Stamp Act, what were they doing during the summer of 1765? For the most part, they were attending to local politics. The most consequential concern of Philadelphia politicians in 1765 was not the Stamp Act but the Quaker party's scheme to convert Pennsylvania to a royal colony. Although the party leaders, Galloway and Benjamin Franklin, had been defeated in the 1764 elections, the Old Ticket still controlled the Assembly. Late in 1764 the Assembly sent Franklin to England with instructions to petition for a change of government. Acutely fearful that Franklin might succeed, the Proprietary faction sought, from the beginning of 1765, to gain enough Assembly seats in the October elections to recall Franklin and to quash the movement for a new government. The Stamp Act provided Proprietary leaders a potentially powerful issue with which to assail their Quaker opponents: having been enacted by royal government, it could be pointed to as evidence that royal government in Pennsylvania would similarly assault the people's liberties. Motivated partially by considerations of ideological principle, but also by calculations of political advantage, supporters of the Proprietary interest spearheaded protest against the stamp tax in Philadelphia. Before the election, however, most of their persuasive efforts were devoted, not to elucidating the broad constitutional and imperial issues raised by the Stamp Act, but to utilizing the act as a rhetorical club with which to bludgeon the Quaker party and its proposal for royal government.[14]

The Whig leader most responsible for arousing discontent with the Stamp Act in Philadelphia was not John Dickinson, Charles Thomson, Thomas Mifflin, or any other noted writer, but William Bradford, publisher of the *Pennsylvania Journal*. Today the only identifiable member of the city's Sons of Liberty, Bradford was one of the few Philadelphians actively and centrally committed to the Whig cause from 1765 through the Declaration of Independence. An uncompromising foe of British "tyranny," he served on the committee that demanded the resignation of stamp distributor John Hughes in 1765, initiated agitation against the Tea Act in 1773, enlisted in the militia in 1775, and fervently backed the drive for independence in 1776. But it was as a printer that Bradford contributed most to the protest movement. Through the decade of protest his *Journal* was among the most important and widely read outlets for Whig rhetoric, not only in Pennsylvania, but in other colonies as well. It was reputed to be the newspaper "more generally read by those calling themselves the Sons of Liberty" than any other.[15]

In the summer and fall of 1765 Bradford played an especially vital role in shaping public opinion in Philadelphia. While Quaker and Proprietary politicians railed at each other about altering the colony's form of government, Bradford took the lead in promoting opposition to the Stamp Act. By reprinting in the *Journal* such essays as those by "Freeman," he infused Philadelphians with the constitutional case against parliamentary taxation. By publishing the often inflammatory protest resolves of town meetings and provincial legislatures throughout the colonies, he informed Philadelphians that resistance to the Stamp Act was widespread and respectable. By reporting, at times with favorable commentary, the tactics used in other parts of America to nullify operation of the act, he en-

couraged Philadelphians to engage in similar measures. Bradford's activities so animated residents of the city against
Grenville's law that by mid-July Joseph Galloway had decided to
compose his "Americanus" essay in order to "prevent the contagion of rebellion from spreading irrecoverably far." This,
despite the fact that no local author had yet attacked the Stamp
Act in the city press (and none would for another two months).
Bitter testimony to Bradford's rhetorical prowess came from
John Hughes, whose political career was destroyed by his
adamant refusal to discountenance the Stamp Act. Writing to
British officials in October 1765, Hughes complained that the
intensity of Americans' opposition to the act was attributable primarily to printers like Bradford who "stuffed their papers
weekly . . . with the *most inflammatory pieces* they could procure,
and *excluded everything* that tended to cool the minds of the
people."[16]

Philadelphians of all political factions agreed almost
unanimously in 1765 that Parliament could not rightfully tax the
colonies. At the same time, most citizens, even strident Whigs,
granted that Parliament did have the right to levy imposts for
purposes of regulating trade. This concession was complicated,
however, with passage of the Townshend Acts. The duties imposed by this legislation were designed to raise revenue in
America through the familiar process of collecting imposts at colonial ports. Now Whigs faced a distinct problem: for over a
century Parliament had been passing laws regulating colonial
trade, and for that purpose had imposed duties, which brought
some revenue into the exchequer. At this late date
Philadelphians could hardly claim that Parliament had no right
to lay such duties. Must they therefore submit to the Townshend
duties?[17] This dilemma was brilliantly resolved by John
Dickinson's *Letters from a Farmer in Pennsylvania*, the most influential discourse published in Philadelphia before *Common
Sense*.

Dickinson's main task was to demonstrate that the Townshend
duties were in fact taxes and not simply instruments for controlling trade. Once he did this, the duties could be easily
condemned on the same grounds as the hated stamp tax.
Dickinson resolved this problem by arguing that there existed a
clear distinction between duties laid for the legitimate purpose
of regulating trade and duties laid for the illegitimate purpose

of raising a revenue; and Charles Townshend's legislation manifestly sought to accomplish the latter. In the first place, the intention of procuring a revenue was explicitly avowed in the statute itself. Moreover, it placed duties upon items which colonists could import from no country other than England and which they were forbidden to manufacture themselves. Thus there was no reason to lay the duties except to procure booty for the treasury, and they were therefore unconstitutional. If they were allowed to stand, the colonists' "boasted liberty" was but "a sound and nothing else."[18]

Dickinson's discrimination between duties imposed to regulate trade and those designed to raise revenue was not new to Philadelphians.[19] Nor was it unassailable. Thomas Jefferson labeled it a "half-way house." Benjamin Franklin found it a "middle doctrine" difficult to support "clearly with intelligible arguments." According to Franklin, a better case could be made for either extreme: "that Parliament has a power to make *all laws* for us, or that it has a power to make *no laws* for us."[20] Dickinson himself recognized that the distinction was largely theoretical since even duties laid strictly to govern commerce raised money as effectually as duties laid expressly for that purpose. Dickinson's goal, however, was neither to break new ground nor to determine absolutely the degree to which Parliament could legally exercise jurisdiction in American affairs, but rather to explain why the Townshend duties menaced colonial liberties as severely as had the Stamp Act. Whatever its ultimate shortcomings, his distinction between trade duties and tax measures was perfectly suited to the constitutional issues posed by the Townshend duties.

Appearing first as a series of newspaper essays in Philadelphia, the *Letters from a Farmer* were rapidly reprinted throughout the colonies, achieved seven editions in pamphlet form, and generated an almost unanimous chorus of praise for their author. Town meetings and provincial legislatures from Rhode Island to Georgia hailed "the glorious Farmer" as the foremost champion of American liberty. Perhaps the most eloquent testimony to the aptness and persuasiveness of Dickinson's constitutional arguments is that they shortly assumed the force of first principles for other Whig writers. In the *Pennsylvania Gazette* of 14 April 1768, "Monitor" explained that it would be superfluous to discourse upon the "unconstitutional oppression and injustice" of the Townshend Acts "since no one could be unacquainted with the doctrines set forth so fully "in the late, excellent and unanswerable LETTERS of the FARMER."

Although an adroit response to the Townshend duties, Dickinson's discrimination between trade regulations and tax measures does not alone account for the enormous impact of the *Letters from a Farmer* upon their eighteenth-century readers. To explain that impact we must attend to the totality of Dickinson's message and how he presented it.

In the course of all twelve letters Dickinson provided a judicious and comprehensive statement of the Whig cause, firmly grounded in both fact and theory.[21] The first letter was devoted to introducing the "Farmer" and to demonstrating the dangers of Parliament's recent attempt to suspend the New York legislature for failing to carry out provisions of the Mutiny Act. In the second through sixth letters Dickinson developed and defended his constitutional case against parliamentary taxation in general and the Townshend duties in particular. In the next five letters he moved from the issue of taxation to larger questions posed by all of the Townshend Acts. The final letter magnified the dangers of "slavery" and contained a powerful plea for colonial unity. Throughout, Dickinson supported his contentions with a wealth of legal and historical evidence. He enunciated in the *Letters from a Farmer* almost every major belief of "reasonable" Whigs in the late 1760s: the unconditional denial of Parliament's right to lay any kind of direct tax upon Americans; the historically incontestable link between freedom and a people's ability to resist unrepresentative taxation; the value of historical example as an authoritative guide to the future; the danger of allowing the establishment of precedents for arbitrary governmental action; the illegality and perfidy of England's efforts to circumscribe the activities of colonial legislatures; the unfairness of British efforts to extract additional revenues from the pockets of Americans; the threat posed to America by an ambitious, plotting faction of British politicians; the necessity of firm, yet constitutionally proper, methods of protest and resistance; and, no less vital, the inestimable benefits derived to Americans from their connection with England, a connection that could never be terminated without the colonists bleeding, physically and metaphorically, "at every vein." Much of the impact of the *Letters from a Farmer* in their own time was due to the manner in which they articulated the most elemental yet often conflicting political fears and aspirations of those countless colonists who, like Dickinson, were angry over the Townshend Acts and apprehensive of the designs of British conspirators, yet who truly loved the mother country and desired nothing more than the restoration of normal relations with her.

Dickinson's tract was also a masterpiece of argumentative prose. Although Dickinson was not an "eloquent" writer—he possessed neither the "felicity of expression" of Jefferson nor the awesome linguistic resources of Edmund Burke—his prose was characterized by a grace and a power that set it apart from that of almost all his American rivals. His chief accomplishment in the *Letters from a Farmer,* however, was less aesthetic elegance than argumentative perspicuity. His purpose in composing the *Letters* was exhortative—to arouse apathetic Philadelphians to resist the Townshend Acts "immediately, vigorously, and unanimously." Yet his most pressing stylistic necessity was less hortatory than didactic: to instruct readers of the nature of liberty and how its existence in America was imperiled by British politicians. The controlling stylistic requirement of didactic discourse is clarity, for without understanding there can be no instruction. The great popularity of the *Letters from a Farmer* was attributable in large degree to Dickinson's ability to make the principles of the Whig cause explicable and compelling by stating complex legal and philosophical propositions in clear and striking language. The one quality of the *Letters* praised more often than any other was their perspicuity. As one group of admirers stated, the *Letters* "penetrated to the foundations of the Constitution," "poured the clearest light on the most important points, hitherto involved in darkness bewildering even the learned," and, "with amazing force and plainness of argument," established the principles that would "fully instruct ages yet unborn what rights belong to them and the best method of defending them."[22]

Ironically, while the *Letters from a Farmer* made Dickinson a hero in most parts of America, they did not immediately enhance his political stock in Philadelphia. There his views met opposition from two groups. First, some more doctrinaire Whigs held that to deny Parliament the right to tax America while granting it the right to govern her commerce was an "absurd distinction," an incredibly naive "paradox in policy." This position was argued most trenchantly by William Hicks in a series of newspaper essays presented as the work of "A Citizen" and later reprinted in pamphlet form. Unfortunately, little is known of Hicks except that he was a supporter of the proprietor in the dispute over royal government and a firm advocate of the Whig cause in the late 1760s. In contradistinction to Dickinson, he argued that to grant Parliament any legislative power whatever over the colonies was constitutionally unjustified and politically inexpedient. According to Hicks, there was no legislative power Parliament could rightfully exercise in America, for "under a pretense of regulating our trade we may be stripped of our property; and with an appearance of limiting our manufactures, we may insensibly be robbed of our liberty." Hicks presented his position well, but most Philadelphians were no more prepared in 1768 than in 1765 to deny completely the right of Parliament to legislative sovereignty in the colonies. And despite his differences with Dickinson over the extent to which Parliament could legally prescribe laws for Americans, Hicks readily joined Dickinson and Thomson in spearheading the campaign for nonimportation.[23]

Far more damaging to Dickinson personally and to the Whig movement was the counteroffensive orchestrated by Joseph Galloway, Dickinson's long-time political rival. Part of Galloway's larger effort to dampen overt protest against the Townshend Acts and to prevent nonimportation, this counteroffensive consisted of essentially two stages. The first came in the spring of 1768, when Galloway had reprinted in the *Pennsylvania Chronicle* of 25 April a major essay signed "F + S," which was widely known to have been written by Benjamin Franklin. Franklin's essay did not necessarily reflect Galloway's judgment of British colonial policy, for it contained stinging attacks upon the Townshend Acts and upon the whole system of British restraints on American trade and industry. More important for Galloway's immediate purposes, however, was the fact that Franklin's discourse differed from the *Letters from a Farmer* in two important respects: it did not criticize the Galloway-controlled Assembly for its failure to initiate stern measures against the Townshend Acts, and it did not recommend compulsory nonimportation as a means of combatting the acts (though it did urge voluntary nonconsumption of British goods). Galloway's strategy in printing this essay was subtle but shrewd. Franklin had been the acknowledged leader of the Quaker party prior to his departure for England late in 1764, and it was generally assumed in 1768 that his sentiments still reflected those of the party leadership. By circulating Franklin's essay through the city, Galloway hoped to identify himself and the Quaker party with Franklin as patriotic upholders of American rights. At the same time he would stamp Dickinson with the taint of radicalism by contrasting his denunciation of the Assembly and advocacy of nonimportation with the more moderate plan of resistance championed by Franklin, who, despite his absence, was still the city's most respected citizen.

By the summer of 1768 Galloway had lost his touch for subtlety. Through July and August a number of virulent, often blatantly ad hominem essays highly critical of the "Farmer" and his doctrines appeared in the *Pennsylvania Chronicle,* which Galloway and Thomas Wharton had secretly funded as an organ for Quaker party propaganda. The comments of "Machiavel" were typical. He lambasted the *Letters from a Farmer* for containing "the basest misrepresentations, the blackest ingratitude, the most groundless predictions of vassalage and slavery, the warmest incitements to opposition and violence, and no great affection to the King and Parliament."[24]

Galloway's barrage proved temporarily successful. It helped delay the advent of nonimportation and contributed to Dickinson's defeat in the 1768 Assembly elections. But though Philadelphians were not prepared in 1768 to endorse stern measures of resistance against the Townshend Acts, there was no doubt among either Whigs or their opponents that Dickinson's rhetoric had convinced many citizens that Townshend's legislation did indeed pose potentially grave dangers to American liberties. William Franklin reported to his father that Dickinson's ideas passed "very well with great numbers of the common people . . . and with some others." From this and similar testimony, Benjamin Franklin reported to his European acquaintances that the *Letters from a Farmer* had had "a prodigious effect in spiriting the people up against the late duties." As it became evident in the final months of 1768 and the opening months of 1769 that the weak measures of protest championed by Galloway were not going to secure modification of the Townshend Acts, more and more Philadelphians came to agree with Dickinson and his fellow Whigs on the need for mandatory economic sanctions against the mother country. By the spring of 1769 nonimportation was a reality in Philadelphia, and in 1770 Dickinson was elected to the Assembly from the city. Moreover, the *Letters from a Farmer* continued to be accepted until 1774 as the definitive exposition of the Whig viewpoint on the constitutional quarrel with England. As late as the fall of 1773 Philadelphia Whigs felt it unnecessary to detail the case against parliamentary taxation since the matter had been "so clearly discussed, and the conclusions so firmly established by our FARMER, that we need not say anything on this subject."[25]

Indeed, as long as the major question dividing the colonies from England was that of taxation, there was little need to go beyond Dickinson's position. But in the meantime it appeared to increasing numbers of Philadelphians that their rights could be invaded in even more vital ways than by parliamentary taxation. This perception was confirmed early in 1774, when Parliament moved to punish the town of Boston for the "tea party" held in its harbor the previous December. In a series of legislative actions, Parliament closed the port of Boston to shipping until the town made restitution for the destroyed tea, greatly increased the powers of the royally appointed governor of Massachusetts, authorized the quartering of British troops in the private houses of colonists, and provided that British officials indicted for murder in Massachusetts as a result of their efforts to enforce the revenue laws or suppress civil disorders could be tried in another colony or in England. These Coercive Acts, as they have become known, moved the dispute with England onto new and broader ground. Although not aimed at Philadelphia, the acts demonstrated to the city's Whigs that Parliament could undermine their rights as readily by any kind of general legislation as by the specific act of taxation.

Dickinson's distinction between acts for regulating trade and acts for raising revenue was clearly incapable of meeting the exigency introduced by the Coercive Acts. Philadelphia protesters now argued that the constitutional contest with England was reduced to a single question—whether Parliament could righfully make any laws whatever for America. In the Whigs' response to the Coercive Acts the claim that Parliament

could not tax America was superseded by the wider claim that
there existed no line between those cases in which the colonies
should acknowledge the power of Parliament and those cases in
which they should not. Now, in 1774, the established argument
that Parliament could not tax the colonists because they were not
therein represented was brought to its full, logical extension to
support the Whigs' contention that Parliament possessed no
legislative authority in America. For the most part, however,
Philadelphia protesters based their rejection of the sovereignty
of Parliament upon warrants drawn from natural rights. This
subject will be treated shortly.

It is necessary first to consider the argument of some students
of the Revolution that the system of political ideas developed
from 1765 to 1775 to justify opposition to parliamentary legislation was essentially conservative insofar as it was designed to
defend ancient liberties by appeals to principles long recognized
in the British constitution.[26] Whig protesters in Philadelphia
were indeed conservative in the sense that they argued for old
rather than new liberties, for liberties they had long exercised
free of parliamentary interference. This conservatism helps to
explain the persuasiveness of their arguments which conformed with decades of Philadelphians' experience with
government. The men who led the rhetorical agitation against
England in Philadelphia contended not simply for rights
guaranteed by the British constitution, but for a way of life and a
system of autonomous government which they claimed not only
by virtue of the constitution but also by virtue of history. As
argued by the Whigs, and as perceived by the substantial body of
Philadelphians, it was not America but England that had departed from governmental standards and traditions.

But conservative as Whig publicists may have been in seeking
to preserve the past as they understood it, they proclaimed and
defended American constitutional rights in a manner which
radicalized Philadelphia opinion and which helped foster and
intensify a move toward separation from the mother country. By
denying Parliament any constitutional right to legislative
sovereignty in the colonies, they declared America to be, by legal
right, utterly independent of Parliament. The revolutionary implications of this argument were clearly recognized by Joseph
Galloway, who stepped forward again in 1774 and 1775 to
challenge his old adversaries. If it were true that the colonies

had a "free and exclusive legislation" in all matters of internal policy, he warned, then the Commons could have "no more authority over them than the parliament of Paris," and the colonies were "as independent of the one as the other." As long as protesters persisted in their claims to independence of Parliament, "union and harmony" with the mother country could not "long subsist." According to Galloway, Whig leaders were madly leading Philadelphians down "the high road of sedition and rebellion."[27]

As Galloway realized, denying the sovereignty of Parliament brought the Whigs a great distance toward declaring America completely independent of England. Whigs, of course, denied any such intention and insisted that their only aim was to preserve the rights of Philadelphians by establishing the true nature of the constitutional connection with England. That connection was one in which Americans owed no fealty to Parliament but full and complete loyalty to the king, admitting "of no intermediate parliamentary power between an American legislation and his royal throne." Richard Wells voiced the prevailing Whig view when he proclaimed that Philadelphians owed full allegiance to their "good and gracious King," but could not, *"must not,* allow *any kind of authority in his Parliament."*[28]

Despite such professions of loyalty to George III and repeated denials of any desire for independence, the Whigs' constitutional arguments advanced in response to the Coercive Acts actually left little room for compromise in either England or America. By denying Parliament any authority to intercede in American affairs, Whig advocates such as Wells and Wilson created a "legal" rationale for resisting all imperial legislation. The only further constitutional interpretation needed to propel them from protest to revolution was one which abrogated Americans' obligations to George III. Those obligations were not denied until 1776 and will be discussed in a later chapter. Parliament, of course, was not willing to abdicate its power over Americans. Nor was George III prepared to accept an American legislative power independent of and equal to Parliament. Indeed, the very concept of self-governing dominions united to the empire only through the crown was utterly untenable to the British political nation so long as the king actively ruled the empire and controlled Parliament, as he did in the eighteenth century.[29]

The constitutional positions assumed by Philadelphia Whigs
in 1774 and 1775 were clearly different from those they had
adopted in 1765. In their efforts to maintain a persuasive constitutional foundation for resistance, they eventually formulated
what amounted to a wholesale revision of the proper relationships among king, Parliament, and the colonies. Over the
same time, they radically reinterpreted the nature and meaning
of the British constitution.[30] When viewed from this perspective,
the Revolution in Philadelphia emerges as "a collision of two
mutually incompatible interpretations of the British constitution."[31] This view alone is too narrow, however, for Whig rhetoricians defended their rights and resisted the authority of Parliament not only by appealing to the British constitution but also by
appealing to natural law and natural rights. By so doing, they
elevated the controversy to the level of a moral conflict.

The Whigs claimed that Americans possessed natural rights
both as British citizens and as members of the human race. Although some protesters in Philadelphia used "natural" and
"constitutional" interchangeably when speaking of rights, most
distinguished natural, eternal, and inalienable rights from those
which were constitutional, civil, or relative. The natural rights
claimed by Philadelphia Whigs differed little from the general
rights of life, liberty, and property they claimed by virtue of the
British constitution. To these they added happiness, which,
while not embodied in the constitution, was held to be a right
granted to man in his nature. Natural rights differed from
constitutional rights primarily because man had brought his
natural rights with him into society and would take them with
him should he ever return to a state of nature. When natural
rights were specified and protected by charters, compacts, or
constitutions, it was a matter of recognition, not of favor con-
ferred by princes. Natural rights were privileges belonging
inherently to all men, as John Dickinson explained.

We claim them from a higher source—from the King of Kings, and
Lord of all the earth. They are not annexed to us by parchments and
seals. They are created in us by the decrees of Providence, which establish the laws of our nature. They are born with us; exist with us; and
cannot be taken from us by any human power, without taking our lives.

In short, they are founded on the immutable maxims of reason and justice.[32]

Whig spokesmen posited a clear, hierarchical distinction between statutory law and natural law. They held that the legitimacy of statutory law was measurable by the degree to which it conformed to the abstract universals of natural law. By so arguing, Philadelphia rhetoricians gave a philosophical basis to their protest movement. The presuppositions underlying the doctrine of natural rights were intrinsically radical, potentially revolutionary. In its ultimate, logical extension the doctrine granted every individual the right to interpret the positive law as he saw fit; but, as Blackstone pointed out, "obedience is an empty name, if every individual has a right to decide how far he himself shall obey."[33] As Blackstone realized, there was little that could not be legitimized in the name of natural right. By erecting an ultimate standard external to the constitution and the common law by which to judge the propriety of British legislation, Whigs claimed moral, even divine, sanction for the most radical of their arguments and actions.

For much of the period 1765–75, Philadelphia Whigs used natural law side-by-side with the British constitution in developing standards by which to judge acts of Parliament and to justify resistance to those acts. But as the focus of controversy shifted in 1774 from the constitutionality of specific acts of Parliament to the right of Parliament to pass any laws for the colonies, Philadelphia protesters subordinated legal questions to questions of natural rights. Legal complexities and historical precedent, they complained, "too often puzzle the cause." Instead, they urged Philadelphians to found their claims "on the immutable 'ground' of justice and natural right."[34] The Whigs' use of natural rights as an argumentative ground served especially to undergird their claims to total exemption from parliamentary legislation and to justify resistance to any exertion of British authority that was judged to imperil American rights and interests.

In denying the right of Parliament to bind America in this or that particular matter, Whig rhetoricians looked confidently to historical precedent and common law for logical support. But these sources provided little backing (despite occasional American claims to the contrary) for the assertion that Parliament possessed no rightful jurisdiction whatever over the colonies. Positive law did not provide sufficient protection for American rights in the face of the Coercive Acts. Accordingly, the jurisdiction of Parliament over the colonies was now made to depend, not just upon what was "consistent with law," but upon what coincided with the eternal "principles of liberty, and with the happiness of the colonies."[35]

In Philadelphia this viewpoint was most fully mapped out and most convincingly presented by James Wilson in his *Considerations on the Nature and the Extent of the Legislative Authority of the British Parliament*. Although Wilson was a pivotal figure in Philadelphia and Pennsylvania politics from 1774, he was a latecomer to the ranks of Whig writers. Born near St. Andrews, Scotland, he did not set foot on American soil until 1765. A brilliant lawyer who would one day become America's greatest jurist, Wilson was also a rhetorician of considerable skill. Benjamin Rush wrote that his eloquence was "most commanding. . . . He reasoned, declaimed, and persuaded according to circumstances with equal effect. His mind, while he spoke, was one blaze of light. Not a word ever fell from his lips out of time, or out of place, nor could a word be taken from or added to his speeches without injuring them." Although Wilson wrote most of the *Considerations* in 1768, the pamphlet was not published until 1774. It was Wilson's first identifiable contribution to the rhetoric of protest in Philadelphia, and it quickly vaulted him to a prominent position among the city's Whigs.[36]

Wilson's major claim was that the colonies were in no manner subject to the legislative authority of Parliament. Especially noteworthy for our purposes is the way Wilson supported this claim. He began by noting that those who granted Parliament the power to bind the colonies in all legislative matters generally rested their case upon Blackstone's revered judgment that there must in every state be a supreme and uncontrolled authority in which resided the right of sovereignty. According to Blackstone, in the British system of government that supreme authority was Parliament, whose acts had "a binding force" on all members of the empire, including the American colonies. Against this traditional view Wilson argued that Blackstone's maxim was valid only insofar as Parliament promoted the ultimate end of all government—"the happiness of the governed." This end,

Wilson held, was "founded on the law of nature: it must control every political maxim: it must regulate the legislature itself." The question, therefore, was whether it would "ensure and increase the happiness of the American colonies that the Parliament of Great Britain should possess a supreme, irresistible, uncontrolled authority over them." Wilson devoted considerable space to demonstrating that the answer to this question was no. The inescapable conclusion was that Parliament had no right to legislate for the colonies.[37]

Not only did Wilson base his case for exemption from parliamentary authority predominantly upon warrants drawn from natural law, but the natural right he esteemed most highly was that to happiness. Wilson was not alone in assigning priority to happiness; through the rhetoric of Philadelphia Whigs, especially from 1774, one reads time and again that governments existed for one overarching reason—to promote the happiness of the governed.[38] By so arguing, Whig publicists injected into the rhetoric of protest an explicitly revolutionary proposition which previous writers had occasionally skirted but had seldom stated explicitly: as government existed to further the happiness of society, any authority that failed "to procure real felicity" ceased to be "a legitimate authority." Or, stated differently: "That notion of government must be false, and that action unlawful, that is contrary to the happiness of society."[39] From these premises Philadelphia Whigs readily judged that all parliamentary legislation affecting America was illegal by the law of nature since it did not conduce to the happiness of the colonies.

What did Whig rhetoricians mean by "happiness"? It is hard to say, since no Philadelphia essayist or pamphleteer bothered to define happiness in either its personal or communal aspects. They simply asserted the primacy of happiness among political values and judged British actions which subverted it illegal. There was little Philadelphia Whigs could not and did not condemn in the name of happiness. There was also little in the manner of resistance they could not justify as essential to the maintenance of happiness. Beginning in 1774, several writers proclaimed independence itself to be a natural, God-given right to be exercised if and when American happiness could no longer be secured by connection with England.[40]

Justifying the necessity and propriety of extralegal measures of resistance is a major problem for all protest movements, but it was especially crucial in Philadelphia, where the religious principles of Quakers and some of the German church groups firmly discountenanced any form of resistance that coursed much outside established channels. In urging Philadelphians to conduct business without stamped paper, to boycott the dutied items covered by the Townshend Acts, to refuse to accept East Indian tea, to support the Continental Congress, and the like, Whig rhetoricians urged actions that were unlawful, disrespectful of established authority, and, in the final analysis, rebellious. Gradually they formulated a defense of such protest—one that rationalized resistance not only in negative terms (e.g., Parliament had no right to tax Americans without their consent), but also in positive terms. That positive justification was found in the natural right of resistance to arbitrary and unrestrained power.

It deserves emphasis that this justification was not used in Philadelphia through the entire British-American controversy. It seldom appeared before 1773 and did not become commonplace in Whig rhetoric until the Coercive Acts convinced many Philadelphians that their liberty and property could no longer be protected by normal, constitutional methods. Before 1774 Philadelphia Whigs were wont to justify protest by arguing that "true loyalty" did not exist "in a blind attachment to the power and interest" of a prince or parliament, but "in a rational and well-grounded zeal for the constitution and liberties of our country." Since taxation by Parliament was unconstitutional, they held, *not* to resist it would be an act of "disloyalty to our country." Whig spokesmen also legitimated their actions in the early years of protest by proclaiming that resisting oppressive parliamentary legislation would even make the king himself "think the better" of Philadelphians' "loyalty" and "love of liberty." As George III gloried in reigning over "*freemen,* and *not slaves,*" for Philadelphians vigorously to defend their freedom could not "displease, but must endear us to him."[41]

That this argument presupposed a nonexistent bifurcation of power and interest between king and Parliament was not understood by these rhetoricians. They seem to have convinced themselves and sought to convince their audience that protest against the Stamp and Townshend acts constituted acts of loyalty to the crown.[42] It was not until the controversy escalated after 1773, as more American petitions were rejected or ignored at court, as Lord North and his fellow ministers publicly branded protesting colonists "rebels" whom "we must control" or "submit to," and as it became clear that George III did not rejoice in the Americans' "loyal resistance" that Philadelphia Whigs moved beyond their previous justifications and invoked the sacred natural right of the people to resist unjust exertions of power.

The emphasis given in these later years to the natural right to defend one's self against arbitrary authority was also a strategic response to the increasingly shrill and frequent accusations by British sympathizers that the Whigs' activities constituted nothing less than high crimes against the crown. As Galloway and others of similar persuasion assailed the protest movement as "clear, palpable treason and rebellion," protesters countered by arguing that "legal resistance and rebellion" were "essentially different," and that Whiggish Philadelphians were engaged only in legal resistance. Perhaps the most pointed exposition of this argument and its basis in natural law came from the writer who ironically called himself "Pacificus." According to "Pacificus," resistance, including outright rebellion, was a justified, proper, and lawful means for a people

to rescue themselves from the most violent and illegal oppressions; to throw off a tyranny that makes *property precarious* and *life painful*; to preserve their *laws and religion* to themselves and their posterity . . . when no other means are left for the security of everything that is dear and valuable to rational creatures. . . . The happiness and good of the people is the only law by which every contest between the supreme magistrate and the people is or ought to be tried; and the party transgressing against the law are the rebels against the constitution. . . . Governors were made for the people, and not the people for the governors, and therefore it is unlawful for a governor to act against the people, but very lawful for the people to act against the governor whenever his conduct tends to distress them.[43]

Neither "Pacificus" nor most other Philadelphia Whigs sought to encourage an actual rebellion before the beginning of war in 1775. Rebellion was held to be a legal and moral defense against tyranny; but, the Whigs reminded their audience, it was the last resort of a free people determined to maintain their freedom. Rebellion was not justified unless all peaceful means of redress had failed, unless the abuses of government were so glaring that violence was the only alternative to continued submission. Then, "when the laws of the land" provided no relief from despotism, or when the executors of these laws were "unfaithful to their trust," the people could turn to the "perpetual and universally binding law of *self-defense*."[44] Such a state of affairs was not perceived in Philadelphia until after the battles of Lexington and Concord. Before then Whig rhetoricians in the city delimited their objectives to defending themselves against their opponents' charges of rebellion and to securing redress of American grievances within the empire.

Nonetheless, it was a short step from resistance justified by natural law to rebellion, and by 1775 Whigs had provided a complete intellectual rationale for revolution. Moreover, through their repeated affirmations of the rights of resistance and rebellion, they secured general assent to the notion that Philadelphians might justifiably revolt if and when conditions warranted. With the exception of the great majority of Quakers, who stuck firmly to the injunction of their faith against revolution, most Philadelphians believed that "revolutional principles" legalized "resistance against unlawful power." How fully the city's non-Quaker residents adhered to the right of revolt against tyrannical authority is suggested by no less a figure than William Smith, prominent Anglican divine, provost of the College of Philadelphia, and a leading opponent of independence before it was declared. Speaking in 1775, Smith explained that "the doctrine of absolute non-resistance has been fully exploded among every virtuous people" since God himself sanctioned rebellion in "the cause of virtue and freedom." And the next year, speaking in memory of General Montgomery, hero of the battle of Quebec, Smith echoed sentiments we know were held by others among his fellow Philadelphians: that the actions of the colonists from the time of the Stamp Act through the battle of Lexington were fully "dictated by *self-preservation*, the first great law of nature as well as society."[45]

It is appropriate here to note that while the Whigs used warrants derived from natural law to legitimize opposition to British rule, those same warrants could be turned against any authority considered oppressive. Thus John Adams, who argued from natural law when he found it rhetorically useful, nonetheless always "shuddered . . . at the consequences that may be drawn from such premises." He cautioned that all claims "based on nature and eternal and unchangeable truth" ought to be "well understood and cautiously applied." The wisdom of Adams's advice was starkly illustrated by rhetoric and events in Philadelphia during the debate over independence. Through the 1770s appeals to natural law became more and more conspicuous in the rhetoric surrounding local political quarrels, even to the point that as parochial a question as improving the navigability of the Schuylkill River was said to revolve around nothing less than "the rights of mankind." By 1776 the universal applicability of natural law had been often enough exemplified and was widely enough comprehended that Radical Whigs, most of whom were not members of the Philadelphia-centered oligarchy that had long controlled provincial politics, appropriated arguments derived from natural law to help legitimize their overthrow of the Charter of Privileges and institution of a new, republican constitution for Pennsylvania. Many Whigs who had directed the resistance movement in previous years were members of the old oligarchy and staunchly opposed the new constitution. But to some degree they were also responsible for it; by the intense and persuasive utilization of natural law in their quest for home rule, they illustrated and popularized principles which could be used to justify a revolution in local as well as imperial politics.[46]

Natural rights philosophy is no longer an explicit constituent of American political ideology, but we should not allow its demise to obscure its great persuasive force in the eighteenth century. Natural rights doctrines were part of the intellectual heritage that crossed the Atlantic from Europe to America. The immediately visible roots of these doctrines lay in the writings of Enlightenment rationalists such as John Locke and Jean Jacques Burlamaqui, and in the social and political thought of late seventeenth- and early eighteenth-century English radicals such as Algernon Sidney, John Trenchard, and Thomas Gordon. The majority of Philadelphians surely lacked firsthand acquaintance with the tracts of these men, but many were aware of their existence and still more accepted premises of natural rights philosophy as cultural maxims by which to judge political behavior. "The higher law, whether proceeding from God or nature or history, had been a part of men's thinking since the first settlements. By the time of the Revolution it was a universally accepted article of faith."[47]

It is important to recognize, however, that the persuasive power of natural rights theories did not rest on intellectual or purely philosophical propositions; natural rights were believed in at the level of common sense. Granville Sharp was aware of this when he wrote from his vantage point in England that an "accurate and critical knowledge of law" was a necessary qualification for those who sought to deliver their opinions "concerning the nicer and more difficult questions of jurisprudence," but every man could resolve questions of natural rights with "plain conclusions of reason and common sense." So, too, was Thomas Jefferson, who stated that the controversy with England turned upon "the great principles of right and wrong" whose understanding required "not the aid of many counsellors." If we could ask the average colonial Philadelphian why he supported the Whig cause, he would probably answer in terms of liberty or freedom or happiness. He would probably agree with the unknown Philadelphian who explained in 1775 that "it is not a quibble in politics, a science which few understand, which we are contending for; it is this plain truth, which the most ignorant peasant knows, and is clear to the weakest capacity, that no man has a right to take their money without their consent. The supposition is ridiculous and absurd, as none but highwaymen and robbers attempt it." The purely legal definition of the authority of Parliament over the colonies was a complex constitutional matter beyond the ability or interest of many average citizens to resolve. But it required "no Machiavellian head" to understand that no man could rightfully seize another's property by brute force. Nor was a knowledge of political philosophy necessary to explain the propriety of one's attempt to recover his illegally seized property: "It is written with a sunbeam."[48]

Philadelphians could make individual decisions about constitutional and natural rights partially because those rights were ambiguous and highly connotative and thus open to personal interpretation and application. Because these rights could be applied in specific, though often different ways, the affirmation and defense of American rights helped resolve one of the Whigs' most pressing problems—fostering and maintaining unity.

For example, the rhetoric of the Revolution in Philadelphia was replete with salutes to "liberty" and its many blessings. But what did Whig rhetoricians mean by liberty? They certainly meant something different from what their opponents meant. In a slashing attack upon the resistance movement, John Drinker, a colleague of Galloway, bitterly excoriated Whig leaders for making "a notable stalking horse of the word LIBERTY," for using it as a "magic engine for the destruction of the substance." Drinker represented himself and the "sensible" portion of the community as the champions of that genuine "liberty which is essential to human happiness." He accused Whig protesters of fostering only a liberty "destructive" of happiness—"a vile prostitute, a name given to the filthy idol of a sordid few." As the vehemence of Drinker's tirade attests, "liberty" was one of the most emotively powerful terms in the lexicon of eighteenth-century Philadelphians. But while everyone agreed that liberty was "something worth possession," almost no writer, Whig or Tory, explained what he meant when he used the term. Most dwelt more on the necessity of liberty to the good life than on its nature or attributes. As one Philadelphian complained, liberty was a vague term often talked of but seldom identified as more than "a fine thing which everybody likes; and a good quality, which one would not seem to be without."[49]

"Liberty" was an emotive word possessing any number of potential meanings depending on the goals, values, and attitudes of its perceivers. To the merchant, liberty might mean freedom to trade with whomever he pleased without restrictions imposed from across the ocean; to the mechanic, it might mean the freedom to develop his own manufactures free from parliamentary interference; to the devout Presbyterian, it might mean an end to perceived plots to establish an Anglican bishophric in America; to the aggressive colonial politician, it might mean the opportunity to climb the political ladder without having to compete with royally appointed customs commissioners and the like. Liberty might also mean simply freedom from unconstitutional taxation by an arbitrary legislature three thousand miles away. The term served to unite various people with diverse interests in defense of a common value. While only small groups of Philadelphians would sacrifice to save the country from Anglicanism or to serve the ambitions of local politicians—if the issues were so defined—many groups would protest and, if necessary, fight to preserve liberty for themselves and their posterity.

However ambiguous liberty and the other rights claimed by the Whigs, they were held to be absolute in the sense of being inalienable, unalterable, and eternal. They were God-given. Philadelphians possessed them as British citizens and, ultimately, as men. The case for American rights, as the Whigs presented it, rested on universals and absolutes. Naturally, that case could not be compromised without sacrificing the natural and constitutional rights that made life worth living. This was the abstract structure of thought in and behind protest rhetoric in Philadelphia. To many who saw the whole structure it was convincing for reasons we can understand if we understand the Whig leaders' reliance on the doctrines of natural rights. But we cannot assume that the majority of Philadelphians moved from protest to revolution this systematically. *How* the Whigs argued their case for American rights so as to solidify agreement with their political ends also needs examining.

Rhetorical discourses convey meaning and elicit responses through both content and form. Critics studying the genre of argumentation have most often concentrated on the content of arguments and have considered the form, or method, of argument to be merely an integument. At times, however, the method of argument may outweigh and even have an effect independent of the content of argument.[50] Argumentative methods impose upon the content of argument and the audience who receives that argument a way of ordering reality and of responding to it. The impact of a method of argument upon any individual rhetorical transaction would be difficult to detect. But the characteristic use of a method of argument over a long period by one or more parties in a public controversy may, with some confidence, be discovered to help shape the nature, direction, and outcome of that controversy. In asserting and defending American rights, Whig rhetoricians in Philadelphia made special and constant use of argument from principle. By such argument they further precluded compromise as an option for themselves or a desirable goal for their followers.

One who argues from principle declares that the fundamental

aspect of an issue in dispute is its dependence on some ultimate principle or principles. He asserts that universal standards for the regulation and guidance of right conduct exist and stand beyond question or refutation. He then judges all codes and behaviors by uncompromising application of his universal standards. The principle (e.g., all men are brothers, all men are naturally free, etc.) is a general one, and it expresses a fundamental truth by means of which conduct or choice may be judged. Argument from principle declares that there exist but two possible judgments or choices—"right" or "wrong," the "right" choice or judgment being that which conforms to the principle originally given.

Argument from principle stands in obvious contrast to argument from expediency. One who argues from expediency declares that the proper ground for judgment is determined by examining what is politic or expedient rather than from some "received" definition of what is right or just. Of course, the differences between argument from principle and argument from expediency are not total or absolute. One could adopt expediency as an ultimate principle, just as one could identify that which is expedient as that which is right or just. Nonetheless, we may characterize the two modes of argument by saying that he who argues from principle tends to judge issues as right or wrong, good or bad, in an *absolute* sense, while he who argues from expediency tends to judge issues as practical or impractical, advantageous or disadvantageous, in a *relative* sense. The distinctions between argument from principle and argument from expediency help one to identify argumentative patterns and to note when persuasion is encouraging audiences to render one or the other kind of judgment.

The tendency of Philadelphia Whigs to argue predominantly from principle was most evident in their indictments of parliamentary taxation. Although most writers at one time or another attacked the tax provisions of the Stamp, Townshend, and Tea acts as inexpedient, their attacks centered, not on the amount of the taxes, but on Parliament's violation of the principle that no man could be taxed except by his chosen representatives. "It was not the value of the impositions we contended for, but right," recalled one Philadelphian of the protests against the Stamp and Townshend acts. Although the Tea Act reduced the price of legal tea in the city, Whigs again argued from principle and proclaimed that although the act might "promise some pecuniary advantage," the principle of taxation embodied in it was "replete with the most dreadful mischief."

If this insidious attempt is attended with success it will, very justly, be looked upon by all the world as a formal surrender of the principle which is the chief bulwark of our liberties. It will be a standing precedent for future impositions; and to these no bounds can be limited after the principle is once given up. There is no such thing as keeping to it partially: It must be sacredly adhered to in every instance, or totally relinquished. A tax of the value of one penny levied upon us without our consent as effectually takes away our liberty, as if the sum were a million. It is not the value of the tax we object to, but the principle on which it was laid.[51]

One of the most remarkable habits of Whig writers and speakers was their readiness to turn questions of expediency into questions of absolute and uncompromising principle. This habit was strikingly illustrated in Thomas Jefferson's *A Summary View of the Rights of British America*, published in Philadelphia after the passage of the Coercive Acts in 1774. Although Daniel Boorstin exalts Jefferson as a great legalist who founded his claims upon specific historical grievances rather than upon abstract philosophical principles,[52] it was not the argument from history but the argument from principle that controlled Jefferson's indictment of parliamentary authority. The topics of *A Summary View*, as Jefferson announced them, were "the great principles of right and wrong." Its purpose was to secure redress of "the injured rights of colonists." Throughout, Jefferson referred to the arbitrary violations of colonial "rights" by Parliament and the ministry. He denounced the Sugar Act, the Townshend Acts, the Iron Act, and the Hat Act on economic grounds, but the ultimate judgment he passed on all these statutes was that they contravened the "natural right" of Americans to "free trade with all parts of the world." Jefferson also cited the Stamp and Tea acts, the Coercive Acts, the suspension of the New York Assembly, and the stationing of British troops in the colonies as "unwarrantable encroachments and usurpations, attempted to be made by the legislature of one part of the empire, upon those rights which God and the laws have given equally and independently to all." By denouncing these measures on grounds of right and principle, even when recog-

nizing that expediency was also at issue, Jefferson was led inexorably to reject compromise with Parliament. To be sure, Jefferson professed a desire to restore tranquillity with England,
but nowhere in the pamphlet did he advance a plan for settlement other than on his own principled terms. There were no
shades of grey; America was right, England was wrong, and
England could "no longer persevere in sacrificing the rights of
one part of the empire to the inordinate desires of another."[53]

From 1765 to 1775 Whig leaders in Philadelphia refused to
consider compromise with England on any but the most minor
matters. And they justified their dogmatic stance by claiming
that compromising "arguments drawn from a temporary
expediency" were irrelevant to American claims, "which should
only be considered as a matter of right." This unyielding position was most forcefully expressed by William Hicks, who, with
Dickinson and Thomson, led the rhetorical protest against the
Townshend Acts. To act in a spirit of compromise, Hicks exclaimed, would prove disastrous to America.

This is the conduct of an artful politician, not of a steady patriot. To
wave [sic] one legal demand for the better securing another may, in the
common occurrences of *private life*, be a justifiable piece of policy; but in
matters of *national concern*, where the happiness of the whole community is at stake, compositions of this kind are of the most dangerous
nature; and though a superiority of power may justify a peaceable submission, yet nothing can excuse the basely relinquishing our claim to *all
the rights of free men*. . . . If a selfish motive of *temporary expediency*
should draw from the present inhabitants of the colonies any *unguarded
concessions*, they will serve to rivet the chains of slavery upon their
wretched posterity.[54]

This passage merits closer attention. At first sight, the dispute
with England appears to have been a political one which could
be resolved through normal political processes of negotiation,
persuasion, and accommodation. But Hicks explicitly placed the
controversy outside the realm of political jurisdiction. He defined the issue as one of ultimate principle which could be compromised only by "an artful politician"—never by "a steady
patriot." Although he was arguing primarily for the necessity of
vigorous and united protest against the Townshend Acts, Hicks
ultimately denigrated expediency per se as a justifiable ground
for "patriotic" judgment and conduct. By so doing he urged his

audience to perceive all acts of expediency as "fatal and un-
manly" (as Thomas Paine would characterize them in 1776) and
all efforts to compromise British-American differences as cunning and deceitful.

The Whigs' principled opposition to compromise was clearly
exhibited during the furor over nonimportation in 1770. Early
in May, Philadelphians received confirmation that Parliament
had rescinded all of the Townshend duties except that on tea,
which was to remain "as a *badge* of the legislative authority of the
mother country over the colonies."[55] The city's dry goods
merchants thereupon accelerated their efforts to repeal the
nonimportation agreement that had been in effect since March
of 1769. Arguing that continued nonimportation of all British
goods would cause irreparable damage to the city's economy, the
merchants urged that the boycott be lifted on all items save tea.
By such a plan Philadelphians could preserve their liberty and
ensure continued prosperity as well.[56]

The dry goods merchants presented their proposal as the
most expedient means of protesting maintenance of the tea duty
while safeguarding the city's commercial interests. To leaders of
the protest movement, however, the proposal was a symbol of
absolute capitulation to the right of Parliament to tax America.
They accordingly branded all attempts to abandon total nonimportation as "avowed acquiescence in Parliamentary authority,
and an infamous sacrifice of freedom, property, and posterity."
The boycott, Whig rhetoricians claimed, had come into being to
defend the principle of no-taxation-without-representation. To
abandon it now, while the principle was still violated by the tea
tax, would acknowledge the right of Parliament to tax Americans without their consent. If this principle had been worth the
economic price of nonimportation in 1769, surely it was worth
the same price a year later. If Philadelphians had been contending for liberty previously, they surely had the same cause for
contention now. "A Son of Liberty" asked, "Is not the principle
[of parliamentary taxation] as dangerous to our liberties now, as
it was August last? Is *American* liberty of less value than it was
then?" Whig spokesmen based their case upon the need to
defend absolutely the principles of American liberty and cautioned Philadelphians, especially merchants, to "let no arguments from necessity or interest have any weight with you."[57]

The strategy the Whigs adopted in this instance was one designed to solidify public opinion by presenting issues as matters of right and principle which could not be compromised on grounds of temporary expediency. The strategy was representative. Throughout the decade of protest Whig rhetoricians repeated that if Philadelphians were to retain their rights, they had no course but to oppose all proposals that might compromise those rights. This stance, and the kinds of rigid perceptions and uncompromising actions it encouraged, were capsulized by three of the most popular slogans of the prerevolutionary decade. From 1765: "A day, an hour of virtuous liberty, is worth a whole eternity in bondage." From 1768: "Those who would give up *essential liberty* to purchase a little *temporary safety*, DESERVE neither *liberty* nor *safety*." From 1774: "Freemen cannot bear a middle course between liberty and slavery. It is essential to the happiness of liberty that it should be secure and perpetual."[58]

A natural outgrowth of the steady accent upon absolute principle was explicit attack upon moderation in responding to British actions. This outcome became increasingly visible from 1774, partially in response to the alarming events of that year, but also as a logical corollary of argument from principle. To be an outright supporter of Parliament, "Anglus Americanus" exclaimed, would be an act of pure folly. "*Moderation, moderate men and moderate measures* are therefore the spells which are to charm us into a destructive supineness." The record of history, he claimed, presented an "undeniable truth. That it is not the avowedly flagitious and wicked men who have subverted the liberties of states and empires, but the lukewarm, the neutral, the moderate men." Arguing from similar premises, "A Plain Dealer" concluded that "every man in the British empire who is not for us, is against us. . . . Every American who is not willing to adopt the most strenuous and effectual measures is our real, if not our avowed and determined enemy; whether he dress himself in the guise of a moderate man, a political reflector, or any other garb whatever."[59] Clearly, argument from principle could be readily extended to rationalize coercive measures against those deemed by protesters to be "unfriendly to the spirit of liberty."[60]

Consistent with the Whigs' uncompromising concentration on

matters of principle was their contempt for England when that country acted for reasons of practicality. Even when Parliament met colonial demands, as in repealing the Stamp Act, some Whigs condemned the motives behind the action. One speaker, reviewing the course of protest in 1765–66, applauded Philadelphians' determination not to use stamped paper, their closing the city's port to British shipping, and the distress they thereby inflicted on British manufacturers and traders. Then the speaker deplored British motives: "For this reason the ministry found it necessary to change their measures. The Stamp Act was repealed, not because it was unjust and unconstitutional, but because it was dangerous to carry into execution." Another ardent Whig also complained that the stamp tax had not been revoked for being "an arbitrary imposition, but under a specious pretence of favor to a disquieted people, and perhaps more to oblige British tradesmen" than American colonists. William Hicks excoriated Parliament for retracting the stamp tax only as a concession to British merchants affected by the "ill consequences" occasioned by American nonimportation. Protest against the act was based on its illegality, Hicks stated, but its repeal was misguidedly "founded upon the *inexpediency* of the act, [rather] than upon a conviction that they had exerted an *unconstitutional power.*"[61]

Repeal of the Stamp Act was accompanied by passage of the Declaratory Act, which affirmed the right of Parliament to legislate for America in "all cases whatsoever." But Whig writers and speakers did not attack repeal of the Stamp Act because it was coupled with the Declaratory Act. General discontent with that statute did not emerge in Philadelphia until 1774, when protesters saw in it an insidious justification for the Coercive Acts.[62] Complaints about the grounds for retraction of the Stamp Act related solely to the fact that it was rescinded for reasons of expediency rather than principle (although the data for this claim were embodied in the Declaratory Act). Similar arguments greeted repeal of the Townshend duties in 1770. "A Tradesman," for instance, urged continuation of nonimportation, not only because the duty on tea was not repealed, but also because repeal of the other dutied items emanated, "not from a persuasion that the Act was unconstitutional, and repugnant to the rights of America; but because it was anti-commercial."[63]

Looked at individually, the tendencies of Whig rhetoricians to indict parliamentary taxation primarily as a matter of principle, to turn many economic questions into questions of right, to reject expediency as proper grounds for political action, to attack the most minor concessions as total capitulation to the authority of Parliament, and to criticize repeal of the Stamp and Townshend acts as misguidedly expedient, might be seen as isolated strategies arising in response to the vagaries of particular situations. But looked at together and in combination with the substantive legal and philosophical arguments against the authority of Parliament, these responses reveal a rhetorical posture of remarkably singular perspective and direction. As Philadelphia protesters affirmed their rights and attacked Parliament, they held that violation of American rights and interests was much more important as a matter of principle than as a matter of expediency. The principle-expediency dichotomy is crucial to understanding protest rhetoric in Philadelphia from 1765 to 1775. By focusing on matters of right and principle, the Whigs tended systematically to narrow the ground of debate to matters which were not open to compromise. As presented by Whig publicists, the dispute with England became a contest between oppression and freedom, between tyranny and liberty, between injustice and justice, between wrong and right. Issues of economic benefit, social stability, military defense, and political advantage are most often open to compromise; but the Whigs treated these issues as secondary and sometimes as too demeaning to consider. There can be little compromise when the stakes are perceived as freedom, liberty, justice, and right. In this sense Whig rhetoric foreclosed settlement of the British-American conflict, except settlement by surrender of either country.

Some Philadelphians recognized and were alarmed by the Whigs' unyielding emphasis upon matters of right and principle. Joseph Galloway, who often granted that Philadelphians had genuine grievances against Parliament, deeply feared the consequences of the protesters' "idle speculations" about American rights. To discuss such matters, he said with some prescience, was to use "the language of independence," for it broached such fundamental principles as to make compromise "inconsistent with the honor and dignity of Parliament." Benjamin Franklin, who from his post in London saw with special clarity the forces expanding the rift between England and her colonies, also urged protesters to base their case upon prudential considerations rather than upon the question of right. "This question," he warned, "ought, by all means, to be kept out of sight, because there are no hopes of it ever being settled, and any discussion of it will certainly widen the breach."[64] Despite these and other warnings, few Philadelphia Whigs abandoned argument from principle or even granted honor to argument from expediency.

This is not to say that the Whigs' use of argument from principle was always considered strategy; nor that, when deliberate, it was designed to foreclose all possibilities of compromise with England. But the ultimate consequences of discourse are often more momentous than those foreseen at the time of original presentation. No matter how often protesters proclaimed "subordination" to the mother country, they frequently only gave it lip service. The term became, as one keen observer later noted, "a word without any precise meaning to it."[65] If we view Whig rhetoric as movement and cumulation of ideas over time, we can see its long-range results. The ways Philadelphia Whigs began their responses to specific British acts led by a kind of self-contained logic to the impasses of 1775. The rhetoric of protest in Philadelphia moved from point to point in time creating advantages and disadvantages for its spokesmen, opening but chiefly closing options. The repeated insistence upon American rights defended by argument from principle led the Whigs and their partisans to uncompromising premises and conclusions from which they could not retreat by 1775.

Preclusion of compromise is an inevitable consequence of the repeated use of argument from principle. Preclusion of compromise may not invariably ensue in every rhetorical situation, but the advocate who argues from principle over an extended period of time increasingly commits himself and his supporters to that principle and thereby limits rhetorical options more than the advocate who argues from expediency. This, of course, is what Edmund Burke understood when he remarked that to argue about considerations of right and principle was to pursue "metaphysical distinctions." Such questions were not proper grounds for decision in "states and kingdoms" but ought to be left to the schools—"there only they may be discussed with safety."[66] When public discussion centers, as it did from 1765 to 1775, upon matters of absolute principle, the life of discourse must inevitably come to an end; there is no room for argumentative concession. The choices under conditions of continued conflict are victory or surrender, ideationally or physically.

# 4

## THE SPECTER OF
## CONSPIRACY

On the morning of 8 July 1776 "a great concourse of people" gathered in the State House yard for the first public reading of the Declaration of Independence. The crowd registered its approval "by three repeated huzzahs," proclaiming with each, "God bless the free states of North America."[1] The controlling justification for rebellion Philadelphians so heartily endorsed that day was premised upon belief in conspiracy against American freedom within the highest reaches of British government. After affirming the general right of a people to revolt against arbitrary rule, the Declaration states:

Governments long established should not be changed for light and transient causes; and accordingly all experience hath shown that mankind are more disposed to suffer while evils are sufferable than to right themselves by abolishing the forms to which they are accustomed. But when a long train of abuses and usurpations, pursuing invariably the same object evinces a design to reduce them under absolute despotism, it is their right, it is their duty, to throw off such government and to provide new guards for their future security. Such has been the patient sufferance of these colonies; and such is now the necessity which constrains them to alter their former systems of government. The history of the present King of Great Britain is a history of repeated injuries and usurpations, all having in direct object the establishment of an absolute tyranny over these states.

Such a caustic view of British-American relations did not emerge suddenly in 1776; nor was it fully developed in 1765 when George Grenville decided that an American stamp tax would help relieve the financial burdens of a swollen and overextended empire. The seeds of bitterness were planted in Philadelphia at the time of the Stamp Act, were nourished by the repeated violations of colonial rights and interests from 1765 to 1776, and were cultivated by Whig rhetoricians who discerned

96

conspiratorial motives in every act of Parliament and the ministry. The charge of conspiracy grew naturally as Whiggish Philadelphians tried to explain the tyrannous behavior of a parent state that before 1765 had usually been regarded as generous, just, and beneficent. For many Philadelphians there were only two "logical" explanations: the repeated infringements upon American property and liberty could be attributed to stupidity or to concerted policy. At the time of the Stamp Act stupidity seemed as plausible an explanation as any. But as a series of statutes threatened the rights and interests of Philadelphians, Whig spokesmen increasingly charged that selfish and perfidious designs lay behind all British actions.

Allegations of conspiracy were not confined to Whig rhetoric in Philadelphia, of course, but surfaced in the literature of protest throughout the thirteen colonies. One school of thought, argued most vigorously by Bernard Bailyn, holds that such allegations—shrill and apochryphal as they often were—"meant something very real to both the writers and their readers" and that the fear of a comprehensive conspiracy against liberty throughout the English-speaking world "lay at the heart of the Revolutionary movement." Another school, nicely represented by Richard Morris, dismisses much of the language of conspiracy as mere twaddle to which "serious men gave little credence." It is "dubious," Morris states, "whether sensible and sophisticated men put much stock in such talk."[2] The truth surely lies somewhere between. Bailyn's argument, for example, rests predominantly upon examples drawn from the rhetoric of New England Whigs (especially those from Massachusetts), whose views often did not reflect those of more moderate protesters in the middle or southern colonies. On the other hand, there is simply too much preoccupation with the motives of British leaders in the writings of such undeniably "serious" and "sophisticated" men as John Dickinson, Charles Thomson, William Hicks, and James Wilson to be overlooked or hastily disparaged. Charges of conspiracy were present in the rhetoric of Philadelphia Whigs through the decade of protest—though less conspicuous and less fervid than in some parts of America—and contributed importantly to the development of a revolutionary movement in the city, without necessarily being at its heart. The conspiracy theory made sense out of British colonial policy in the years after 1764, furnished an explanation of British motives that a significant, though undeterminable, number of Philadelphians found more and more compelling with the passage of time and events, and further encouraged Philadelphians to perceive the British-American dispute as one that could not be satisfactorily resolved through compromise.

As early as 1765 some Philadelphia Whigs looked for and found an overarching motive behind Parliament's efforts to tax Americans. The Stamp Act, they charged, resulted from "deep-laid contrivances of wicked power and cunning," and was meant to accomplish far more than it professed. One writer termed it an *"entering wedge"*; another, a *"Trojan Horse"* calculated to establish a precedent for introducing "future oppressions and impositions." The argument that the Stamp Act was intended to provide a precedent to justify further taxation was not foremost in Whig rhetoric in 1765. Nor was it uppermost in the minds of most Philadelphians. But as England persevered in her efforts to extract revenue from the colonies by unconstitutional means after 1766, Whig publicists claimed with greater and greater frequency that what British leaders desired most was "a precedent of their right to tax America." This description of British motives seemed persuasive in light of two related questions. For one thing, if Parliament's only desire was to raise money, why did it not use the time-honored method of requesting funds from colonial legislatures? For another, why did Parliament doggedly continue to tax Americans after the almost unanimous opposition to the Stamp Act? To many it was the method of raising funds that was most at issue, and the fact that the sums involved in the Townshend duties and the Tea Act were really very small was taken as evidence of conspiratorial intent. As John Dickinson explained in his *Letters from a Farmer in Pennsylvania,* some persons might "be inclined to acquiesce" in minor taxes and thereby inadvertently bring to fruition years of British scheming.

Nothing is wanted at home but a PRECEDENT, the force of which shall be established by a tacit submission of the colonies. . . . If the Parliament succeeds in this attempt, other statutes will impose other duties . . . and thus the Parliament will levy upon us such sums of money as they choose to take, *without any other* LIMITATION *than their* PLEASURE.[3]

The question, of course, was why England suddenly sought in 1765 to establish its claim to an unqualified right to tax the colonies. According to Philadelphia Whigs, the explanation lay in the widespread corruption that characterized British political life in the eighteenth century.[4] Whig writers and speakers seldom tired of depicting a debauched state of political morality in the mother country. Their accounts were confirmed by similar accounts from the mother country herself. Virtually every issue of the city's newspapers carried reports from colonists visiting London as well as reprints of essays originally published in the British press. From these sources Philadelphians received first-hand "news" that the home government was "totally corrupted from head to heels" and that the ministry had "already begun to give away in PENSIONS the money THEY have lately taken out of OUR pockets WITHOUT OUR CONSENT." Philadelphians were consistently given a picture of the mother country in which their money supported corrupt and rapacious ministers, placemen, and pensioners, whose voracious appetites—once whetted with a new portion of American resources—threatened, indeed promised, to devour the whole. According to many protesters, this avarice explained Parliament's repeated attempts to establish a precedent for taxing the colonists. The fullest single statement of the logic of this argument was addressed to Philadelphians in 1776 by the unknown author of *Four Letters on Interesting Subjects*.

If a general review be taken of the conduct of Britain, it will confirm the suspicion which many discerning men, both on this and the other side of the water, had at first, which was, that the British court wished from the beginning of this dispute to come to an open rupture with the Continent, that she might have a colorable pretence to possess herself of the whole. The long and scandalous list of placemen and pensioners, and the general profligacy and prodigality of the present reign, exceed the annual supplies. England is drained by taxes, and Ireland impoverished to almost the last farthing, yet the farce of state must be kept up, every thing must give way to the wants and vices of a court. America was the only remaining spot to which their oppression and extortion had not yet fully reached; and they considered her as a fallow field, from which a large income might be drawn, if politically broken up; but the experiment of the Stamp Act had taught them to know that they must not hope to effect it by taxation. It is generally believed that Mr. Grenville had nothing more in view in getting the Stamp Act passed than the raising a revenue in America quietly; and it is fully believed by many that the present king and ministry had *no revenue* in view in passing the Tea Act; their object was a quarrel, by which they expected to accomplish the whole at once, and taxation was only the bone to quarrel about. To see America in arms is probably the very thing they wished for—the unpardonable sin which they wanted her to commit; because it furnished them with a pretence for declaring us rebels; and persons conquered under that character forfeit their all, be it where it will or what it will, to the crown. And as Britain had no apprehension of the military strength of the Continent, nor any doubt of easily subduing it, she would, from motives of political avarice, prefer conquest to any mode of accommodation whatsoever; and it is on this ground only that the continued obstinancy of her conduct can be accounted for.[5]

Claims of conspiracy against American property were voiced by Philadelphia Whigs across the decade of protest, but they were most prominent before 1770. As early as 1768 increasing numbers of the city's protesters began to allege a plot more comprehensive than one designed to rob Americans of their material possessions. They began to interpret the actions of the ministry and its supporters in Parliament as a pattern of aggressively despotic behavior revealing "a settled plan . . . adopted for absolutely and permanently enslaving" the colonies.[6]

The fullest exposition of this accusation during the conflict over the Townshend Acts appeared in a letter written by Charles Thomson and published in both the *Pennsylvania Journal* and *Pennsylvania Gazette* of 10 May 1770. The essay is particularly noteworthy for its extensive treatment of the evidence and reasoning undergirding its contentions. Thomson began by stating that attitudes in Philadelphia had hardened to the point that a partial redress would do little "to allay the heats and quiet the minds of the people," who were coming more and more to "see plainly that the Ministry have adopted a settled plan to subjugate America to arbitrary power; that all the late acts . . . tend to this purpose." He then discussed the measures which revealed this "settled plan": the Stamp and Townshend acts; the Declaratory Act, which asserted the right of Parliament of make laws for America "in all cases whatever"; the arbitrary proroguing of the New York legislature "for daring to dispute" parliamentary commands; the extension of the jurisdiction of vice-admiralty courts; the use of the army to enforce "obedience to the will of Parliament"; and the unfailing tendency of British leaders to treat colonial petitions "as sedition" and to deem all efforts to secure redress as "rebellion and treason." According to Thomson, British plotters sought to take "the purse strings into their own hands," not simply for the ostensible economic reasons, but because "every other power" must invariably follow from that of taxation. Taken together, he warned, the acts and regulations of the previous five years pointed unmistakably to a plot to poison and uproot the flourishing tree of American liberty. "How much farther they may proceed is uncertain, but from what they have already done the colonies see that their property is precarious and their liberty insecure."[7]

The logic of Thomson's argument was compelling to Whig partisans because it gave order and meaning to the otherwise unfathomable chain of statutes and circumstances from 1765 to 1770. Still, it is not certain to what extent the mass of Philadelphians shared such a disaffected view of British motives. Although allegations of conspiracy were considerably more evident in Philadelphia during the Townshend Acts crisis than during the Stamp Act controversy, most such allegations still centered on England's quest to strip Americans of their hard-earned property rather than on a general plot against liberty itself. It was not until the spring of 1774 that charges of British collusion against American liberty became commonplace in Philadelphia.

After imposition of the Coercive Acts virtually every piece of Whig rhetoric published in Philadelphia maintained, directly or indirectly, that there could no longer be any doubt of England's intentions toward America. As one writer put it, "Everyone who is acquainted with the late transactions must be convinced of *a settled plan to enslave this country*." The dangers facing Philadelphians were painted in vivid terms in an essay signed "A Mechanic." It warned that "a corrupt and prostituted Ministry" was conspiring against "the sacred liberties of the Americans," attempting "by every artifice to enslave" them "and plunder them of their property, and, what is more, their birthright *liberty*." In an important series of essays published in the spring of 1774, John Dickinson traced step by step the history of British-American relations since 1765 and reached what seemed to many Philadelphians an inescapable conclusion: "that a plan has been deliberately framed and pertinaciously adhered to, unchanged even by frequent changes of Ministers, unchecked by any intervening gleam of humanity, to sacrifice to a passion for arbitrary dominion the universal property, liberty, safety, honor, happiness, and prosperity of us unoffending yet deeply devoted Americans."[8]

We could continue to cite similar remarks at length, but those already quoted illustrate the prominence of the conspiracy theme after 1773. Almost all anti-British rhetoric in Philadelphia now attributed the actions of the mother country to the deliberate machinations of sinister men determined to undermine and ultimately to destroy the foundations of American liberty. The proof of the allegations rested in the *progression* of parliamentary and ministerial acts in the years after 1764. Taken individually the series of "unwarrantable encroachments and usurpations" upon American rights and interests might, as one writer acknowledged, "be ascribed to the accidental opinion of a day." But taken together and in sequence they reflected a coherent and clearly explicable logic of behavior, for "a series of oppressions begun at a distinguished period and pursued unalterably through every change of ministers too plainly prove a deliberate and systematical plan of reducing us to slavery."[9]

Of all the dreadful consequences potentially resulting from the conspiracy against America, none received more mention in Philadelphia than "slavery." From the time of the Stamp Act through the period of the Coercive Acts, the city's Whigs insistently cited slavery as the absolute political evil. Every piece of legislation adversely affecting Philadelphians foretold or sounded "the footsteps of slavery." The Stamp Act was labeled "the SLAVE ACT" which brought with it "slavery and destruction of liberty and property to thousands of freeborn and loyal subjects." The Townshend duties were held to portend the clanking of chains, for "*those* who are *taxed* without their own consent, expressed by themselves or their representatives, are *slaves. We are taxed* without our consent, expressed by ourselves or our representatives. *We* are therefore SLAVES." The chests of tea sent to Philadelphia under the Tea Act were said to contain in them "a slow poison, in a political as well as a physical sense. They contain something worse than death—the seeds of SLAVERY."[10] The Coercive Acts were deemed the most oppressive of all, for if Parliament could freely tax Americans, alter colonial charters, close colonial ports, and abridge the right of trial by jury, then "the vassals of an eastern monarch" were "*as free* and *as happy* as the subjects in America" and "every American" would soon "wish that he had never been born, for *not to be* is better than *to be a slave.*"[11]

Friends and foes alike pointed to the incongruity between the Whigs' exclamations regarding British slavery and the presence in America of more than half a million black slaves. This incongruity was less blatant in Pennsylvania than in most provinces. Still, there was no escaping the fact that while Whiggish Philadelphians contended unctuously for natural rights to liberty and property, those same rights were being denied to some one thousand black slaves in the city and hundreds of thousands more throughout the continent.[12] During the decade of protest there appeared in the Philadelphia press a steady stream of literature linking the cause of American freedom with that of freedom for blacks. As one resident stated in 1774, the plight of African slaves "appears to be so remarkably blended with ours that it seems almost impossible to claim our own rights without acknowledging that we have deprived them of theirs." Richard Wells was less tentative. How, he asked, could Philadelphians conceivably "reconcile the *exercise of* SLAVERY" with their *"professions of freedom, 'founded on the law of god and nature, and the common rights of mankind'?"* How could they ever expect Englishmen to grant the validity of American claims while colonists were "deeply involved in the inconsistent practice of *keeping their fellow creatures* in *perpetual bondage?"*[13] Although such appeals did not provoke immediate elimination of the peculiar institution, abolition did prove to be a salutary by-product of the Revolution in Pennsylvania. In 1780, a year before the surrender at Yorktown, the Pennsylvania legislature provided for the gradual extinction of slavery in the state. Significantly, the preamble to this law acknowledged the influence of the revolutionary ideology. It recalled the struggle against England and stated that Pennsylvanians felt called upon to manifest the sincerity of their professions of freedom by extending a portion of their liberty to others "who, though of a different color, are the work of the same Almighty hand."[14]

The disparity between Whig rhetoric and the practice of slavery in America notwithstanding, many Philadelphians shared the protesters' fears that British colonial policy opened the door "through which slavery will enter into America if we are not extremely vigilant to prevent it."[15] Far from being mere

hyperbole, slavery was a central concept in eighteenth-century
political discourse and had specific meanings—apart from those
associated with African bondage—which it no longer possesses.
It was among the most powerful and loaded words in the lexicon
of colonial Philadelphians and was used by writers of all political
persuasions to disparage that of which they disapproved.[16] No
single word better expressed the dangers Whigs apprehended in
the actions of British conspirators. Economically, slavery meant
having nothing a person could call his own. Politically, it meant
"the want of every right, and the deprivation of every privilege."
It meant ultimately being subject in all humanly significant matters "to the arbitrary will of others"—as were the citizens of European and Asian despotisms. While a freeman exercises control
over his own destiny, "a slave holds everything at the pleasure of
his master, and has no law but the will of his tyrant."
Philadelphians' anxiety regarding the "enslaving" measures of
Parliament and the ministry thus sprang from a set of associative
meanings attached to "slavery" that unleashed powerful emotive
reactions in the face of an alleged conspiracy to usurp American
property and liberty. To those who accepted the Whigs' claims,
there could be no doubt that Philadelphians would indeed be
reduced to the vassalage of Poles, Russians, or Turks if they
submitted to the will of England, for "it may, with truth, [then]
be said . . . 'that they hold their lives, liberties, and properties
by the precarious tenure of the will of others.' "[17]

   Allegations of a British plot to rob Philadelphians of their
property and liberty—to reduce them to slavery—clearly
reflected Whiggish belief rather than political reality. British colonial policy from 1763 to 1774 was marked more by confusion
than by consistency. Central though American affairs were, any
uniform approach to them was all but impossible in the rapid
succession of ministries that came and went in the years 1763–
70. Nor did there exist any single agency in London holding exclusive responsibility for the colonies. Until 1774 the mother
country did not adhere to any clear line of American policy. Her
actual steps were a series of menaces and warnings, advances
and retreats. The Stamp Act was passed and repealed, but repeal was accompanied by the Declaratory Act affirming the right
of Parliament to bind Americans in all cases whatsoever. The
Townshend duties were passed and retracted, yet the duty on
tea remained as a symbol of the authority of Parliament. The

fumblings and vacillations in British policy after 1763 reveal anything but a deliberate scheme to establish absolute tyranny in America.[18]

Yet a goodly number of Philadelphians—precisely how many we can never know—seem to have believed that there really was a deliberate scheme to enslave them. The question, of course, is why. In the broadest sense, they believed because during the decade of protest they confronted a steadily accumulating mass of evidence that seemed to verify the existence of conspiracy. No barrage of propaganda, no matter how brilliant, could have persuaded Philadelphians of ministerial and parliamentary collusion against their most cherished liberties unless there existed concrete referents from which conspiratorial motives could plausibly be deduced. As John Adams noted, no rhetorician could "persuade a large people, for any length of time together, to think themselves wronged, injured, and oppressed unless . . . they saw and felt it to be so."[19] The primary evidence of conspiracy rested, as we saw earlier, in the succession of British encroachments upon Philadelphians' political freedom and economic security in the years after 1764. Crucial secondary corroboration was provided by the "news" Philadelphians received of opinion and events in England.

The prerevolutionary years were tumultuous ones in England as well as in America and witnessed a mounting volume of criticism toward fundamental aspects of British life. To Adam Smith and his Scottish precursors there was immediate need to replace mercantilism. To evangelists like John Wesley and George Whitefield only a return to Christian principles could save the people and the state from degradation. The most vocal group of protesters were men such as James Burgh, Joseph Priestly, John Cartwright, and Richard Price who saw in the unrepresentative nature of Parliament, in the widespread corruption and prejudice of the ministry, and in the heavy-handed tactics of George III threats of tyranny that jeopardized the beneficent, constitutional balance of power achieved in the Glorious Revolution. Similar, though less thoroughgoing, criticisms were voiced by opposition politicians such as Edmund Burke, Isaac Barré, William Pitt, Charles Fox, and others, who, whether from conviction or opportunism, sought to convince the British people that constitutional principles were being deliberately eroded by the king and his ministers. Although such dissatisfactions at no time reached revolutionary proportions, they reflected widespread unease about the moral and political health of the nation. At much the same time that Americans began to announce they were being victimized by tyranny, many Englishmen were beginning to develop exactly the same attitude toward their own government.[20]

Much of the criticism of British leaders and institutions was regularly reprinted in the Philadelphia press and helped strengthen the fears of many residents that they were being conspired against by cunning and powerful forces. Almost every week Philadelphians could read one or more of the following: speeches by Pitt, Burke, or Barré condemning the quest to tax Americans as unconstitutional and destructive of fundamental liberties; essays by "Junius" and other writers taking the crown to task for its excessive reliance upon prerogative at the cost of regular channels; detailed accounts of the government's persecution of John Wilkes, including the adamant refusal of the House of Commons to acknowledge his lawful election to that body on three successive occasions; petitions from towns in England accusing the ministry of seeking to reinstitute Star Chamber proceedings to silence the press; accounts of massive subornation at all levels of political life; reports that properly framed and delivered petitions from both sides of the ocean were haughtily scorned at court and in Parliament; stories of arbitrary interference in judicial processes to shelter the misdeeds of highly placed friends of the administration. Similar denunciations were often contained in the large number of pamphlets by British authors published in Philadelphia during the years 1765–75.[21] The picture of the mother country Philadelphians received from these sources led to one overarching conclusion, which was trenchantly stated by the unknown Englishman who authored the fourth installment of "The Crisis."

The steady and uniform perseverance in a regular plan of despotism, since the commencement of this reign, makes it evident to the meanest capacity that a design was formed (and it has with too much success been carried into execution) for subverting the religion, laws, and constitution of this kingdom, and to establish, upon the ruins of public liberty, an arbitrary system of government.[22]

Not all of these discourses from England explicitly alleged the existence of a plot against America. Most British writers were concerned primarily with the dangers to their own country; the conspiracy they envisioned was predominantly one against British rather than colonial liberty. Still, by exposing and castigating the methods and motives of governmental leaders, they lent considerable credence to the charges of Philadelphia Whigs. After all, if the ministry were actively engaged in reducing "the free and manly government of England" itself "to the dark, assassinating system of eastern despotism," was there any reason to believe they would spare America—especially given the often striking parallels between events on both sides of the ocean? Indeed, it seemed to some Philadelphians that the situation pointed to an administration plot against both British and American freedom, that the battle was not only for colonial rights, but for "the liberties of the whole empire."[23] In addition, reports from England fortified the ever-growing feeling of Whiggish Philadelphians that the differences with Whitehall could not be settled through normal, constitutional methods, for not even British discontents were being so resolved.

Accusations of governmental conspiracy were further accredited by what was written in "private" but published letters from Englishmen and Americans living in London to friends in Philadelphia. From the time of the Townshend Acts an extraordinary number of these letters echoed the opinion that "the grand object of the present Ministry is to facilitate the establishment of tyranny in the colonies." To one writer, sending troops to Boston, establishing powerful admiralty courts, and continuing efforts to tax Americans could not "leave a doubt that a settled plan" had been "adopted for absolutely and permanently enslaving" the colonies. "Everything I see here confirms me in this opinion." To another, the ministry had secured a majority in the Commons by bribery and now stood "determined to carry their point against the freedom of America." Still another reported, this time in 1774, that "there is now no doubt of a regular system being laid to subvert the liberties, religion, and constitution of this country as well as that of America. This is now generally believed in England, and it is well known that the attempt is only first made on America.[24]

Thus the "news" available to Philadelphians from the mother country tended almost uniformly to substantiate what Whig rhetoricians were saying about the character and motives of British leaders.[25] Equally important is the fact that such news—

whether contained in letters, essays, pamphlets, or speeches—
possessed special credibility and exerted an incalculable effect
upon opinion in the city, for it was advertised as and was widely
believed to be reported by men close to events in London, men
well situated to judge the designs of administration officials,
men "with a knowledge of public affairs beyond the line of ordinary information."[26]

Not only was there ample evidence of a plot to establish arbitrary power in the colonies, but there existed strong predispositions among at least a portion of the Philadelphia audience to interpret that evidence as pointing unmistakably to conspiracy.
The conspiracy theory was accepted partially because it
explained British political behavior in a fashion which conformed with, and grew out of, the dominant political presuppositions of the age. The configuration of attitudes and ideas
that constituted the revolutionary ideology was present a half-
century before there was an actual revolution. Cardinal elements in this pattern were fears of corruption and of the menace
of ministerial collusion. Apprehension of conspiracy was a major
ingredient in the rhetoric of early eighteenth-century British
radicals and opposition writers—commonly called "Common-
wealthmen" or "Real Whigs"—and it was an important
constituent of informed American political thought by the mid-
eighteenth century.[27] This apprehension was primary "in the
sense of forming assumptions and expectations, of furnishing
not merely the vocabulary but the grammar of thought, the apparatus by which the world was perceived."[28] Given this in-
tellectual-political heritage, the natural and immediate reaction
to British legislation which threatened fundamental colonial
rights and interests was to presume conspiratorial motives on
the part of its movers. Seen from this perspective, the problem
of Whig rhetoricians was not to get their audience to think in
conspiratorial terms, but only to convince them that evidence of
conspiracy existed. That problem was in large part solved, albeit
unwittingly, by England herself.

At the same time, we need to beware the tendency to overestimate the impact of the "Commonwealth ideology" upon the
thought of ordinary Philadelphians. We cannot assume that the
city's great mass of citizens were versed in the rather intricate
body of political and social ideas advanced in England by such
men as John Milton, Algernon Sidney, John Trenchard,

Thomas Gordon, and Benjamin Hoadly, whose writings constituted the most influential source shaping the basic political presuppositions of literate and highly educated Whig
spokesmen. But such an assumption is not essential to account
for the persuasiveness of the conspiracy theme. The widespread
public belief in a governmental plot to divest Philadelphians of
their liberty and property was not necessarily predicated upon
knowledge or acceptance of Real Whig political philosophy.
Allegations of conspiracy comprise a persistent strain in the
rhetoric of virtually all American social and political movements.[29] In fact, such allegations are not restricted to the discourse of mass movements, but commonly appear whenever
social groups perceive a temporal situation of unusual stress and
complexity that cannot be readily comprehended by reference
to normal causative agents. At such times belief in conspiracy
provides a "logical" explanation for what may not otherwise be
explicable or acceptable, simplifying the search for causes and
providing a ready target for hostility. In the last analysis,
Philadelphians accepted the Whigs' conspiracy theory because it
made sense of the mosaic of trends and events of the prerevolutionary decade. Only the existence of a perfidious plot to establish arbitrary rule in America could explain the attitudes and
actions of British leaders as they emerged from 1765 to 1775.
Ultimately, Whiggish Philadelphians believed in conspiracy because, as one stated in 1776, "it is on this ground only that the
continued obstinacy of [England's] conduct can be accounted
for."[30]

To this point we have been concerned with the dimensions and
persuasive appeal of the Whigs' claims that Philadelphians were
being victimized by a consciously framed and executed plot to
usurp their property and liberty. Our next task is to determine
what strategic functions these claims fulfilled and how they influenced the intensity and direction of the resistance movement
in Philadelphia. We shall see that the conspiracy theory defined
the enemy and his motives and invigorated the Whigs' campaign
for intercolonial unity. In both ways it intensified a sense of
alienation from England and reinforced Philadelphians' opposition to compromise.
     A central requirement of any protest movement is to define

and castigate an identifiable enemy. When a person protests he seeks to inculcate in his followers an attitude of opposition. Thus a group of people, a set of beliefs, or a system of government must be singled out, held up for public disapproval, and rendered contemptible. Defining the enemy is vital inasmuch as support is more likely to be secured when ideological statements are presented as generalized beliefs which simplify social, political, or economic problems.[31] It is almost invariably true that "mass movements can rise and spread without belief in a God, but never without belief in a devil."[32]

Protesters can use either or both of two major strategies in defining the enemy: vilification and objectification. Vilification is the use of language to degrade the enemy's person, actions, or ideas and is typically achieved by the use of caustic language in personal attack upon a conspicuous leader of the opposition.[33] Philadelphia Whigs frequently used this strategy, as when they characterized Lord North as "a monster in nature, an infernal spirit stole into the world in human shape," the Duke of Grafton as "a man of loose morals" willing to sell American rights "for the sake of a present pecuniary gratification," or General Gage as "a common highwayman . . . who perpetuates a robbery upon the property and liberty of a whole province."[34] Attacks of this nature allowed Philadelphians to personalize the struggle with England.

Whig writers and speakers also employed the strategy of objectification—the use of language to direct the grievances of a particular group toward another collective body such as an institution, nation, political party, or race that is deemed responsible for all or most of the misfortune that befalls the agitator's votarists.[35] The Whigs' use of objectification was most clearly evident in their attacks upon the "cursed cabal"—"that unseen hand which governs the momentous affairs of this great empire." Although the members of this cabal were frequently vilified individually, the rhetoric of protest in Philadelphia was replete with denunciations of vague but "powerful legislative usurpers," "a lordly faction at home," "pestilent disturbers of the empire," "an arbitrary faction," "men of perverted understanding, greatly depraved by ambition."[36] Objectification is generally a safer strategy than vilification. The relatively stable nature of ill-defined bodies allows objectification to continue to be effective as individual enemies pass from the scene through resignation, political defeat, or death. By focusing Philadelphians' discontent on an ill-defined, aggregate enemy as well as on specific individuals, Whig publicists were able to keep up their attacks after prominent British officials had fallen from positions of responsibility.

Neither vilification nor objectification necessarily involves accusations of conspiracy. As rhetorical strategies they are ways of identifying adversaries, affixing blame, and enlarging the distance between the enemy and the protesters. But to be effective the agitator must not only denominate the enemy, he must also persuasively portray him in the darkest of terms. For colonial Philadelphians few things could have been more patently evil than an organized enemy determined to reduce them to political and economic slavery. Describing British leaders as conspirators not only identified the enemies of America, but assigned to them vicious motives which seemed both to determine and explain their behavior. It was the assignment of motive that constituted the most telling part of the Whigs' allegations. England's acts identified the enemy in a general sense; rhetoric was necessary to interpret those acts and to define the motives behind them.

Depicting an enemy motivated by conspiratorial designs allowed the Whigs to reduce the struggle with England to one between "good" and "evil" and to fasten all responsibility for it upon leaders in the mother country. In the process, they further strengthened the perception that British-American differences could not be settled through compromise, for compromise with an enemy determined to destroy every vestige of American property and liberty was unthinkable. Indeed, the very act of painting one's adversary in conspiratorial hues inevitably reduces controversy to a two-valued battle for survival demanding immediate and uncompromising resolution. The rhetorician who arouses fears of conspiracy does not present social conflict as something to be mediated through normal processes of give-and-take. Since what is at stake is a choice between absolute good and absolute evil, the quality needed is not a willingness to compromise but the will to fight things out to a finish. Since the enemy is thought of as being totally unappeasable, nothing but complete victory will do.[37] To the perceiver of conspiracy, compromise will only enhance realization of the enemy's perfidious ambitions and therefore must be avoided at all costs. Thus those

Whigs who for a decade exposed and reviled England's "plan of despotism" inexorably encouraged Philadelphians to believe that they could save themselves from "this dreadful bondage," not by seeking a middle path of negotiation and accommodation, but only by *"unanimous, determined, permanent opposition."*[38]

This is not to say that Philadelphia Whigs who alleged the dangers posed by British conspirators did so in order to foreclose all possibilities of settling the conflict with England short of revolution. Quite the contrary. But as in their use of argument from principle, they simply seemed unaware of the propulsively divisive direction of their rhetoric and did not comprehend the degree to which charges of conspiracy must inevitably reduce the grounds for compromise. This was true of even so skilled an advocate and sensible a politician as John Dickinson, in whose writings one finds recurrent paeans to the British nation and repudiations of severing the connection with it intermingled with equally frequent charges that governmental forces were scheming to deprive Philadelphians of their most treasured political and material possessions. There can be no doubting the sincerity of Dickinson's commitment to imperial union—he so dreaded the prospect of separation that he refused to sanction independence when the question came before the Continental Congress in 1776. But there can also be no doubt that by telling Philadelphians for the ten years before 1776 "that a regular plan has been invariably pursued to enslave these colonies" he helped convince them that England's intentions were "UNALTERABLY HOSTILE" and, by extrapolation, that American liberties could never be adequately safeguarded within the empire.[39]

To understand further how the conspiracy theory worked to preclude compromise we need to look more closely at whom Dickinson and his colleagues defined as their enemy.

During the period 1765–75 Philadelphia protesters most often assailed Parliament and the ministry while generally exempting George III from complicity in the plot against America. As one Whig explained in 1768, the king only gave his assent to bills prepared by the ministry and passed by the Commons, "and the best and greatest of monarchs, as frail men, may often be deceived by pernicious schemes which plausibly advance their revenues, or any other favorite purpose." Some Philadelphians even imagined that the sovereign power of the crown itself was being undermined by ministerial intrigue, as Dickinson informed Arthur Lee in 1774: "It is suspected here that a design is regularly prosecuted by the ministry to make his majesty dethrone himself by the calamities and convulsions his reign is likely to bring on his whole people. Please to inform me what is thought on this point in England." Not all Whiggish Philadelphians saw the problem as Dickinson stated it, but most continued at least until the fall of 1775 to agree with James Wilson that King George was a decent man "under whose venerable name" ambitious ministers "daringly attempt[ed] to shelter their crimes."[40]

Despite this consensus, some residents began by 1774 to suspect that King George himself might be involved in the conspiracy to enslave the colonies. These suspicions were founded at first upon events in the mother country, notably the major role played by the king in the Wilkes case, and were intensified by several virulent British letters and essays attacking the king republished in the Philadelphia press. These criticisms in a sense authorized the city's Whigs to scrutinize more carefully the structure of British government and the role of the king in it. By the time of the Coercive Acts at least a few had concluded that, as ultimate responsibility for governmental affairs rested with the crown, George III could not be the innocent so widely believed.

This line of reasoning was pursued most vigorously in two important essays published in Philadelphia in the latter half of 1774. "Phocion's Letter to the K——" began by observing that Englishmen and Americans alike had been raised "under the courtly influence of that ill-famed sentiment, *that the King can do no wrong*," according to which the ministry must be held accountable for all governmental blunders. It was now time, "Phocion" exclaimed, to discard such an antiquated notion "and charge on your Majesty alone the execution of measures which promise to disgrace your government." To be sure, Parliament legislated for the empire, but as "sole head" of the nation the king had the power to reject its vicious schemes. It was therefore misleading to censure the actions of, say, a minister of state, for he was "the mere tool of a day." According to "Phocion," the duty of patriots in Philadelphia and throughout America was to investigate the ultimate "cause of our grievances," and that investigation led directly to the throne, "from whence, though they might not originate, they have ultimately issued, nor could they have affected us without your approbation."[41]

Six weeks later, an open letter by "Scipio" charged the king with failing to fulfill his duties toward his American subjects. Citing the Boston massacre, the increasing list of pensioners, a Parliament corrupted and awed "under your countenance" to support a venal administration, the Wilkes affair, and the Quebec Act, "Scipio" expostulated: "These, Sir, and numberless other hideous calamities have generally been attributed to your Ministers, but I am bold to say they become chargeable to YOU, as responsible for the conduct of those men whom YOU, YOUR-SELF, nominate to office." Such unwarrantable behavior could only be charged to "the weakness of your understanding" or "the wickedness of your heart." In either case, "instead of being hailed as the happy guardian of your people, you are becoming their tyrant and oppressor! Instead of being styled the darling and well-beloved of hundreds of thousands of your subjects, you are becoming the most hated object of millions!"[42]

Both letters were atypical in their extremism, and all the implications of their challenges were not to be stated until Thomas Paine's full-blown attack upon monarchy in *Common Sense*. Still, it is noteworthy that some Whigs in the city had begun by 1774 to assign ultimate responsibility for American matters to the crown. If found plausible, these attacks chipped away at King George's sanctity and suggested that he could be implicated in the conspiracy against America. They also helped prepare Philadelphians for the wholesale indictments of the king which ensued during the debate over independence in 1776.

In a very real sense, however, Whig writers and speakers identified Philadelphians' most dangerous adversary as one above Parliament, the ministry, and even George III. The ultimate enemy was not just evil men but evil institutions—the entire corrupt system of British government. It was this system that spawned greedy and malfeasant leaders such as Bute, Grenville, Townshend, and the rest. To many Philadelphia Whigs the debauched ambitions of such men were the natural outgrowths of a general moral malaise afflicting the parent state. The more Philadelphians witnessed of British policy in the colonies and the more "news" they received from across the ocean, the more it seemed that the British nation as a complex of men and institutions was "totally indifferent about liberty, and lost to every sense of honor or virtue." Some said the root of the problem rested in the "commercial" character of a people "accustomed to view[ing] all objects through the medium of self-interest." It was therefore a vain illusion to pretend that Philadelphians' liberty and property would not be sacrificed to "the ease and greatness" of England: "The relation which she stands in to us, as the parent state, is a bond of amity too feeble to suspend for a moment the operation of such selfish and powerful passions as avarice and the lust of empire."[43]

By indicting the system of government in the mother country the Whigs once more stripped away the intellectual room for compromise. If the conspiracy against American freedom grew out of the nature of British life and politics, it would persist regardless of the ministry or sovereign in power. Individual administrations could come and go, but the grasping avarice of power-hungry politicians would remain, ensuring, as one correspondent from London put it, "a number at all times sufficient to keep you in bondage." Or as another stated: "To establish a despotic power over America is the unalterable sentiment of so many persons of influence that, in truth, we have little to expect from any changes, since administration will always be modeled to the purpose, and a great majority will be found ready  . . . to aid in trampling upon the liberties of America." To be sure, wrote yet another, there were many eloquent friends of America in Parliament, "but what can eloquence do against a corrupt majority"—a majority that promised always to be corrupt? The answer was clearly nothing. The inescapable inference was that Philadelphians could look only to themselves for protection: "If we mean to establish our liberties on an immovable basis, we must not rely on British patriots or orators, but must do it for ourselves."[44] Again, the full extension of this line of thought was not presented until 1776. Yet it is important to notice that Philadelphia Whigs bruited it as early as 1769 and repeated it thereafter, until by 1774 many had defined the enemy in a fashion that anticipated and implicitly encouraged a decision that American destiny could be fulfilled only by revolution and not by compromise with a perpetually corrupt and tyrannous parent state.

In addition to enhancing the definition and defamation of the enemy, the conspiracy theory also invigorated the Whigs' efforts to inculcate a spirit of intercolonial unity among Philadelphians. Persuading their audience to perceive the struggle with England in continental rather than local terms was not a problem unique to Whig leaders in Philadelphia. As John Adams later remarked,

"The colonies had grown up under constitutions of government so different, there was so great a variety of religions, they were composed of so many different nations, their customs, manners, and habits had so little resemblance, and their intercourse had been so rare, and their knowledge of each other so imperfect, that to unite them in the same principles in theory and the same system of action, was certainly a very difficult enterprise." That enterprise was especially arduous in Philadelphia because many of the "enslaving" measures of Parliament and the ministry did not affect Philadelphians as directly as they affected residents of other cities such as Boston, New York, and Charleston. Writs of assistance were not a pressing issue in Philadelphia; civilian-military relations were cordial until all royal troops were removed in 1774; the Pennsylvania Assembly was allowed to function as freely after 1765 as before; nor was there a royal governor whose actions could be vilified as arbitrary or tyrannous. All this meant that the sense of grievance was not felt as strongly in the city on the Delaware as in other places where the citizenry was squarely confronted with a standing army, with suspension of the legislature, or with royally appointed provincial officials working in concert with the British to suppress dissent.[45] Inducing Philadelphians to identify with the sufferings of colonists in other areas and instilling an attitude of intercolonial cooperation were among the major demands facing the city's Whigs through the decade of protest. Those demands became especially severe during the campaign against the Coercive Acts in the spring and summer of 1774.

Through the opening months of 1774, Philadelphians, as other Americans, waited apprehensively to see how Parliament would respond to the Boston Tea Party. They found out on 14 May, when word arrived of the Port Act, which closed the port of Boston, except for the passage of food and fuel, until full payment was made for the destroyed tea. Five days later Paul Revere rode into Philadelphia with a circular letter from the Boston Committee of Correspondence requesting aid and support. The letter contended that although the Port Act affected only Boston immediately, it actually attacked every colony. "You will be called upon to surrender your rights," the Boston Committee told Philadelphians, if ever administration leaders "should succeed in their attempts to suppress the spirit of liberty *here*."[46] Even before Revere reached Philadelphia, however, the city's Whig leadership—composed at this time of Charles Thomson, John Dickinson, Joseph Reed, and Thomas Mifflin—had reached the same conclusion. Over the succeeding weeks they advanced a program of resistance for Pennsylvania that included sending aid to Boston, participating in economic sanctions against the mother country, and joining with other colonies in a general congress.[47] This program was far more ambitious and potentially treasonous than anything offered to Philadelphians during the previous eight years. Not surprisingly, it met resistance from several quarters.

One source of resistance came from moderate Whigs such as William Smith and Thomas Wharton, Jr., who were alarmed at the degree to which radicals such as Thomson and Mifflin had seized control of the protest movement during the Tea Act controversy, and who now stood poised "to interpose and not suffer those warm and violent men to carry measures as they pleased." The moderates did not condone the Port Act, but unlike the radicals they were not ready to commit Philadelphia to vigorous opposition against an act that did not strike directly at the city. Another impediment to the radicals' plans was presented by the Pennsylvania Assembly, which was "known to be under the influence of Galloway and his party."[48] At no time since the Stamp Act had the Assembly put itself forcefully on record against the obnoxious measures of Parliament. True to form, it was not prepared in 1774 either to speak out against the blockade of Boston or to facilitate any move toward intercolonial union. Overcoming the obstacles posed by moderate Whigs and by the Assembly required considerable acumen and involved the radicals in a complex pattern of political machinations which, though interesting, are not of central concern here.[49] The important point for our purposes is that these machinations could not succeed without substantial popular backing for the radicals' resistance program. To secure that backing the radicals needed first to arouse and intensify Philadelphians' discontent with the Port Act.

Radical rhetoricians attacked this problem by turning once again to the theme of conspiracy. And as was so often true during the years before 1775, John Dickinson assumed a central position in the battle for public support. The day before Paul Revere arrived with the circular letter from Boston, Dickinson and Charles Thomson met and "secretly concerted" the measures to be employed against the Port Act. To "prepare the minds of the people," Dickinson subsequently published a series of four letters "well calculated" to "awaken the attention of" Philadelphians, to "raise them to a sense of their danger," and to "point out the fatal consequences of the late acts of Parliament and the plans of the British administration."[50] Entitled "To the Inhabitants of the British Colonies in America," these letters appeared in successive issues of the *Pennsylvania Journal* from 25 May to 15 June.[51]

Dickinson's task was clear: Philadelphians would ally with Bostonians, subscribe to nonimportation agreements, and support an intercolonial congress only if convinced that their interests were vitally endangered by the Port Act. Thus he devoted the full series of letters almost entirely to refuting the view, shared by a goodly number of Philadelphians, "that the late act of Parliament, abolishing the privileges of the port of Boston, was occasioned by the particular imprudence of the inhabitants, and in no manner concerns the other colonies." According to Dickinson, such a view was the most dangerous that could be imagined because it would allow parliamentary and ministerial conspirators to consummate their "deliberately framed" scheme to strip all Americans—Philadelphians included—of their liberty and property. Carefully reviewing British colonial policy since the end of the Seven Years' War, Dickinson sought to demonstrate that there could be no plan of domination more complete "than that now meditated, avowed, and in part executed on this continent." And that plan was irrefutably aimed, not just against Boston, but *against the colonies in general.*" All intelligence from London pointed to only one conclusion: "that a regular plan has been invariably pursued to enslave these colonies, and that the act of Parliament for blocking up the port of *Boston* is a part of the plan." Intercolonial unity was therefore the most pressing consideration of the moment as the freedom of "every man of us is deeply interested in the fate of our brethren in Boston."

Dickinson further buttressed his case by turning, as he so often did, to historical example. Why, he asked, were the ancient states of Greece broken down to submission by Philip of Macedon and later by the Romans? "Because they contended for freedom *separately*." Why had the Swiss and Dutch remained free in the face of repeated attempts at conquest by much more powerful countries? "Because they wisely regarded the interest of *each* as the interest of *all.*" Only such an enlightened perception could now save Philadelphians from succumbing to the designs of administration conspirators who, unable to subject the colonies all at once, were resorting to the age-old strategy of conquering by dividing. If England were allowed to get away with the Port Act, even though it was ostensibly aimed only at Massachusetts, the remaining colonies would soon find themselves "attacked and humbled [one] after another" until all Americans had become "the slaves of *Britons.*" Philadelphians could therefore preserve their liberties only by uniting behind the people of Boston, who were "suffering in a cause common to us all."[52]

Dickinson was not alone in arousing Philadelphians against the Port Act and in pleading for unity. He was supported by a large cast of writers whose arguments differed little from his and thus need not be recounted here.[53] The success of this rhetorical barrage was obliquely testified to by John Penn, who reported late in June that the people of Philadelphia "look upon it that the chastisement of Boston is purposely vigorous and held up by way of intimidation to all America, and in short that Boston is suffering in a common cause."[54] With the mind of the people thus properly "prepared," to use Thomson's term, radical Whigs were able to realize their political objectives. By the end of July they had sufficient public support both to defuse the moderates' quest to rein in the resistance movement and to pressure the Assembly into sanctioning the formation of a continental congress. Indeed, the radicals' triumph was so decisive that one can point to the summer of 1774 as a turning point in the development of a revolutionary movement in Philadelphia. That triumph was accomplished to an important degree through an artful series of political maneuvers which have rightfully been much scrutinized by historians. What has not been recognized is that it was also predicated upon the ability of radical Whig rhetoricians to convince Philadelphians that the closing of the port of Boston and the other Coercive Acts (word of which reached Philadelphia the second week in June), while confined in their immediate operation to Massachusetts, actually constituted conspiratorially conceived threats to the rights and property of all Americans and thus demanded immediate, vigorous, and united opposition. That such a scheme did not in fact exist was not as important as the fact that many citizens believed it existed. Belief in conspiracy provided the indispensable psychological warrant that allowed Philadelphians to accept the plight of Boston as important to themselves, for if conspiracy were afoot there could be no doubt that the principles of the Coercive Acts would soon be extended "to every inch of America" and that, "as sure as there is a God in Heaven, the [other] provinces will soon *suffer one by one*."[55]

Of course, not all Philadelphians believed in a British plot to enslave Americans in 1774 or at any time during the decade of protest. In fact, there were some who saw a conspiracy of quite a different kind from that portrayed by Whig rhetoricians. As early as 1766 Joseph Galloway attributed anti-British protest to a faction of Presbyterians who had seized upon the Stamp Act as "a favorable opportunity of establishing their republican principles, and of throwing off all connection with their mother country." Ten years later he was even more firmly convinced that this "malevolent sect" was to blame for all the disturbances that had disquieted British-American harmony and brought the colonies to the brink of revolution. Galloway was not the only Philadelphia Tory to see conspiracy in the actions of Whig agitators. Others shared his perceptions, and though most did not express specific fears of a "Presbyterian" plot, many felt the greatest danger to American freedom was posed, not by British officials, but by "dangerous men" in the city of Philadelphia "who have designs, and are carrying on intrigues unknown, unsuspected but by too few." By 1776 a sizeable number of those Philadelphians who continued loyal to England had come to accept a distinctly conspiratorial explanation of the Revolution. Their attitudes were expressed in the words of the unknown resident who stated: "The present breach with *England* is not the device of a day, and has not arisen with the question about taxation (though that has been a favorable plea), but is part of a system which has been forming here even before the late war."[56]

This accusation was naturally voiced most often after 1774, when the specter of independence loomed most ominously. During the years 1765–74 the most persistent charge of conspiracy leveled by Philadelphia Tories was that Whig leaders were using the dispute with England to advance their own political fortunes. Not surprisingly, this charge was made most consistently during periods of intense political conflict in the

city. In the summer of 1768, for example, at the peak of the em-
broilment over nonimportation, there appeared in the *Pennsylvania Chronicle* a succession of attacks upon Whig leaders in
general and Thomson and Dickinson in particular as "designing
men" who, "to aggrandize themselves," were purposefully leading the people on "to violence and outrage." Week after week,
Galloway and his "pack of small scribblers" (as William Goddard
characterized them) reviled Dickinson and "his unlucky man,
C.T.," for drawing *well-meaning persons* to their interest by a
*specious concern* for their country."[57] The most sustained assault
came from the writer who adopted the pseudonym "Machiavel"
in three essays published during the latter half of August.
Among other things, this author compared Whig leaders to the
ancient Roman demagogues—"artful, ambitious, and wicked
men" who "took advantage of the times" to pave a way "to
absolute power."[58]

Six years later similar charges again circulated through the
city, this time as part of the campaign by Galloway and other
conservatives—Abel James, Jabez Fisher, Samuel Shoemaker,
John and Henry Drinker—to dampen protest against the
Coercive Acts and to curtail the movement toward a continental
congress. A conspicuous feature of this campaign was the claim
that Whig leaders were duping the people "by the fallacious
spirit of a pretended patriotism" as a means to acquire public
popularity and advancement.[59] The notion of a Whig conspiracy
was most fully developed in two scathing essays, probably by
John Drinker, which were published together as a pamphlet in
late August. Drinker's goal, as he stated it, was to look behind
the so-called "noble struggles for freedom" presently convulsing
Philadelphia in order to "understand their origin and
tendency." As to origins, Drinker found them in the schemes of
"designing men" who were "seeking personal or party emolu-
ments from public distractions." He identified the major participants in this plot as, on the one hand, unscrupulous
merchants and smugglers who used the language of liberty to
justify their "exorbitant thirst of gain" and, on the other hand, as
"ambitious spirits . . . fond of *any* opportunity of giving
themselves consequence with the populace." According to
Drinker, the Whigs' true character was revealed by their reliance
upon abuse and coercion "to enforce their opinions, and deter
their neighbors from inspecting the honesty of their motives or

the utility of their measures." Although Whig rhetoric was replete with heady references to "LIBERTY and RIGHT," Dickinson, Thomson, and other "popular demagogues" were actually only making cunning "use of those high-sounding names, and applying them as magic engines for the destruction of the substance."[60]

Philadelphians were thus offered two competing explanations for the unsettled state of affairs in the years 1765–75. One attributed the disruption of British-American relations to the ambitions of administration conspirators in London; the other to the ambitions of Whig conspirators in Philadelphia. Seen in this light, the coming of the Revolution can be understood as the outcome of Philadelphians' acceptance of one conspiracy theory over another. That they would accept the Whigs' explanation was not foreordained, however. The Tories' allegations that Whig leaders were concerting to fatten their pocketbooks and to take over Pennsylvania's government did not spring simply from the overactive imaginations of a few embittered defenders of the old order. Like the Whigs' charges of British collusion, the Tories' charges began with certain observable facts which could reasonably be interpreted as pointing to conspiracy. It was true, for example, that the Presbyterian party was since its formation the moving force behind organized opposition to British policy in the city. It was likewise true that tea smugglers had a considerable stake in preventing implementation of the Tea Act. Perhaps most crucial, it was also true that while Whig partisans contended for liberty with England, they frequently seemed willing to deny liberty locally to those of different opinion. Although the coming of the Revolution in Philadelphia was not marked by the frequency or intensity of violent mob activity that occurred in some parts of America, at various times during the decade of protest resistance leaders in the city threatened or provoked coercive measures against those whose words or deeds they deemed "unfriendly to the cause of liberty."[61]

These actions provided the proof of the Tories' allegations. That the allegations may have possessed fairly broad appeal—at least at one juncture—can be inferred from the fact that charges of a Whig conspiracy were central to Galloway's successful 1768 campaign to prevent nonimportation and to keep Dickinson out of the Assembly.[62] By 1775, however, most Philadelphians were clearly more concerned with British than Whiggish conspirators. One reason is that a lot of strong Tory literature did not see print in Philadelphia after 1770, partly because staunch British supporters feared reprisals from Whig zealots, partly because the city's publishers were unwilling to print it.[63] Equally important, much of the Tory discourse circulated in the city from 1773 was too run through with personal invective, shoddy reasoning, and aristocratic biases to convince anyone who was not already fully prepared to accept its claims. In the later years Tory publicists appealed most strongly to their own followers and thus sacrificed whatever chances they may have had for generating broad public support. Above all, however, the acceptability of any conspiracy theory rests in its explanatory power, and with the passage of time and events the Whigs' theory of a British plot against American liberty seemed to explain more satisfactorily what had happened since 1765. To the majority of Philadelphians, the most puzzling feature of the years 1765–75 was the conduct of the British government, not the behavior of colonial protesters. While Tories had much to say about the latter, they had comparatively little to say about the former. By focusing upon the motives and methods of Whig leaders, Tory spokesmen revealed that they saw the major problem of the day, not as British tyranny, but as the reorientation of the political order in Pennsylvania. Thus as more and more Philadelphians apprehended danger from parliamentary and ministerial conspirators and became more and more willing to sanction radical departures from established political procedures to fend off that danger, Tory spokesmen increasingly relegated themselves to a small corner of Philadelphia's political landscape.

One question remains: Did Philadelphia Whigs truly see collusion in the activities of British leaders or did they seize upon the theme of conspiracy as a rhetorical ploy? The answer to both parts of the question is yes. There is no evidence to suggest that men like Dickinson and Thomson did not genuinely fear the kinds of plots they trumpeted in their public rhetoric; much of their private correspondence reveals the same fears, albeit less dramatically. Their depictions of the motives of British

politicians were not always factually true, but they were invariably psychologically true.[64] The rhetoric of Whig protesters
in Philadelphia was frenzied and apocalyptic largely because the
Whigs' fears of a perfectly wicked and immoral enemy determined to violate and ultimately to destroy American liberty
and property were real and threatening. At the same time, it is
equally evident that Philadelphia protesters used allegations
of British conspiracy as deliberate strategy to intensify
Philadelphians' anger with the mother country and to engender
a spirit of intercolonial union. The strategy naturally became
more effective in the 1770s as the evidence of conspiracy seemed
to pour in from all sides. Whig publicists did not simply dupe an
inert and passive populace into believing that their material
possessions and political rights were under cunning and
systematic assault. It is inconceivable that Philadelphians would
have accepted the Whigs' claims had there not been verifiable
actions by British leaders that could reasonably be interpreted as
betokening conspiracy. The importance of Whig rhetoric was
that it lent order and meaning to those actions.

  Belief in a British conspiracy against American liberty and
property did not alone propel Philadelphians into revolution,
but it strengthened the conclusion that they could never maintain their most coveted rights and interests through connection
with England. Ascribing conspiratorial motives to British leaders
circumscribed the range of responses to Parliament and the
ministry at every stage of the conflict. If British leaders were
conspiring against American liberty, then liberty could be
preserved only by unyielding resistance to their policies. And if
to resist British policy were to defend freedom, then to compromise was to sacrifice freedom. Thus the conspiracy theory
also legitimized every act of the Whigs, no matter how radical,
for any act of resistance became by definition an act of moral
courage and social necessity. To Whiggish Philadelphians there
but two mutually exclusive choices: submit and become slaves or
resist and strive to remain free men. As argument from principle reduced the grounds for judgment to a choice between
right and wrong, the conspiracy theory reduced the grounds for
judgment to a choice between good and evil. Once again Whig
rhetoricians portrayed the dispute in absolute terms and encouraged those who accepted their claims to choose between

moral extremes. Once again they helped shape the belief that compromise was neither politically expedient nor morally justifiable. This mental rigidity was reinforced further by the ways Philadelphia Whigs redefined the images of England and America during the decade of protest.

# 5

## THE APOTHEOSIS OF
## AMERICAN DESTINY

In 1765 most Philadelphians held an idealized image of their connection with England. They loved the mother country, thought of it as home, and considered it the intellectual and spiritual center of Western civilization. They thought there was more freedom, prosperity, and opportunity for individual fulfillment in England than anywhere else in the world. As one writer explained at the time of the Stamp Act, Philadelphians were a people "long habituated to entertaining a high veneration" for the British nation.[1] That veneration ran so deep that most residents tended to look to England for normative values and standards of behavior, for conceptions and models of what they would like themselves and their society to be.[2] Benjamin Franklin believed that his fellow Philadelphians—like other Americans—were so devoted to England at the close of the Seven Years' War that they could have been governed

at the expense only of a little pen, ink and paper. They were led by a thread. They had not only a respect but an affection for Great Britain, for its laws, its customs and manners, and even a fondness for its fashions, that greatly increased the commerce. Natives of Britain were always treated with particular regard; to be an Old England-man was, of itself, a character of some respect, and gave a kind of rank among us.[3]

This is obviously not the sort of image one holds of a country against which one is about to do battle. Revolution was impossible as long as Philadelphians held such an exalted view of England. Yet by 1776 that image had been reshaped so that revolt had become not only possible but, from the standpoint of many Philadelphians, necessary to maintain the purity and vitality of American life against the debauched and corrupt influence of the mother country. This chapter is concerned with how Philadelphia Whigs redefined the images of American and

British life during the years 1765–75 and how this process helped shape the direction and intensity of the resistance movement in Philadelphia.

The question of identity is often near the heart of revolutionary rhetoric. This question is manifested most prominently in two themes. One is the redefinition and apotheosis of the "self"—whether that self be an individual, an oppressed class, a race, or a society. Another is the identification and denigration of an "enemy" placed in opposition to the redefined and apostrophized self.[4] The themes of apotheosis and denigration complemented one another in the rhetoric of Philadelphia Whigs through the decade of protest, revealing and shaping the progressively revolutionary nature of the city's resistance movement. At times the themes were developed in the overt ideological content of Whig rhetoric; at other times they were insinuated by the protesters' figurative and connotative language. The presence of these themes did not always result from deliberate strategy. Sometimes—especially before 1770—they appear to have been unconscious reflections of the Whigs' own changing perceptions of British and American life, changes of which individual Whigs may themselves have been only dimly aware. But however they were expressed and whatever the intentions of their authors, recurrent and insistent apotheoses of America and Americans, coupled with equally repeated and strident denigrations of England and Englishmen, strengthened Philadelphians' feelings of psychic separation from the mother country, invigorated a sense of American identity and community among the city's Whiggish residents, and further precluded compromise.

Several forces contributed to the erosion of England's positive image during the prerevolutionary decade. Primary were the economic restrictions upon colonial commerce and manufacturing, the repeated infringements of Philadelphians' natural and constitutional rights, and the belief that these actions were purposefully undertaken by conspirators against American property and liberty. Together these forces led many Philadelphians to question the benevolence of the parent state and helped foster feelings of economic, political, and moral resentment against British leaders. This process of redefinition was intensified by the Whigs' depictions of and attacks on the corrupt and luxurious excesses of British political and social life.

Not all Philadelphia Whigs agreed on the extent to which Parliament could legally legislate for America or on the proper mode of opposition to British policy, but they were remarkably united in the belief that in England "the state of the nation was never so bad as it is at this moment, for it is totally corrupted from head to heels." Philadelphians were warned time and again to beware a government controlled by "rapacious sycophants" utterly "abandoned in morals, desperate in fortune, and despicable in abilities."[5] They were further informed that the weakness of the administration reflected "the universal prevalence of luxury, corruption, and dissipation" at all levels of British life. Americans visiting in London informed their friends in Philadelphia that the English were "a people stupified by luxury and the opium *vice*," while Whig rhetoricians intoned that "infidelity, irreligion, venality, and vices of every kind have never prevailed in greater degree, and cannot well rise to a higher pitch than they have lately gained."[6] Philadelphia protesters frequently described England's moral disintegration in terms of disease—witness "A.B." in the *Pennsylvania Gazette* of 8 June 1769:

> The great increase of riches in this nation, with its natural concomitant luxury, have introduced a licentiousness and corruption amongst all ranks of people, unknown to former times. The inferior sort are regardless of all order and decency and impatient of all restraints, even of those which are essential to true liberty; while ministers, actuated by the same principle, are assuming unconstitutional powers to quell these disorders, under pretence that the power of the civil magistrate is insufficient to check and control them. These innovations have produced such a fermentation in the nation as, if not timely prevented, seems likely to shake the foundations of the constitution. Every action, both of governors and governed, seems dictated by violence and passion. Effects are treated as causes, and opposed only by temporary expedients, and counteracted by little chicanery; all which, instead of correcting the humors, increase the disease.

The luxury-and-corruption-as-disease metaphor tended to reinforce Philadelphians' apprehension that the decadence of England was not temporary. A disease, of course, could ideally be cured by speedy diagnosis and treatment. But there seemed no doctors equal to the task. As one writer reported from

London, the nation was "infected with many dreadful diseases." Worse still, he added, those men of power and responsibility "who should be its doctors are its disease." Thus Whiggish Philadelphians were not surprised that when they looked to Whitehall for "the temper and firmness of a great minister," they found only "the enervated languor of a consumption; or the false strength of a delirium." Beguiled by the false goddess, luxury, and betrayed by the corruption of evil men, Englishmen were on the verge of committing "the most horrid parricide on their country," Richard Wells direly warned his fellow Philadelphians in 1774.[7]

As with the Whigs' allegations of conspiracy, their visions of the mother country's moral and political health were frenzied, exaggerated, and unduly apocalyptic.[8] Yet these images gained wide credence in Philadelphia. Georgian England seemed to many citizens to have fallen from the great heights achieved during the Glorious Revolution. The poverty of the lower classes, the rotten boroughs, the open bribery at elections, the conspicuous consumption and moral laxity of the upper classes all grated harshly on the perceptions of Philadelphians living hardy (but comfortable) lives on the edge of a largely untamed wilderness. Some Philadelphia merchants and lawyers lived in luxury rivaling that of British country gentlemen whose lifestyles they consciously imitated, but they were nonetheless appalled at the extravagance and public immorality of the British aristocracy. The image of British life presented in the Philadelphia press must have especially aroused the ire of those middle-class artisans and shopkeepers accustomed to the austerity of Quaker and German piety or Scotch-Irish frugality. No doubt circulation of this "new" image of the mother country created dissonance among Philadelphians habituated to rendering deference to all things British, but the new description was enunciated so commonly by local Whigs and was confirmed so consistently by essays and correspondence from England printed in the city's newspapers that by 1775 it assumed perceptual dominance.[9]

By focusing on luxury and corruption, Whig publicists redefined England in terms that possessed special meaning for eighteenth-century Philadelphians. Like other Americans, Philadelphians appear to have accepted the maxim that freedom and liberty were direct descendents of virtue and morality. And they believed there was no more reliable index of a nation's virtue than its ability to resist the corroding influences of luxury and its concomitant, corruption. Whig rhetoric reflected and reinforced this consensus. It should be recognized, however, that Philadelphia protesters tended to fasten attention more upon the dangers of luxury than of corruption, warning that corruption was actually symptomatic of a more fundamental moral malaise that stemmed from a people's inability to resist the temptations of that luxury "with which liberty is incompatible."[10]

"Luxury" was among the most conspicuous devil-terms in the lexicon of Whig writers and speakers. Some equated it simply with "the sordid love of gain." Others defined it with scholastic dispassion as "an excessive or superfluous indulgence in anything which our circumstances will not reasonably afford." Still others identified it more sensationally as "that which consists in dull, selfish, animal enjoyment; in minds stupified, and bodies enervated, by wallowing forever in one continual puddle of voluptuousness."[11] But no matter what specific meaning individual Whigs attached to luxury, almost all portrayed it as an addiction which, if allowed to continue unchecked, would tempt Philadelphians "to turn their backs on virtue, and pay their homage where they ought not," ultimately sapping their will to resist tyranny. From the excesses of luxury, nations fell easily into corruption and "a servile dependence upon power" from which only slavery could result. The narcotizing and enervating effects "attending the growth of luxury among a free people" were dramatically capsulized by "An Old Mechanic." "Luxuries," he counseled, "will become necessaries and the people will grow so fond of them that they will even sell themselves and their children for slaves to purchase them."[12]

A good portion of the anti-luxury diatribes published in Philadelphia were intimately linked to the Whigs' campaigns for nonimportation. One of the protesters' chief strategies in soliciting support for economic sanctions against the parent state was to demean imported British goods—especially clothing and tea—as "pernicious luxuries" Philadelphians would be better off without. Importing fewer items from abroad and relying more upon locally grown and manufactured commodities, the Whigs stressed, would prevent "European luxuries and vices" from corrupting Philadelphians' virtue and dedication to liberty.

Given the known dangers of luxury, they advised, nonconsumption of foreign goods "would be the best political as well as moral virtue that we could possibly exercise."[13] Indeed, by the 1770s some Whigs began to advocate nonimportation not only as a means of forcing retraction of oppressive parliamentary legislation but as prudent and virtuous in and of itself.

The immediate context of this Whig rhetoric is less important, however, than its long-range implications. By repeatedly amplifying (in whatever context) the ways luxury inexorably destroyed a people's public virtue and devotion to liberty, Philadelphia Whigs further invigorated their redefinition of England's once positive image. Before 1765, Philadelphians generally perceived the parent state as strong, healthy, and virtuous. By 1776 they tended to see her as luxurious, corrupt, immoral, and by extrapolation, weak, diseased, and on the way to destruction, but nonetheless vicious.

This change in image complemented the Whigs' allegations of ministerial and parliamentary conspiracy. A necessity of all revolutionary rhetoric is to strike a balanced characterization of the enemy. The enemy must be sufficiently evil and cunning to elicit widespread contempt, but he must not be so powerful and artful that he cannot possibly be defeated. If he is too humane, revolution is not necessary; if he is too formidable, revolution is not possible. By alleging a plot against American property and liberty Whig publicists rendered an adversary known, hated, and feared. It was, however, identification of a vulnerable adversary. Although still physically strong, England was morally weak. Being morally weak she could successfully be resisted by virtuous, patriotic Americans—as the Dutch had resisted Spain, as the Greeks had resisted Persia, as good naturally resists evil.

Of course, a revolutionary perspective on British-American relations included a peculiarly proud view of Americans—a view Whig spokesmen in Philadelphia encouraged at every stage of the imperial conflict.

━━◄══════►━━

During the Stamp Act controversy John Dickinson predicted that British restrictions on colonial commerce and manufacturing would eventually set America apart from England by forcing her to rely upon those resources "within herself, of which she never otherwise would have thought." Four years later, at the

height of agitation over the Townshend duties, Charles
Thomson noted that Dickinson's forecast was fast becoming
reality.

From the genius of the people and the fertility of the soil, it is easy to
foresee that in the course of a few years they will find at home an ample
supply of all their wants. In the meanwhile their strength, power and
numbers are daily increasing, and as the property of land is parceled
out among the inhabitants and almost every farmer is a freeholder, the
spirit of liberty will be kept awake and the love of freedom deeply
rooted; and when strength and liberty combine it is easy to foresee that
a people will not long submit to arbitrary sway.[14]

These passages from Philadelphia's two most influential Whig
leaders reveal an important dimension of thought in the city
during the decade of protest. As the controversy progressed,
Philadelphians looked increasingly to themselves for the
physical and spiritual assets upon which to rest claims to
strength, vitality, and freedom. When they reflected on their
own present and future, Whiggish Philadelphians saw a robust
and virtuous people blessed with powerful natural and moral
resources and possessing a special destiny realizable only outside
the confining structure of the British empire. This dramatic
shift in the way Philadelphians perceived themselves, other
Americans, and the empire was hastened, guided, and reinforced by Whig rhetoric.

From the time of the Stamp Act, Philadelphia Whigs
consistently portrayed America as potentially stronger and more
powerful than its parent country. One feature of that portrait
was a representation of America as the economic bulwark of the
empire. This representation was grounded upon two generally
uncontested premises: "Great Britain stands upon her commerce. The American colonies are the *pillars of that commerce*." As
early as 1765 Whig publicists pictured England as economically
dependent upon America. Should the colonies adopt nonimportation agreements and deprive England of her customary
American trade revenue, one writer contended in September
1765, British merchants would suffer irreparable losses and
"thousands of her useful laborers and their families must
starve—so great a dependence has the mother upon her
children." Four months later "Philoleutherus" developed the
same theme in more detail. Those who held that England would
crush opposition to the Stamp Act exhibited "great ignorance"

of America's true strength: "Whatever courtiers may pretend, Great Britain is more dependent on us than we on her; and so it will prove to be if the matter is ever put to a fair trial." According to "Philoleutherus," at least half a million Englishmen relied "entirely on their commerce with the colonies for their daily bread." Deprived of the lucrative American market, one of only two from which she accrued a favorable balance of trade, England's entire economic structure would topple; her merchants would be forced out of business, her workers would be jobless and reduced "to a starving condition."[15]

Some of the most convincing demonstrations of the colonies' economic value to the mother country were written by Benjamin Franklin. A belated arrival to the ranks of those who spoke against the Stamp Act, Franklin was among the earliest opponents of the Townshend duties. From early in 1768 through the next two years he composed a series of essays over various pseudonyms criticizing the Townshend duties and calling for their repeal. He wrote these essays in London for a British audience, but he forwarded most of them to Philadelphia, where they were faithfully reprinted. A recurring feature of the essays was a warning that Parliament and the ministry ran the risk of seriously weakening the economy of the mother country by forcing the colonists into boycotting British imports in order to combat the Townshend Acts. Franklin buttressed his claim by citing official records which made clear the importance of the American trade to British merchants and manufacturers. Writing as "A Briton," he conservatively estimated the annual value of England's exports to the colonies at two million pounds sterling—at least half of which would be lost through nonimportation. He calculated that 15,400 laborers would forfeit their jobs should nonimportation take hold, in addition to which there would be losses incurred by shippers and sailors normally employed on American routes. Such computations had little impact upon the British audience for whom they were originally intended, but they were of considerable interest to readers in Philadelphia. There they reinforced the contentions of local Whigs and induced many residents to ponder seriously the question Franklin posed in the *Pennsylvania Gazette* of 19 January 1769: *"Whether the mother country, in consequence thereof, is not rather dependent upon the colonists, than the colonists upon the mother country?"*[16]

Viewed retrospectively such estimates of America's economic importance were clearly exaggerated, but they gained such wide circulation as to become by 1770 undefended premises of Whig rhetoricians in Philadelphia. In the first place, events had given credence to these formulations. England's dependence upon American trade seemed conclusively demonstrated when British merchants rapidly forced repeal of the Stamp Act following adoption of colonial nonimportation agreements in 1765. Moreover, "news" from the mother country reaffirmed the conclusions of Philadelphia protesters. Philadelphians received word from London that "America is now almost the only market for our manufactures" and that America made England the most powerful nation in Europe as "its trade is of more consequence to us than all our other trade together." Across 1768–70, Philadelphia newspapers reported vast British business losses due to the colonial embargo, while British pamphlets and essays reprinted in the city predicted economic ruin should the colonial trade be lost. For instance, the British author of the aptly titled *Power and Grandeur of Great Britain, Founded on the Liberty of the Colonies* urged Parliament to heal the breach before it was too late. Exclaiming that British economic and political superiority were founded on the connection with America, he presented a remarkable vision of what would occur should the colonies be driven to independence: "I see Britain reduced in her trade; depopulated by the transmigration of her people to America; her populous trading [and] manufacturing cities deserted; her nobles, for want of tenants, tilling their own grounds; and calling on oppressed, disaffected America to relieve and defend her against the power of her enemies. In short, I see Britain in America and America in Britain."[17] Philadelphia Whigs themselves drew no more devastating images of England without America.

Under the pressures of rhetoric and events many Philadelphians thus came to hold a set of perceptions later described by David Ramsay:

Instead of feeling themselves dependent on Great Britain, they conceived that, in respect to commerce, she was dependent on them. It inspired them with such high ideas of the importance of their trade, that they considered the mother country to be brought under greater obligations to them, for purchasing her manufactures, than they were to her for protection and the administration of civil government. The

freemen of British America, impressed with the exalting sentiments of
patriotism and of liberty, conceived it to be within their power, by future combinations, at any time to convulse, if not to bankrupt, the nation from which they sprung.[18]

Such perceptions were reinforced and extended by the Whigs'
emphasis on America's wealth in the two resources considered
most valuable in the preindustrialized eighteenth century: land
and people. That America was geographically larger and would
one day hold more people than the mother country were immensely important "facts" often amplified in the Philadelphia
press. One of the most provocative ideas injected into
eighteenth-century American political discourse was Franklin's
discovery that the population of the colonies was doubling every
twenty years. Franklin's demographic calculations, formally advanced in his *Observations Concerning the Increase of Mankind*
(1751), exerted a powerful influence. The *Observations* were
widely quoted in the years after 1751 and by the 1760s were
regarded as authoritative on both sides of the Atlantic. The conclusions were echoed by various Philadelphia protesters through
the decade of protest and contributed significantly to a general
redefinition of the image of the colonies vis-à-vis that of England.[19]

It is significant that Philadelphia Whigs seldom pointed to
America's projected population increase without linking it to the
vast expanse and the natural resources of the American
continent. While England could, biologically, double in population every two decades, she was territorially restricted by her
insular boundaries. America faced no such barriers and
therefore would "in less than half a century . . . contain more
inhabitants than Great Britain and Ireland" together. According
to the unknown author of the pamphlet *Observations of Consequence in Three Parts, Occasioned by the Stamp-Tax,* there were almost no limits to America's potential development. In his esti-
mation, the extensive North American territory contained 1
million square miles of land, which parceled out to the incredi-
ble total of 640 million square acres—"more than twelve times
the area of England and Wales" and capable of supporting
"more than a hundred million inhabitants."[20]

The most important presentation of these ideas in
Philadelphia before 1776 came in a series of six newspaper
essays published in the *Pennsylvania Packet* between 20 June and

8 August 1774. So well received were the essays that they were reprinted together late in August as a pamphlet entitled *A Few Political Reflections, Submitted to the Consideration of the British Colonies, by a Citizen of Philadelphia*. The author was Richard Wells, a moderate Whig in the city's resistance movement during the 1770s.[21] Wells's pamphlet was notable in several respects and deserves more attention than it has heretofore received. It denied the right of Parliament to legislate for America but rejected all riotous measures of protest (including the Boston Tea Party, for which Wells thought the East India Company deserved compensation). It presented a sound rationale for calling a continental congress but rejected political independence. It defended the efficacy of intercolonial nonimportation agreements as a means of resisting the Coercive Acts but attacked proposals for nonexportation as economically unwise. It decried England's efforts to enslave Americans and called upon patriotic Pennsylvanians to practice their Whiggish preachings by abolishing the wicked practice of black slavery. In substance and in tone *A Few Political Reflections* is an excellent representation of the political attitudes of the moderate majority of Philadelphians during the summer and fall of 1774. It is significant, then, that the pamphlet also contained a lengthy and powerful discussion of America's territorial and demographic potential.

Citing Franklin, Wells said that America would continue to double its population every twenty years. Within a century there would be 96 million inhabitants—"a multitude beyond conception," and the growth would continue "till the land is full." And here lay the key to America's future glory; the vastness of the North American continent promised continual growth and development. Wells calculated the size of the continent at more than 7 million square miles, enough to provide 47 million farms of 100 hundred acres each. If each farm maintained five people, the land of North America would one day support almost 235 million industrious inhabitants. By comparison, England held only 32 million acres, and the total population of Asia, Africa, and Europe amounted to no more than 300 million people. The conclusion, said Wells, was portentous and inescapable: "America *must* grow—England *must* perceive it."[22]

Wells also took note of America's other resources. There was nothing America needed, he explained, "which the various climes of this extensive continent will not indulge." In America could be found stone, clay, lime, timber, iron, oils, and lead. From these resources colonial workmen could produce glass, paints, ships, and weapons, while fertile farm lands yielded hemp, flax, cotton, wheat, tobacco, and rice, and provided ample pasture for the cattle and sheep from which artisans could manufacture leather and woolen goods. To be sure, America lacked the silks of China, the spices of India, the gold of Peru. But such luxuries were hardly vital. If one considered the essential resources, Americans possessed "every necessary for *shelter from the weather*" and "the means of procuring every *necessary* implement of labor and husbandry." Wells concluded his discussion of America's prospects by exclaiming, "I am struck with wonder at the immensity of the view before me."[23]

Contemplating American commercial might, a steadily increasing population, and a vast continent of plentiful resources, large numbers of Philadelphians moved with Wells and other Whig rhetoricians to redefine their images of America. Whereas Philadelphians had once seen England as the center of the empire, by 1775 they tended to share John Dickinson's judgment that "THE FOUNDATIONS OF THE POWER AND GLORY OF GREAT BRITAIN ARE LAID IN AMERICA."[24]

Given the paeans we have been reviewing, it is not surprising that some Philadelphia Whigs began to portray America itself as destined to become the center of a mighty empire. One writer forecast that the rapid growth of colonial population and economic prosperity would make America the physical center of the British empire, "and not many generations may pass away before one of the first monarchs of the world, on ascending his throne, shall declare with exulting joy, *'Born and raised amongst you, I glory in the name of* AMERICAN.' "[25] Not only would America replace England as the seat of empire, "Rationalis" predicted, but there was little doubt that in time hers would become "the greatest and most prosperous empire the world has ever seen." Richard Wells believed that nothing could obstruct or retard "the rapidity of our progress," and one day America would surely be an "amazing" empire ranking in "splendor, independence, and riches with all the united powers of the Eastern World."[26]

Not all Philadelphia Whigs envisioned American destiny explicitly in terms of empire, but most agreed that the time was coming "when the knee of empires and splendid kingdoms"

would bow to America. "The name of AMERICAN will carry
honor and majesty in the sound—and men will esteem it a blessing to wear the venerable and commanding style." Equally illustrative of the way Philadelphians were encouraged to see
themselves and their destiny were the remarks entitled
"Observation".

As the colonies are blessed with the richest treasures of nature, art will
never be idle for want of stores to work upon; and they being instructed
by the experience, the wisdom, and even errors, of all ages and all countries, will undoubtedly give rise superior to them all in the scale of
human dignity. No people that ever trod the stage of the world have
had so glorious a prospect as now rises before the Americans—there is
nothing good or great but their wisdom may acquire; and to what
heights they will arrive in the progress of time, no one can conceive.[27]

By 1776 some Whigs would urge independence on grounds
that continued alliance with England would prevent America
from realizing the glorious destiny so freely forecast during the
preceding decade. Before the outbreak of war in 1775, however,
separation was far from the minds of most Philadelphia
protesters. They pointed to America's boundless potential partly
to arouse Philadelphians to assert their rights "with manly
dignity," partly to elicit support for nonimportation and
domestic manufacturing, and partly to convince Parliament to
rescind restrictive trading and taxing schemes. Wells, for
example, was "astonished" at England's obdurate refusal to "be
satisfied for the present with the immediate advantages resulting from our mutual intercourse." His stated aim was simply to
present "the strongest and clearest proofs" to persuade the
rulers and people of England that it was *their interest* to attend to
our grievances and grant us redress." Similarly, the anonymous
author of *Some Observations of Consequence in Three Parts* urged
Parliament to recognize the present and future benefits of
alliance with America and rescind its "preposterous measures."
The colonies, he explained, should not be "rashly scourged" but
treated with kindness: "They ought to be tenderly guarded by a
jealous love, that valuable fruits may proceed timely, and even
abundantly from their very promising blossoms, which the
storms of a jealous tyranny would blast and prevent."[28]
    Although no doubt sincere, such disclaimers could not
eliminate the divisive logic implicit in the Whigs' apotheosis of

American physical resources. By picturing the colonies as potentially and in some respects actually stronger than the mother country, they helped to develop and intensify Philadelphians' feelings of distinctness from and superiority to England. At the same time, they provided an additional rationale for opposing specific acts of Parliament and eventually for denying it any legislative authority in America. Wells explained, for example, that Parliament was composed of "insignificant creatures" who boldly uttered "pompous display[s] of imaginary power" like "lords of the earth," whereas in truth the "combined numbers of an English Parliament" paled to insignificance "when weighed against the growing majesty of this growing continent." Indeed, the anomaly of a mighty continent's being ruled by an island seemed increasingly silly. If America would one day be the seat of empire, how logical was it for her to be treated imperiously by those who would shortly become subordinate? "That Great Britain should continue to insult and *alienate* the growing millions who inhabit this country, on whom she greatly depends, and on whose alliance in future time her existence as a nation may depend," was to Whig partisans "as glaring an instance of human folly as ever disgraced politicians or put common sense to the blush." The inexorably revolutionary direction of the Whigs' lionization of America's physical strength was revealed by the writer who aptly titled his essay "Look-Out." It was inconceivable, he stated, that England could continue to

tax and control at pleasure this vast country, with its countless millions of people, and situated in the finest and most advantageous part of the world. . . . Be it known to all men, the *Americans* will not suffer these insults but a very little time longer—they have the means of redress in their own hands, and they will soon use them. . . . Such is the present increasing and flourishing state of the colonies, many think they will become an independent commonwealth within five years, unless they are treated in a very different manner from what they have been of late. It is a settled point that they can do it whenever they are disposed, and every step of administration tends to this disposition.[29]

In addition to apotheosizing America's physical resources, Philadelphia Whigs portrayed the colonies as spiritually superior to the mother country. As Whig rhetoricians denigrated the splendor and sophistication of life in England, they correspondingly redefined as assets the rusticity and simplicity of life in

America. This redefinition became more pronounced as the
British-American controversy progressed, but it was evident as
early as the Stamp Act crisis. The remarks of "Rationalis" are
illustrative. Americans, he exclaimed, were "a rough and hardy
people, uneffeminated with the luxury and uncontaminated
with the vices that are preparing the inhabitants of the mother
country to be slaves." He urged Philadelphians to be proud that
they had "not yet been intoxicated with the Circean cup of
pleasure," that "effeminancy" had not yet "enervated their
bodies or minds." While Englishmen devoted themselves to
worthless pursuits "to kill time," Americans were frugal, industrious, and determined "to subsist in their labors in the independence of freemen." While Englishmen dallied with the false
arts of luxury and corruption, Americans led the virtuous lives
of "simple rustics," steadfastly believing "that liberty, and not
pleasure, is the greatest blessing of life."[30]
   In short, by 1775 England was identified with vice and
America with virtue.[31] Whig spokesmen had transformed the
controversy with England at least partially into a dispute over
life-styles. They enjoined their audience not just to do or believe
something but to *be* something.[32] They urged Philadelphians to
be, quite simply, American rather than British. By trying to
emulate Englishmen, the Whigs said, Philadelphians aimed at
unhealthy goals which could only undermine American virtue.
Rather than strive after the sophisticated life-style of British society, Philadelphians should retain their own "innocence and
simplicity." Rather than emulate the luxurious fashions of
British aristocrats, Philadelphians should disregard "all the
pageantry, and the robes, and the plumes" and wear American-
made apparel as "the symbol of dignity, the badge of virtue."
There were ample resources in America to live "within
ourselves . . . without gadding abroad after every knick-knack
and trinket that is worked up in Great Britain." And, of course,
by being American, Philadelphians could more effectually resist
England's corrupt political schemes. After all, Wells pointed out,
"the independent spirit of a free American" would never "sink
prostrate at the unworthy feet of luxury and surrender up our
dearest rights for the paultry [*sic*] pomp and pageantry of un-
manly tinsel."[33]
   The protesters' exaltations of American virtues and resources
can be seen as important indices of the inherently revolutionary

nature of much Whig thought after 1765. Revolutions are many things. They are political, economic, institutional, and social struggles. They are also battles between competing cultural and moral systems. A central characteristic of revolutionary movements is their preoccupation with reconstituting the values underlying old orders. Severe, irreconcilable conflict over basic cultural values is a cardinal feature setting revolutionary movements apart from reform movements, which generally seek to restore, preserve, or create normative standards within the framework of existing cultural values.[34] When one appraises the consciously articulated demands for change advanced by Whig spokesmen across the years 1765–76, it is evident that the "revolutionary movement" began as a reform movement and remained so until its latest stages. But when one looks at the latent meanings of Whig discourse—at what might be called its subideological dimension—one sees how persistently the Whigs perceived America and England as protagonist and antagonist in a great moral drama being played upon the stage of world history. From this perspective the shift of the Whig movement from a stance concerned predominantly with reform to one directed overtly toward revolution can be seen to have occurred when Whigs came to full, conscious realization that the imperial conflict centered not only on issues of political privilege and economic interest but also on questions of cultural and moral values.

The apotheosis of American values also reduced the perceived grounds for compromise and helped prepare Philadelphians as a receptive audience for the introduction of overtly revolutionary appeals. A common argument for separation during the debate over independence in 1776 was that the luxury, corruption, and dissipation of England would ultimately spread across the ocean and infect "the bosom of perfect liberty and freedom in America." This argument was seldom stated explicitly in Philadelphia before the outbreak of war in the spring of 1775, but it grew naturally out of Whig rhetoric from 1765 on. If America were pure and England defiled, the danger of contamination obviously increased the longer America remained within the empire. This view was nascent in Philadelphia as early as 1770, when "A Son of Liberty" asked whether America could remain free when freedom was being subverted in England: "Will the streams be pure when the foun-

tain is corrupted?" "'Tis impossible," he answered. By February
1775 Benjamin Franklin had concluded privately that continued
connection would inevitably "corrupt and poison . . . the glorious public virtue so predominant in our rising country." Six
months later "Caractacus" expressed similar sentiments publicly.
Philadelphians, he warned, should not lose sight of the evils
which beset the parent state—evils which promised to "spread
desolation and slavery through every part of the empire. . . . I
will not say that it is high time we should be taken from her
breasts, but I will say that she has played the harlot in her old
age, and that if we continue to press them too closely we shall extract nothing but disease and death."[35]

The emphasis on British moral decline, the lionization of
American commercial strength and natural resources, the
exhortations to think and be "American," and the apotheosis of
American virtues also encouraged Philadelphians to perceive
England and America as two separate countries rather than as
constituent elements of a unified empire. Occasionally this distinctness was stated explicitly, as when "N." declared the Stamp
Act nothing more than "a foreign tribute," or when other Whigs
referred to America as "this country" and to England as "that
country."[36] More often, especially before 1773, the distinctness
was stated only implicitly. If the colonies were superior to England, they must in some sense have been separate from her.
Whig spokesmen established a long series of imagistic equations
which accented the differences between England and America.
England was corrupt, America was pure; England was opulent,
America was frugal; England was effeminate, America was
manly; England was descendent, America was ascendent; England was weak, America was strong; England was decadent,
America was robust; England was small, America was spacious;
England was oppressive, America was free. As Philadelphia
Whigs presented them, the differences between England and
America were far more than political or economic. They were
also geographical, social, institutional, and perhaps most important, moral. And they were not differences readily dissolved
by compromise.

One set of images posed special problems for the Whigs: the
image of England as parent or mother and of America as child.
This analogy was widely accepted and regularly employed on
both sides of the Atlantic. But being a figurative analogy, it
could sustain various interpretations. In one sense, it suggested

that America was subordinate and bound by duty to her parent, who nourished and protected her. In another sense, it suggested that the colonies' subordination was only temporary, that they, like all children, would one day reach maturity and become independent. Despite the inherent tension between these interpretations, neither England nor America had special reason to push the logic of one or the other before 1765. As long as British-American relations remained generally cordial, there was no need to probe alternative meanings. But with the reassertion of British authority after the Seven Years' War, the ambiguities of the analogy could no longer be tolerated. Consequently, the analogy—and more important, its "proper" interpretation—assumed a central position in the rhetoric of all major parties to the imperial controversy.

To most British politicians and polemicists there was no confusion over the parent-child analogy. Those who supported the government's American policy did so by pointing to England's parental prerogatives and to the colonies' filial obligations. As Thomas Blacklock put it, nothing could be "more analogous to the natural relation between a parent and a child than the political relation between a country and its colonies." It was the responsibility of the mother country to support, protect, and guide its children "from their infancy to their maturity." Correspondingly, it was the duty of the colonies to obey their parent state and to provide "all the returns which they can properly make for her maternal care and liberality." From these premises it was an easy step to sanctioning coercive measures against the willful and ungrateful American child. England "has long had reason to complain of American ingratitude," one writer held in 1776, "and she will not bear longer with American injustice. . . . The law of God and of nature is on the side of an indulgent parent against an undutiful child; and should necessary correction render him incapable of future offense he has only his obstinancy and folly to blame." So deeply were the imperatives of the familial analogy rooted in British thought that even opposition leaders who supported America's resistance to unconstitutional taxation refused to abjure England's parental supremacy in other areas. William Pitt himself declared that the colonies "must be subordinate. In all laws relating to trade and navigation especially, this is the mother country, they are children; they must obey and we prescribe."[37]

Philadelphia Tories decried England's efforts to tax Ameri-

cans without consent as a violation of the parent state's obliga-
tion to treat her children justly. But, they added, it did not
follow that the colonies ought to disobey their mother country or
to sever the bond with her. The tie between England and
America bore "a true resemblance to that between parent and
child," Joseph Galloway contended.

> Their rights and duties are similar. Should a child take umbrage at the
> conduct of a parent, tell him that he was not his father, nor would he
> consider himself, or act, as his child *on any terms,* ought the parent to
> listen to such undutiful language, or could he be justly censured for
> treating it with neglect, or even with contempt?

The most notable Tory interpretation of the parent-child
analogy in Philadelphia was that presented by Isaac Hunt, a
Quaker lawyer and long-time political ally of Galloway, in his
aptly titled pamphlet *The Political Family.* Hunt made two important concessions: he acknowledged the colonies' growing
strength and maturity, and he admitted that with nations, as
with children, "the state of minority is temporary. When that
state ceases, the parent's right of chastisement and absolute command ceases also." To Hunt's way of thinking, however, neither
concession mitigated America's obligations to England. Citing
Francis Bacon's definition of colonies as "the children of more
ancient nations," Hunt argued:

> Children receive nourishment from the milk of their mothers till they
> are capable of digesting other food! And they receive from the hands of
> their parents, protection from the insults and injuries to which their
> feeble infant state is exposed. They ought, therefore, when they have
> attained the state of youth, or manhood, to evidence their gratitude by a
> pious love and filial obedience. . . . Honor, reverence, esteem and
> support, when wanted, in return for nourishment, education, and pro-
> tection are *perpetually* due to the parent.[38]

There is no way of knowing the extent to which ordinary
Philadelphians accepted the British-Tory reading of the parent-
child analogy at the outset of the imperial controversy. Probably
a fair number agreed with its major tenets, but that reading was
for obvious reasons anathema to the city's Whig leaders.
Psychologically, the interpretation connoted American sub-
servience and inferiority; politically, it demanded quiescence
and obedience. To sustain protest against British policy
Philadelphia Whigs had to advance their own interpretation of

the analogy. Across the years 1765–75 they persuasively redefined the status and obligations of both members of the British
political family in a fashion that broadened the acceptable
sphere of resistance to an unjust parent, provided a more
exalted depiction of the growing American child, and gradually
highlighted the inherently revolutionary implications of the
analogy.

Philadelphia Whigs responded to the British-Tory interpretation of the parent-child analogy in three general ways. The first
response, most evident during the periods of agitation against
the Stamp and Townshend acts, was that America was obliged to
comply with British commands only as long as the mother
country fulfilled her parental responsibilities. Foremost among
these responsibilities was protecting the colonies "in their constitutional liberties, taking nothing from them but what they
choose voluntarily to give to the support of government." As "legitimate" and "dutiful" children, said one Philadelphian, the
colonists deserved "a constitutional patrimony." And although
just parents were entitled to absolute obedience, England could
not be obeyed while she cruelly drove America "into bondage,
with the scourges of ambition or avarice." According to
Dickinson, the indignation aroused by the Stamp Act was "but
the resentment of dutiful children who have received unmerited
blows from a beloved parent." "An infant that tottered along a
walk in a garden, and loaded with flowers had presented them
to her mother, would as soon have expected to be knocked down
by her." To hold that Philadelphians had no course but to bow to
such a cruel and unfaithful parent was absurd, said "Justice and
Humanity" in arguing against the Townshend duties. A proper
filial obedience was one thing; servility was quite another. Given
the repeated assaults upon colonial liberty, it was now up to "the
mother country" to show "some marks of her paternal [sic] affection if she wishes to receive a willing obedience from her
American children."[39]

Portraying the colonies as loyal, affectionate, but protesting
children put the blame for disruption of harmonious family
relations squarely upon the heartless parent. The portrayal also
intensified Philadelphians' sense of alienation from England, for
only a depraved and demonic parent would willfully turn on its
own offspring. Inevitably, some Philadelphia Whigs began to
charge the mother country with the horrid and unnatural crime

of infanticide. How terrifying to think, said Richard Wells, that America's "once fond mother" had "trained up her children, like calves in the stall, to fall bloody victims by her own unnatural cruel hands." It was perfectly evident, said an outraged John Carmichael shortly after the battle of Lexington, that the British were now prepared "to murder and butcher their own children in America, that have been so obedient, useful, and affectionate." According to another writer, there could now be no doubting either the enormity of England's wickedness or the propriety of Philadelphians' efforts to defend themselves: "Whoever considers the unprincipled enemy we have to cope with, will not hesitate to declare that nothing but arms or miracles can reduce them to reason and moderation. They have lost sight of the limits of humanity. The portrait of a parent red with the blood of her children is a picture fit only for the galleries of the infernals."[40]

Obedience, then, was due England only as long as she fulfilled her parental obligations. Effective as this argument was in justifying resistance to British policies that threatened Philadelphians' rights and interests, it did not question the colonies' filial subordination to the mother country or challenge her parental right to superintend the colonies. By 1774, however, some Philadelphia protesters were beginning to stress the incontrovertible right of all children to grow up and make their own way in the world. In her infancy, they granted, America was indeed beholden to England. But now she was a maturing country, no longer to be treated as an insolent youngster. As they dwelt upon America's commercial strength, her boundless natural resources, her steadily increasing population, and her special spiritual vitality, more and more Whigs were led to deny the validity of identifying America as a child, subordinate and inferior. No Philadelphian expressed this idea and its potentially revolutionary implications more clearly or forcefully than Richard Wells. Wells granted all that Englishmen had done for America during its infancy and childhood: "They took us as babes at the breast; they nourished us, and leading us gently along, supported and instructed us—with pleasure they viewed our ripening years, and gloried in the goodly figure to which we were attaining." Because of that assistance America had grown swiftly to become the equal of its parent.

We look to manhood—our muscles swell out with youthful vigor; our sinews spring with elastic force; and we feel the *marrow of Englishmen in our bones.* The day of independent manhood is at hand—we *feel* our strength; and, with a filial grateful sense of *proper* obedience, would wish to be esteemed the *friend* as well as *child* of Britain. In *domestic* life, we all allow there is a time when youth shall no longer be subject to the control of age; when reason forbids, and when nature denies. May Britain think seriously on this important subject; let her weigh the connection in the strict balance of justice; nay, let her try it on the graduated scale of causes and events, and her judgment will join hand in hand with her equity, and declare we are *men.*[41]

While some Whigs confronted the implications of the parent-child analogy by citing America's arrival at "independent manhood," a few looked back to the origins of the colonies and declared that Americans were never truly the children of England. These writers argued that Philadelphians, like other Americans, were in fact outcasts, orphans, and not the nurtured offspring of England. America, they said, was settled at the expense of the inhabitants. The colonists' "own blood was spilt in acquiring lands for their settlement; their own fortunes expended in making that settlement effectual; for themselves they fought, for themselves they conquered, and for themselves alone they have right to hold." Not one shilling was issued from the British treasury until recent years, "after the colonies had become established on a firm and permanent footing." It was only when America became "valuable to Great Britain for her commercial purposes" that she began to claim the colonies as her children. In short, contemporary Americans, according to "John Hampden," inhabited a glorious continent "settled at the expense of the possessors and sealed with the blood of their ancestors."[42]

As the preceding paragraph suggests, there was in the rhetoric of Philadelphia Whigs a veneration of the original American settlers comparable to that accorded in later ages to the Founding Fathers. This veneration was conspicuous throughout the decade of protest, whether a child-parent relationship with England was recognized or not. Increasingly conscious of their identity as Americans, Philadelphia protesters apostrophized their forefathers and gloried in their American heritage. The most important elements of this heritage were said to be the blessings of freedom and liberty. These blessings were purchased by "our brave forefathers . . . with their blood, and with a father's care" were handed down "to us, their children," exclaimed one writer. To another, they comprised a "sacred trust consigned to us for the happiness of posterity." Surely, then, patriotic Philadelphians could never allow "the pestilential breath of tyrants to approach this garden of our forefathers and blast the fruit of their labors." "A Friend to the Colony" made much the same point as he exhorted Philadelphians not to dishonor their ancestors, themselves, or their duty to posterity.

We have received our liberties as an inheritance from our fathers, and we are bound to transmit them to our children unimpaired. If we do so, we shall do our duty; if we do otherwise, we shall act with the basest treachery and impiety. We shall deservedly incur the censure, the contempt, and the abhorrence of all honest men, and entitle ourselves to the curses of posterity.[43]

Philadelphia Whigs portrayed American liberty as an inherited condition whose continued growth was threatened by the poison of British tyranny and whose continued existence could only be secured by acting in the spirit of those courageous men who crossed a turbulent ocean to establish a reign of freedom in an untamed wilderness. If accepted, this portrayal could only intensify Philadelphians' resistance to compromise. Compromise would not only endanger the freedom and liberty of living Americans, but would threaten the freedom and liberty of generations yet unborn. This perception of the stakes in the imperial controversy was broadened still further after passage of the Coercive Acts by introduction of the claim that the American cause was the cause of all mankind. From 1774 many Whiggish Philadelphians felt animated, as Benjamin Rush later exulted, by a belief that they were "acting for the benefit of the whole world and of future ages."[44]

Belief in a special American destiny was most pronounced in New England, where the Puritan founders had hoped to establish "a city set upon a hill," but it was also perennially present in Philadelphia, which was itself founded as an ideal community, a citadel to freedom, a "holy experiment."[45] Given this heritage, some of the city's Whig publicists understandably equated the cause of America with the will of God. They assured their audience that "you may surely, without presumption, believe that ALMIGHTY GOD himself will look down upon your righteous conduct with glorious approbation." To God, they declared, "you can look up with confidence, and in him you may trust." Obviously not all Philadelphians saw the Whig cause as divinely sanctioned, but belief in a heavenly ordained American destiny was widespread in the city. Even William Smith, Philadelphia's most outspoken foe of independence during the first part of 1776, confessed in 1775 that he was possessed "with a strong and even enthusiastic persuasion that Heaven has great and glorious purposes towards this continent which no human power or human device shall be able finally to illustrate." If Philadelphians and other Americans guarded against the snares of luxury, venality, and corruption, "the GENIUS OF AMERICA" would rise triumphant "with a power at last too mighty for opposition." America *"will be free,"* Smith declared, and will be "for ages to come, a chosen seat of *freedom, arts,* and *heavenly knowledge:* which are now either drooping or dead in most countries of the old world."[46]

Smith's final remark discloses what by 1775 became a widely held belief in Philadelphia, as in other parts of America. Philadelphians had seen England as the world's strongest bastion of freedom and liberty. But now the mother country herself seemed infected and fast going the way of France, Spain, Russia, Poland, Turkey, and all the other once-free nations which labored under oppression and tyranny. Now there seemed "scarce a spot on the globe inhabited by civilized nations where the vestiges of freedom" were to be observed. Throughout Asia, Africa, and South America freedom was unknown. More alarming still, warned Dickinson,

the passion of despotism raging like a plague, for about seven years past, has spread with unusual malignity through *Europe. Corsica, Poland,* and *Sweden* have sunk beneath it. The remaining spirit of freedom that lingered and languished in the Parliaments of *France* has lately expired. . . . What kingdom or state interposed for the relief of their distressed fellow creatures? The contagion has at length reached *Great Britain.* Her statesmen emulate the *Nimrods* of the earth and wish to become "mighty hunters" in the woods of America. What kingdom or state will interpose for our relief? . . . We have not the least prospect of human assistance.[47]

To Philadelphians jealous of their rights, apprehensive of conspiracy, fearful of luxury and corruption, convinced of their patriotic virtue, proud of their growing strength, and determined to bequeath liberty to their offspring, the impending demise of freedom in England meant that America was nearly the world's last, and surely its best, hope. From 1774 the city's Whigs echoed no conviction more consistently than this. "Amidst the wide *waste of empires,* this one corner of the globe" stood alone as "the last asylum of truth, righteousness, and freedom." Consequently, Philadelphians possessed an especially burdensome responsibility bestowed by God, who had "appointed this land of liberty as a refuge to the distressed of all nations." Philadelphians were bound to preserve liberty for future generations the world over and "to show the world this asylum, which, from its remote and unconnected situation with the rest of the globe might have remained a secret for ages."[48]

Acceptance of America's transcendent destiny broadened the scope of the resistance movement and lent it a regenerative urgency which, though largely secular, bore the rhetorical trappings of a religious crusade. The struggle against England could now be discussed as a moral cause with Americans allied on the side of freedom and justice on behalf of the entire world—past, present, and future. Philadelphians were not challenging England simply for themselves, they were protesting (and eventually fighting) for divinely ordained liberty everywhere. This claim gave moral sanction to radical action against the parent state. And, of course, universalizing goals and associating them with divine intentions further precluded any negotiable middle ground. If the ultimate Whig arguments were believed, the American cause could not be compromised because compromise would signal the worldwide demise of liberty. By transforming the American cause into a global cause the Whigs made Philadelphia patriots no longer just the defenders of their colony or even of their country, but "the champions and patrons of the human race." But champions and patrons though they might be, Philadelphians—with other Americans—stood alone. There was no state to whom they could look for relief or support. All had fallen to the plague of despotism. Still, the only course was to stand resolutely and uncompromisingly behind the Whig cause. By 1775 large numbers of Philadelphians had been brought by events and Whig rhetoric to agree with John

Dickinson that "the preservation of our freedom and every attendant blessing must be wrought out, under providence, *by ourselves*."[49]

By the spring of 1775 most Philadelphians had become nascent revolutionaries. They were not prepared to compromise with England, but neither were they prepared to separate from her. They agreed with Whig rhetoricians on the need for vigorous and determined resistance to British assaults upon colonial liberty and property. Resistance and revolution, however, are two different processes. While most Philadelphians clearly supported the former, most did not support the latter. Yet by the spring of 1775 Philadelphia opinion had hardened to the point where precipitate action by either England or America could turn protest into rebellion. Such action occurred at Lexington and Concord on 19 April 1775, and by January of 1776 the period of protest had come to an end. Revolution was at hand.

# PART III

# FROM PROTEST TO REVOLUTION

## THE DEBATE OVER INDEPENDENCE

# PROLEGOMENON

THE battles of Lexington and Concord were transforming events. From 19 April 1775 America and England were at war; consequently, their relationship could never again be what it had been before that date. The commencement of hostilities dramatically altered the grounds for and the tenor of debate regarding the role of the colonies in the empire. As Thomas Paine stated, most plans and proposals voiced before the outbreak of war were "like the almanacs of last year; which, though proper then, are [now] superseded and useless." Philadelphians no longer needed to argue about their rights and interests or whether they had been violated. Any remaining doubt about these matters was sealed in most minds by the events in Massachusetts. What had previously been a contest over propositions of value became one regarding propositions of policy. "We all agree in this," explained one Philadelphian, "that Great Britain is unjust and arbitrary." Disagreement existed over "the mode of opposition."[1] The alternative modes of opposition were, of course, independence and reconciliation.

The possibility of revolution was not happily received in Philadelphia. Most residents supported the war with England as an unfortunate but necessary course to preserve American freedom. At the same time, they were not yet convinced that independence was either inevitable, desirable, or feasible. Despite vast differences in economic, political, and religious outlook, a preponderance of Philadelphians could find common ground in the hope that British-American disagreements could still be resolved within the empire. That hope was sufficiently broad and sufficiently intense through the remainder of 1775 to prevent pro-independence Whigs from mounting a concerted public campaign for leaving the empire. Widespread public debate on separation from England did not begin in Philadelphia until

publication of *Common Sense* early in January 1776. For the ensu-
ing six months pro- and anti-independence spokesmen competed for the support of the city's great middle majority.

The contest between these two groups of rhetoricians was one
of the great public debates in American history. Not surprisingly, it has attracted the attention of many historians and
critics.[2] Yet despite all that has been written on the subject, we
still lack a satisfactory appraisal of the extent to which and the
manners in which the public discourse of revolutionary and anti-
revolutionary rhetoricians influenced the final determination of
the contest over independence in Philadelphia. Most scholars, to
the extent that they seek to resolve this question at all, do not go
beyond the general and somewhat facile judgment that the
journalistic agitation over independence, though doubtless important, was but one of a complex of factors whose exact influence cannot be readily discerned.[3] A more precise accounting
is possible, however, if we analyze the rhetoric of the competing
groups of advocates with careful and steady regard to the
Philadelphia audience at whom they directed their appeals. To
be sure, evaluating the impact of discourse upon specific
audiences is often difficult. Nonetheless, such evaluation is
possible and, in this instance, vital if our inquiry is to yield valuable dividends.

Few periods in the revolutionary era rival the special complexity of political opinion, rhetoric, and events in Philadelphia
during the first six months of 1776. Pennsylvania was the scene
of not one but two revolutions in 1776. The first culminated in
the repudiation of British moral and governmental authority.
The second was essentially the child of the first and culminated
in the overthrow of the Pennsylvania Assembly and institution
of a radically new state government. In the next two chapters we
shall deal strictly with the efforts of pro- and anti-independence
rhetoricians to persuade Philadelphians of the respective merits
and demerits of separation and reconciliation. Although our
controlling concern is with what Joseph Reed called the "terrible
wordy war" waged in Philadelphia on the subject of American
independence,[4] the imperial and internal revolutions were so
closely allied that we cannot fully appraise the rhetoric surrounding the former without also attending closely to the rhetoric that accompanied and helped to bring about the latter.
This conjugance was especially vital in May and June, and it will

be treated in Chapter 8. Our immediate task is to sketch the
competing factions of rhetoricians and the nature of the
audience they faced as 1775 turned into 1776.

The popular debate over independence in Philadelphia was not
so much between Whig and Tory as among competing groups of
Whigs. By 1776 the Tories, those who placed loyalty to England
before colonial liberties, possessed little public credibility and
limited access to the press. Their position was well illustrated by
the plight of Joseph Galloway, who had been the Whigs' most
persistent and persuasive foe during the decade of protest.
Embittered by the failure of his Plan of Union, stripped of his
position as speaker and no longer able to marshal a majority in
the Assembly, stigmatized by his shrill, capricious railings
against the Continental Congress, alienated from Philadelphia
mechanics, bereft of power and prestige, Galloway had retired
from politics the previous May and was no longer willing to
take up the pen against his Whig tormentors.[5] Deprived of
Galloway's leadership and rhetorical talents, discredited and
ideologically isolated from their fellow citizens by the continuing
state of war between England and America, staunch defenders
of British authority were not in a position to mount an effective
public campaign for their views.

   While the outbreak of war unified public opinion against
those who urged capitulation to the parent state, it also raised
the specter of independence, which by late 1775 shattered the
unity that had existed among Philadelphia Whigs since autumn
of 1774. By the beginning of 1776, Whig leaders divided into
two opposing factions. One group, known as "Moderates,"
"Reconcilers," or "Dependents," included men such as John
Dickinson, James Wilson, Robert Morris, William Smith,
Andrew and James Allen, Thomas Willing, Samuel Howell, and
Alexander Wilcox. For the most part, these were men associated
with the elite factions that had traditionally overseen the
province's political and economic affairs. Most were affluent,
well educated, politically prominent, and had been attached at
one time or another to the Proprietary faction. Many had been
at least marginally active in the protest movements of the previous decade; some had at times led the city in challenging
British authority. All were now alarmed and fearful when faced

with what Galloway called "the ill-shapen, diminutive brat, IN-DEPENDENCY."[6] Unlike Tories, however, Moderate Whigs generally supported the war then in progress as both justifiable and necessary if Americans were to retain their liberties. But unlike Radical Whigs, the Moderates did not believe that the war had to be or ought to be waged for independence, but simply to force from England just and reasonable terms for a settlement within the empire. The positions of the Moderates ranged from implacable resistance to independence to reluctant acceptance of its premature imposition; their identifying characteristic was a faith that reconciliation consistent with American liberty was still possible.

The acknowledged leader of the Moderate faction was John Dickinson. Dickinson had been a powerful advocate of vigorous resistance to British measures in previous years, but he opposed any precipitate move toward independence while there existed even a remote possibility of reconciliation and before the colonies had formed a stronger military and political union among themselves. He gave his talents and prestige to the Moderates' cause, but because he was preoccupied with directing the anti-separation forces in both the Continental Congress and the Pennsylvania Assembly, he contributed little formal discourse to the public dialogue over independence.[7]

The most influential public spokesman for reconciliation was William Smith, the acerbic, talented Anglican divine and head of the College of Philadelphia. One of the city's most learned, dynamic, and successful men, Smith was more than capable of shouldering the Moderates' rhetorical campaign against independence. In addition to being one of America's most gifted pulpit orators, he was an inveterate political activist and an immensely skillful secular controversialist. Conservative by nature, training, and conviction, Smith sought in 1776 a middle path that would preserve both the "dignity" of British politicians and the "essential rights" of American colonists. He took his viewpoint to the public in a series of eight letters which appeared over the name "Cato" in most Philadelphia papers in March and April. Smith's "Cato" essays constituted the most effective presentation of the case against independence in Philadelphia.[8]

The most notable pamphlet in support of reconciliation was *Plain Truth,* written by James Chalmers, a Maryland landowner who eventually became a Loyalist. Chalmers was not a Pennsylvanian, but his pamphlet deserves inclusion here because it was the first full response to *Common Sense* in Philadelphia. Almost immediately upon publication *Plain Truth* became an object of derision among those who supported independence. John Witherspoon, president of Princeton College and a frequent contributor to Philadelphia newspapers, called it "so contemptible that it could not procure a reading on a subject as to which the curiosity of the public was raised to great height." Thomas Paine ridiculed it as "a performance which hath withered away like a sickly, unnoticed weed, and which even its advocates are displeased at, and the author ashamed to own." Historians and critics have generally accepted these judgments, denigrating Chalmers's tract as grammatically inept, argumentatively incompetent, and intellectually impoverished. In truth, these indictments are overdrawn; more important, they obscure the fact that *Plain Truth* was influential in its own time and appears to have exerted an important impact upon public opinion. In less than two months it went through two editions and four printings in Philadelphia alone. John Adams, never given easily to acknowledging those who disagreed with him, nonetheless observed that *Plain Truth* "contributed very largely to fortify and inflame the party against independence, and finally lost us the Allens, Penns, and many other persons of weight in the community."[9]

In opposition to the spokesmen for reconciliation stood the "Radicals," "Independents," or "Disunionists," who looked to immediate independence as the only guarantee of American freedom. This faction included some men who were well known to Philadelphians—Thomas McKean, Joseph Reed, George Clymer. But it was headed largely by men who had recently risen to positions of political authority—James Cannon, Thomas Paine, Benjamin Rush, Christopher Marshall, John Bayard, Timothy Matlack, Thomas Young, Daniel Roberdeau, David Rittenhouse, Owen Biddle. None of this latter group was a member of the Whig hierarchy that had directed the resistance movement during the previous decade. Most were, as Rush characterized himself, "neglected, or unknown," by "the persons who called themselves great in the city." The Radicals had assumed strategic positions in Whig political organizations during the last half of 1775 as established Whig leaders had either backed away when confronted by the real possibility of inde-

pendence or had curtailed their involvement in local politics to
assume posts in the Continental Congress or the military. The
Radicals solidified their position early in 1776 when they acquired decisive control of the Philadelphia Committee of Inspection and Observation. Relative newcomers to Philadelphia
politics, Radical Whigs proved to be effective politicians and
highly skilled rhetoricians.[10]

The Radicals did not have a recognized leader of the stature
of John Dickinson or William Smith. Their campaign was very
much a collaborative effort,[11] but one that relied to a considerable degree upon the rhetorical talents of Thomas Paine. When
Paine arrived in Philadelphia in November 1774 there was little
to suggest that he would prove any more remarkable than most
immigrants to the New World. Born into England's teeming
lower-middle class, possessed of a meager formal education,
unsuccessful in marriage, undistinguished in any profession, he
appeared destined to live out his remaining years as inauspi-
ciously as he had the previous thirty-eight. But he soon found
employment, companionship, and, in the cause of American independence, a dignity and a purpose which had previously
eluded him. Endowed, as John Adams remarked, with "a capacity and a ready pen," Paine became the most influential
spokesman for independence in Philadelphia. Not trained in the
classical style that dominated, one might say stultified, literary
education in eighteenth-century England and America, he
wrote freed of the standard conventions of style and argumentative method that burdened most of his contemporaries. Most
crucially for a popular movement, he had what Rush correctly
discerned to be "a wonderful talent of writing to the tempers
and feelings of the public." His monumentally popular
pamphlet, *Common Sense,* was by far the most powerful and effective presentation of the case for separation, while his
"Forester" essays spearheaded the Radicals' counteroffensive
against Smith's "Cato" series. Paine's greatest works would be
written in other countries in later years, but his rhetoric in
Philadelphia during the first half of 1776 alone would suffice to
secure his reputation as one of the Western World's great revolutionary publicists.[12]

Among the most effectual Radical rhetoricians was James
Cannon, a mathematics tutor at the College of Philadelphia who
had emigrated to America from his native Scotland. Cannon's

greatest contribution to the campaign for independence lay in his organizational abilities: it was he who directed the Committee of Privates from behind the scenes, and it was he who engineered many of the crucial activities of the Provincial Conference and Pennsylvania Constitutional Convention of 1776. Cannon was also an able advocate, however, and his "Cassandra" essays were an important addition to the Radicals' public rhetoric.[13]

Other Radical authors of note included Jacob Green, whose *Observations on the Reconciliation of Great Britain and the Colonies* was the least contentious pamphlet arguing for separation; Benjamin Rush, who, as he later revealed, "wrote under a variety of signatures, by means of which an impression of numbers in favor of liberty was made"; Thomas Young, whose pen was "frequently employed in the common cause"; and the unknown who styled himself "Salus Populi" in a series of newspaper essays published periodically from January through March.[14] These writers were at times aided by pro-independence members of the Continental Congress, then meeting in the city. Samuel Adams, in particular, contributed several useful newspaper pieces over the signatures of "Candidus" and "A Religious Politician."[15]

As the prospect of independence fragmented Philadelphia's Whig leadership, so it also vitiated the city's traditional political divisions and allegiances. As one resident observed early in 1776, the dispute over separation "has greatly changed our political landscape, and has driven all our little distinctions of parties entirely out of sight."[16] By the opening of 1776 Philadelphians were divided into three relatively distinct political groups regarding independence, only one of which constituted a significantly influenceable audience for Radical and Moderate publicists. In the first place, there were those already committed to independence. This group was made up of the Radical Whigs and their supporters. It included many of the city's mechanics and most of its militia. The size of the pro-independence portion of the Philadelphia audience is not fully determinable, but we can reasonably estimate it to have encompassed perhaps 25–35 percent of the city's politically relevant inhabitants.[17] In the second place, there were those who opposed independence under any circumstances. The most prominent members of this alliance were orthodox Quakers and well-to-do supporters of the Proprietary faction, though it embraced some citizens from virtually all of Philadelphia's religious denominations and economic classes.[18] A reasonable estimate would set the size of this group at 15–25 percent of the city's politically relevant population.[19]

We could recount the aims and motives of both the above groups in considerable detail. Such is not necessary for our purposes, however, since neither was likely to be converted by anything Radical or Moderate publicists could say or write. Nor was either group large enough to block or effect any final move toward separation. The outcome of the debate over independence would thus depend upon a third group, composed of those Philadelphians who at the opening of 1776 had yet to make a final decision on the question. This uncommitted group, whom we shall designate as centrists, occupied the political middle, comprised a significant minority, perhaps a majority, of Philadelphians, and held the balance of power by January 1776. These centrists constituted the target audience for revolutionary and anti-revolutionary advocates, for upon their verdict would rest the fate of independence as a popular measure. Clearly, their attitudes require special deliniation.

Before the clashes at Lexington and Concord, Philadelphians had made few preparations for military defense; but word of the engagements in New England generated a more martial spirit. One observer said the news of war set the city on fire "like a lightning stroke." By the middle of 1775 Philadelphia boasted a militia of over two thousand men—three battalions, plus an artillery company, riflemen, and light-horse and light-infantry rangers.[20] John Adams, long a critic of the pacific nature of Philadelphia's citizens, exclaimed that "so sudden a formation of an army never took place anywhere." According to Christopher Marshall, many of those who had previously sympathized with England softened their language and "so far renounced their former sentiments" as to take up arms and join the militia. The transformation was major. "Even our women and children," one Philadelphian said, "now talk of nothing but of the glory of fighting, suffering and dying for our country."[21]

To some observers these developments meant that Philadelphians were rapidly committing themselves to independence. Roger Sherman, a delegate to the Continental Congress from Connecticut, remarked that people in Philadelphia seemed "as spirited in the cause as in New England." Benjamin Church, who was soon to be exposed as a British conspirator, lamented that the spirit of independence was spreading like a plague: "The people of *Connecticut* are raving in the cause of liberty. . . . The *Jerseys* are not a whit behind *Connecticut* in zeal. The *Philadelphians* exceed them both."[22]

In fact, most Philadelphians were not prepared at any time in 1775 to sever their ties with England. Their martial response to the battles in Massachusetts represented an immediate reaction to dramatic events as well as a pragmatic adjustment to the outbreak of war. They were caught up in the excitement generated throughout America in the middle of 1775. But by January of 1776 the situation had calmed. The torrent of "patriotic" speeches and writings during the previous spring and summer stemmed to a trickle in the fall. Centrist Philadelphians remained staunchly opposed to British usurpations of colonial rights, adhered to the system of values and propositions established during the previous decade, joined their fellow Americans in condemning the "wanton British aggression" at Lexington, and favored continued military battle with England if such were necessary to preserve their freedom. But they were not prepared to abandon the hope that American liberties might yet be maintained within the empire and thus were disinclined to support any group that outspokenly advocated independence. As late as March 1776 Joseph Reed complained that, "notwithstanding the act of Parliament for seizing our property, and a thousand other proofs of a bitter and irreconcilable spirit, there is a strange reluctance in the minds of many to cut the knot which ties us to Great Britain." This reluctance did not indicate a softening of attitudes toward the mother country. Rather, centrist Philadelphians simply felt that the time for independence had not yet come, that all chances of reconciliation were not yet extinguished. Their position was astutely summarized by John Adams, who, as a leader of the pro-independence forces in the Continental Congress, kept close tabs on public opinion in the city.

I find that the general sense *abroad* [outside Congress] *is* to prepare for a vigorous defensive war, but at the same time to keep open the door of reconciliation—to hold the sword in one hand and the olive branch in

the other. . . . Petitions, negotiations, everything which holds out to
the people hopes of a reconciliation without bloodshed is greedily
grasped at and relied on, and they cannot be persuaded to think that it
is so necessary to prepare for war as it really is.[23]

At the beginning of 1776 centrist Philadelphians were temporizing. A number of reasons for this can be assigned: a certain
suspicion of the New England "rebels"; apprehension about the
economic consequences of separation; skepticism about the
prospect of victory in a war against the world's greatest military
power; lack of confidence in the ability of a new, republican
government to maintain political liberty and civil order; a linger-
ing sentimental attachment to the British nation and monarch;
the operation of a powerful natural fear of the unknown and a
consequent inclination toward caution; and above all, the hope,
slim as it may have been, that reconciliation might yet somehow
be possible. Each of these psychological barriers to independence will engage our attention in considerable detail later.
For the moment it is enough to note that as 1775 turned into
1776 they were of sufficient concern to enough uncommitted
citizens to constitute the topics which Radical and Moderate
Whigs had to address if their treatments of independence were
to be relevant to centrist Philadelphians.

The reticence of many centrists to embrace independence was
strengthened by the fact that Philadelphia was still comfortably
removed from the war. While some other parts of America were
undergoing the physical and economic hardships of war,
Philadelphia remained economically prosperous and militarily
untouched. Under these conditions centrists saw little reason not
to persevere in their dreams of reconciliation; their attitudes
and behavior confirmed Patrick Henry's judgment that "men
would never revolt against their ancient rulers while they
enjoyed peace and plenty." As late as May 1776 John Adams lamented that while the cause of independence was strongly supported in the northern and southern colonies, it was less secure
in the middle colonies: they "have never tasted the bitter cup;
they have never smarted, and are therefore a little cooler."[24]

Of course, there was nothing Radical or Moderate spokesmen
could do through their discourse to regulate British or
American war plans. As Adams and Henry realized, the situation in Philadelphia early in 1776 had developed to an equilibrium in which events, apart from discourse, were bound to con-

trol the outcome of the debate over independence in crucial ways. John Adams compared America with "a great unwieldy body" whose progress must be slow. It was "like a large fleet sailing under convoy" in which "the fleetest sailors" (such as the New Englanders) "must wait for the dullest and slowest" (such as the Philadelphians). Those who favored independence could support their cause with rhetoric, but they unfortunately could not "force events." In Philadelphia the equilibrium in public opinion would remain, Adams thought, until "some critical event" took place.[25]

The capacity of competing rhetoricians to determine the outcome of the contest over independence was also circumscribed in another fashion. At the opening of 1776 the colonies were already in a de facto state of independence. America was at war with its parent state, and Congress had assumed virtually all the functions of government in the colonies. It had raised armies and navies, fought battles with British troops and ships, assumed control of commerce and the currency, made overtures for foreign assistance, and declared England the enemy of America. "It cannot surely after all this be imagined that we consider ourselves in any state but that of independence," Samuel Adams exclaimed. "But moderate Whigs are disgusted with our mentioning the word!"[26] In retrospect, it seems that the corner had already been turned by late 1775, when Benjamin Franklin stated that separation was both probable and practicable.[27] By early 1776 Franklin's judgment was shared by many other observers who realized that opinion in England and America allowed little room for compromise.[28]

But important as the flow of events undoubtedly was and inevitable as independence may have been, rhetorical advocacy of separation was nonetheless vital in Philadelphia for political and psychological reasons. Politically, it was essential that an independent America be united in support of Congress. That unity was impossible as long as the continent's leading city and most prosperous colony remained fissured on the necessity and feasibility of separation. To effect prematurely a final break with England would alienate many citizens from Congress, intensify divisions throughout society, and divert attention from the war effort. If America were to succeed as an independent nation, its formal assertion of independence had to be legitimated (though not officially ratified) by popular sanction. As Elbridge Gerry explained to James Warren in March 1776, America had already "gone [to] such lengths she cannot recede." But, he added, while the people in New England were ripe for affirming the colonies' nationhood, "the fruit must have time to ripen" in more moderate colonies such as Pennsylvania.[29]

Psychologically, it was not unease about resisting (which they were doing) or unease about the propriety of rebelling (which they accepted) that held back centrist Philadelphians. Rather, they confronted a truly momentous decision: whether to recognize and assert their identity as supporters of irrevocable independence. St. John de Crèvecoeur empathically described their predicament. Each had to determine, "shall I discard all my ancient principles, shall I renounce that name, that nation which I held once so respectable? . . . On the other hand, shall I arm myself against that country where I first drew breath, against the playmates of my youth, my bosom friends, my acquaintance?— the idea makes me shudder!" As de Crèvecoeur recognized, the decision was so formidable, so painful, so irrevocable that a person would put it off until it could no longer be delayed or ignored.[30] Understandably, many Philadelphians temporized. In January 1776 those uncommitted Philadelphians who held the balance of power were not yet ready to renounce their spiritual and moral allegiance to England and to affirm a unique and solely American identity.

In sum, Moderate and Radical spokesmen faced a centrist audience firmly committed to protest but not yet ready for revolution. The task of the Radicals was to win over a large portion of the political middle. The task of the Moderates was to hold enough support from the middle to ward off any immediate declaration of independence. But neither could succeed without help from England. If the conflict did not suddenly escalate, if Philadelphia remained unhurt by the war, if England appeared willing to negotiate a just settlement, the Moderates' framework of thought would be persuasively enhanced. If the conflict escalated dramatically, if Philadelphia became directly involved in the war, if it became clear that no chance of reconciliation existed, the Radicals' framework of thought would be persuasively enhanced. Within these boundaries Radicals and Moderates who hoped to persuade centrists with rhetoric faced certain special problems. It is to these problems, and how competing rhetoricians dealt with them, that we now turn.

# 6

## RHETORIC
## OF SEPARATION

To secure the support of Philadelphia centrists, Radical Whigs had to meet several requirements with their rhetoric. First, openly propose disunion. Second, destroy the sanctity of the king, the last intellectual link with England. Third, so discredit reconciliation as to make it an utterly unacceptable alternative to independence. Fourth, emphasize the advantages of separation. Fifth, demonstrate that the colonies stood a plausible chance of winning the war. By attending to these requirements clearly and forcefully, Radical Whigs helped create a powerful public endorsement of independence.

The notion of independence was not novel. European writers had for years predicted that America would one day become "naturally" independent of her parent state. Philadelphia Whigs had occasionally raised the subject during the decade of protest but in almost all instances had dismissed it as an ultimate and undesirable alternative which might one day be forced upon the colonies.[1] It was not until November 1775, when the Pennsylvania Assembly enjoined its delegates to the Continental Congress to reject utterly any proposals that might "cause or lead to, a separation from our mother country," that the prospect of independence received serious attention in the Philadelphia press. The Assembly's instructions touched off a series of exchanges in the newspapers. But although independence was clearly the fundamental issue in dispute, the journalistic debate centered on the right of the Assembly to instruct the colony's congressional delegates. Only one writer, "Independent Whig," forthrightly affirmed that he was for "independency," at least until England offered "better terms than slavery or grape shot."[2] Although the possibility of separation was clearly on people's minds, outright advocacy of it was still not considered respectable. Despite George III's rejection of the Olive Branch petition of July 1775, despite the steadily escalating level of warfare between colonial and British forces, despite the Restraining Acts and the Proclamation of Rebellion, "independence" remained an opprobrious word in Philadelphia as late as December 1775.[3] That opprobrium was removed and the debate over independence initiated by Thomas Paine's *Common Sense*.[4]

Momentous events often have inauspicious beginnings. So it was with the publication of *Common Sense*. No fanfare, no avalanche of advance publicity, no sneak previews preceded its appearance at Robert Bell's bookstore on 10 January 1776. "No plan was formed to support it," Paine recalled a few months later. "The book was turned upon the world like an orphan to shift for itself." That the work might have an extraordinary impact appears not to have been foreseen by Paine; nor by Benjamin Rush, who originally urged Paine to take up the project; nor by Benjamin Franklin, Samuel Adams, or David Rittenhouse—all of whom read and criticized the essay before its publication.[5] It was soon apparent, however, that this was no ordinary pamphlet. Demand for it in Philadelphia was so heavy that within two weeks of its release Bell had a second edition on the shelves. During the first six months of 1776 Paine's "orphan" went through the unprecedented total of eight editions in the city, including a German translation which, one observer recorded, worked "on the minds of those people amazingly." It would not be hyperbolic to concur with Rush's effusive judgment that *Common Sense* "burst from the press . . . with an effect which has rarely been produced by types and paper in any age or country."[6] This powerful and monumentally popular pamphlet was ideologically distinctive—especially in its forthright advocacy of immediate divorce from England and in its fervent denunciation of monarchy and George III—and radically shifted the grounds for public debate and persuasive appeal.

Until the appearance of *Common Sense* almost all Philadelphia Whigs had spoken or written of the restoration of American rights within the empire as their goal. Paine moved far beyond this position by arguing for immediate independence as the only solution to an intolerable situation. Reconciliation, he exclaimed, was no more than "a fallacious dream" terminated by the battle of Lexington: "Arms as the last resort [now] decide the contest; the appeal was the choice of the King, and the Continent has accepted the challenge." It was "idle and visionary" to believe that England and America could ever be reunited on firm and lasting principles of trust and justice. Reconciliation would simply allow the king to "ACCOMPLISH BY CRAFT AND SUBTILITY [*sic*], IN THE LONG RUN, WHAT HE CANNOT DO BY FORCE AND VIOLENCE IN THE SHORT ONE." Anyway, it was rather absurd for a mighty continent to be governed by a tiny island: "There was a time when it was proper, and there is a proper time for it to cease."

Paine coupled his denigration of continued dependence with an optimistic assessment of the colonists' prospects of winning their independence on the battlefield. To be sure, America was not the military power England had long been, and yet Americans possessed all the physical and spiritual resources necessary to stand up to British forces. With foreign as well as divine assistance America could not be bested. "The sun never shined on a cause of greater worth," Paine assured his readers, for the cause of America was "in a great measure the cause of all mankind." Now was the time for America to affirm its coming of age and declare its emancipation from the Old World: "Everything that is right or reasonable pleads for separation. The blood of the slain, the weeping voice of nature cries, 'TIS TIME TO PART."[7]

Paine's arguments about the necessity and feasibility of independence were not new; John Adams characterized them as "commonplace."[8] What was new, and so very important, about *Common Sense* was the totality of Paine's case for American moral and political autonomy. He brought together into one coherent, comprehensive, persuasive statement all those "commonplace" arguments for independence which, in Philadelphia at least, had heretofore been disconnected and only occasionally voiced. The case for separation presented in *Common Sense* was grounded upon most of the major beliefs enunciated by Whig protesters during the preceding decade—beliefs also held by many of those Philadelphians who were yet undecided on the issue. Paine's great achievement was to synthesize and extend those beliefs to demonstrate why divorce from England was now the only reasonable course for America. Although *Common Sense* is justly famed for its stylistic ardor, much of its impact was due to the manner in which Paine patterned his arguments for independence. He clarifies the direction of the essay early, the mood develops swiftly and forcefully, the ideas unfold easily and spontaneously. Each argument is positioned to attain maximum ideational and emotional effect. So carefully articulated are the parts that to change the position of one would seriously impair the whole. Clearly, forcefully, systematically, Paine exposes first the futility and foolishness of reconciliation, then the advantages of separation, and finally the probability of military success. Thus he brings his readers step by step to the conclusion that independence is necessary, beneficial, and practical.

Paine's essay was also distinguished ideologically from previous Whig writings by its scathing indictment of the British constitution and monarch. With but a few exceptions, Philadelphia Whigs had directed their attacks against Parliament and the ministry throughout the decade of protest.[9] Even after the commencement of hostilities in April 1775 many of the city's protesters had continued to express reverence for the constitution and allegiance to the crown.[10] In *Common Sense* Paine took a large step toward revolution by arguing that the most formidable barrier to colonial liberty was neither Parliament nor the ministry but the king—the "overbearing part in the English constitution," the "Royal Brute of Great Britain." Unrelentingly, he vilified George III as "an inveterate enemy to liberty," the "hardened, sullen tempered Pharaoh of England," the so-called "FATHER OF HIS PEOPLE" who could "unfeelingly hear of their slaughter, and composedly sleep with their blood upon his soul."

The problem was not simply George's "thirst for arbitrary power," however, but the unnatural and tyrannizing institution of monarchy. Government by kings, Paine informed his readers, was a vile, pernicious, and unholy practice—"the popery of government," "the most prosperous invention the Devil ever set on foot for the promotion of idolatry"—and had perverted even the British constitution. Paine averred that the constitution had originally been protective of human rights, but he insisted it was now sickly and unfit for Americans to live under because "monarchy hath poisoned the Republic; the Crown hath engrossed the Commons." "One honest man," he concluded, was of more worth "to society and in the sight of God, than all the crowned ruffians that ever lived."[11]

Paine's indictment of George III invigorated his case for independence. At one point he defined the entire question as a choice between "whether we shall make our own laws, or, whether the king, the greatest enemy this continent hath, or can have, shall tell us, *there shall be no laws but such as I like.*' "[12] Well aware that many Philadelphians still possessed an "ill-placed confidence" in the abilities and intentions of the king, Paine understood that his readers could not avow independence without first disavowing George III. So concerned was Paine with undermining "the unmeaning name of King" that he contrived to have *Common Sense* issued on the same day that George's virulently anti-American speech to the Parliament of 26 October 1775 arrived in Philadelphia.[13] By attacking the sovereign, Paine personalized the contest with England. He provided a clearly defined antagonist against whom revolutionary Philadelphians could focus their anger; and he provided a devil-figure so depraved, so utterly iniquitous that centrist Philadelphians might justifiably wish to be free of it forever.

The enemy depicted in *Common Sense* was not merely an evil man, however, but an evil system; the wickedness of George III was portrayed as symptomatic of the evils of monarchy. By denigrating monarchy as an institution Paine forwarded an additional and powerful warrant for revolution, for the evils of monarchy would remain—would continue to pervert the principles of the constitution and threaten the liberties of Americans—regardless of who might occupy the throne at any given time. Only by erecting a government of their own could Americans save themselves from monarchical superstitions and thereby "prepare in time an asylum for mankind."[14]

One aspect of Paine's diatribe against monarchy deserves special notice. After *Common Sense* other Radical writers continued the crusade against the king, but none came close to matching the sustained verbal intensity with which Paine assailed his ruler. In *Common Sense,* and in other of his American writings, Paine assaulted George III and the institution of monarchy with a passion sufficiently unusual to solicit the attention of his contemporaries. One wrote: "he seems to be everywhere transported with rage—a rage that knows no limits and hurries him along like an impetuous torrent. . . . Such a malignant spirit I have seldom met with in any composition." This same observer added that "such fire and fury" could not be seen as "genuine marks of patriotism. On the contrary, they rather indicate that some

mortifying disappointment is rankling at heart; or that some
tempting object of ambition is in view; or probably both."[15] It is
scarcely possible to question Paine's patriotic devotion to the
ideas and principles enunciated in *Common Sense*. But it is conceivable that the uncommon and almost consuming ardor with
which he derided monarchy in general and the British sovereign
in particular was also a function of the more than three decades
of failure and frustration he had spent in England before emi-
grating to America and of his inclination, perhaps largely unconscious, to displace his bitterness onto the most prominent
symbol of British life—the crown. Paine began a new life in the
New World, but he could not easily forget his old life in the Old
World, or forgive those he held responsible for it. From this
perspective, his attack on the king was at once cathartic and redemptive: cathartic insofar as it vented the accumulated
hostilities of a lifetime, redemptive to the extent that identifying
and execrating the cause of his previous disappointments
allowed Paine to absolve himself of personal accountability for
them.[16]

Important as *Common Sense* was to the maturation of revolutionary thought in Philadelphia, we cannot account for its
enormous impact on ideological grounds alone. Other Radicals
might have brought together many of the ideas contained in
Paine's tract, but none possessed his remarkable verbal
resources and stylistic abilities. To be sure, those resources were
not fully explored and those abilities not fully developed at the
time Paine wrote *Common Sense,* the style of which was overly
ornate, involved, and artificial in comparison with the more
even, stately, terse, and epigrammatic prose style embodied
fifteen years later in the *Rights of Man.*[17] Paine recognized as
much in later years when he remarked, "it was the American
Revolution that made me an author." Be that as it may, he
displayed in *Common Sense* a stylistic power seldom found among
eighteenth-century American writers. Thomas Jefferson, no
mean penman himself, knew of no one who exceeded Paine "in
ease and familiarity of style, in perspicuity of expression, happiness of elucidation, and in simple and unassuming language."
John Adams marveled at the "clear, simple, concise, and
nervous style" of *Common Sense* and commented that Paine's
"manly and striking" mode of expression "had as much weight
with the people as his arguments."[18]

We know today that Adams's distinction between style and argument is overdrawn—that there exists an integral and reciprocal relationship between thought and language, between form and matter. Recognizing this, we are led to see the stylistic power of *Common Sense* not just as the "dress" of Paine's thought, but as an essential element of the total argumentation. Paine claimed to offer his readers "nothing more than simple facts, plain arguments, and common sense." In truth, he also tendered striking characterizations, riveting analogies, piquant metaphors, stunning aphorisms, even an occasional touch of wit—all of which lent psychological impact to those "simple facts" and "plain arguments" and imbued them with the ineluctable logic of "common sense." Although examples abound, a few will suffice. On government and monarchy: "Government, like dress, is the badge of lost innocence; the palaces of Kings are built on the ruins of the bowers of Paradise." On William the Conqueror: "A French bastard landing with an armed Banditti and establishing himself King of England against the consent of the natives." On George III: "In England a King hath little more to do than to make war and give away places. . . . A pretty business indeed for a man to be allowed eight hundred thousand sterling a year for, and worshipped into the bargain!" On the possibilities of reconciliation: "As well can the lover forgive the ravisher of his mistress, as the Continent forgive the murders of Britain." On the natural relationship between England and America: "In no instance hath nature made the satellite larger than its primary planet, and as England and America with respect to each other reverses the common order of nature, it is evident they belong to different systems. England to Europe: America to itself." On the American cause: "The sun never shined on a cause of greater worth. 'Tis not the affair of a city, a county, a province or a kingdom; but of a continent—of at least one eighth part of the inhabitable globe. 'Tis not the concern of a day, a year, or an age; posterity are virtually involved in the contest, and will be more or less affected even to the end of time by the proceedings now."[19]

The stylistic appeal of *Common Sense* has often been acknowledged;[20] less recognized is how adroitly Paine tailored his pamphlet to the psychological demands of centrist Philadelphians. Paine well understood the renitence of many Philadelphians to divorce themselves forever from a system of government and a way of life that, on balance, had not treated them badly and to commit themselves to an audacious and unexampled venture whose outcome was highly uncertain. How well Paine comprehended the psychological state of uncommitted Philadelphians and how astutely he sought to resolve their apprehensions is best exhibited in the sensitive and comforting closing passages of *Common Sense*.

> These proceedings may at first appear strange and difficult, but, like all other steps which we have already passed over, will in a little time become familiar and agreeable; and until an Independence is declared, the Continent will feel itself like a man who continues putting off some unpleasant business from day to day, yet knows it must be done, hates to set about it, wishes it over, and is continually haunted with the thoughts of its necessity.

Like most works of enormous and seemingly instantaneous popularity, *Common Sense* ministered to the psychological needs of its audience.[21]

Whether by accident or design, Paine solved the Radicals' most pressing problem: when to inaugurate a concerted campaign for complete division. *Common Sense* settled the matter. The popularity of the pamphlet attests to both the rhetorical skills of its author and the superb timing of its publication. The greatest single shift of Philadelphia opinion in favor of independence occurred within the month following its release. This at least is the testimony of contemporaries. Early in February a Moderate deplored how quickly "the most important revolution in the fundamentals of our policy can pervade a continent" and cited "the progress of the idea of colonial independency in three weeks or a month at farthest." William Franklin, governor of New Jersey and a frequent participant in Philadelphia's political intrigues, attributed much of that shift in sentiment to Paine's "most inflammatory pamphlet" and lamented that because of it "the minds of a great number of the people have been much changed." Franklin's judgment was confirmed by the unknown Philadelphian who informed a friend in England that *Common Sense* was "read by all ranks; and, as many as read, so many become converted; though, perhaps, the 'hour before were most violent against the least idea of independence.' "[22]

These and similar commentaries testify to the enormous impact of *Common Sense* upon centrist Philadelphians, but they can be misleading. In light of the outcome of the special Assembly election of 1 May 1776, in which the anti-independence faction captured three of the four seats contested in the city,[23] we obviously need to beware of the tendency to overestimate the persuasive effects of the pamphlet. It did not convert a majority of Philadelphians to the cause of independence (nor did any other individual piece of rhetoric). It no doubt crystallized the opinions of some residents who had been leaning toward separation, and it surely convinced a fair number of previously undecided citizens that independence was worthy and expedient. Its great immediate accomplishment, however, was to guarantee a public hearing for the Radicals. "Independence" lost much of its pejorative meaning for Philadelphia centrists after the issuance of *Common Sense*. At a time when most Philadelphians clung psychologically, if not logically, to hopes for reconciliation, *Common Sense* forced open discussion of independence.

That *Common Sense* did not singlehandedly assure the outcome of the debate over independence does not mitigate its importance. It was by far the most influential discourse published in Philadelphia during the first six months of 1776. Indeed, of all the pamphlets and essays of the prerevolutionary years, only John Dickinson's *Letters from a Farmer in Pennsylvania* could begin to rival its sheer rhetorical artistry or its impact upon popular attitudes. But given the antipathy of many Philadelphians toward independence at the opening of 1776, it would be foolish to expect any piece of rhetoric—no matter how brilliant—to have been capable of dispelling that aversion entirely. Paine's tract did perform the indispensable function of taking the Radicals off the defensive and allowing them to campaign openly and vigorously for separation, something they had heretofore been unable to do. Moreover, its case for separation was so well conceived, so soundly structured, so engagingly written that it likely created a public presumption in favor of independence. Given the nature of the situation in Philadelphia at the beginning of 1776, to expect much more would be unrealistic. *Common Sense* signaled the beginning, not the end, of the debate over independence.

By focusing his attack upon the king, Paine laid the argumentative foundations for destroying the deference many Philadelphia centrists still accorded George III. Following

publication of *Common Sense,* Paine and other Radical
spokesmen continued to excoriate "the encroachments of the
Crown," the usurpations of "an obstinate and blood-thirsty
Prince."[24] Again and again they portrayed King George as a
man unworthy of either affection or loyalty: a "ROYAL
CRIMINAL," a "full blooded Nero," the "whining King of Great
Britain."[25] Above all, they sought to rivet upon the consciousness of centrist Philadelphians the idea that the king was the ultimate cause of all of America's problems. Typical of the Radicals'
strategy was Paine's masterful "Dialogue between General Montgomery . . . and an American Delegate." In this imaginary
conversation Paine addressed one by one the major arguments
of Moderate spokesmen, including the contention that George
III could not be assigned full responsibility for British policy.

> *Delegate.* You should distinguish between the King and his ministers.
> *General Montgomery.* I live in a world where all political superstition is
> done away. The King is the author of all the measures carried on
> against America. The influence of bad ministers is no better apology for
> these measures than the influence of bad company is for a murderer,
> who expiates his crimes under a gallows. You all complain of the cor-
> ruption of the Parliament and of the venality of the nation, and yet you
> forget that the crown is the source of them both. You shun the streams,
> and yet you are willing to sit down at the very fountain of corruption
> and venality.[26]

The Radicals' charges were well timed. They played upon the
growing belief, even among many who still hoped for reconciliation, that King George could not be as innocent as had been
believed. Despite growing evidence of the king's hostility to
America across the decade of protest, many Philadelphians
continued to presume into 1775 that he was above reproach,
that "everything may yet be attributed to the misrepresentations
and mistakes of ministers."[27] By 1776, however, it was becoming
clear to many centrists that the actions of Parliament and the
ministry could no longer be dismissed as contravening the will of
the king. In the first place, America and England were at war, a
condition that could scarcely have continued for close to a year
without approval from the throne. In the second place, George's
official denunciations of the colonists' actions and motives had
grown increasingly virulent. In July 1775 the Continental
Congress forwarded another remonstrance to the crown. Avoid-
ing any mention of American rights and couched in terms of

deep fealty, the Olive Branch petition, as it became known, beseeched King George personally to take steps toward effecting "a happy and permanent reconciliation." This petition reached London in August. Two days after it was delivered to Lord Dartmouth, George III issued his famous proclamation of 23 August accusing the colonists of "traitorously preparing, ordering and levying war against Great Britain" and pledging full military action "to suppress such rebellion and to bring the traitors to justice." The text of this Proclamation of Rebellion arrived in Philadelphia on 31 October. Charles Thomson later recalled that King George's crude rejection of the Olive Branch petition exerted "a powerful effect" upon the development of revolutionary sentiment in the city.[28]

Actually, the royal decree of 23 August may not have been a direct answer to the Olive Branch petition, but coming when it did it was easily interpreted as such. In fact George refused to accept the petition: "as his majesty did not receive it on the throne, *no answer would be given*," was the official word. But the king did give a veiled reply on 26 October in his speech opening the new session of Parliament. The speech reiterated his stern disapproval of the "rebellious war" being waged by the Americans as well as his determination "to put a speedy end to these disorders by the most decisive exertions." Word of this address arrived in Philadelphia on 8 January 1776 and, like the Proclamation of Rebellion, was printed in all of the newspapers. Correspondence from England further confirmed what was becoming more and more evident with every passing day: that George III was "unalterably determined, at every hazard, and at the risk of every consequence, to COMPEL THE COLONIES TO ABSOLUTE SUBMISSION."[29]

Taken together, the escalation of warfare, the king's disregard of the Olive Branch petition, his proclamation for suppressing rebellion, his acrimonious address of 26 October, and intelligence from the mother country lent persuasive credibility to the Radicals' insistence that George III was the guiding force behind England's efforts to oppress America. A good many centrists must have been finding King George's acts a problem to their loyalty even before Paine focused attention on the crown. Radical rhetoric from January on crystallized dissatisfaction with the monarch and directed that dissatisfaction into revolutionary channels.

The indictment of the king brought to completion the legal and philosophical argumentation of the previous decade. By 1775 Philadelphia Whigs appear to have gained substantial assent to the claim that Americans were subject only to the crown and that that subjection obtained only as long as the crown protected the rights of the people. Now that George III was seen to be seriously and willfully involved in depriving Philadelphians of their liberty and property, they were no longer required theoretically to submit to his sovereignty. Once the king violated the compact with his subjects—as George III was now said to have done—the people were free, indeed duty bound, to exercise their natural right of rebelling against an oppressive ruler. According to traditional Whig principles, the shift of blame from Parliament and the ministry to the crown meant that a revolution existed, that the authority of government as embodied in the king was dissolved. The king was not accused simply because of discovery of his guilt, but because by British revolutionary tradition a people protested against Parliament or the ministry, but they rebelled only against the crown.[30] By reviling George III as a tyrant, Radical Whigs presented a consummate ideological rationale for moving from protest to revolution.

While the accusation of the king had special meaning in Whiggish political thought, it was likely most meaningful to ordinary citizens because, as one Philadelphian stated, it "cut the Gordian knot" that had heretofore firmly bound America to England.[31] If believed, it meant that George III was actively involved in the conspiracy against America; this in turn meant there no longer existed any real possibility of reconciliation. Most Philadelphians already despaired of securing redress from Parliament or the ministry. But many centrists had continued to believe that the king was being hoodwinked by his ministers and undermined by Parliament. Now, however, Radical spokesmen argued with impressive force that George III would always side with Parliament and the ministry whenever there was a dispute with America, for the members of Parliament were nothing but "his tools; and their illegal claims . . . only a specious covering for his endeavors after arbitrary power." Any chance of maintaining freedom within the empire was now totally dissolved, said "An American." Anyone familiar with the plots against the colonies had to recognize that they could have been authorized only by a "higher power" than Parliament, "and whoever believes this cannot but wish to be instantly and forever removed from under such a power."[32]

If they were to abjure continued British dominion, Philadelphians had to disavow not only George III but the entire institution of monarchy upon which his rule was grounded. No Radical writer other than Paine, however, attended more than expeditiously to the evils of kingship per se, though many detailed the iniquities of George III. Several explanations for this might be suggested; the one germane to present purposes is that most Philadelphians were not deeply committed to monarchy as an institution, and denigration of it was therefore not especially important. To be sure, expressions of affection for and devotion to the crown were commonplace in the city through the years preceding the Revolution. Genuine as those expressions were, one suspects they were as much the product of habit as of deeply rooted belief. As in most other parts of America, monarchy was more nominal than real in Philadelphia. George III and his predecessors were three thousand miles and several weeks away by sea. Moreover, in a proprietary colony such as Pennsylvania there was no royal governor to present an immediately visible symbol of the crown and its authority. Philadelphians had long been accustomed to governing themselves with relatively little interference or assistance from royal officials across the ocean. Some residents, especially those of German ancestry, may even have harbored potent resentments against royal government.[33] In any case, the commitment of many centrist Philadelphians to monarchy was forged less by conviction than by custom—and one custom, as Paine understood, was easily enough supplanted by another of comparable utility and attraction. By symbolically killing George III, Radical spokesmen successfully laid to rest "the unmeaning name of king" and helped smooth the way for republican government.[34]

Destroying the sanctity of the crown was central to the case for independence, but it was only one of the several major requirements confronting the Radicals. Samuel Adams complained that despite the obvious contrivance of George III in the schemes to subjugate America, "too many" Philadelphians were "still amused with vain hopes of reconciliation."[35] Those hopes were

never fully extinguished before July; indeed, they were greatly
buoyed early in February, when word reached the city that
British peace commissioners were enroute to the colonies. In
fact these commissioners were empowered only to accept the
submission of the colonies, not to negotiate a settlement that
would guarantee American liberties within the empire.[36] But
such would not become evident for some while. In the meantime
Moderate spokesmen argued strongly that any decision on independence ought to be delayed until after the terms of the commission had been received and scrutinized by the Congress.
More than a few centrists were receptive to the Moderates' reasoning. John Adams thought the commission no more than an
"egregious bubble" that had nonetheless "gained credit like a
charm" among Philadelphians. Joseph Reed remarked that the
expectations raised by the commission had "laid fast hold of
some here" and added what many Radical tacticians were thinking: "I am infinitely more afraid of these commissioners than
their generals and armies." The problem created by the
emissaries was clearly perceived by James Cannon, the Radical
leader most in touch with middle-class Philadelphians: "Too
many have already lost sight of the King and our real enemies,
and are so fascinated with the prospect of Commissioners, that I
begin to dread the snare."[37]

A "snare" is exactly what the Radicals portrayed the commissioners' project as being. While the Moderates claimed the commissioners' mission was proof that England might at last recognize the validity of America's constitutional claims, the Radicals
insisted that there had been no such change of heart. England
still possessed conspiratorial designs upon America, she had
merely changed strategies. "These commissioners," one writer
cautioned, comprised "the wooden horse . . . to take those by
strategem whom twelve years hostility could not reduce." If
Lord North truly desired peace, why were American petitions
scorned in Parliament and at court? The answer was clear—because the emissaries' errand was to "cajole and deceive" the
colonies through "promises, lies, bribery, and corruption."
Their exclusive power and intent was "to tempt towns, counties,
and colonies into a defection from the American union."
"Swallow the bait," Radicals warned, "and you are undone
forever."[38]

It is not possible to determine the extent to which Radical

rhetoric undermined the commission's credibility with centrist Philadelphians. Efforts to discredit the ambassadors were especially intense in February and March, when their arrival was most keenly anticipated. By June the turn of events had disclosed the true nature of their task and substantiated the Radicals' claims.[39] Anti-commission rhetoric, however, was part of a larger vilification of reconciliation of any sort. As long as continued union with the mother country appeared attractive on any terms, the Radicals stood little chance of success. Accordingly, they devoted their greatest attention to demonstrating why reconciliation was the "fallacious dream" Paine declared it to be.

The Radicals' overarching strategy in demeaning the value and expediency of reconciliation was to preclude the middle ground by admitting of only two mutually exclusive alternatives—immediate separation and indefinite tyranny. They defined the stakes of the American cause as nothing less than liberty and happiness; to compromise either was not only inexpedient but immoral. Thomas Paine, as usual, put the point most trenchantly. The question of independence, he wrote in the third of his "Forester" letters, was fundamentally a moral issue and was "not to be settled like a schoolboy's task of pounds, shillings, pence and fractions." To discuss expediency was "below the mark: for the first and great question, and that from which every other will flow is *happiness*. Can this continent be happy under the government of Great Britain?" James Cannon put the matter somewhat differently but employed a strikingly similar strategy of reducing complex questions to a choice between polar extremes. Theoretical discussions of the British constitution, he stated, were actually "wide of the mark." It was of little consequence whether the constitution was historically sound or was well-suited to the people of England (as the Moderates claimed) "if dependence on that excellent form of government is big with *slavery* and *ruin* to America. . . . The point with me has ever been, *what will secure our liberties?*"[40]

These formulations derived from an argumentative perspective familiar to centrist Philadelphians, who by 1776 characteristically viewed the controversy with England as one involving happiness and liberty. This certainly did not retard the Radicals' prospects for victory, but it did not assure their success, for Moderate spokesmen also defined the general aims of their cause as happiness and liberty.[41] Radical rhetoricians still needed to convince uncommitted Philadelphians that only independence could secure their freedom and felicity, that the price of reconciliation was necessarily *"absolute surrender of all our rights, liberties, and property."*[42]

To secure adherence to this proposition the Radicals wisely built upon and extended premises established during the decade of protest. They combined enumeration of past violations with charges of British conspiracy to buttress the claim that reconciliation could produce only protracted tyranny. Building upon Philadelphians' deep, long-standing sense of grievance against the mother country, Radicals reviewed the evils of British rule in the past and projected those evils into the future on the strategic assumption that centrist Philadelphians would refuse to continue a mode of government they had already decided was oppressive and arbitrary. Perhaps the most striking use of this strategy was in an unsigned essay in the *Pennsylvania Gazette* of 13 March. Capitalizing upon the power of repetition, its author dredged up in a desultory procession the black roll of impositions that comprised British colonial policy over the past decade and exhorted Philadelphians to

Remember the Stamp Act, by which immense sums were to be yearly extorted from you.

Remember the Declaratory Act, by which a power was assumed of binding you, in all cases whatsoever, without your consent.

Remember the broken promises of the ministry, never again to attempt a tax on America. . . .

Remember the massacre at Boston, by British soldiers. . . .

Remember the massacre at Lexington. . . .

Remember the cannonading, bombarding, and burning of Falmouth.

Remember the shrieks of the women and children. . . .

Remember the broken charters. . . .

Remember the act for screening and encouraging your murderers. . . .

Remember the altering your established jury laws.

Remember the hiring foreign troops against you. . . .

Remember the rejection of all your numerous humble petitions. . . .

Remember the contempt with which they spoke of you in both houses. . . .

Remember the long, habitual, base venality of British parliaments.

Remember the corrupt, putrified state of that nation, and the virtuous, sound, healthy state of your own young constitution. . . .

Remember the obduracy and unforgiving spirit of the tyrant, evident in the treatment of his own brothers.

Remember that an honorable death is preferable to an ignominious life; and never forget what you owe to yourselves, your families, and your posterity.

The Radicals' essential argument was that England simply could not be trusted and reconciliation could therefore produce nothing more than "a temporary, shim sham, patched up, inglorious peace." Those who thought that settlement would thwart the designs of British politicians were either fools or enemies to their country, "Salus Populi" stated, for "there never was an instance of disappointed ambition sitting down contented." The most to be expected from reconciliation was that future schemes would be "concerted with more cunning and artifice."[43] Even if the present Parliament granted the validity of American claims, there was no guarantee that the next one would not reinstitute oppressive legislation.[44] Given all that had happened over the past ten years, the Radicals pointedly asked, was it possible ever again to feel secure and protected under British rule?

Can reconciliation restore unviolated confidence? Can reconciliation make us believe that Great Britain never will, never can be unjust and arbitrary? Can reconciliation be built on any foundation that a future Minister in conjunction with a future Parliament may not remove at pleasure, whenever an opportunity shall offer that shall favor their ambitious views? Can reconciliation remove from us a jealousy founded on fatal experience?[45]

The answer to each of the above questions, according to the spokesmen for independence, was a resounding no. As Thomas Paine reasoned, reconciliation could no more "restore to us the time that is past" than it could "give to prostitution its former innocence." Aware that some centrists romanticized their relationship with England as it had existed before the Stamp Act, Radicals contended that the interests of England and America were now so disparate that no plan of reconciliation could restore the harmony that had existed before 1765. Although Philadelphians had once enjoyed peace, happiness, and prosperity under British rule, the mother country was no longer what she had been "in those happy days of former connection." In addition, some Radicals argued that even if it were possible to recreate the state of affairs before reorganization of the empire, such would prove utterly undesirable: Philadelphians would still be governed by a Parliament in which they were unrepresented, would still be subject to the unpredictable whims of a capricious monarch, would still be sacrificed for the interests of British sycophants, would still be exposed to all the suffocating impositions and unconstitutional encroachments they knew only too well. According to Radical Whigs, to seek reconciliation on any terms was to seek bondage, for "he who is dependent has a master, and he who has a master is a servant, if not a slave."[46]

The Radicals coupled their attacks upon reconciliation with a bitter ad hominem crusade against the Moderates. For one thing, they sought to equate "Moderate" with "Tory" and thus discredit all those who sought continued union. The Radicals well knew that initial credibility rested with men like John Dickinson and William Smith who had long been politically prominent in Philadelphia and to whom its citizens habitually turned for guidance in times of crisis. If the leadership of these men were accepted now, the cause of independence would be seriously jeopardized. This the Radicals understood, and at the beginning of 1776 they identified as their most dangerous opposition, not outright Tories, but "a certain class of moderate men who think better of the European world than it deserves." As the Moderate counterattack increased in intensity and effectiveness, however, Radical spokesmen tagged all opponents of immediate disunion "Tories" and identified all its proponents as "Whigs." By June "a Tory" had been redefined as "a pretended moderate man."[47]

Calumniating Moderate rhetoricians by labeling them Tories was no doubt gratifying to those Philadelphians already committed to independence. That it appealed to the city's undecided residents is less certain. At least one such citizen was sufficiently distressed by the "illiberal reflections" of both Moderate and Radical writers to complain publicly that name-calling and excessive language could be of no use to men searching for truth: "It is the matter, and not the man, that the public are concerned with."[48] Still, efforts to stigmatize Moderates as Tories were probably more successful than they otherwise might have been because repeated attacks had been made through the previous decade upon "moderate men," "ministerial tools," "colonial sycophants," and other so-called "Tories." By 1776 "Tory" was a devil-term carrying opprobrious overtones similar to those attached to "communist" in our own time. As one Moderate

explained, Tory was a name "so odious" and "so very obnoxious" that "a merited wearer of it" could not "find rest for
the sole of his foot on the free continent of America." Seeking to
defend "Cato" against his accusers, this same writer lamented:
"Let the cry of Tory be once effectually raised against him, and
they know his business will be done."[49]

Some Radical publicists sought to play upon middle- and
lower-class social and economic prejudices by linking Moderates
with an *"aristocratical junto"* that, according to James Cannon,
was "straining every nerve to make the common and middle
class of people their *beasts of burden.*"[50] The most blatant use of
this class appeal was in the short essay "To the Electors of the
City of Philadelphia," which ran in the *Pennsylvania Evening Post*
of 30 April. Primary among the enemies of American freedom
in Philadelphia, asserted the unknown author, were the city's
great merchants, who had made their immense fortunes "at the
hands of the people" and who now relished "the *certain prospect*
of *rising* on the ruins of their country." If the present unresolved
state of affairs continued for any time, these "gentlemen" would
soon "have the whole wealth of the province in their hands." But
should independence be declared, their "golden harvests"
would end "and all ranks and conditions would come in for their
just share of the wealth."

These class-oriented arguments will be discussed further in a
later chapter. At this point it is sufficient to note that although
Radical publicists took no pains to document the existence of a
merchant-aristocrat conspiracy, the resistance to independence
of leading Quaker merchants and wealthy backers of the Proprietary faction was well known and lent credence to the charge.
It is conceivable that the Radicals' allegations carried weight with
some centrists who may have harbored animosity against the
city's mercantile aristocracy. But it must be stressed that few
Radical authors exploited class antagonisms before the
Assembly election of 1 May, perhaps because such antagonisms
did not operate powerfully enough among Philadelphia
centrists to constitute a potent persuasive topic. Those citizens
not yet decided on independence appear to have been more
interested in substantive issues than in name-calling and personal innuendo.[51]

The Radicals were most convincing in arguing against compromise because they had a decade of festering resentment to

draw upon. But to secure the allegiance of Philadelphia centrists, without whose support the cause of American independence could not succeed, the advocates of disunion had also to argue persuasively *for* independence.

Not surprisingly, the advantage of independence Radical writers stressed most was that Philadelphians would be free of all the disadvantages attending reconciliation. "Salus Populi" exclaimed that independence would produce "a perfect state of political liberty, a good sound wholesome constitution, a free and enlarged trade, and peace to the end of time." Another writer proclaimed that it would deliver Americans from the influence of crown officers and allow restoration of the true constitution in each colony. Still another contended that by leaving the empire Philadelphians would "avoid tyranny and oppression."[52]

These vague and ill-defined assurances meant most to those Philadelphians who accepted the Radicals' stand, but they probably did not persuade many centrists. The position of uncommitted Philadelphians was well expressed by "A Common Man" in the *Pennsylvania Ledger* of 30 March. Although some citizens might be satisfied with general assertions such as, " 'the state will be much benefited by the change,' " most desired "full and positive demonstration" of "the advantages of an Independence—the benefits to be derived from a new mode of government; how it will affect individuals; the additional happiness and freedom it will produce—particularized in a number of plain, clear instances." The Radicals were not always able or willing to provide that "full and positive demonstration," but they did devote considerable attention to the economic, moral, and political benefits of independence.

To judge by economic conditions, Philadelphia did not appear to be a city poised on the verge of revolution early in 1776. Adversity undeniably existed. Shipping was depressed after March because of the British blockade at the mouth of the Delaware; the Committee of Privates complained that the press of military duty was preventing some of its members from attending to their occupations. Yet things were going well for most Philadelphians. Employment was high, prices were stable, and goods were relatively plentiful. Economic conditions began to deteriorate quickly in late spring, when shortages of goods, price

gouging, and the instability of the dollar set off a dizzying infla-
tionary spiral. In the meantime most Philadelphians were enjoy-
ing a surge of wartime prosperity.[53]

Given the apparently healthy state of the city's economy,
Radical spokesmen could not argue that independence would
produce immediate economic benefits. In the short run, independence could only disrupt commerce and manufacturing—as
Moderates were quick to point out. The Radicals therefore
focused on the long-range advantages of independence. Above
all, they reminded their readers and listeners that separation
would free Philadelphians of all the "numberless acts" passed by
the mother country "to restrict our commerce, to clog [our
trade] with impositions and duties, to discourage manufactures
and employments for our poor, and to give advantages, at our
cost, to the lordly *West-Indians.*" With independence, the
Radicals claimed, Philadelphia merchants and mechanics would
have access to "the lowest and best markets for every com-
modity" and would produce "such immense additions" to the
wealth of the community that commerce, agriculture, and
manufacturing would all attain heretofore unimagined pin-
nacles.[54] "A.B." explained that the alliance with England allowed
the colonies to grow slowly and only to a limited degree—as "a
tree in a little earth between two rocks." Once freed of that
alliance and "able to spread its roots," America would naturally
grow and prosper and "might soon become the largest tree of
the forest."[55]

In a general sense, the Radicals' contentions about the long-
range economic advantages of independence were the natural
outgrowths of various of the second-order economic arguments
forwarded by Philadelphia Whigs through the decade of
protest. Despite the veneer of prosperity in the city during the
first months of 1776, many centrists believed that much British mercantile legislation unduly sacrificed the interests of
American traders, manufacturers, and consumers to those of
West Indian planters and British merchants. Specifically, the
promises of free trade must have looked inviting to many
merchants who chafed under past regulations and looked forward to the prospect of expanded foreign markets, while the expectation of unlimited home manufacturing must have been
enticing to many mechanics who resented past restrictions and
anticipated substantial improvements in business.[56]

Predictions of the blessings of freedom were also warrants for the claim that separation would ensure realization of the glorious American destiny forecast by Whig protesters in previous years. Jacob Green enthusiastically predicted that independence would make America "an asylum for all noble spirits and sons of liberty from all parts of the world. Hither they may retire from every land of oppression; here they may expand and exult; here they may enjoy all the blessings which this terraqueous globe can afford to fallen men." The most famous invocation of America's role as the protector of liberty and freedom was that offered in *Common Sense*. The colonial cause, Paine exclaimed, was "in a great measure the cause of all mankind."

O ye that love mankind! Ye that dare oppose not only tyranny, but the tyrant, stand forth! Every spot of the old world is over-run with oppression. Freedom hath been hunted round the globe. Asia and Africa have long expelled her. Europe regards her like a stranger, and England hath given her warning to depart. O! receive the fugitive, and prepare in time an asylum for mankind.[57]

The final benefit claimed for independence was that only through independence could the peace of the continent be maintained and civil wars averted. This "advantage" was the Radicals' counter to the Moderates' charge that removal of the restraining hand of England would produce severe internal divisions and quarrels among the colonies. The Moderates' argument was lent credence by the long history of intercolonial jealousy and rivalry, and it acquired special strength in Philadelphia as a result of the dispute between Pennsylvania and Connecticut over title to the Wyoming Valley, a dispute that exploded into violence late in 1775 and smoldered into 1776.[58] Many uncommitted Philadelphians shared the Moderates' anxiety about the stability of an autonomous American government. "Intestine confusions, continual wars with each other, republican and Presbyterian governments compose the bugbear of the day," one Radical moaned early in March, "and the very name of them frightens people more than the whole force of Great Britain."[59]

The advocates of independence could not deny the existence of long-standing territorial and commercial embroilments among various colonies. Nor could they resolve the Wyoming Valley affair. In their rhetoric, they chose to ignore both present and past intercolonial quarrels and asserted that to imagine a society of farmers, tradesmen, and merchants quitting their peaceful pursuits to war with one another was "absurd and irrational." The colonies had remained united the past eleven years "without law, without authority, and without restraint" in the face of British tyranny, reminded "Salus Populi." That same union would undoubtedly be strengthened when "established under a continental legislature and supported by public authority." Another writer explained that dissension could spring only from the ambitions of the more powerful colonies, but there was little possibility that two or three could unite to subdue the rest. As for religious upheavals, these were utterly inconceivable in an age of increasing religious toleration.[60]

The concern of some centrists about civil disorders was also a reflection of their uncertainties about republican government. As one Radical observed, the mere mention of republics, democracies, or commonwealths (all of which were used more or less interchangeably in popular discourse) excited in many Philadelphians "the idea of anarchy."[61] It was accepted political wisdom in America through three-quarters of the eighteenth century that a republic could not fulfill the needs of a modern state and that limited monarchy as developed in England was the least of all existing governmental evils.[62] Through the decade of protest Philadelphia Whigs had continued to sing the praises of the balanced British constitution—"the glorious fabric of Britain's liberty—the pride of her citizens—the envy of her neighbors," as James Wilson exclaimed in 1774. "May it be maintained entire by numerous generations to come!" As late as the fall of 1775 Benjamin Rush cautioned Paine to avoid using the term "republicanism" in *Common Sense* if he wished to escape the wrath of the public.[63]

Of course, it was evident to any reader of *Common Sense* that its author was an ardent champion of popular government. Yet Paine tried to sidestep advocating republicanism, democracy, or a commonwealth by name. Similarly, in his "Dialogue between the Ghost of General Montgomery . . . and an American Delegate" Paine strove not to champion candidly any form of government.

*Delegate.* But if we become independent, we shall become a commonwealth.

*General Montgomery.* I maintain that it is your interest to be independent of *Great Britain*; but I do not recommend any new form of

government to you. I should think it strange that a people who have
virtue enough to defend themselves against the most powerful nation in
the world, should want wisdom to contrive a perfect and free form of
government. . . . I would only beg leave to observe to you, that
monarchy and aristocracy have in all ages been the vehicles of slavery.[64]

Paine's efforts to avoid explicitly advocating a commonwealth by
name while obviously favoring it in substance was characteristic
of most Radical rhetoric. Recognizing the pejorative connota-
tions attached to "republic," "democracy," and "commonwealth," the proponents of independence shied away from using
these words before 1 May and left them largely to Moderates.[65]
    Although Radical rhetoricians could evade championing "re-
publicanism," they were nonetheless forced to defend the con-
ceivability of its succeeding in America, for it was generally
assumed that an independent government would necessarily be
a republican one. As we shall see in the next chapter, Moderate
spokesmen charged over and over that separation was doomed
to fail because history proved repeatedly that republican rule
was inevitably followed by tumults, uprisings and finally either
anarchy or tyranny. The Radicals replied that comparisons with
ancient or modern commonwealths were unsound unless it
could be demonstrated that their problems "were necessarily
and unavoidably produced by the nature of a democratic
government." Even if such causality could be drawn, America
was not obligated to adopt precisely the same details of government as previous republics: "Well aware as we are of their incon-
veniences, can we not form such a model as will ensure us the
benefits without *all* the evils to which such forms are liable?" In
fact, the Radicals held, republics were more stable than monar-
chies, for the crown incessantly sought out opportunities for
conquest abroad and was "a temptation to enterprising ruffians
at *home*." Paine pointed out that in England itself thirty kings
and two regents had reigned since the conquest, and in that time
there had been no less than eight civil wars and nineteen rebellions. It was therefore "truly childish and ridiculous" to
project civil disorder as a concomitant of independence. In fact,
the Radicals argued, a contrary prediction would be more accurate since separation would remove every cause for quarrel.
As one writer put it: "America will be the country and all of us as
much one people as the inhabitants of any one colony are at
present."[66]

The importance of arguments such as these should not be treated lightly. The Radicals' defense of popular government was in many ways the most impressive aspect of their campaign for independence. Unlike their excoriations of reconciliation, which frequently seemed overly shrill and hyperbolic, their analyses of forms of government were strikingly restrained and circumspect. They recognized the legitimacy of many centrists' doubts about republicanism and tried to deal with them thoughtfully and judiciously. Whether Radical rhetoricians persuaded Philadelphians that commonwealths were in fact superior to other modes of government is impossible to determine. Nor is it necessary. The important point is that by defending the value and efficacy of republicanism, they helped to neutralize the apprehensions of a portion of the centrist audience. Correspondingly, they contributed to the creation of a public presumption in favor of republicanism as the best type of government for an independent America.[67]

Finally, the Radicals faced the problem of convincing uncommitted Philadelphians that America could defeat England on the battlefield. All the evils of reconciliation and benefits of independence notwithstanding, many centrists were understandably reluctant to undertake a lengthy and costly war with little assurance of success. Here the Radicals' task was to demonstrate that winning independence was possible.

To begin with, the advocates of disunion predicted that an independent America would receive the assistance of outside nations, notably France and Spain. Paine developed this argument as well as any of his colleagues. Writing as "The Forester," he held that as long as the British-American controversy remained a "family quarrel" it would be as indelicate for other states to intervene as it would be for a third party to interfere in a quarrel "between a man and his wife." A declaration of independence, however, would make the conflict a "regular war," at which time neutral powers could "kindly tender their mediation." In *Common Sense* he postulated that a manifesto asserting the colonies' independence would ensure foreign alliances that would do more for American freedom "than if a ship were freighted with petitions to Britain."[68] This argument served a double purpose: in addition to dealing with one of the centrists' apprehensions about the feasibility of separation, it provided yet another reason to support the Radical cause, for only with an official affirmation of independence could America acquire the foreign assistance that would guarantee her liberties.

Prognosticating the likelihood of military aid from France and Spain created a subsidiary problem since there were some Philadelphians who feared that if America did win its freedom with the help of more powerful nations, it might then become easy prey for them. Moderate publicists sought to exploit this concern by arguing that France and Spain still harbored dreams of North American empires.[69] The Radicals responded that such forebodings were groundless because American trade would prove such a boon to all the countries of Europe that none would allow another to conquer America and monopolize its great commercial and agricultural resources. Jacob Green wrote: "If we were once independent, it would be the interest of all the European nations to keep us so." Paine put the point more drolly when he remarked that an autonomous America would fear no danger of subjection "while eating is the custom of Europe." In the same year that Adam Smith published his *Wealth of Nations*, Philadelphia Radicals adopted the premises of free trade and assured their audience that America's commerce would guarantee its freedom from foreign influence and vice versa.

> Our trade will protect itself. It never will be the interest of any nation to disturb our trade while we trade freely with it, and it will ever be our interest to trade freely with all nations. As long as the wide Atlantic Ocean rolls between us and Europe, so long will we be free from foreign subjection were we once clear of Great Britain: And as long as we remain free from foreign subjection, so long will our trade protect itself.[70]

Although foreign alliances would bolster America's strength, the Radicals contended that the main assurance of victory lay in the great military resources of the American people and continent. Their strategy here was to denigrate the martial capabilities of the mother country while exalting those of America. It was true, Paine averred, that the colonies had no navy to speak of, but no country in the world was "so happily situated, or so internally capable of raising a fleet as America." The British, on the other hand, boasted a formidable roster of ships, but no more than one-tenth were fit for service at any given time and of those only a small portion could be dispatched to America. Another writer sought to demonstrate the superiority of colonial troops to the vaunted British regulars and their Hessian mercenaries. He explained that the men who composed a European army had "neither property nor families to fight for" and had "no principle either of honor, religion, public spirit, regard for liberty, or love of country to animate them." But men equally armed and animated by principle, though without discipline, were always superior to mercenaries even when only equal in numbers. When principle and discipline were conjoined, as in the colonial army, "treble the number of mere mercenaries" were "no match for such a militia." This last point was one the Radicals stressed frequently. America was an infant country without the established agencies of war common in Europe, but Americans were fighting for liberty, and there was almost no limit to what "enthusiasm, indignation, and the love of one's country" could accomplish.[71]

Advocates of independence also pointed to key strategic advantages possessed by the colonies. These included familiarity with the American terrain, the inability of England to supply her troops from three thousand miles away, and the presence in America of every necessary resource for the colonists to raise and maintain their armies and fleets.[72] Moreover, should England fail to gain an immediate victory, the decay of trade and the domestic unpopularity of a prolonged war would occasion serious divisions which "would almost certainly prevent a full exertion" of her strength. Perhaps most important, claimed the Radicals, America could win by not losing while England could only win by vanquishing the colonies, a most improbable task: "She is conquered in not conquering us, whether we defeat her or not; and would be obliged to quit the Continent on the same principle that she quitted Boston, could we embarrass her in the same manner. . . . In short, we may conquer without a battle, but she cannot."[73]

In retrospect some of the Radicals' claims for colonial military capacities appear exaggerated and naive. Others proved to be remarkably prescient—such as those dealing with strategic questions of supply and tactical advantage. As John Shy has shown, the British army in America on the eve of the Revolution was ill-prepared to fight the kind of war pressed upon it by colonial leaders.[74] Centrist Philadelphians, however, did not have the

benefit of such hindsight in 1776; they had to evaluate the
Radicals' contentions on the basis of information available at that
time. On the one hand, that information pointed to the superiority of British forces. The "mere unprincipled mercenaries"
belittled by the advocates of disunion had a long and acknowledged history of success. Recent events also belied the
Radicals' claims. In October of 1775 British forces burned the
town of Falmouth, Maine; in December of the same year colonial troops were beaten back in their quest to invade Quebec;
in January 1776 the British destroyed Norfolk, Virginia, in a
devastating naval bombardment.[75]

Still, there were reasons to believe that American forces could
hold their own with the British army and navy. Some colonists
had been unimpressed with the performance of British troops
fighting in America during the Seven Years' War, and optimistic
assessments of American military potential had appeared in the
Philadelphia press at regular intervals through the decade of
protest.[76] That potential had appeared confirmed by the colonial successes in New England during the spring and summer
of 1775. While the reverses of the succeeding fall and winter
campaigns worked against the Radicals' cause, the British
evacuation of Boston in March 1776 came at an auspicious moment in the debate over independence, and the Radicals
predictably hailed it as dramatic proof that the Continental army
could indeed defend American liberties. Most important for the
revolutionary movement in Philadelphia, early in May of 1776 a
group of Pennsylvania provincial gunboats bested a brace of
royal schooners in a two-day battle on the Delaware slightly
downriver from Philadelphia. This confrontation had a powerful impact on opinion in the city and lent persuasive, firsthand
evidence to the claims of American military prowess.[77]

In addition to the colonists' own capabilities and support from
foreign allies, said the Radicals, they also had the benefit of
divine approbation and assistance. One Radical righteously
asserted, "We know we have virtue, truth and right on our side."
Another predicted the success of independence on grounds that
"our cause is good, and we have the Great Disposer of all things
to apply to."[78] The most notable invocation of divine support
published in Philadelphia came from Samuel Adams writing as
"A Religious Politician" in the *Pennsylvania Journal* of 7 February. According to Adams, "Less than Divine wisdom" could

not have fixed "a conjuncture more favorable to independence" than the present. Consequently,

> it need not be asked, Are we able to support the measures which will secure independency? The answer is plain and easy. Though all the world may think we are not, yet, *God*, it appears, thinks otherwise. . . . I say, *God* thinks otherwise, because every part of his providential proceedings justifies the thought. We may then know what part we ought to take. God does the work, but not without instruments, and they who are employed are denominated his servants. . . . We may affect humility in refusing to be made the servants of Divine vengeance, but the good servant will execute the will of his master. *Samuel* will slay *Agag; Moses, Aaron,* and *Hur* will pray in the mountain; and *Joshua* will defeat the *Canaanites.*

As Adams presented it, independence was part of God's master plan to make America a sanctuary for freedom and to punish England for her iniquity. By this logic at least two major propositions could be sustained: America was assured of victory, and to oppose separation was to oppose God himself. Independence was not only expedient, it was ultimately right.

How convincing the Radicals' logic was to centrist Philadelphians is difficult to determine. In some respects the exhortations of Samuel Adams's "Religious Politician" were more attuned to a Boston than a Philadelphia audience. But even Thomas Paine, despite his deistic principles and strong aversion to overt displays of religious piety, did not hesitate to invoke "the will of the Almighty" when he found it useful. Notwithstanding the fact that by 1776 ecclesiastical passions were much less publicly intense throughout America than they had once been, the religious impulse still operated powerfully among most Philadelphians on the eve of the Revolution. Those residents who eagerly sought manifestations of the will of God during ordinary times would surely have been especially concerned about His intentions on the momentous question of independence.

The Radicals' invocations of divine blessing and support were also a function of their efforts to defend the revolutionary movement against Philadelphia's Quaker hierarchy. The rhetorical dispute between Quakers and Radicals in 1776 was the final manifestation of a long-standing rivalry. Although Quakers were as opposed as any other segment of Philadelphia society to England's encroachments upon American rights and interests in the 1760s, many were distressed by the increasingly extralegal and coercive aspects of Whig protest during the nonimportation campaigns of 1768–70. The estrangement of Quaker leaders from the city's Whigs grew more acute after the summer of 1774, when it became clear that agents of moderation were no longer able to exert more than a tenuous influence upon the resistance movement. In January 1775 the Meeting for Sufferings, located in Philadelphia, issued two statements of opposition to the movement. Although the second of these was especially severe in its denunciation of those who sought to "excite dissatisfaction" with established government, Whig leaders regarded it as an outgrowth of discord within the Society of Friends itself and elected to let it pass more or less unchallenged.[79] The wisdom of this strategy was demonstrated in July 1775, when the Meeting, the most prestigious and powerful local Quaker organization, published an address urging Friends to contribute funds for relieving the "afflictions and distresses" of colonial patriots in New England.[80]

Within a few months, however, it was apparent that Quaker patriarchs were not about to countenance what was becoming more and more a revolutionary movement. In the fall of 1775 the Meeting issued a memorial sternly opposing any program that required Quakers to participate in the war either by bearing arms or by paying a fee in lieu of military service. Nor, it decreed, could Friends conscientiously pay taxes levied to prosecute the war.[81] This was a statement the Whigs could not overlook, for it not only insinuated disapproval of opposition to England but also threatened efforts to ready the province for military defense. Accordingly, the Philadelphia Committee of Inspection and Observation appointed a subcommittee to draft a reply.[82] Responses were also published by the officers of Philadelphia's military Association and by the Committee of Privates.[83] To the dismay of Quakers, in November the Assembly passed a law making the Association a regular militia (it had heretofore been a voluntary organization) and requiring military duty, or a payment for exemption, of all males between the ages of sixteen and fifty.[84] Friends grudgingly complied with the new law, but the hostility of the Quaker hierarchy continued to intensify through the remainder of 1775. That hostility burst forth in January 1776 in a widely distributed

testimony in which the Philadelphia Meeting expressed
unequivocal and irrevocable opposition to the campaign for independence.

Very likely intended as a reply to *Common Sense*,[85] the
testimony of 20 January proved to be the Meeting's final effort
rhetorically to stall the escalating drive toward separation. For
the most part the document was similar to prior Quaker
pronouncements. It was the last two substantive paragraphs that
aroused the Radicals' ire. First, the statement reaffirmed the
ancient Quaker principle that "setting up and putting down
kings and governments is *God's* peculiar prerogative, for causes
best known to himself, and that it is not our business to have any
hand or contrivance therein; . . . but to pray for the king and
safety of our nation, and good of all men; that we may live a
peaceable and quiet life, in all goodness and honesty, under the
government which *God* is pleased to set over us." From this
patently anti-revolutionary set of propositions the testimony
counseled "the abhorrence of all such writings and measures as
evidence a desire and design to break off the happy connection
we have hitherto enjoyed with the kingdom of *Great Britain,* and
our just and necessary subordination to the king and those who
are lawfully placed in authority under him."[86]

This was not an admonition the Radicals could afford to ignore. Far from being an in-house communiqué, the testimony
was addressed to "the people in general" and avowedly sought to
influence the Quakers' "friends and fellow-subjects of every de-
nomination." By 1776 Quakers numbered no more than one-
seventh of Philadelphia's population and, for a variety of
reasons, no longer exerted as compelling an influence upon
opinion in the city as in previous decades. Nonetheless, Quaker
leaders still possessed noticeable moral and political leverage,
and the Meeting's epistles and addresses commonly assumed the
status of public documents and circulated far beyond the limits
of the Society.[87] Most critically for the advocates of independence, Philadelphia's considerable German population had
traditionally been "much under the influence of the Quakers,"
as Charles Thomson stated. Yet, as he also noted, the Radical
cause could not succeed without placing a "principal reliance"
upon support from the German sector.[88] Although a significant
proportion of the city's Germans favored independence by

1776, it was essential that the Radicals rapidly and forcefully rebut the testimony of 20 January in order to solidify their base in the German community.

Moreover, the testimony did not necessarily represent the views of all members of the Society of Friends in Philadelphia. The final statement was hammered out at long, repeated sessions, and its harsh condemnation of the revolutionary cause may well have expressed the sentiments of a relatively small group of Quaker politiques such as James Pemberton, Abel James, and Henry Drinker. There is no doubt that the vast majority of Philadelphia Quakers declined to support the Revolution. But there were those who disagreed with the testimony and who were inclined to ally with the Radicals.[89] Through an adroit response to the testimony Radical publicists could profitably exploit this split in Quaker ranks and weaken the principal source of organized opposition to independence.

By the end of January the testimony had been widely reprinted and circulated through the city. For the next three weeks Radical spokesmen sniped at its premises and conclusions. Their strategy was two-fold. First, they denied the assertion that the way to acquire God's blessing was "to guard against and reject all such measures and councils as may increase and perpetuate" the growing rift between England and America. It was evident to anyone who studied the historical record, they said, that the American cause operated with divine assistance. Supporting it was therefore the way to acquire divine approval. As one writer concluded, "We are not brought into our present critical circumstances for nothing. And if we neglect to make the best of them we will scarcely obtain the approbation of the Almighty."[90] This argument was most fully and effectually employed in Samuel Adams's "Religious Politician" essay, already discussed, which was a direct response to the testimony of 20 January.

In addition to disputing the Quaker leadership's reading of divine intent, the Radicals also sought to discredit the motives of those Quakers who opposed the cause of American freedom. The most vociferous assault came from Thomas Paine in his "Epistle to Quakers," which he appended to the third edition of *Common Sense*. Paine sought first to undermine the Quakers' moral authority by indicting them as hypocrites who piously invoked "pretended scruples . . . against the mammon of this world" while they hunted it "with a step as steady as time, and an appetite as keen as death." He then stripped away the guise of religious principle behind which the Quaker hierarchy hid its secular judgments and excoriated the testimony as a patently political document designed to perpetuate British rule imperially and Quaker rule locally. Finally, Paine tried to aggravate existing divisions within the Society of Friends by charging that the testimony was so incompatible with true Quaker tenets that it could not represent the whole Society but only "the narrow and crabbed spirit of a despairing political party." Quakers could conscientiously support the American cause, Paine contended, because its ultimate aim was *"peace forever"* and because the military conflict with England was undertaken strictly for "unavoidable defense."[91]

It is unlikely that Paine's "Epistle to Quakers" convinced many members of the sect to side with the Radicals, although it did have the potential to reinforce the attitudes of those leaning in the direction of revolution. Despite the title of the essay, Paine's target audience was composed less of Quakers than of those Philadelphians who had yet to make a firm decision on independence and who might be influenced by the testimony of 20 January. His purpose was not as much to persuade members of the Society of Friends to abandon their religious principles as to render the testimony "weak and contemptible" with centrist Philadelphians.[92] From this viewpoint the epistle was soundly wrought. By indicting the testimony as politically motivated, Paine helped undermine any moral force it might carry outside the Society of Friends. By citing the distinction between offensive and defensive warfare, he employed a religious justification familiar and sensible to most non-Quakers.[93] By exposing the inconsistencies between the Quakers' amaterialistic principles and their obvious temporal prosperity, he played upon resentments held by some Philadelphians. Quaker leaders continued to work against independence from behind the scenes until July, but one suspects that their withdrawal from the public arena was prompted at least partially by the Radicals' devastating attack upon the testimony of 20 January.

There can be no doubting the efficacy of the Radicals' discourse in behalf of independence. Whereas roughly 25–35

percent of Philadelphia's politically relevant citizens favored independence in January, slightly less than 50 percent of the city's voters signified their approval of it in the 1 May special election. A 15–25 percent shift of opinion in only four months bespeaks a most effective rhetorical campaign (especially since these were months devoid of highly dramatic events that might have exerted compelling influence upon public perceptions and attitudes). A definitive move of opinion toward independence, however, did not occur until after the May election. Consequently, final assessment of the Radicals' persuasive efforts cannot be reached apart from the pulse of rhetoric and events from January through June. That assessment will be made in a later chapter. First we turn to the rhetorical campaign of Moderate Whigs in behalf of reconciliation.

# 7

# RHETORIC
## OF RECONCILIATION

THE major requirements of Moderate spokesmen were the obverse of those faced by the Radicals: to defend reconciliation as a tenable option, to impugn the efficacy of separation, and to demonstrate that America stood little chance of military success. The advocates of continued union directed themselves to what they saw as the practical issues; the questions for discussion, as one writer stated them, were *"is a change necessary,* and *is this the time for it?"*[1]

The situation in Philadelphia at the beginning of 1776 favored the Moderates in several crucial respects. Although separation was obviously becoming more and more a conceivable rather than simply a possible outcome of the dispute with England, most Philadelphians were far from prepared to endorse it. Even the word "independence" was one Radicals hesitated to use publicly. The advocates of reconciliation did not encounter the problem of securing a public hearing, for their beliefs were essentially the same as those of centrist Philadelphians. Not only was there a public presumption in favor of remaining within the empire, there was also an official one: virtually every declaration of the various colonial legislatures—including the Pennsylvania Assembly—and the Continental Congress had heretofore disclaimed any intention or desire to terminate the connection with England. Finally, whereas the Radicals could succeed rhetorically only by convincing a fair portion of the centrist audience to modify their attitudes and perceptions, the Moderates needed only to confirm and strengthen the views already held by the city's large bloc of uncommitted citizens. The Moderates' task was thus less one of persuasion than of reinforcement.

Despite these initial advantages, the Moderates labored through much of the debate over independence under some major handicaps, partially of their own making. Since the offensive belonged inherently to the Radicals as the proponents of change, it made no sense for Moderate spokesmen to launch an intensive public campaign for remaining within the empire until the Radicals had openly and emphatically declared themselves in favor of leaving it. This declaration came with the publication of *Common Sense* in the second week of January. Yet the Moderates did not launch an effective counterattack until the second week of March, when James Chalmers's *Plain Truth* and the first of William Smith's "Cato" essays appeared within a few days of each other.[2] Some reasons for this delay can be suggested. The most obvious is that it took some time to compose and publish a comprehensive reply to *Common Sense,* which Paine had spent several months writing.[3] Still, this does not explain the Moderates' failure to defend reconciliation in shorter newspaper essays or broadsides. The most likely conjecture is that many were unprepared for the enthusiastic public response to Paine's tract and did not understand the degree to which revolutionary ideas were taking hold in the city until late February, when the Radical-controlled Philadelphia Committee of Inspection and Observation called for a provincial convention to assess the affairs of the colony.[4]

Whatever the reason, the Moderates' failure to speak out against the Radicals during January and February was a major strategic blunder. For two months Radical opinion ran unchallenged in almost every issue of the city's five newspapers and created the impression that the opponents of independence were unable to refute the claims of Paine and his colleagues. By dominating the public's attention for so long, the Radicals undermined many of the advantages that had initially favored the Moderates. Significantly, through the first six months of 1776 the Radicals published a little more than twice as much material as did writers favoring reconciliation.

The Moderates were also hampered by the fact that their argumentative premises were in large part the same as those of Radical Whigs. Some Moderates had been actively involved in the Philadelphia resistance movement in years past; almost all were convinced of the unconstitutionality and inexpediency of British colonial legislation over the previous decade. They wished as fervently as any advocate of independence to see American rights restored upon a firm footing. They, too, saw the stakes of the dispute as liberty and happiness. But they denied that immediate disunion would ensure Philadelphians' freedom or felicity. Their identifying claim was that the true interest of America lay in reconciliation with the mother country upon constitutional principles, excluding all taxation by Parliament.[5] But while they opposed any precipitate move toward disunion, most Moderates were willing to admit that an autonomous American state might one day prove necessary. Even William Smith, who as "Cato" was the most effective writer in favor of continued dependence, declared his willingness to opt for separation when it became clear that Philadelphians could "be no longer free, nor secure in [their] rights and property, in connection with Britain."[6] The Moderates' fundamental, irreducible claim was that now was not the time for independence, that there might yet be a turn for the better. Moderate Whigs stood where centrist Philadelphians stood at the beginning of 1776. But by their own reasoning Moderate Whigs could expect to hold the support of the centrist audience only as long as caution and temporizing appeared defensible means of preserving Philadelphians' liberty, property, and happiness.

The Moderates' defense of reconciliation was as noteworthy for what it did not say as for what it did say. Moderates made no serious attempt to defend England's past conduct toward the colonies. They generally agreed that she had acted improperly, imprudently, and immoderately toward her American subjects. But while the colonies deserved just treatment from the parent state, they were not yet entitled or ready to become independent of it. The keystone of the Moderates' campaign was the proposition that separation was, at the moment, too radical a solution to an admitted problem. "The remedy," they claimed, was "infinitely worse than the disease. It would be like cutting off a leg because the toe happened to ache."[7]

By admitting most of the Radicals' charges against England, the proponents of reconciliation placed themselves at a severe tactical disadvantage inasmuch as the Radicals' major argument against compromise was that England's past conduct toward the colonies proved she could not be trusted. Moreover, to admit the existence of a problem, as the Moderates willingly did, is implicitly to grant the need for a solution. But unless the

Moderates could demonstrate that Parliament was willing to relinquish sovereignty over the colonies, which they could not do, reconciliation, their solution, appeared to offer only continuation of the detested status quo. From this point of view the Moderates offered no solution at all. Yet given the state of Philadelphia opinion, they had no way of escaping their predicament. Disapproval of Parliament, the ministry, and the king was sufficiently intense among centrist Philadelphians that to defend England was to invite the Radicals' ready charge of Toryism and to sacrifice all public credibility.

On the other hand, while centrists applauded vigorous measures of resistance, they were not prepared to abandon all hope of reconciliation and plunge headlong into declared revolution. It was this hope that Moderate spokesmen played upon more than anything else. Unable to defend England's actions toward America over the past decade, Moderate Whigs nonetheless urged Philadelphians to oppose an immediate assertion of independence because it would irrevocably extinguish any possibility of settlement within the empire. Writing in the *Pennsylvania Gazette* of 1 May, "Civis" argued that it was not at all necessary to withdraw formally from the empire, for America was already "to every necessary purpose independent of Great Britain" and was fighting valiantly "to secure good terms of reconciliation." Should America continue steadfastly its present course, the mother country would "soon be brought to reason" and Philadelphians' liberty "established on the most lasting foundation." To adopt a formal statement of separation, added another writer, would "unite the whole *British* nation" against the colonies and thereby end forever any chance of renewing the once happy connection with the mother country.[8]

The Moderates' argument obviously rested upon the presumption that England desired reconciliation and was willing to grant Americans their proper rights and privileges. This presumption was understandably difficult to support given a decade of perceived British oppression and conspiracy, the continuing state of war between England and the colonies, and the mounting tide of damning evidence against George III. The Proclamation of Rebellion of August 1775, the king's vitriolic anti-American speech of 26 October, the Prohibitory Act of late December, the British offensive against American coastal towns during the winter of 1775–76, the proliferation of rumors in

January 1776 that England planned to supplement royal troops with Hessian mercenaries—all pointed to the inescapable intentions of British leaders to compel America into submission. Then, early in February, word reached Philadelphia that Whitehall was sending commissioners to the colonies bearing peace overtures. Here, at long last, was something the opponents of separation could use to certify their claim that reconciliation was still possible. Not surprisingly, they made much of the emissaries.

While the Radicals argued that the intent of British tacticians was to disrupt the American union rather than to offer genuine plans for peace, the Moderates insisted that no such conclusion could be drawn before colonial leaders had actually met with the commissioners and studied their measures. Writing as "Cato," William Smith urged Philadelphians to hear the commissioners' proposals "with patience and consider them with candor." If those proposals were unacceptable, they could then be rightfully rejected; but only an "enthusiast or madman" would refuse to hear them out. Smith also dismissed as ludicrous and insulting the Radicals' suggestion that the ambassadors would bribe congressional negotiators into surrender. Turning the Radicals' frequent apotheoses of the Congress to his favor, Smith held that it was preposterous to think that men who had risked their lives and fortunes for American freedom would now sell it for "a mess of pottage."[9] The most extended defense of the commissioners came in an essay signed "T.L." in the *Pennsylvania Evening Post* of 26 March. Like "Cato," this unknown author defended the virtue of Congress, urged reception of the emissaries, and cautioned Philadelphians not to "precipitate matters into a state from whence" they could not be recalled. He also added a new and thought-provoking argument: if a settlement could not be obtained and a war for independence must finally ensue, any time gained in negotiation would work to America's advantage. "If England has any advantage over us," he contended, "it is because we are not quite so ready to defend as she is to attack." Consequently, the discussions should be spun out as long as possible, for in the interim Americans could train soldiers, manufacture arms, and import ammunition—"in short, every day of the treaty will add strength to America."

For the most part, the Moderates portrayed the commissioners' visit as little more than a stopgap. Still, from all in-

dications, many centrists were inclined to agree with their reasoning. Joseph Reed, James Cannon, John and Samuel Adams
all complained in March and April that the prospect of peace
ambassadors had buoyed the hopes of many Philadelphians that
reconciliation might yet take place.[10] By late spring, however, it
was clear that the commissioners' errand was much as the
Radicals described it—to grant pardons and receive the subjection of individual colonies, not to arbitrate a comprehensive
resolution of the conflict. We see illustrated here what was the
Moderates' most recurrent and surely their most frustrating
handicap—their inability to control the actions of the home
government. They counseled a temperate reception of the
emissaries, but they willingly granted that independence might
be justified if the commissioners' terms proved disappointing.
When those terms did in fact prove disappointing, revolution
could be warranted by the Moderates' own words.

Like their Radical counterparts, Moderate rhetoricians were
wont to speak and write about economic questions in rather
general terms. William Smith, for example, blithely asserted that
if a plan of reconciliation were adopted, "our trade will be re-
vived. Our husbandmen, our mechanics, our artificers will
flourish." Another writer stated simply that continued dependence would restore tranquillity and return everything to its
"pristine state": "Agriculture, commerce and industry would
resume their wonted vigor. . . . Emigrants will flow in as usual
from the different parts of Europe. Population will advance with
the same rapid progress as formerly, and our lands will rise in
value."[11] Qualitatively there was little to distinguish these
general benefits of reconciliation from what the Radicals offered
as benefits of separation. Both sides envisioned and presented
strikingly similar visions of the good life. The issue was how best
to secure it.

According to the Radicals, the economic potential of
Philadelphians could be realized only by severing the alliance
with England and escaping all the rules and regulations that had
heretofore encumbered colonial commerce and industry. According to the Moderates, America had progressed and pros-
pered because of its dependence upon England. British fleets
protected colonial vessels from the plunderings of ruthless
pirates and foreign powers; British troops guarded vulnerable
colonists from the maraudings of savage Indians and the en-

croachments of French adventurers; British statesmen provided bounties on almost every item exported from the colonies without which traders, farmers, and mechanics alike would suffer irreparable losses. No doubt, admitted "Cato," England had recently "acted the part of a cruel step-dame, and not of a fostering parent." But it was also undeniable that without British aid the middle colonies would not have risen to "wealth and prominence," the land would not have been transformed from "a barren wilderness" into "hospitable abodes of peace and plenty," the "solitary haunts of wild beasts" would not have become "well cultivated fields or flourishing cities." Philadelphians would therefore do well to remember the past and keep in mind that they accrued significant economic benefits from the connection with England, benefits they could "expect to reap nowhere else."[12]

The Moderates' arguments were not without appeal. In the three-quarters of a century since its founding, Philadelphia had become the commercial center of the colonies and one of the major cities of the empire. Its citizens had grown ever more prosperous and secure. It was true that the guardianship of the mother country was to some degree responsible for that advancement, a fact the Radicals generally acknowledged. It was even possible to argue without great exaggeration, as did James Chalmers, that the years before 1763 constituted a "Golden Age" in Pennsylvania—a period during which "no part of human kind ever experienced more perfect felicity." Most Philadelphians would certainly have been inclined through much if not all of the decade of protest to agree with Benjamin Franklin's advertisement of Pennsylvania as a "flourishing" province, "where the climate is healthy, and the government mild and good, and where, if anywhere, competence and happiness are within the reach of every honest, prudent and industrious man."[13]

All this notwithstanding, the Moderates' argumentation failed to take into account the events of the past twelve years and thus was not well adapted to those Philadelphia centrists who shared the Whiggish discontent with the mother country's practice of sacrificing American interests to those of West Indian planters and British merchants and manufacturers. Nor did it possess the buoyant optimism that helped make the Radicals' lionization of free trade so appealing to those merchants and mechanics who chafed under mercantile regulations and wished to advance their fortunes unhampered by interference from across the ocean. Moderate rhetoric predicted only that reconciliation would restore economic conditions as they had existed before the controversy with England. It did not hold out promise that the future would be better than the past; only that it would be no worse. It appealed strongly to the instinct for caution and thus was likely of greatest appeal to those Philadelphians who had the most to lose by a sudden shift from the old order. But it failed to stir the acquisitive impulses of the city's middle-class citizens, who had less to lose and perhaps much to gain by revolutionary change.

The Moderates' most insistent argument in defense of reconciliation was that reconciliation continued to be the expressed aim of every official colonial body, including the Continental Congress. Virtually every American remonstrance and petition since 1765 had followed the lead of the Stamp Act Congress in extolling dependence upon England as "one of our greatest blessings." Even the congressional declaration of 6 July 1775, justifying taking up arms, had disavowed any "ambitious designs of separating from Great Britain, and establishing independent states." As late as November 1775 the Pennsylvania Assembly had instructed its delegates to Congress to reject any proposals that might sever "that union and harmony between *Great Britain* and the colonies so essential to the welfare and happiness of both."[14] In sum, as 1776 began the Moderates could legitimize their position as the officially held stance of Whig organizations in Philadelphia and throughout America. Again and again they reminded centrist Philadelphians that independence was "wholly inconsistent" with the original purposes of protest and had been repeatedly discountenanced by "every public declaration of the Continent." Not only had the colonies announced individually for reconciliation, but "reunion with Great Britain upon constitutional principles" was also irrefutably "the favorite object of the *Continental Congress*." "Cato" put the point most decisively: "The sword was drawn in defense of our laws and liberties. Till these are rendered *safe*, let it not be returned to the scabbard; but still let not the scabbard be thrown away."[15]

Moderates moved from the above arguments to defend themselves against the Radicals' accusations of Toryism and self-seeking by claiming that as opponents of independence they were the "true Whigs" who sought peace on the principles of the British constitution and not on the "visionary schemes" of a few "modern law-givers." William Smith made much of the "fact" that independence could count no supporters among the "men of consequence" who had long directed the Whig cause in Philadelphia. Its only advocates were unknowns who had been "exalted by the present confusions into lucrative offices" and who sought "to subvert all order . . . and rise on the ruins of their country."[16] Much the same dichotomy was presented in a broadside circulated on the last day of April entitled "To the Electors and Freeholders of the City of Philadelphia." According to this publication, those citizens who advocated reconciliation were courageously upholding the pronouncements of Congress and representing "the ardent desires of multitudes of good men deeply interested in the consequences." On the other side were a host of "nameless writers, setting themselves up in opposition to public bodies, striving to inflame the passions, and lead us on to schemes of dangerous and uncertain event, wholly inconsistent with our original purposes."

By identifying themselves with Congress, the Moderates sought to lend official sanction to their position. Their reasoning was straightforward. They admitted England had acted arbitrarily toward the colonies. But, they added, even Congress continued to proclaim against the desirability of independence. Therefore, patriotic Philadelphians should side with their "government" and also disavow separation. While the Radicals argued from experience by claiming that a history of deliberate British tyranny proved that American rights and interests could never be adequately safeguarded within the empire, the Moderates argued from authority by maintaining that independence had never been an acknowledged goal of the resistance movement and was still repudiated by Whiggish assemblages throughout the continent. This difference in argumentative mode is revealing; it capsulizes the different kinds of claims made and judgments encouraged by the two groups of spokesmen. By arguing from experience, Radicals played upon centrist Philadelphians' long-established sense of grievance with various aspects of British rule. By arguing from authority, Moderates played upon centrist Philadelphians' respect for the Continental Congress and desire to keep their options open as long as possible. But their argument was of limited flexibility and efficacy, for should Congress change its stance and come out for independence, the argument from authority could constitute a reason for uncommitted Philadelphians also to favor independence.

One of the Moderates' most telling shortcomings was their inability to provide positive justifications for reconciliation. Their pressure for negotiations with the commissioners was not a defense of reconciliation per se, but a call for moderation and temporizing. The same was true of their efforts to couple reconciliation with the will of Congress. Nor were they able to show that settlement within the empire could be accomplished without sacrificing at least some of the rights and interests considered essential by uncommitted Philadelphians. Although the Moderates never spelled out their position fully, any benefits to be gained from reconciliation could conceivably accrue in one of two ways—if England returned to the colonies the system of government which had operated before the Stamp Act, or if she restored conditions as they had existed before the outbreak of war in 1775. But Moderates were unable to establish that England would do the former, and the latter was clearly unacceptable to a majority of centrist Philadelphians. John Dickinson comprehended the Moderates' dilemma as early as the spring of 1775, when he lamented that the commencement of hostilities cut the ground from under those Philadelphians who hoped to bring the British-American conflict to a peaceful resolution.

What topics of reconciliation are now left for men who think as I do, to address our countrymen? To recommend reverence for the monarch, or affection for the mother country? Will the distinctions between the prince and his ministers, between the people and their representatives, wipe out the stain of blood? Or have we the slightest reason to hope that those ministers and representatives will not be supported throughout the tragedy, as they have been through the first act? No. While we revere and love our mother country, her sword is opening our veins.[17]

Bereft of persuasive "topics of reconciliation," Moderates devoted their greatest efforts, not to arguing the advantages of reconciliation, but to amplifying the disadvantages of independence.

━━▶

The Moderates' most repeated argument against independence was that America stood no conceivable chance of military success. It was preposterous, they explained, for the colonies, with no navy or army to speak of, to think themselves capable of besting the world's foremost military power. One Moderate ridiculed the Radicals for attributing magical qualities to the word "independence" in the belief that "the moment Great Britain hears the sound, her heart will sink into the bottom of the ocean and all her forces will be blown up into the air, . . . that all Europe will run mad with joy upon the occasion and toss their assistance as mad men toss about their straws." Either assumption was "to frighten England with a phantom." Whereas Radical publicists pointed to various colonial successes on the battlefields of New England during the spring and summer of 1775 as evidence of American military strength, Moderate spokesmen contended that the only reason America had not yet been utterly quashed by the mother country was because British leaders were holding their forces in check pending the outcome of attempts to reach a reconciliation. A formal declaration of independence would force England to treat America as mercilessly as she would any other enemy. Then, one writer prophesied, "ruthless war with all its aggravated horrors will ravage our once happy land, our seacoasts and ports will be ruined and our ships taken. Torrents of blood will be spilt, and thousands reduced to beggary and wretchedness."[18]

This line of argument was pursued most energetically by James Chalmers, who devoted a considerable portion of *Plain Truth* to denigrating the optimistic assessment of America's martial capabilities presented in *Common Sense*. According to Chalmers, Paine was woefully "ignorant of the true state of Great Britain and her colonies." Chalmers calculated that once one eliminated women, children, men too old to fight, slaves, Tories, and conscientious objectors, there were in all of America no more than sixty to seventy thousand men capable of bearing arms in the revolutionary cause. Even assuming these to be "equal to the Roman legions" in skill, it was still farfetched to suppose them competent to defend the continent. Against battle-proven British regulars the colonial militia would fall like so many toy soldiers. America might be fighting for freedom and liberty, but its troops had heretofore displayed "few marks of Spartan or Roman enthusiasm." Moreover, Chalmers continued, America possessed no navy to keep its ports open and to defend itself against the bombardments of the vaunted imperial fleet. To be sure, Paine had provided a blueprint for building an American flotilla. But, Chalmers caustically noted, it existed "on paper only" and provided little protection against England's four hundred ships of wood and iron.[19]

Besides pointing to the inadequacy of colonial defenses, Moderates also deemed the hope for foreign assistance improbable at best and a positive threat to American freedom at worst. Smith held that France was hardly in a position to help the colonies given the "ruinous state of her finances and feeble condition of her fleets." Even if financially or militarily capable, both France and Spain were avowed enemies of liberty and were unlikely to assist a revolutionary movement. Chalmers pointedly asked whether Philadelphians could actually believe that French and Spanish rulers would "offer an example so dangerous" to their own oppressed subjects. Another writer flatly asserted that both countries had already offered their aid to England.[20]

More important, the Moderates held, if America enlisted mercenary foreigners as allies, independence might be lost as quickly as it was gained. At best, she would simply be trading British dominion for control by either France or Spain. Neither would risk another war with England unless "sure of some extraordinary advantage by it, in having the colonies under her *immediate jurisdiction*," warned one writer. Moving from similar premises, "Hamden" exclaimed that only "a very short-sighted politician" would build his hope of freedom on the assistance of France, which only fifteen years ago had tried to conquer America. The most extensive assault upon the feasibility of receiving foreign assistance came in the fourth and fifth of William Smith's "Cato" letters. Playing upon many Philadelphians' habitual distrust of France, suspicion of Roman Catholicism, and fear of mercenary armies, Smith argued at length that little faith could be placed in "Popish princes" who were themselves "strangers to *liberty*." By calling in foreigners America would surely "bleed at every pore" and, like Poland and Germany, be ravaged for years by "the unholy violence of mercenary soldiers rioting through every corner of a land not their own, insolent in victory and barbarous in defeat." Surely the friends of America in England were still "of more worth" than "whole nations of foreigners" drawn into the continent "by mercenary or interested views."[21]

Arguments such as the above were well calculated to reinforce what was for many uncommitted Philadelphians a major barrier to embracing independence. The prospect of war is seldom happily received in any society, and colonial Philadelphia was no exception. Most centrists were willing to take up arms only as a last resort. England was, after all, the acknowledged ruler of the seas, and the exploits of her armies were well known to Philadelphians. While Radicals glorified the strength and courage of colonial soldiers, the burning of Falmouth, Maine, in October 1775, the unsuccessful invasion of Quebec in December, and the devastating bombardment of Norfolk in January 1776 pointed up American military impotence and lent persuasive weight to the Moderates' claims that a war for independence would transform America into "one field of blood and carnage for a length of years." Moreover, most Philadelphians had long perceived France and Spain as dangerous adversaries—both were aggressively Roman Catholic and had long cherished dreams of North American empires. The Moderates' anti-war arguments on behalf of reconciliation also appealed to the natural conservatism and fear of the unknown felt by at least a portion of the centrist audience. While the present system was hardly the best imaginable, it was surely not the worst. And whether America or England won the war, there seemed slight doubt that it would be unpleasant, costly, and protracted.

In addition, there hovered the monumental task of constructing a new government should independence be won. Moderates argued that even in the unlikely event America did achieve a military victory, she would gain little from it. Once the restraining hand of the mother country was removed, there would likely follow a series of intercolonial rivalries, quarrels, and disruptions. One writer gravely warned that independence would burst the time-honored bonds "of religion, of oaths, of laws, of language, of blood, of interest, of commerce, of all those habitudes" that had heretofore kept Americans *united* among themselves, under the peaceful influence of their common parent." Were every colony to become a separate state, said another, "jealousy and a hundred other passions, which so early divided the wise states of Greece," would plague the continent and render it once again ripe for foreign conquest. Another writer predicted that as a result of separation all "property throughout the continent would be unhinged; the greatest confusion, and most violent convulsions would take place." Still another wrapped himself in the mantle of prophesy and forecast that in the race for glory and power colony would be set against colony: "our fertile fields will be deluged with blood, our wives and children [will] be involved in the horrid scene; foreign powers will step in and share in the plunder that remains, and those who are left to tell the story will be reduced to a more abject slavery than that you now dread."[22]

While the Moderates' visions of intercolonial strife were no doubt exaggerated, they might not have seemed hyperbolic to centrist Philadelphians given the long history of jealousies and quarrels between Pennsylvania and her neighboring colonies over lands and boundaries. The boundary dispute with Maryland had smoldered from the 1680s until completion of the Mason and Dixon survey in 1767. Then in the 1770s Virginia laid claim to the western country beyond the Alleghenies which Pennsylvania said belonged to her. This set off a controversy that simmered into the Revolution itself. The rivalries with Maryland and Virginia were largely restricted to diplomatic bickerings among colonial officials. The dispute with Connecticut over title to the Wyoming Valley, however, arrayed the people of the two colonies against one another, often tempestuously. This contest broke into open violence again in late 1775, when Pennsylvania authorities sent a force of more than six hundred men to depose the Connecticut settlements on the east branch of the Susquehanna, near the present location of Wilkes-Barre. The Pennsylvanians were opposed by some four hundred Connecticut settlers, and a five-day battle ensued with casualties on both sides.[23] When news of the battle reached Philadelphia early in January, it enhanced the Moderates' claim that separation would allow such quarrels to multiply and eventually destroy any measure of liberty that might be gained through independence.

Word of the embroilments in the Wyoming Valley also fanned the fears of some uncommitted Philadelphians that New Englanders harbored aggressive intentions toward the other colonies. Suspicion of Yankees was most intense among Philadelphia's Quakers and Roman Catholics (for religious reasons), but it was not confined to those groups. One of the recurrent themes in the letters written from Philadelphia by Samuel and John Adams during their terms as delegates to the Continental Congress was the degree to which Philadelphians of all political and religious persuasions shared some degree of bitterness and distrust toward their neighbors to the north. As late as the summer of 1776 one Philadelphian remarked that while most residents seemed reconciled to independence, "above all they fear the New Englanders should the Americans gain the day." Some Moderate publicists played openly upon this fear. Chalmers held that if independence did take place "the New England men" would "assume a superiority, impatiently to be born [sic] by the other colonies." Moreover, Chalmers added, it was "madness" for religious minorities to expect "angelic toleration from New England," where they had "constantly been detested, persecuted, and execrated." Smith was more subtle, but there could be no mistaking the meaning of his charge that Philadelphia Radicals were no more than "the avowed instruments and dependents of some, who, having no concern in our domestic affairs, are nevertheless intermeddling with them, to the great disturbance of the province and injury of the public cause."[24]

In depicting scenes of turmoil and devastation Moderate rhetoricians also sought to reinforce Philadelphians' apprehensions about republicanism and democracy. As we observed in the last chapter, advocates of independence strove at the beginning of 1776 to avoid using the words "republic," "democracy," and "commonwealth" for fear of adverse public reaction. Still, it was generally believed in Philadelphia that with independence would come democracy or republicanism. And like other Americans, Philadelphians had long regarded the British constitution as the ideal mixed government; many continued to hold "monarchical superstition[s]" into 1776. Although one can question the intensity of ordinary citizens' concern with republicanism as an issue, it was true, as one Radical bemoaned, that the prospect of republicanism aroused in many Philadelphians "the idea of anarchy."[25]

The public identification of republicanism with social and political disorder was strong enough in the city to provide a potent topic for Moderate rhetoricians. They stigmatized Radicals as republicans and pointed out that "the idea of separation from Great Britain" was firmly enmeshed "with that of erecting a republic in America." What the Radicals really desired was the establishment of "independent republicanism"—this was their "principal object" and all other things were "only men-

tioned as conducive to that end."[26] Moderates also amplified
standard arguments against republicanism, one of which was
that the lessons of history pronounced against popular governments. After some historical review, for example, "Civis"
reminded his audience that there was nothing to view in previous Greek, Roman, and European commonwealths "but scenes
of domestic violence and rapine, war and bloodshed." "Rationalis" recounted the "constant scenes of blood and devastation" presented by earlier republics and concluded that such
governments inevitably reverted to "downright aristocracy" as in
Holland, or to "arbitrary power" as in Cromwellian England.
Another claim was that republicanism was suitable only for a
country of limited geographical size. It might do well for a single
city or small territory, "but would be utterly improper for a
continent such as this. America is too unwieldy for the feeble,
dilatory administration of democracy." A third major contention
was that republicanism had been roundly condemned by impec-
cable Whiggish authorities such as Locke and Montesquieu and
even by "Independent Whigs" such as Algernon Sidney and
Thomas Gordon. Chalmers, for instance, quoted freely the reservations of various political scientists regarding "democracy,"
including Montesquieu's weighty admonition that "no government is so subject to CIVIL WARS, and INTESTINE COMMOTIONS, as
that of the democratical or popular form." Smith smugly arrayed a half-dozen publicly acclaimed writers against republicanism, among them "the great *Sydney*" and "the famous
*Gordon*."[27]

In attacking republicanism the Moderates were careful to
dissociate themselves from defending monarchy. Several writers
devoted considerable effort to refuting Paine's lengthy argument in *Common Sense* that Holy Scripture revealed God's
unequivocal disapproval of all forms of kingly rule; but they
strictly disavowed any notion that kings ruled by divine right.
Rather, they claimed that an accurate reading of the Bible disclosed that no form of government was either divinely blessed or
cursed.[28] The true test of governmental systems therefore could
only be that of experience. And by this measure only one could
be held up for universal approbation—that of England with its
equipoise of monarchical, aristocratic, and democratic elements.
In contrast to the drawbacks of independent republicanism
Moderates pointed to the glories of the British constitution, "the

praises of which have adorned and filled the volumes of the greatest men in our own and other countries." Against these paeans the ravings of the Radicals seemed "to flow from insanity, and to be rather the effusions of a distempered brain, than the language of a person possessed of *common,* or any other, *sense.*"[29] To be sure, the Moderates averred, there were at present some shortcomings in British government, but these sprang from corruption and luxury rather than from any inherent defect in the constitution. As "Cato" argued, there was always "the power left in the people for bringing it back to its first principles." It would therefore be far wiser, according to "Civis," to persevere in efforts to maintain the constitution in America than "to explore the dark and untrodden way of independence and republicanism."[30]

Spokesmen for reconciliation combined their injunctions against republicanism with denunciations of the methods and motives of Radical leaders. For one thing, Moderates accused their opponents of employing abusive and coercive tactics. According to "Cato," Radicals found themselves unable to persuade with "ungrounded suggestions and delusive arguments" and were consequently resorting to "personal invectives and calumnies" against all who would not "swallow, at a venture, every crude notion" advanced as "the politics of the day." "Seek Truth" launched similar charges. According to this unknown author, "the grand political question of independence" was one upon which all citizens had "an undoubted right to speak their minds . . . without being charged with sentiments inimical to *America.*" But that right was being traduced everyday by rash and intemperate revolutionaries seeking "to suppress an[y] opposition" by menacing those of different opinion with "intolerable abuse." Surely, "Seek Truth" concluded, Philadelphians would be wise to reject such illiberal practices and cast their lot with Moderate men, who were "most inclined to grant an unlimited indulgence to a freedom of speech and freedom of the press."[31]

Moderates compounded these charges by maintaining that the Radicals' readiness to employ coercion was symptomatic of their true character and aims. No one pursued this theme more doggedly or effectively than William Smith. From the first through the last of his eight "Cato" essays, he scathingly portrayed the champions of independence as a small group of "designing men" who were prostituting the cry of liberty "to cloak an ambition" for personal advancement. According to Smith, no "men of consequence" could be counted among the Radical hierarchy, only "adventurers" who had "nothing to lose" by separation, soldiers of fortune "exalted by the present confusions into lucrative offices" which they could hold "no longer than the continuance of the public calamities." Smith sought to discredit his adversaries further as outsiders having "neither 'character nor connections'" in Philadelphia—"strangers intermeddling in our affairs, and avowedly pressing their republic[an] schemes upon us, at the risk of all we hold valuable." It was essential to recall, Smith warned, that those Englishmen who deposed Charles I "were not themselves friends to republics. They only made use of the name to procure the favor of the people; and whenever, by such means, they had mounted to the proper height, each of them, in his turn, began to kick the people from him as a ladder then useless."[32]

One is tempted to dismiss these imputations (as well as their counterparts in Radical discourse) as typical of the mudslinging apparent in the political rhetoric of any age and of the verbal gusto with which eighteenth-century polemicists characteristically assailed their adversaries. To do so would be a mistake, however, for embedded in the ad hominem accusations of both Radical and Moderate spokesmen were substantive claims of special salience to the Philadelphia audience. According to Radical rhetoricians, Moderate opponents of independence constituted a desperate band of wealthy, elitist, Tory aristocrats whose overarching motive was to retain their positions and power at the expense of the rights and interests of the great bulk of Philadelphians. According to Moderate rhetoricians, Radical proponents of independence comprised a small group of immoderate conspirators who cared little about the true interests of the people and whose controlling ambition was to enhance their own political schemes by rushing Philadelphians into divorce from the mother country. Some of the issues addressed, suspicions excited, resentments fanned, and fears kindled by these sets of charges were of long historical standing in Philadelphia; others were peculiar to conditions and alignments in the city during the first half of 1776. All came together and exploded during the controversy over Pennsylvania's frame of government in the spring of 1776. That dispute, and the rhetoric surrounding it, will be evaluated in the next chapter. For the moment several points may be made about the Moderates' efforts to deprecate their Radical antagonists.

The Moderates' charges often appeared to be directed toward citizens of more than average property and position, toward those "men of consequence" who comprised "the thinking part of the community." The proponents of reconciliation made relatively few direct attempts to gain the active support of the middle-class small businessmen, tradesmen, and artisans who composed the greatest part of the city's politically active population. By contrast, these were the special targets of Radical writers and speakers. Although some members of the "middling" class had already decided in favor of independence by the opening of 1776, many had not.[33] A good portion of the centrist audience was made up of "average" Philadelphians, but Moderate rhetoricians tended at times to argue "in such terms as to alienate rather than enlist the sympathies of the average man." They portrayed the advocates of independence as "political quacks" and "demagogues" who held out promises of democracy "to seduce the people into their criminal designs."[34] Such characterizations no doubt proved satisfying to those Philadelphians already committed against independence and may have appealed to more conservative and to wealthier portions of the centrist audience. At the same time, however, they revealed the rather condenscending opinions of some Moderate leaders about the worth and abilities of ordinary citizens and surely insulted any middle- or lower-class centrists who already had cause to resent the social, economic, and political pretensions of their more affluent neighbors. Perhaps most damaging, by these arguments the Moderates lent credibility to Radical charges that the primary opponents of independence were wealthy Philadelphia "Nabobs" and other self-seeking elitists who feared the power of the common people above all else.

It would be misleading, however, to suggest that the Moderates' attacks upon Radical leaders were poorly received by all or even most middle-class Philadelphians, most of whom were respectful of social order, jealous of individual liberties, and wary of "visionary schemes."[35] It was true that some prominent advocates of separation in Philadelphia—Paine, Thomas Young, Samuel and John Adams—were "outsiders," as the Moderates charged. It was also true that most Radical

movers were not among the "men of consequence" who in previous years had directed political activity in the city, but were
"new men" who had risen to power because of their work in the
resistance movement and who exhibited no intentions of abdi-
cating their recently won authority. Most critically, the
Moderates' censure of the Radicals' intolerant attitudes and
coercive tactics were sufficiently grounded in fact to possess
considerable public credence and persuasive force. The
Philadelphia Committee of Inspection and Observation, created
in 1774 to enforce adherence to the Continental Association,
had gradually expanded its power and the scope of its operations through 1775. By 1776 it was devoting more and more attention to disciplining those Philadelphians deemed "ENEMIES TO
THEIR COUNTRY." This discipline normally consisted of extract-
ing public recantations of "seditious" statements; occasionally of
more drastic measures such as confiscating firearms or prescrib-
ing jail sentences. Radical writers justified the committee's encroachments upon open expression by claiming that free speech
could realistically be allowed only "so far as is consistent with the
peace and welfare of society."[36] Most centrists were willing to
countenance reasonable coercive measures against monopo-
lizers, hoarders, active supporters of the crown, and others
whose actions might seriously impair the war effort; but many
had misgivings about the willingness, even eagerness, of Radical
leaders and partisans to circumscribe the opinions and
expressions of those who disagreed with them.[37]

These misgivings were invigorated by an address in the *Penn-
sylvania Packet* of 29 April over the signature of "An Elector."
This preelection exhortation was the work of Dr. Thomas
Young, a long-time Whig firebrand who had arrived in
Philadelphia in 1775 by way of Albany, Boston, and Newport.[38]
Young began by lambasting the Moderates as "advocates for
absolute tyranny." He then excoriated Pennsylvania's Charter of
Privileges as a "*Shibboleth*" designed to keep the people from controlling public affairs and which the Moderates industriously exploited to blunt the drive toward independence. Warming to his
task, Young next railed against the province's preclusion from
the franchise of men possessing less than £50 real personal
property as well as the requirement prohibiting Germans from
participating in elections until naturalized. Every man, he said,
who "pays his shot and bears his lot" should be permitted to

vote, including all of Pennsylvania's military associators, regardless of age or property. This proposal was bound to disquiet even some pro-independence Philadelphians insofar as it would abrogate basic provisions of the Charter of Privileges designed to guarantee a responsible electorate. More disquieting yet was Young's concluding remark that "every non-associator and stickler for dependency" should be kept "well away" from the public councils.

Young's proposals were stunningly subversive not only of Pennsylvania's established constitution but also of fundamental eighteenth-century tenets of representative government. Coming just two days before the pivotal special election of 1 May, the essay was a strategic blunder of some proportion. Moderate publicists responded quickly and forcefully. The day following publication of Young's address a broadside entitled "To the Electors and Freeholders of the City of Philadelphia" ripped his "novel system" and warned that the proposals of "An Elector" starkly revealed "what we are to expect should we suffer such men professing such principles to get the direction of our affairs." The next day an unidentifiable Moderate writing as "Civis" artfully flayed the Radicals for trying to take the election "out of the hands of the lawful electors" as a final step toward consummating their "thinly covered" plot to subvert Pennsylvania's "happy constitution" and assume total control of the province. According to this author, the goal of "An Elector" and his fellow revolutionaries was to "destroy the right of election" by disfranchising all opponents of separation and limiting the vote only to those who had "already fixed their sentiments in favor of independence, without regard to their age, condition, or their knowledge of our constitution." There could no longer be any doubt, he concluded, that should the Radicals carry the day, the most basic principles of free government would be "laid waste, to let in the ambitious republican schemes of a set of men whom nobody knows."[39]

The Moderates' admonitions reinforced the anti-revolutionary forebodings of a portion of the centrist audience. More specifically, Young's daring essay, and the swift and skillful Moderate response to it, were likely telling factors in the Moderates' narrow victory at the polls on 1 May. But however useful in the short run, the Moderates' injunctions against the Radicals could not stem the tide permanently, for they were not directed as much against independence as against its agents. If and when uncommitted Philadelphians determined that reconciliation was in fact a "fallacious dream," they would willingly take their chances with the Radicals and opt for independence as the only alternative to British tyranny. Once again the Moderates' argumentation was ultimately tied to the turn of events and contained within itself an implicit, occasionally explicit, admission that independence might finally prove inescapable. Even William Smith, after blasting the Radicals for their nefarious ambitions and crude tactics, acknowledged that "when the last necessity" arrived and separation could no longer be avoided, he too would have no choice but to cast his lot with the revolutionaries "for better and for worse."[40]

Underlying and unifying the diverse arguments Moderates used to extol reconciliation and to stigmatize independence there reverberated an insistent appeal to caution that possessed considerable psychological power for centrist Philadelphians. Sometimes this appeal was evident in the ideological content of Moderate discourse; at other times it was revealed in imagery, metaphor, and symbol. In remarkably similar language Moderates time and again attacked independence as "dangerous and uncertain" and castigated its advocates for rushing into "new schemes" and risking "all the evils which may follow" without "waiting to know clearly" whether compromise could be worked out.[41] Over and over they portrayed separation as a fateful "leap in the dark" and urged Philadelphians to persevere in their "ancient forms of government" rather than explore "the dark and untrodden way of independence and republicanism."[42]

Nowhere was the appeal to caution as conspicuous as in William Smith's influential "Cato" essays. A veteran of many heated controversies in the city, Smith well understood that Philadelphians were characteristically "cautious and backward in entering into measures."[43] He therefore defined as his target audience "the great and respectable number of good men who will always be averse to changes, except in the last necessity." Throughout the eight letters Smith identified himself and his program with the goals, values, and attitudes of these prudent Philadelphians by appealing to their penchant for order and impulse for caution. In one instance he described independence as "a tempestuous ocean, of which we know not the other shore." In another he compared it with journeying "into untried regions, full of tremendous precipices and quagmires, treacherous to the foot, whither the wise and considerate think it is not safe to follow." In yet another he characterized it as a "leap in the dark" whose outcome "may be worse than it is described." Consistently he warned that Philadelphians had "much to lose" by taking such a "precipitate step" and could only benefit "by the exercise of deliberation and choice." Should they opt for the Radicals' "hasty resolutions," they could conceivably "have nothing of the least stability or permanence upon the earth."[44]

The appeal to caution constituted the bottom line of the Moderates' campaign. The core of their total message can be summarized thus: Independence is a great and momentous question which Philadelphians must resolve wisely or suffer disastrous consequences. To be sure, England has not acted judiciously toward America these past eleven years, and the colonies are now fighting to maintain their essential rights and interests. But they ought not to abandon hopes for reconciliation as long as it remains the official goal of Congress and as long as there exists even the slightest chance of compromise. An immediate declaration of independence will foreclose any possibility of ever restoring the happy and prosperous connection of former years and will plunge the entire continent into an abyss of uncertainty, turmoil, and devastation. Therefore, Philadelphians ought to continue to exercise circumspection and restraint and delay any final decision on independence until all other options are irrevocably extinguished and until the outcome of separation can be more optimistically foreseen.

The Moderates were fighting a holding action. They argued not so much for reconciliation per se or against independence per se as for indecision and temporizing. Their fundamental claim was that disunion was not the best course for Philadelphians *now,* but they readily granted that separation might one day be necessary. On issue after issue one sees the narrow range of argumentative options open to the advocates of continued union. Neither their own beliefs nor those of centrist Philadelphians allowed them to vindicate the mother country's past or present conduct. Lacking the power to control or predict the actions of British leaders, they were unable to demonstrate

that reconciliation was still possible or to offer a plan of reconciliation that would be acceptable to both England and America.
Likewise, they could not defend George III from Radical attacks
or endorse allegiance to the crown. And though often adroitly
attuned to the values and attitudes of centrist Philadelphians,
their arguments against the feasibility of independence were
necessarily theoretical and appealed most powerfully to the instinct for caution.

There was no lack of ability among Moderate Whigs, some of
whom were public controversialists of proven skill. With the crucial exception of waiting too long to initiate a concerted campaign against disunion, they mounted as able an effort as could
have been expected under the circumstances. But by their
own admission they could presume to keep uncommitted
Philadelphians uncommitted only as long as events made caution and temporizing defensible—only as long as the potential
perils of independence seemed more formidable than the actual
perils of persevering in the connection with England.
Spokesmen for reconciliation were undermined partly by the
Radicals' adroit campaign for independence, partly by the mo-
mentum of events in the spring of 1776. As we shall now see,
they were also defeated by the machinations of a group of men
determined to bring Pennsylvania immediately into the independence column regardless of the expressed wishes of the electorate.

# 8

## DENOUEMENT

At its commencement in January the debate over independence was a more or less open-ended controversy over the timeliness and relative merits of separation and reconciliation. The situation changed dramatically early in March when the Pennsylvania Assembly announced plans to hold a special election on the first of May to fill seventeen newly created seats in the legislature. Four of the new representatives were to be chosen by the city of Philadelphia. Coming when it did, the election became a referendum on independence.

In retrospect the election of 1 May provides a unique barometer by which to measure Philadelphia opinion in the spring of 1776. Its significance to the participants, however, was that its outcome would determine the official stance of the colony on independence. As the legal governing body of Pennsylvania, the Assembly appointed and instructed the province's delegates to the Continental Congress. Under the leadership of John Dickinson it had heretofore strictly enjoined its delegates to oppose any measure "that may cause or lead to a separation from the mother country, or a change of the form of this government."[1] As long as Moderates and conservatives retained control of the Assembly those instructions would remain in effect. The Radical minority was large enough, however, that a sweeping victory at the polls on 1 May would swing control of the legislature into their hands. Radical leaders thus saw the election as their chance to put Pennsylvania into the forefront of the revolutionary movement, while Moderates saw it as an opportunity to ward off challenges from the Radicals until general elections were held in October.

To the disappointment of the Radicals, Moderate candidates won three of the four seats contested in Philadelphia and enough in the backcountry to retain their grip on the Assembly.

Although the election was so close in the city that a minor shift of votes would have reversed the results, its outcome signaled that the advocates of separation had not yet convinced enough Philadelphians that immediate disunion was desirable.[2] Radical leaders appeared stymied; independence seemed little closer now than it had in January. Yet by July, only two months after the May election, a majority of Philadelphians were ready to sever their alliance with England, Pennsylvania's delegates to the Continental Congress voted in favor of separation, and the newly independent state of Pennsylvania was well on its way to possessing a radically new frame of government. In this chapter we shall deal with the public discourse that accompanied and helped to bring about these changes of opinion, policy, and government.

Independence was the overriding political issue of the day, but it was not the only question under debate in Philadelphia during the first half of 1776. As one reads through the newspapers, pamphlets, and broadsides, one quickly discovers that discussion of independence frequently brought up matters indigenous to local and provincial politics—especially the character of the Pennsylvania Assembly as a representative institution. The interlacing of these topics, evident at almost every stage of the debate over independence, was most conspicuous and most vital between the special election of 1 May and the Declaration of Independence early in July. During these weeks Radical publicists complemented their arguments for separation with challenges to the right and ability of the Pennsylvania Assembly to govern the province in such troubled times. By so doing they helped to cripple the Assembly as a governing body and promulgated a cluster of publicly acceptable warrants for the revolutionary reconstitution of government in Pennsylvania. To attend properly to this subject, however, we must first account for the presence of the "Assembly issue" in the rhetoric of Radical and Moderate publicists before the May election and assess its salience to those uncommitted Philadelphians upon whose ballots both groups of advocates depended. Our analysis should also bear upon long-standing historiographical disputes regarding the nature of the revolutionary experience in Philadelphia.

By 1776 the Pennsylvania Assembly was estranged from the

revolutionary movement. Only at the time of the Stamp Act had it responded strongly to what Whig partisans perceived as British tyranny. From 1767 through 1773, under the leadership of Joseph Galloway, it had at times actively sought to retard the growth of the resistance movement in Pennsylvania. In the fall of 1774 John Dickinson and Charles Thomson were elected to the Assembly, and Galloway was unseated as speaker. From this time until its collapse in the summer of 1776, the Assembly followed Dickinson's blend of resistance and moderation. It was committed to protecting the province against British aggression, but it was equally committed to maintaining the connection with England. By the fall of 1775 it was embroiled with Radical Whigs on a number of fronts. One set of disputes centered upon military defense—the amount of money and materials allocated for defense, the military obligations of Quakers and other conscientious objectors, the drafting of new rules for the militia. But above all, Radical Whigs objected to the Assembly's consistent and unyielding opposition to independence.[3]

The Radicals' dissatisfaction became ever more acute in November, when the Assembly issued instructions forbidding Pennsylvania's congressional delegates to countenance any proposals that might produce a permanent rift between England and America. Some writers now began to assail not only the instructions but also the Assembly's right to issue any such directions in the name of the people of Pennsylvania. According to "A Lover of Order," the legislature had usurped one of the basic privileges of a free society, for the authority to instruct was "as sacredly the right of the people as election." Thomas Paine attacked the Assembly for being nothing more than "a small number of representatives" echoing the wishes of "a small number of electors." Of all the issues facing the province, he stated, none was more pressing than assuring the people "a large and equal representation" in the legislature. Early in March 1776 an especially skillful attack appeared over the signature of "The Censor." In the opinion of this unidentifiable author, the will of the people was more fairly represented by local committees of inspection and correspondence than by the Assembly, whose members had too long displayed "a great inattention to the rights of their constituents." "Our Assembly has as good a right to elect a king for us," he claimed, "as to appoint one man to represent us in Congress." This privilege, "The Censor" concluded, could not be retained "but at the expense of our liberties."[4]

There could be no doubt that the Radicals' overriding concern was actually with the content of the Assembly's instructions, as Moderate spokesmen readily discerned.[5] Nonetheless, by impugning the Assembly the Radicals hit upon a potentially puissant issue, for it was undeniable that representation in the legislature was grossly disproportionate in favor of Bucks, Chester, and Philadelphia counties. By 1776 these three eastern, Quaker-dominated counties controlled 24 of the 41 Assembly seats, more than twice those to which they were entitled by virtue of population and taxes paid. Despite its 30,000 inhabitants and huge tax assessments, the city of Philadelphia sent only two men to the Assembly, less than one-half those to which it was entitled. Backcountry counties were even more disproportionately underrepresented.[6]

The situation was manifestly unfair and came to a head late in February 1776, when the Philadelphia Committee of Inspection and Observation called for a provincial convention to consider "the present state of the province."[7] According to the committee, a convention was necessary to provide a forum in which the views of all segments of the colony would be equally and fairly represented. Faced with a potentially fatal threat to its authority, the Assembly agreed to create seventeen new seats to equalize its representation. Reapportionment may not have been the committee's major goal in calling for a convention, but it accepted the proposal for a special election in the belief that enough of the new seats would be filled by men who favored independence to give the Radicals control of the legislature.[8] Upon announcement of plans for the May election, the committee retracted its call for a convention, stating that "the present unequal representation is the ground of every other complaint."[9] It would seem there should now have been no further cause to castigate the Assembly as unrepresentative; indeed, if the Radicals planned on winning control of the legislature on 1 May there were good reasons for them not to undermine its integrity further. Yet the issue cropped up again between March and May. Why?

It was the Moderates who reintroduced the Assembly issue. The day after the legislature appointed a committee to draft a bill increasing the membership of the Assembly,[10] William Smith opened his first "Cato" letter by claiming that the advocates of independence sought to destroy the Pennsylvania Charter and to seize "into their own hands our whole domestic police, with legislative as well as executive authority." To prepare the way for this internal revolution, Smith charged, the Assembly had been intimidated by "the most scurrilous misrepresentations of patriotic exertions." From here Smith moved to an attack upon the Philadelphia Committee, which had issued the call for a provincial convention. The general committee system, he averred, deserved commendation in many respects, but the committees had not been instituted to assume legislative functions of government. In fact, Smith held, the committees were actually less representative than the Assembly. Although the Philadelphia Committee contained one hundred members, they had been elected by no more than two hundred people; the situation was even worse in some of the outlying counties, where committeemen were chosen by six or seven people. Smith vigorously denied that any committee possessed a popular mandate to call a convention. Should a convention now be called to assume the reins of government, all power would be placed in the hands of "a *few men* who consider themselves leaders in the city of *Philadelphia;* and the province in general have but little to say in the matter."[11]

Smith's essay was the most devastating assault upon the Radicals and the Philadelphia Committee yet published in the city and seemed to stun the revolutionaries. The first extended response came from James Cannon, writing as "Cassandra" in the *Pennsylvania Gazette* of 20 March. In a pattern followed in subsequent Radical rebuttals, Cannon did not deny Smith's allegation that the Radicals' aim was to overturn the Assembly. Indeed, he as much as confirmed the charge by contending that independence would never be approved by a legislature whose members took oaths to the British sovereign and whose acts were subject to approval by the governor. Cannon bitterly attacked "Cato" as a Tory but addressed himself only peripherally to Smith's charges of usurpation by the committees. In a generally inept fashion Cannon implied that the committees better represented the people than did the Assembly.

Three days later Smith responded to Cannon's address by stating that the initial "Cato" letter had been written before the Philadelphia Committee dropped its call for a convention. The issue being now settled, Smith expressed his willingness to forebear further discussion of the committees and the Assembly "except so far as relates to independence." And here, he argued, lay the crux of the matter, for all the agitation against the Assembly had been on account of its instructions against separation. But these instructions represented the will of the people and should remain until "an uncorrupted majority" of the people voted to change them. The liberties of all Pennsylvanians were guaranteed under the Charter of Privileges, Smith told his audience, and could "nowhere be so safe as in the hands of your representatives in Assembly."[12]

Thomas Paine was the only Radical other than Cannon to deal significantly with Smith's allegations before the May election. In his initial "Forester" letter, published on the first of April, Paine devoted a lengthy paragraph to attacking Smith's opening essay as "insipid in its style, language, and substance." Like Cannon, Paine did not deny intentions of overthrowing the Assembly or altering the charter. In fact, he attacked the charter as a tool of the proprietors which had been "cunningly changed" upon two former occasions to serve the Penn family's selfish desires. Surely, then, the people could "make such alterations in their mode of government as the change of times and things requires." By impassioned pleas for "our *chartered constitution*," said Paine, "Cato" was trying to lead the people away "by the jingle of a phrase."[13] After this essay Smith, Cannon, and Paine all dropped discussion of the internal issues and concentrated on defending or attacking independence.

The internal issues surfaced again two days before the May election, this time in Thomas Young's controversial "Elector" essay. As we saw in the preceding chapter, Young attacked Pennsylvania's Charter of Privileges and called for elimination of various restrictions upon the franchise. He also introduced an idea that had not heretofore found its way into Radical discourse—that the addition of seventeen new representatives to the Assembly constituted only a "partial" and "very late" effort to redress one of the charter's most glaring injustices. According to Young, the "patriots" agreed to the scheme only as an expedient way to reform the Assembly without creating the severe dissensions that would attend any quest for "radical reformation" of government, though they fully believed at the time that only such reformation could produce "a real free

constitution" which would obviate the injustices of the charter.
Young's essay was quickly seized upon by Moderate publicists as
irrefutable evidence of the Radicals' lack of respect for "the
happy constitution of this province" and proved to be a tactical
blunder that helped produce a Moderate victory at the polls on 1
May.[14]

Several points warrant discussion here. First, contrary to one
school of historical thought, these interchanges about Pennsylvania government did not represent the culmination of a long
quest by Philadelphia mechanics to wrest power from the proprietary and Quaker elites that had controlled city and provincial politics for decades.[15] The attacks upon the Assembly in late
1775 and early 1776 grew out of the frustration of Radical
Whigs with the Assembly's cautious military and political
policies, especially its refusal to support independence. It was
this discontent that led to the call for a provincial convention
and to the compromise which resulted in the May election. Once
the Radicals agreed to the election, they had no immediate
reason to denigrate the Assembly. Indeed, it seems possible that
had Smith not broached the subject in his initial "Cato" essay, it
might not have surfaced prominently at all between March and
May. But once attacked, the Radicals probably felt a need to
defend themselves, and they did so by turning to the familiar
strategy of lambasting the Assembly and hailing the committees
as the true voice of the people. Only a small portion of the discourse published in Philadelphia from 8 March to 1 May was devoted to the issue of government in Pennsylvania. It would thus
be a mistake to see this issue as more than a minor part of the debate over independence before 1 May, though it would become
central after that date.

This is not to say that internal control of Pennsylvania politics
was not a significant issue to some Philadelphians. Through the
years from 1765 the resistance movement had increasingly
drawn into its ranks middle-class citizens who had previously been excluded from meaningful participation in
politics. By 1776 there existed an undeterminable number of
Philadelphians who harbored potent animosities toward the
province's ruling elites, who had a taste for better things, and
who saw in independence a chance to displace the old oligarchies and to broaden the lines of power and privilege. But this
group would surely have recognized its opportunity by March

when the Moderates began their campaign against separation and could probably be counted among those already committed to the Radical position. On the other hand, many members of the governing oligarchies feared that independence would occasion a change in Pennsylvania government and a corresponding diminution of their status and influence. This group must have recognized its danger by March and could probably be counted among those already committed against the Radical position. But for Philadelphia centrists Pennsylvania politics were of secondary consequence in the months before the first of May. Their overriding concern was whether it was "expedient or inexpedient . . . to cut the Gordian knot and establish independence," and it was on this question that the May election was decided.[16]

Emotions ran high in Philadelphia on the first of May; the election proved to be "one of the sharpest contests" in memory.[17] Both sides hoped for victory; each knew the outcome would be close. When results became known the next day, most Philadelphians assumed that the Moderates' victory settled the question of independence, at least until the general elections five months hence. Only one week later, however, appeared an indication that some did not.

On 8 May the fourth and final of Thomas Paine's "Forester" letters appeared in the *Pennsylvania Journal*. In this lengthy, somewhat rambling essay Paine offered an interesting analysis of the recent election. The balloting, he insisted, did not accurately reflect public sentiment because military associators who were away on duty had not been able to vote and because a considerable number of Germans who were known "zealots in the cause of freedom" had been barred from voting by the naturalization requirement. Given this, the election of even one Radical candidate was a considerable accomplishment. In any case, Paine continued, the election had been simply an "experiment" undertaken by the friends of liberty "for the sake of knowing the men who were against us." The experiment now conducted, a provincial convention was more vital than ever. Whereas Paine had called for a convention before the election on grounds that the Assembly was unrepresentative, he now justified the call by claiming that since the Assembly sat under authority of the British crown, it was actually no more than "a branch from that power against whom" Pennsylvanians were fighting. According to Paine, the election had settled nothing. In fact, he contended, by enlarging the size of the legislature it had merely increased the necessity of a convention "because the more any power is augmented which derives its authority from our enemies, the more unsafe and dangerous it becomes to us."

Paine's essay foreshadowed the direction Radical strategists would turn in the weeks ahead. Defeated in the election, the Radicals now turned their attention to circumventing the results of that contest and to bringing Pennsylvania to the side of separation with or without electoral consent. They were aided by various pro-independence members of the Continental Congress, notably Samuel and John Adams, who knew that Congress would not sanction independence as long as Pennsylvania opposed it. Pennsylvania set the pace for the middle colonies; as long as her delegation voted against leaving the empire so too would those of New York, Delaware, and New Jersey.[18] Thus the Adamses colluded with leading Philadelphia Radicals—Paine, Cannon, Young, Benjamin Rush, David Rittenhouse, Christopher Marshall, Thomas McKean, Timothy Matlack, and others—to destroy the authority of Pennsylvania's government and to institute one more amenable to their revolutionary wishes.[19] Much of the activity through which this plan was realized naturally took place behind the scenes, but the redirection of political strategy also necessitated a corresponding shift in rhetorical strategy.

The authorization for reconstituting Pennsylvania's government came from the Continental Congress. In the week following Paine's final "Forester" letter, John Adams introduced and guided through Congress a resolution urging Americans to adopt whatever governments they considered essential to their happiness and safety "where no government sufficient to the exigencies of their affairs has hitherto been established." By itself this resolution posed little threat to the Assembly, which, as Charles Thomson explained, was fully capable of providing for the welfare of its constituents.[20] It was Adams's preamble that justified the Radicals' designs and signaled the beginning of the end for the Pennsylvania legislature. The preamble declared it foreign to "reason and good conscience" that the people of America should continue to take the "oaths and affirmations necessary for the support of any government under the crown of Great Britain."[21] If the preamble were accepted as a direction to the colonies, the Pennsylvania Assembly would be discredited as an official organ of government inasmuch as its members sat under the authority of the crown and professed allegiance to it. John Adams deemed his resolution (and preamble) "the most important" yet passed by Congress, for it amounted to "a total, absolute independence." James Allen, one of Philadelphia's most vociferous champions of continued union, agreed. "Moderate men look blank," he wrote after hearing of the action by Congress. "A convention chosen by the people will consist of the most fiery Independents; they will have the whole executive and legislative authority in their hands."[22]

Upon announcement of the resolution of 15 May, Radical rhetoricians went to work, but not on another attempt to convince centrist Philadelphians of the merits of independence. Close study of the Philadelphia press reveals that the real debate over independence in the city did not take place in the first six months of 1776 but in the first four. The barrage of Radical and Moderate rhetoric was heaviest in March and April, the two months immediately preceding the May election. In May the number of essays on the position of the colonies in the empire fell 75 percent below the totals for each of the previous two months. There was no increase in the volume of published literature regarding independence during June; there was, if anything, a slight decrease. Equally significant was the disappearance of polemics over the familiar pseudonyms adopted by the most important Radical writers. "Cassandra," "Candidus," "A Religious Politician," and "Salus Populi" did not appear at all in May or June. "The Forester" published only once—to complain about the election results and to propose a provincial convention. Radical spokesmen now directed their primary efforts elsewhere—toward lambasting the Assembly and promoting their scheme to reorganize Pennsylvania's government.

Since the Radicals lacked demonstrable majority support for independence, their new tactic was to create the appearance of such support. They staged a series of well-planned public meetings which issued carefully rehearsed declarations, all enthusiastically announcing for separation and calling for a provincial convention to put in motion machinery for revising the charter. To create the illusion that virtually the entire city was on the bandwagon for independence, they inundated the press with protests, resolutions, petitions, and memorials denying the authority of the Assembly and clamoring for a new state constitution and immediate disunion.

The first volley in this new campaign was fired in a broadside entitled "The Alarm," which circulated through the city on 19 May in both English and German editions. "The Alarm" was designed partially to arouse enthusiasm for the mass meeting scheduled by the Philadelphia Committee for the next day and partially to acquaint the public with the issues to be taken up at that meeting. It addressed one overriding question—who were "the proper persons to be entrusted with carrying . . . into execution" the congressional resolve of 15 May? Securing a proper public response to this question was critical, for it was the opinion of at least some Philadelphians that the "recommendation of Congress was certainly meant to go to the Assemblies, where there were such who had authority" to act upon it.[23] According to "The Alarm," the Pennsylvania Assembly could not possibly implement the congressional directive because the people had not vested it specifically with the power to create a new government. Besides, the legislature sat under authority of the crown and Congress had called for action founded "on the authority of the people." Who, then, ought to put the resolve into operation? "The Alarm" contended that conventions were historically "the only proper bodies to *form* a constitution" while legislatures were "the proper bodies to make laws agreeable to *that* constitution." Indeed, it alleged, the Pennsylvania legislature could no longer even meet "without either breaking the resolve of Congress, or assuming . . . arbitrary power." Consequently, a convention had to be called immediately "to take charge of the affairs of the province."

"The Alarm" served its purposes well. On 20 May some four to five thousand people braved a driving rain to attend the public meeting in the State House yard. Following a reading of the congressional directive of 15 May, the gathering approved half a dozen resolutions. The first, passed unanimously, attacked the Assembly's congressional instructions for their "tendency to withdraw this province from that *happy union* with the other colonies, which we consider both as our *glory* and *protection*." The remainder, passed with only one dissenting vote, proclaimed that the Assembly could not form a new government without "assuming arbitrary power" and urged that a convention be called to establish a new state constitution.

The crowd also gave its assent to a protest addressed to the Assembly. Embedded in the protest was the claim that, in denying the authority of the Assembly to reconstitute Pennsylvania's frame of government, "we mean not to object against its exercising the proper powers it has hitherto been accustomed to use, for the safety and convenience of this province," until such time as a new constitution founded on " *the authority of the people*' shall be finally settled." No evidence exists by which to judge the sincerity of those who composed this disclaimer; but by discrediting the Assembly as a body that derived its power solely "from our mortal enemy, the King of *Great Britain,*" the Radicals provided grounds for rejecting its authority in all instances. After all, how logical was it to have the defense of the province directed by "a body of men, bound by oaths of allegiance" to the enemies of America? William Bradford, Jr., himself a backer of independence, exulted that the actions of the State House meeting had lent the "coup de grace to the King's authority" in Pennsylvania.[24]

The Moderates understood only too well the implications of the Radicals' denigration of the Assembly and on 21 May they began circulating a remonstrance denouncing the protest adopted the previous day. When presented to the Assembly on 29 May, the remonstrance carried the signatures of some six thousand residents of Philadelphia city and surrounding counties. Claiming that the congressional resolution of 15 May was erroneously taken by the Radicals to be "an absolute *injunction*" whereas it was actually "only a constitutional recommendation," the remonstrance denied the necessity of proroguing the Assembly in order to frame a new government. The Moderates supported this contention by noting how efficiently the Assembly had governed, and continued to govern, the province in trying times. There was nothing in the present situation to dictate that Pennsylvanians should sacrifice their charter, especially since other colonies with similar charters continued to be governed by their regular legislatures "without conventions." The remonstrance did not explicitly defend the Assembly's stance against independence, but it did assert that no legislature in America exceeded that of Pennsylvania for its "noble exertions in the common cause of liberty."[25]

The Philadelphia County Committee of Inspection and Observation took a different tack. In an address approved on 18 May and published in Philadelphia newspapers on 29 May, this Moderate-controlled organization charged that the Radicals had "totally changed" the original basis of opposition to England by abandoning the goal of a "constitutional reconciliation." The County Committee affirmed its willingness to support independence should such a drastic measure become necessary, but it stressed that "a happy, permanent" settlement within the empire could best ensure Philadelphians' "happiness and security." Thus it urged the Assembly to retain its instructions against separation and to oppose any alteration "of our invaluable constitution, under which we have experienced every happiness."[26]

It is important to note that in each of these documents Moderate spokesmen seemingly tried to dissociate the question of independence from that of constituting a new government for Pennsylvania, perhaps because they sensed that by keeping these two matters separate they might at least be able to save the charter even if independence could no longer be forestalled.[27] In neither discourse, though, was the disengagement complete. In any case, it was probably too late to attempt it. Throughout the debate over independence Moderate rhetoricians tended to equate opposition to independence with support of the Assembly and defense of the Charter of Privileges. This equation became somewhat less explicit after the May election, but by then it was already too firmly stamped upon Philadelphians' minds to be easily erased. By mid-spring the Moderates had accustomed Philadelphians to thinking they could not achieve independence from England without dismantling the charter and the institutions legitimated by it. This was unfortunate in at least two respects. First, it was incorrect: there was no necessary reason why the charter could not have continued as the constitution of an independent Pennsylvania.[28] Second, by so arguing, the Moderates encouraged Philadelphians to believe that they had to choose between independence and the charter. When independence finally seemed inescapable, Philadelphians acquiesced in the Radicals' overthrow of the Assembly and destruction of the charter in the belief that Pennsylvania's established frame of government had to be sacrificed to the larger good of escaping British tyranny. Thus Moderate writers unwittingly helped rationalize the internal revolution they sought so desperately to prevent.

In response to the Moderates' challenges to the State House meeting of 20 May, Radical publicists accelerated their activities. In the succeeding month they published a spate of essays, notices, and broadsides abusing the Assembly and calling for a new government. Two major arguments recurred through these writings. First, that by its obstinate refusal to adopt pro-independence instructions the Assembly had failed to serve the people and had defected "from its union with the other colonies." Second, that since the Assembly derived its authority from "the Crown of Great Britain," it was not only unqualified to carry out the congressional resolve of 15 May, but could not take any action without posing as severe a threat to the liberty of Pennsylvanians as the "unlimited exertions" of Parliament and George III.[29]

Moderate rhetoricians were either unable or unwilling to counter these arguments. Almost no Moderate discourse of note appeared in any of Philadelphia's five newspapers following publication of the remonstrance of 21 May and the Philadelphia County Committee's address of 18 May. Henceforth one would think from reading the papers that no one but the rankest Tory possessed any desire for reconciliation or loyalty to the Assembly.

It was now up to the Assembly to defend itself. Under the guidance of John Dickinson, Moderate members moved to preempt the Radicals' two major charges against the Assembly. Their first response was swift and skillful. When the legislature reconvened on 20 May, its seventeen new members were permitted to take their seats without swearing allegiance to the crown.[30] By suspending this time-honored custom the Assembly took a major step toward blunting its critics and complying with the directive of Congress. Three weeks later, but only after considerable deliberation, the Moderates finally approved new instructions empowering the province's congressional delegates to adopt such "measures as shall be judged necessary for promoting the liberty, safety, and interests of *America;* reserving to the people of this colony the sole and exclusive right of regulating the internal government and police of the same."[31] Drafted by Dickinson, this carefully chosen language allowed but did not compel the delegates to vote for independence. It also reaffirmed the Assembly's opposition to congressional interference in the internal affairs of the colony.

Radical publicists responded to both of these actions with disdain. The Committee of Privates, in one of its numerous publications, found it curious that while the new members were admitted to their seats without swearing fealty to the king, the whole legislature still took care to head its resolves, as usual, "Votes of Assembly, John Penn, Esq., Governor." According to the committee, the Assembly thereby acknowledged "the King's representative" to be a proper governor and obviated any good it might have done by abolishing the oaths. This line of reasoning was extended in a skillful essay entitled "To the People," published in the *Pennsylvania Gazette* of 26 June. Written by an unidentifiable Radical legislator, this piece deprecated the Assembly's conduct regarding oaths as no more than a guileful expedient designed to circumvent the directive of 15 May. Not only did the Assembly continue to acknowledge the authority of the Penn family, thereby retaining its link with the king, but it refused to abolish the loyalty oaths required of all German citizens before they were admitted to the franchise, despite the inescapable fact that "if allegiance was no longer a necessary qualification for a Representative, it was no longer a necessary qualification in an elector." If one examined closely the much ballyhooed actions of the Assembly on the matter of oaths, "it will appear they have gone through nothing—spent their time to no purpose."[32]

Radicals attacked the new instructions for Pennsylvania's congressional delegates as too little too late. Rather than forthrightly standing for American autonomy, the Radicals complained, the instructions continued to hold out "the doctrine of reconciliation." While freeing the delegates to vote as they pleased, the Assembly had not directed them to stand for separation; consequently, there was "no reason to believe that their conduct in Congress" would be altered. In fact, contended the author of "To the People," far from representing a genuine change of conviction by Moderate legislators, the new instructions were no more than "an artful and selfish compromise for the safety of the persons" who promoted them. Had the Assembly truly favored separation, it would have responded favorably to the resolution of the Virginia convention asking Congress to declare the colonies free and independent states.

Rather, it tabled the matter—an incivility which weakened "the friendship, and consequently the union of the colonies."[33]

The Assembly was damned if it did and damned if it did not. Radical spokesmen assailed it from every direction on an ever proliferating number of issues, many of which involved military defense. From the summer of 1775 the Assembly had been involved in a number of disputes with the province's military associators. Among its most vocal critics was the Committee of Privates. This organization was probably more genuinely revolutionary than any other in Philadelphia. Moderates deprecated it as "a body founded in faction and growing in insolence" and ridiculed its chairman, Samuel Simpson, as "a drunken shoemaker." Its members were largely lesser mechanics; many were servants and apprentices. Its leaders—Simpson, James Cannon, Joseph Stiles—were "new men" devoted not only to independence but also to reforming the elitist structure of Pennsylvania politics. Under Cannon's guidance, the committee began a concerted drive in February 1776 to publicize the grievances of the lowest-ranking associators and to undermine the authority of the Assembly. By spring Cannon had turned the committee into a potent political force.[34]

Illustrative of the committee's efforts was a protest published during the third week in June. The stated purpose of this document was to demonstrate why the two brigadier-generalships assigned to Pennsylvania by the Continental Congress ought to be filled by vote of the associators themselves rather than by appointment from the Assembly. In fact, the reasons advanced in support of this contention constituted a general indictment of the Assembly's right and capacity to determine any questions about the defense of the province. Among the committee's claims were these: that the Assembly was "not properly constituted" to deal with military affairs; that many members were Quakers, who being "totally averse to military defense," could "not be called the representatives of Associators"; that some legislators were "well known'" to be "disposed to break the union of the colonies, and submit to the tyranny of *Great Britain*." Most remarkable was the following convoluted claim:

Because as this House was chosen by those only who were acknowledged the liege subjects of *George* our enemy, and derived their sole right of electing this House from that very circumstance, we conceive that the moment they undertook to set aside this allegiance [by eliminating the oath of allegiance], they, by that very act, destroyed the only principle on which they sat as Representatives, and therefore they are not a House on the principle on which they were elected; and having derived no new authority from the people, freed from such allegiance, they are a representative body on no principle whatever, and therefore can in no manner undertake to do the business of Representatives further than the people indulge them, without usurping authority and acting arbitrarily.[35]

The inconsistencies of the protest seem not to have bothered Cannon or the committee. Their singleminded aim was to disparage the Assembly. For this purpose, it seemed, almost any argument would do.

The Radicals took advantage of every opportunity. Early in May a dispute broke out between the captains of Philadelphia's fleet of row-galleys—armed whaleboats commissioned to repulse any effort to invade Philadelphia by water—and the Committee of Safety, which had been organized under the aegis of the Assembly and had responsibility for the day-to-day direction of Pennsylvania's defense. The details of the controversy are not crucial here. The important point is that by June what had begun as a minor military question had become a major political issue.[36] Radicals predictably sided with the captains, but their rhetoric was concerned less with clarifying the merits of the case than with impugning the integrity of the Committee of Safety and, by extrapolation, the Assembly. The Committee of Privates, for instance, confessed to having "not the least confidence" in the Committee of Safety, which was composed largely of men "who endeavored to withdraw us from the Continental Union" and therefore ought not to have "too great weight in the councils which regard our safety." Six weeks later Radicals were still airing the same accusation. One wrote: "several of the Committee of Safety are suspected Tories, have signed the Remonstrance [of 21 May], and are highly improper to be at the head of military secrets and affairs. . . . I cannot see how any man, especially a military man, holding independent principles, can think himself safe under the direction of those who oppose him."[37]

While assailing the Assembly in the press, Radical leaders pushed ahead with plans for a provincial convention to carry out the congressional resolution of 15 May. In a desperate attempt to save Pennsylvania's established government, a band of

Moderate legislators advanced plans for electing delegates and holding a constitutional convention under the direction of the Assembly. To thwart these plans—which, according to one Radical representative, would simply have fanned "the spirit of disunion"—Radical Assemblymen from the first of June attended only those legislative sessions devoted to formulating new instructions. All others they boycotted. Unable to procure a quorum, remaining members of the Assembly adjourned to 26 August.[38] The adjournment came on 14 June, the day the public elected delegates to the Provincial Conference.

The decision to adjourn was fateful. It gave credence to the Radicals' oft-repeated charge that the Assembly was incapable of superintending the affairs of the colony. Missing no bets, Radical rhetoricians now cited the adjournment as final evidence that the liberty and safety of Pennsylvanians could not be adequately safeguarded without a change of government. In recognizing the Radical-controlled Provincial Conference as the legal government of Pennsylvania, the Patriotic Society gave as its rationale:

there being now no other provincial representation in existence here; and because we likewise conceive that the late House of Assembly, by breaking up and dispersing in the very crisis of danger and difficulty, and that without a sufficient number present to authorize such an act, has thereby deserted the public cause, dissolved themselves and left the people, so far as respects that House, unrepresented.

One Radical legislator, who had himself likely contributed to the Assembly's inability to muster a quorum, blithely castigated it for deserting "the public trust in a time of greatest danger and difficulty. Like *James II* they have abdicated the government, and by their own act of desertion and cowardice have laid the Provincial Conference under the necessity of taking instant charge of affairs."[39]

The Radicals' censure of an adjournment they had helped bring about was markedly disingenuous. Still, it was undeniably true that by its action the Assembly had left government "all afloat." The legislative vacuum it created was quickly filled, first by the Provincial Conference, then by the Constitutional Convention. The Provincial Conference began meeting in Carpenters' Hall on 18 June to formulate plans for a convention to erect a government "on the authority of the people only." By the time it disbanded on 25 June it had also taken a number of legislative actions on behalf of the province, despite the fact that it was not convened to do so. It justified its conduct on grounds that "the sudden and unexpected separation of the late Assembly" left no other body to assume vital legislative functions. The Constitutional Convention opened its sessions in Philadelphia on 15 July. In addition to drafting a new state constitution, it acted as a legislature until adjourning on 28 September. When the old Assembly reconvened in August, it found itself without a quorum, public support, or significant duties. After one last attempt to recover its authority, the Assembly recognized that the end had come and dissolved itself. "Thus ended legislation under the proprietary government in Pennsylvania."[40]

The Assembly emasculated, Radical strategists lined up support for independence. On 6 June the Committee of Privates published a notice requesting a poll of the city's battalions to determine "whether they will support the resolve of Congress of the 15th ultimo, and the proceedings of the public meeting held the 20th following." Four days later, the first, second, fourth, and fifth battalions of the Philadelphia militia declared their approval of the actions of Congress and the town meeting. In addition, the soldiers signified their almost unanimous desire that Pennsylvania "be a free and independent state, and united with the other twelve colonies represented in Congress." Among some two thousand officers and men only twenty-nine negative votes were recorded. In a move no less predictable, the Provincial Conference two weeks later announced its willingness "to concur in a vote of the Congress, declaring the United Colonies FREE and INDEPENDENT STATES."[41]

The Radicals' maneuvers were designed to create the impression that the Assembly was inherently incapable of governing and that the people had willingly declared for independence. In fact, the people—at least those who disagreed with the Radicals—were not consulted. The Radicals were determined to bring Pennsylvania into the affirmative column of the independence ledger and to do so were willing to abridge locally the principles of natural right and free expression for which they were contending on the imperial level. One Philadelphian later recalled that the cause of the revolutionaries "was essentially that of freedom, and yet all the freedom it granted was, at the peril of tar and feathers, to think and act like themselves."[42] After the May election freedom of speech in Philadelphia was a right reserved for the proponents of independence.

To guarantee "popular support" for separation the associators circumscribed the activities of Moderates in the city (and backcountry), while the Philadelphia Committee forced outspoken opponents of independence to recant publicly under penalty of being declared "enemies to their country." The day after the mass meeting of 20 May a short broadside circulated through the city. It cautioned Philadelphians to beware of the "specious imprecations" contained in the Moderates' remonstrance against the meeting. Signed, *"Seven thousand who appeared at the State House, and have sworn to support the Union,"* this notice served warning in no uncertain terms: "The sense of this city hath been publicly taken, and we will not be belied by Tories. We protest against private machinations, and we shall consider the authors of such as enemies, and treat them accordingly. Let the men come forth who are endeavoring privately to undermine the Union; we will seek to find them out; we dare them to it at their peril." These were not idle words. On 10 June Christopher Marshall recorded the following incident in his diary.

Just about this time, part of the Fourth Battalion seized a Jew, for malpractice, cursing the Congress, declaring his willingness to fight against them, etc., but upon their treating him roughly [he] excused himself by informing against Arthur Thomas, a skinner, who, he said, instructed him in those points. Now, as this Thomas was one [who] had been frequently complained of ever since Dr. Kear[s]ley's affair, and with whom it's said, he now corresponds, the mob flew to his house. Not finding him as he ran away on their appearance, they wreaked their vengeance on his house, furniture, cash, skins, breeches, etc., etc., etc.[43]

Nor were those of Moderate persuasion allowed to influence their fellow citizens at public meetings or demonstrations. At the tumultuous gathering of 20 May, for example, all those who proclaimed confidence in the Assembly were "insulted and abused" by the Radicals and their supporters, who "behaved in such a tyrannical manner that the least opposition was dangerous." According to the same observer, the Committee of Privates used "every method . . . to force men into Independency." When the question of separation was put to the city battalions on 10 June, "any man who dared oppose their opinion was insulted and hushed by their interruptions, cheers and hissings." The proceedings of the meeting could only be described as "unfair and partial." "Republicus" expressed clearly the Radicals' attitude toward those of differing opinion. "Reconciliation," he declared, "is now thought of by none but knaves, fools and madmen." Independence constituted the only safe course for America and "every man that is against it is a traitor."[44]

In addition to censoring, threatening, and coercing their opponents, Radicals also restricted their right to vote. When the Provincial Conference established procedures for electing delegates to the Constitutional Convention, it imposed tests and oaths designed to limit the number of potential opposition voters. Disqualified from the election were all those whom the committees of inspection or safety had declared "an enemy to the liberties of *America*" as well as all who refused to foreswear allegiance to George III and to promise "to establish and support a government in this province on the authority of the people only."[45] This ruling guaranteed a Constitutional Convention composed of men sympathetic to both the imperial and internal revolutions.

On 2 July the Continental Congress approved Richard Henry Lee's resolution that "these united colonies are, and of right ought to be, free and independent states." Two days later it issued the Declaration of Independence. Their major goal accomplished, the Radicals now set about consolidating their power in Pennsylvania. The Constitutional Convention opened its sessions in the State House on 15 July and assumed control of the existing state government while creating a new one. After more than two months of deliberation the new Pennsylvania Constitution was ready to present to the people. Under the press of wartime expediency, however, it was never submitted for popular ratification but was proclaimed into existence by the convention on 28 September. When plans were announced the next day for electing a new legislature, every voter was required to swear not to "do any act or thing prejudicial or injurious to the constitution or government [of Pennsylvania] as established by the convention." Once again the Radicals disfranchised many of their opponents. As James Allen explained, the test oath split the adversaries of the new constitution to pieces, "the majority

disliking the frame and therefore not voting for the new
assembly, which was of course chosen by very few."[46]

Not all Radicals were happy with the convention's handiwork.
Even before the constitution was fully formed, Christopher
Marshall had broken from his revolutionary comrades. Finding
the religious oath required for officers of the new government
too vague to prevent "Turks, Jews, infidels, and what is worse,
Deists and Atheists" from making laws, Marshall rejected the
constitution and joined ranks with Dickinson, Smith, and others
who had fought in vain to preserve the Charter of Privileges.
There were other backsliders, including Benjamin Rush,
Thomas McKean, George Clymer, John Bayard, and John
Morton. These men had backed the drive to abuse the Assembly
and destroy the charter in order to hasten independence. But
unlike men such as Paine, Cannon, Young, and Rittenhouse,
they were not eager to put into practice the egalitarian principles
expressed so stridently in Radical rhetoric. They found the new
constitution "too much upon the democratical order," and they
objected particularly to its creation of an all-powerful unicameral legislature, relaxation of suffrage requirements, and
imposition of the test oath. Unhappiness with the new frame of
government was so severe in Philadelphia that, despite the
loyalty oath, Anti-Constitutionalists swept every seat in the
November election. The Constitutionalists were victorious
elsewhere, however, and dominated the new Assembly. In the
succeeding months they solidified control of the new government.[47]

In retrospect great historical happenings often appear to have
been inevitable. Not so with the revolution in Pennsylvania
politics in 1776. If there were compelling historical forces leading inexorably to a drastic reconstitution of Pennsylvania
government, they were not apparent at the time and are today
impossible to detect. The Pennsylvania Assembly was replaced
because it lost the confidence of the people. A number of factors
contributed to the erosion of that confidence. In some respects
the Assembly fell victim to the errors and weaknesses of its
Moderate leaders and champions. By linking the question of
maintaining the Charter of Privileges with that of maintaining
the connection with England, the Moderates helped convince

Philadelphians that they could not leave the empire without destroying the charter and thus the Assembly. By failing to respond strongly to the needs of the military associators, Moderate legislators created a formidable organized opposition to the authority of the Assembly and contributed to the public impression that the Assembly might fail to guarantee the defense of the province (as it had failed in previous crises). By adjourning at a most critical juncture, the Assembly substantiated charges that it could not govern and created a legislative void the Radicals eagerly and promptly filled. Perhaps most important, by obdurately refusing to amend its explicit instructions against independence, it appeared "adverse to the cause of freedom" and prompted Radical leaders to set in motion machinery for circumventing its authority. Had Moderate leaders perceived more clearly and responded more astutely to the revolutionary currents swirling about them, a radical upheaval in Pennsylvania government would not have been necessary. As Charles Thomson explained to John Dickinson in August 1776, it was partly the miscalculations of Dickinson and his colleagues that finally threw "the affairs of this state into the hands of men totally unequal to them." The people "did not desert you," Thomson stated. "You left them."[48]

Thomson did not hold the Moderates entirely accountable, however. In a narrative written several years after the Revolution, he recalled that the Charter of Privileges was actually "very favorable and well adapted" to the exigencies of 1776. Recognizing this, many Whigs were willing to "temporize and make use of the Assembly rather than a convention" but were thwarted "by a body of men from whom they expected to derive the firmest support." That "body of men," Thomson noted, comprised more zealous Whigs who had been "suddenly raised to power" and were "impatient of any kind of opposition." This group finally prevailed over their Moderate counterparts, and as a consequence, Pennsylvania was "rent to pieces by parties."[49] As Thomson understood, the Assembly fell victim not only to its own ineptitude, but also to the skillful rhetoric and political machinations of Radical Whigs. Beginning the week after the May election, Radical leaders subjected the Assembly to unrelenting pressure. They capitalized upon its every error, took advantage of its every misjudgment, outmaneuvered its Moderate defenders at every turn. Unable or unwilling to offer

the bold and decisive leadership demanded in a revolutionary
time, the Assembly lost the confidence of its constituents and, as
a result, the ability to govern. In the last analysis, Philadelphians
acquiesced in the destruction of the Assembly because they were
persuaded—by events and by Radical rhetoric—that it was
necessary in order to escape British tyranny and to ensure the
defense of the province.

One factor remains to be discussed. The Radicals could not
have succeeded had there not occurred between May and July a
subtle shift in public opinion in which many Philadelphians
came to look more favorably upon the notion of independence
and to back the drive to overturn the Assembly. The outcome of
the May election signaled that a majority of Philadelphia voters
were not yet prepared to withdraw from the empire. As we have
seen, the Radicals moved to circumvent the election results by
dismantling Pennsylvania's existing government. But had they
read the election results more carefully, and had they
persevered in their efforts to convince Philadelphians of the
merits of separation, they would likely still have succeeded. The
May election did not indicate an unalterable resistance to independence in the city. It indicated that many people had yet to
make a final decision on the matter. The only groups who knew
with certainty what they wanted were the ardent Tories and the
staunch revolutionists. By the first of May, "Philadelphia neither
lagged in enthusiasm for independence nor embraced the idea
with fervor. It simply hung in delicate balance between the
two."[50]

Until May the war which was actively raging in some colonies
had yet to touch Pennsylvania. Philadelphia was not in the position of cities such as Boston or Norfolk, where there had already
been skirmishes with British land and naval forces. In fact, no
royal troops had been stationed in Philadelphia since September
1774. For most of its citizens the war was a distant matter. What
the Radicals most needed was some dramatic happening to
kindle the fire of separatism. As Samuel Adams explained on 30
April, "We cannot make events. Our business is wisely to
improve them." Heretofore, he observed, circumstances had favored the Moderates, for "there has been much to do to confirm
doubting friends and fortify the timid." "One battle," he
thought, "would do more towards a Declaration of Independence than a long chain of conclusive arguments in a provin-

cial convention or the Continental Congress." Almost as if in response to Adams's wishes, England unwittingly came to the Radicals' aid. Between May and July there took place a series of incidents that dramatically punctuated many of the key claims regarding the necessity and feasibility of separation and helped promote a spirit of independence in the city.[51]

The first event was confirmation of British plans to escalate the war. On 15 May the *Pennsylvania Gazette* announced that a fleet of fifty-seven warships and three armies totaling 35,000 men had been dispatched to the colonies. This report was confirmed a week later when the *Pennsylvania Journal* reported that the ministry intended "to have an army of 30,000, mostly Germans, in America by June."[52] The hiring of Hessian mercenaries especially disturbed centrist Philadelphians. As Arthur St. Clair later explained, the news "cast the die" for "many worthy men" who had heretofore argued for reconciliation but who now felt that "if foreign troops were employed to reduce Americans to absolute submission, . . . independence or any other mode was justifiable." Joseph Shippen, long an advocate of continued union, lamented that regardless of the objections "we and thousands of others may have to . . . independence, it appears to me, beyond a doubt, that a public declaration of it will be made as soon as it is fully ascertained that a large army of foreigners has been taken into British pay to be employed against the colonies."[53]

The second catalytic event was news of British plans to march through Virginia and attack Philadelphia by land and, if possible, by sea. There could now be no doubt that the city was destined to become involved in the war regardless of its position on independence. And along with involvement would come exposure to the "execrable barbarity" of British and Hessian soldiers. Atrocity stories had been standard newspaper fare in Philadelphia since the occupation of Boston in 1768, but they were never more prevalent than in 1776. The catalogue of British enormities cited by the Continental Congress was typical:

burning our defenseless towns and villages, exposing their inhabitants, without regard to age or sex, to all the miseries which loss of property, the rigor of the season, and inhuman devastation can inflict, exciting domestic insurrections and murders, bribing the savages to desolate our frontiers, and casting such of us, as the fortune of war has put into their power, into jails, there to languish in irons and in want; compelling the inhabitants of *Boston,* in violation of the treaty, to remain confined within the town, exposed to the insolence of the soldiery, and other enormities, at the mention of which humanity and decency will forever blush.

Equally abhorrent to centrist Philadelphians were reports that England had enlisted large numbers of slaves and Indians to slaughter innocent colonists. One particularly horrifying tale concerned an engagement near Montreal in which a party of one hundred colonials was attacked by an equal number of Canadians and four hundred Indian "savages" who disarmed the Americans and, with "savage barbarity," "butchered" them in "cold blood."[54] Faced with such evidence of British cruelty and rapine, centrist Philadelphians were increasingly inclined to agree with Thomas Paine that the time of argument was indeed past.

Finally, the "battle" which Sam Adams hoped for occurred on 8 and 9 May, when thousands of Philadelphians lined the shore of the Delaware to view a confrontation between thirteen armed provincial boats and two royal schooners which had ventured too close to the city. The fight began about three o'clock in the afternoon of 8 May. After some four hours of heavy cannonading by both sides, one royal vessel ran aground and the other dropped anchor to protect her. When the battle resumed the next day, the row-galleys chased both royal ships down the river past New Castle, several miles from the original scene of action. Although one Pennsylvanian was killed and two others wounded, the provincials proved their courage and their ability to defend Philadelphia against two representatives of the vaunted British navy. As one observer noted, the contest produced "a very happy effect upon the multitudes of spectators on each side of the river," and henceforth "British ships of war will not be thought so formidable. A few long boats drove, and apparently injured, those sized ships that seemed best calculated to distress us." John Adams voiced similar thoughts. He explained that the battle "diminished, in the minds of the people, . . . the terror of a man-of-war."[55] Uncommitted Philadelphians could no longer escape the painful fact that all of America, their fair city included, was undeniably at war with England. But they could now take heart in the ability of Americans to win that war.

◄════►

By January 1776 a declaration of independence was probably inevitable given still hardening American and British attitudes. Americans were unwilling to compromise their rights, and England was unwilling to abdicate her sovereignty. Moreover, the colonies were already in a de facto state of independence. Still, unity was essential if an independent America were to survive. The subject of separation had to be publicly broached and persuasively advanced to legitimate any final action by the Continental Congress. This was especially important in a moderate-minded colony such as Pennsylvania, as Dickinson, Thomson, and Wilson recognized in 1775. Other, more zealous Whigs misread opinion in Philadelphia and Pennsylvania and were eager for revolution before the public was prepared. Even John Adams, who anticipated independence for close to a year before its declaration and who helped engineer the change in Pennsylvania government, agreed that the six-month public debate over leaving the empire had been psychologically and politically indispensable. Writing to his wife the day after Congress voted to terminate the connection with England, Adams confided that while he had hoped for independence in January, delaying until July had "many great advantages attending to it."

The hopes of reconciliation, which were fondly entertained by multitudes of honest and well meaning, though weak and mistaken people, have been gradually and, at last, totally extinguished. Time has been given for the whole people maturely to consider the great question of independence and to ripen their judgment, dissipate their fears, and allure their hopes, by discussing it in assemblies, conventions, committees of safety and inspection, in town and county meetings, as well as in private conversations, so that the whole people, in every colony of the thirteen, have now adopted it as their own act. This will cement the union, and avoid those heats, and perhaps convulsions, which might have been occasioned by such a declaration six months ago.[56]

What was the importance of public rhetoric to this final decision in Philadelphia? Certainly it was not the whole story. As Samuel Adams realized, "mankind are governed more by their feelings than by reason" and "events which excite those feelings will produce wonderful effects." We can never know how long uncommitted Philadelphians might have persevered in their dreams of reconciliation without the fortuitous chain of events of May and June. There is little doubt that, as one colonist explained, the effects of even so influential a piece of rhetoric as *Common Sense* were secondary "compared with the effects of the folly, insanity, and villainy of the King and his Ministers."[57]

To acknowledge the importance of events, however, does not mitigate the consequence of rhetoric. Discourse always occurs within a context, and that context will always influence the ways language shapes perceptions, attitudes, and beliefs. The task of revolutionary publicists, as Samuel Adams so shrewdly understood, was "wisely to improve" upon events.[58] By discerning the symbiotic relationship between rhetoric and events we can arrive at an evaluation of the debate over independence that is at once critically satisfying and historically scrupulous.

At the beginning of 1776 centrist Philadelphians were poised between protest and revolution. Unable to turn back, they were not yet willing to go forward. Intellectually, they were still bound to the person and office of the king. Politically, they were unconvinced of the hopelessness of reconciliation. Militarily, they were unsure of besting British land and naval forces. Psychologically, they were not yet ready to renounce irrevocably their spiritual allegiance to England and to assert a uniquely American identity. In the months between the publication of *Common Sense* and the special Assembly election of 1 May, Radical rhetoric generated a demonstrably significant movement of opinion in favor of separation. Whereas at the beginning of January even the word "independence" was one its advocates shied away from using, on the first of May just less than a majority of the city's voters signified their readiness to support the Radicals and their plans.

Less than a majority, however, was not enough to give the Radicals enough seats to control the Pennsylvania Assembly and amend its official instructions against independence. Consequently, Radicals now moved to circumvent the results of the May election by displacing the Assembly. Some Radicals continued to write in the press of the merits of separation; most turned to discrediting the Assembly and promoting the scheme to constitute a new state government. The revolution in Pennsylvania government succeeded partly because the Radicals' skillful rhetorical assaults helped undermine public confidence in the Assembly. It also succeeded because a significant, albeit undeterminable, number of previously uncommitted Philadelphians came in May and June to agree with the Radicals that the "last necessity" had finally arrived. On the first of May many centrists were still unswayed by Radical arguments, but by July those same arguments had become persuasive within the frame of events that brought the war closer to Philadelphia, demonstrated the futility of compromise, and revealed the possibility of victory. Events from May to July were the catalysts finally prompting a broadly based decision to separate; Radical rhetoric from January to July provided and maintained the necessary authorizing warrants which had to be presented if that decision were to come without the "heats" and "convulsions" John Adams recognized as might-have-beens in the American revolutionary experience.

# AFTERWORD

In addition to being a potent factor in the onset of imperial rebellion, Whig discourse also had far-reaching domestic consequences. Most significantly, as the rhetoric of Philadelphia Whigs hastened the dissolution of British-American union, so too did it help shape the character of political discourse and participation in the city.

The years of revolutionary turmoil which brought an end to British rule in Philadelphia also irrevocably undermined the politics of deference that had predominated in the city through most of the colonial period.[1] Although historians have long debated the degree to which the American Revolution grew out of and/or spurred the growth of democratic values and institutions,[2] there is no question but that the years of imperial strife accelerated popular participation in and control over government in Philadelphia and Pennsylvania. The patrician elite did not relinquish the reins of power altogether. Nor did the hierarchical structure of Philadelphia society disintegrate with the coming of independence. Nevertheless, a new democratic order began to take shape in the city as both a cause and a consequence of the quickening pulse toward revolution. As early as 1770 some Philadelphians noticed a growing disinclination on the part of ordinary citizens to defer to the opinions and wishes of their social superiors.[3] These changes of mood and attitude were shortly translated into political activity, especially by the city's mechanics, who began to seek greater influence within established political structures and, more important in the long run, within the city's protest movement. Between 1773 and 1776, middle-class Philadelphians steadily increased their representation on Philadelphia's Whig committees and played ever more consequential roles in resistance activities.[4] Most of the Radical Whigs who led the city into revolution and who engineered the coup in Pennsylvania's government in 1776 were "new men" unassociated with the colony's ruling oligarchies and committed to both independence and what in the parlance of the day were known as leveling principles. The constitution these new men created for Pennsylvania in the fall of 1776 institutionalized those principles. It thereby earned the undying enmity, as William Shippen wrote, of those patrician Philadelphians who had "been heretofore at the head of affairs" and who now found themselves "brought down to a level with their fellow citizens." Whereas in 1765 politics in Philadelphia had been firmly controlled by a privileged, self-conscious minority of individuals possessing great wealth, family standing, and connection, by 1777 the power of government in the city had been stripped from the established oligarchies and placed "in the hands of those who were governed."[5]

This expansion in the political consciousness and influence of common citizens was reflected in and partly occasioned by a profound transformation in the nature of political discourse in Philadelphia during the dispute with England. Many of the men who led protest against British authority were "gentlemen" of rank and eminence who were not inclined to view the "middling sort" of Philadelphians as a meaningful audience for political discourse.[6] Much of their rhetoric exemplified what may be called the gentlemanly mode of colonial public address. Highlighted with Latin quotations, run through with references to learned authorities, laden with citations from Greek and Roman history, sprinkled with complex circumlocutions, accented with literary allusions, their writing bespoke their patrician values, advanced educations, elitist upbringings, and aristocratic presuppositions. Much of the literature of protest published in Philadelphia during the dispute with England was produced by gentlemen who tended to make few concessions to the needs of readers from lesser social groups and who frequently wrote as if they were addressing only other gentlemen. The gentlemanly mode of public address was at once a symbol and an instrument of social privilege and political authority. Its underlying but nonetheless inescapable message was that matters of state were naturally of interest only to and would properly be resolved only by persons who possessed the background, interests, tastes, and habits of mind of the patrician class; to their judgment the people appropriately submitted and to them average citizens correctly "consign[ed] the care of their rights."[7]

The gentlemanly mode of public address was intimately connected with an elitist social and political order. As that order began to crumble, so did its distinguishing style of public literature. Although the gentlemanly mode of discourse survived well into the nineteenth century—as did the patrician culture whose values it reflected and reinforced—even by the time of the Declaration of Independence it was being seriously challenged and to a degree supplanted in Philadelphia by what we may call the popular mode of public address. The popular mode was distinguished by its lack of literary and scholarly trappings, by its acknowledged appeal to a wide public, by its colloquial idiom and direct style, by its disdain for polished subtleties of image and figure, and at times by its outright denigration of the gentlemanly way of life. In contrast to the gentlemanly mode, the popular mode insisted—in its content, in its form, and in its style—that issues of state were not above discussion by ordinary citizens, that political affairs were not the business only of well-to-do, privileged, and lettered aristocrats, that the community at large had a vital stake in government and ought to participate directly in its day-to-day operation.

Distinctions between the gentlemanly and popular modes of public address are well illustrated by comparing John Dickinson's *Letters from a Farmer in Pennsylvania* and Thomas Paine's *Common Sense*. Comparing these works is especially instructive, not because they were totally dissimilar, but because in some respects they were quite alike. Both were enormously popular. They were by far the two most influential political tracts printed in Philadelphia during the British-American controversy. Both were marked by their wide sweep. The *Letters from a Farmer* constituted a full, learned, and judicious explication of what most Philadelphia Whigs were thinking during the years 1768–73; *Common Sense* advanced a comprehensive case for independence encompassing a range of topics from the origins of government to the marksmanship of colonial militiamen. And both were notable for their literary style. Dickinson's pamphlet received scores of encomiums for its perspicuity and boldness; Paine's tract elicited widespread praise for its "striking, nervous, and manly" mode of expression.[8]

These similarities notwithstanding, the two works reflected conflicting political and cultural universes. Although both pamphlets reached a wide readership, Dickinson clearly conceived of his audience far differently from the way Paine thought of his. Dickinson did not address ordinary readers in their idiom, but in the manner of cultured and erudite gentlemen. The *Letters from a Farmer* read at times like a scholarly dissertation, at other times like a legal disquisition. The seventy-one pages contain almost as many footnotes, some of which run on for several pages. There are citations from Coke, Plutarch, Montesquieu, Hume, Tacitus, Locke, Cicero, and Demosthenes, among others, as the *Letters* move from one well-documented and closely reasoned argument to the next. Although Dickinson's condemnation of British policy was uniformly forceful, he seldom appealed blatantly to the emotions of his readers. His language was consistently reserved, serious, and decorous. He urged strenuous opposition to the Townshend Acts, but he counseled against "hot, rash, disorderly proceedings." The cause of liberty, he stated, was best maintained by "wise and good men" who possessed "a sedate, yet fervent spirit, animating them to actions of prudence, justice, modesty, humanity, and magnanimity." Perhaps most revealing was the persona Dickinson adopted as author of the *Letters*.

I am a *Farmer*, settled, after a variety of fortunes, near the banks of the river *Delaware,* in the province of *Pennsylvania.* I received a liberal education, and have been engaged in the busy scenes of life; but am now convinced that a man may be as happy without bustle as with it. My farm is small; my servants are few, and good; I have a little money at interest; I wish for no more. . . . Being generally master of my time, I spend a good deal of it in a library, which I think the most valuable part of my small estate. . . . I have acquired, I believe, a greater knowledge in history, and the laws and constitution of my country than is generally attained by men of my class. . . .

From my infancy I was taught to love *humanity* and *liberty.* Enquiry and experience have since confirmed my reverence for the lessons then given me, by convincing me more fully of their truth and excellence. . . .

These being my sentiments, I am encouraged to offer you, my countrymen, my thoughts on some late transactions that appear to me to be of the utmost importance to you. Conscious of my own defects, I have waited some time in expectation of seeing the subject treated by persons much better qualified for the task; but being therein disappointed, and being apprehensive that longer delays will be injurious, I venture at length to request the attention of the public.

These passages from the opening paragraphs of the first letter present as good a picture as we have of the character and spirit of the colonial gentry. Although Dickinson's persona was

carefully selected to appeal to popular American convictions
about the superiority of agrarian life, it was no accident that the
model for his persona was the gentleman farmer, not the strug-
gling backcountry settler. The essential qualities of Dickinson's
"Farmer" were stateliness, scholarship, equanimity, detachment,
virtuous leisure, moderate wealth, humility, and a powerful
sense of public responsibility.[9] A latent message of the *Letters* was
that men possessing such attributes were best qualified to deliberate upon political matters and that people without such attributes ought to defer to the judgment of their betters.

In *Common Sense,* on the other hand, one finds none of the
gentlemanly ethos that informed Dickinson's *Letters.*[10] Most of
the controversy surrounding Paine's tract stemmed from its
vigorous advocacy of immediate withdrawal from the British
empire. But as Gordon Wood has noted, "some of the awe and
consternation the pamphlet aroused came from its deliberate
elimination of the usual elitist apparatus of persuasion and its
acknowledged appeal to a wider reading public."[11] Whereas
most Whig pamphleteers set forth detailed arguments buttressed by legal precedents, historical illustrations, and quotations from respected authorities, Paine forwarded "nothing
more than simple facts, plain arguments, and common sense."
Rather than writing in the cultured lexicon of the patrician elite,
Paine professed to adopt the "simple voice of nature and
reason." In truth the profession was somewhat disingenuous,
for Paine was a careful and accomplished writer who consciously
used language with an eye not only toward producing persuasive prose but also toward achieving that elusive quality known
in the eighteenth century as sublimity and today as eloquence.
But all the same, Paine did pioneer "a style of thinking and
expression different to what had been customary" in American
political discourse.[12] The style of *Common Sense* was more akin to
that of sloganeering than to that of the usual Whig political
pamphlet. Paine's metaphors were not drawn from classical
literature but from everyday experience and were couched in
everyday language. Moreover, Paine forthrightly appealed to
the emotions of his audience throughout, contending that "the
passions and feelings of mankind" should be engaged in all matters of consequence to society. Indeed, the dominant tone of
*Common Sense* was one of rage—a bitter, almost savage anger all
but unique in the literature of the Revolution.[13] Gone were the

amenities of formal address habitually employed by the better classes: George III was not "His Majesty," but the "Royal Brute of Great Britain." The author of *Common Sense* was quite clearly not a gentleman. Just as clearly, he scornfully rejected the notion that meaningful participation in politics was the exclusive domain of the gentry. The sustained assault upon monarchy and hereditary rule, the virulent indictment of the British constitution, the apotheosis of the people, and the plan for American government advanced in the pamphlet all made it clear to any reader of *Common Sense* that its author was an ardent champion of the rights and privileges of "the people at large." Paine's tract was not only a strident plea for American independence, it was also a powerful indictment of the politics of deference and the hierarchical ordering of eighteenth-century society.[14]

Thus we find in the *Letters from a Farmer* and in *Common Sense* ideological and rhetorical tokens of competing political cultures. What wants special notice, however, is not just that the literature of the Revolution revealed emerging changes in Philadelphia's political order, but that Whig rhetoric was a potent catalyst behind those changes. As the British-American controversy progressed, Whig publicists tended increasingly to orient their discourse toward the literary requirements and political and economic interests of ordinary Philadelphians.[15] Although it was evident as early as the Stamp Act crisis that the most effective weapon of anti-British protesters was an aroused and incensed populace, it was not until the fall of 1768 that Philadelphia Whigs began systematically to solicit the backing of middle-class citizens. The circumstances surrounding this shift in Whig rhetorical strategy have been explored elsewhere.[16] Suffice it to say here that during the 1768–70 controversies over nonimportation, Charles Thomson, John Dickinson, and their colleagues began to establish a popular constituency for the resistance movement. They continued to court and to expand that constituency during the dramatic years 1773–75. In the process they helped to forge a coalition that eventually carried Philadelphia from protest to revolution.

The decision to expand the popular base of protest activity did not necessarily signal a change in the deeply rooted belief of Whig gentlemen that average colonists were ill-equipped to make informed and intelligent political decisions. Nor were they interested in broadening the lines of power and privilege within the city. Throughout the years before 1776, Whig leaders solicited only the *support* of ordinary Philadelphians, not their active *participation* in the resistance movement. And they sought even this support as a matter of necessity rather than choice, for the Whig cause could not sustain itself against its opponents on either side of the Atlantic without the backing of a substantial portion of the general population. But to secure this backing, Whig spokesmen had to modify their discourse to appeal to a popular readership. By so doing, they inadvertently hastened the eventual demise of the gentlemanly mode of public address and inexorably encouraged ordinary citizens to see themselves as legitimate participants in affairs of state. This consequence of Whig rhetoric was alluded to by Joseph Reed, himself the scion of an eminent family. Writing to Lord Dartmouth at the close of 1773, Reed stated that since the agitation against British policy in Philadelphia had "originated and been conducted by some of the principal inhabitants," there had heretofore "been no mobs, no insults to individuals, no injury to private property; but the frequent appeals to the people must in time occasion a change, and we every day perceive it more and more difficult to repress the rising spirit of the people."[17]

Reed's concern was well founded. In the years after 1768, Whig publicists not only appealed frequently to the people, but some explicitly encouraged the people to see themselves as vital participants in the political process. Writing in 1770, one Whig, who adopted as his motto "Libertas et Natale Solum," urged Philadelphians not to allow a handful of selfish merchants to terminate the nonimportation accords that had been in effect since the spring of 1769. Since matters of liberty affected the entire community, he argued, "every freeman, whether he be farmer, merchant, or mechanic," should forcefully "insist upon his right to vote in so important an affair." Equally portentous, Whigs encouraged the people to interfere in the business affairs of Philadelphia merchants by arguing that nonimportation should be continued because it was favored by the colony's farmers and mechanics, who comprised "the most substantial part of the province." Whig gentlemen, who had habitually perceived the great mass of Philadelphians as "not fit to be the guardians of their own rights," found themselves in the curious position of apostrophizing "the virtue and integrity of the middling sort of people, . . . who despise venality and know best the sweets of liberty." Thus, in trying to prevent the resumption of trade with England in 1770, "A Citizen" proclaimed: "Let the powers of patriotism be drawn from their *proper source*. Let the landholders, artificers, and independent freemen of this province take upon themselves the defense of those liberties in which they have the greatest and most substantial interest."[18]

The inescapable conclusion that the people were rightfully entitled to play an active role in politics was further strengthened by the penchant of Philadelphia Whigs to argue from premises of natural rights. If all men were equal in a state of nature, as the protesters contended, then run-of-the-mill artisans and shopkeepers could make as substantial a claim of right to enter politics as the best educated and most cultured of gentlemen.

This incipiently democratic view of society and politics rippled just beneath the surface of much Whig rhetoric during the years 1768–75. Then early in 1776 it burst to the surface in the literature of Radical Whigs during the debate over independence. As Radical publicists defended the feasibility of republican government in an independent America and denied the authority of the Pennsylvania Assembly to instruct Pennsylvania's congressional delegates to vote against separation, they exalted the innate abilities of common citizens and called for government that put "all the servants of the public under the power of the people." In responding to William Smith's charge that divorce from England would destroy social and political stability in America, Thomas Paine contended that "the safest asylum, especially in times of general convulsion when no settled form of government prevails, is *the love of the people*. All property is safe under their protection. Even in countries where the lowest and most licentious of them have risen into outrage they have never departed from the path of *natural* honor." In fact, James Cannon charged, the greatest danger to America was not the prospect of republicanism, but the reactionary zeal of an entrenched *"aristocratical junto"* that feared the just aspirations of "the common and middle class of people" more than anything else. Another writer cautioned Philadelphians to beware the insidious claims of Moderate men of wealth and position and to remember that "a freeman worth only £50 is entitled, by the laws of our province, to all the privileges of the first nabob in the country." The claims of well-to-do gentlemen to the contrary, the only necessary qualifications for governing wisely were "honesty, common sense, and a plain understanding." According to Thomas Young, the reins of power should therefore be readily accessible to "every man who pays his shot and bears his lot."[19]

The differences between the rhetoric of Radical and Moderate Whigs were formal as well as ideological. Most Moderate discourse was written in the gentlemanly mode of public address that was at once a symbol, a product, and an agency of a deferential society, but the bulk of Radical literature prefigured the popular mode of public address that came to predominate in the new republic. *Common Sense* showed the way, and most Radical publicists, consciously or not, adopted many of the more obvious formal strategies and nuances of Paine's tract—its colloquial idiom, its disdain for literary convention, its direct appeal to popular emotions. In fact, as Radical and Moderate spokesmen assailed one another's arguments, they frequently vilified one another's literary style, perhaps because they understood that the two were inextricably interwoven.[20] For as Philadelphia's political order was being transformed by powerful revolutionary currents, so too was the character of its public rhetoric. By mid-1776 a new kind of political discourse was becoming established in the city—a kind of discourse that helped deepen and strengthen the democratizing aftershocks of the upheaval in British-American relations. Seen in this light, the rhetoric of the Revolution not only helped resolve the issue of home rule, but materially affected the question of who was to rule at home. And therein rests its most distinctive legacy.

# NOTES AND INDEX

# NOTES

## ABBREVIATIONS

| | |
|---|---|
| *Chronicle* | *The Pennsylvania Chronicle* |
| *Evening Post* | *The Pennsylvania Evening Post* |
| *Gazette* | *The Pennsylvania Gazette* |
| *Journal* | *The Pennsylvania Journal* |
| *Ledger* | *The Pennsylvania Ledger* |
| *Mercury* | *The Pennsylvania Mercury* |
| *Packet* | *The Pennsylvania Packet* |

## FOREWORD

1. To Hezekiah Niles, 13 Feb. 1818, in Charles F. Adams, ed., *The Works of John Adams* (Boston, 1856), 10: 282–83.

2. Douglass Adair and John A. Schutz, eds., *Peter Oliver's Origin and Progress of the American Revolution* (Stanford, 1967), p. 159; [Daniel Leonard], "Massachusettensis," in *Novanglus and Massachusettensis; or, Political Essays Published in the Years 1774 and 1775* . . . (Boston, 1819), p. 169; [Joseph Galloway], *Historical and Political Reflections on the Rise and Progress of the American Rebellion* . . . (London, 1780), pp. 3–4.

3. Adair and Schutz, *Peter Oliver's Origin and Progress,* p. 145; Leonard, "Massachusettensis," pp. 208–9, 150, 156.

4. William Gordon, *The History of the Rise, Progress, and Establishment of the Independence of the United States of America* . . . (London, 1778), 2: 379, quoted in Merrill Jensen, "Historians and the Nature of the American Revolution," in Ray A. Billington, ed., *The Reinterpretation of Early American History* (New York, 1968), p. 112; David Ramsay, *The History of the American Revolution* (London, 1793), 2: 319–20; Adams to Hezekiah Niles, 13 Feb. 1818, in Adams, *Works of Adams,* 10: 283.

5. Kenneth Boulding, *The Image: Knowledge and Life in Society* (Ann Arbor, 1956), p. 14; Murray Edelman, *Politics as Symbolic Action* (Chicago, 1971), p. 66; Murray Edelman, *The Symbolic Uses of Politics* (Urbana, 1964), p. 131; Kenneth Burke, *Attitudes toward History* (Boston, 1937), p. 4. Cf. Peter L. Berger and Thomas Luckmann, *The Social Construction of Reality: A Treatise in the Sociology of Knowledge* (New York, 1966); Ernst Cassirer, *Language and Myth,* trans. Suzanne K. Langer (New York, 1946); Joseph Church, *Language and the Discovery of Reality*

(New York, 1961); Hugh Dalziel Duncan, *Communication and Social Order* (New York, 1962); Suzanne K. Langer, *Philosophy in a New Key: A Study in the Symbolism of Reason, Rite, and Art* (Cambridge, 1942); Claus Mueller, *The Politics of Communication: A Study in the Political Sociology of Language, Socialization, and Legitimation* (New York, 1973); Charles K. Ogden and I. A. Richards, *The Meaning of Meaning: A Study of the Influence of Language upon Thought and of the Science of Symbolism* (New York, 1923); Ch. Perelman and L. Olbrechts-Tyteca, *The New Rhetoric: A Treatise on Argumentation*, trans. John Wilkinson and Purcell Weaver (Notre Dame, 1969); Robert F. Terwilliger, *Meaning and Mind: A Study in the Psychology of Language* (New York, 1968); Benjamin L. Whorf, *Language, Thought, and Reality* (New York, 1956).

6. James R. Andrews, *A Choice of Worlds: The Practice and Criticism of Public Discourse* (New York, 1973).

7. Moses Coit Tyler, *The Literary History of the American Revolution, 1763–1783* (1897; reprint ed., New York, 1957), 1: 8–9, v.

8. Philip Davidson, *Propaganda and the American Revolution, 1763–1783* (Chapel Hill, 1941), pp. xiv–xvi, 410. Other prominent propaganda studies of the Revolution are Carl L. Becker, *The Declaration of Independence: A Study in the History of Political Ideas* (New York, 1922); Arthur M. Schlesinger, *Prelude to Independence: The Newspaper War on Britain, 1764–1776* (New York, 1957); John C. Miller, *Sam Adams: Pioneer in Propaganda* (Boston, 1936).

9. Bernard Bailyn, *The Ideological Origins of the American Revolution* (Cambridge, 1967), pp. vi, 19, ix. Also see Bailyn's *The Origins of American Politics* (New York, 1968), and his "Central Themes of the American Revolution: An Interpretation," in Stephen G. Kurtz and James H. Hutson, eds., *Essays on the American Revolution* (Chapel Hill, 1973), pp. 3–31. Other notable neo-Whig studies include Pauline Maier, *From Resistance to Revolution: Colonial Radicals and the Development of American Opposition to Britain, 1765–1776* (New York, 1972); Edmund S. Morgan and Helen M. Morgan, *The Stamp Act Crisis: Prologue to Revolution* (Chapel Hill, 1953); Edmund S. Morgan, *The Birth of the Republic, 1763–1789* (Chicago, 1956); Thad W. Tate, "The Coming of the Revolution in Virginia: Britain's Challenge to Virginia's Ruling Class, 1763–1776," *William and Mary Quarterly,* 19 (July 1962): 323–43; Gordon S. Wood, *The Creation of the American Republic, 1776–1787* (Chapel Hill, 1969). For more detailed reviews of the propaganda studies and the neo-Whig studies consult Gordon S. Wood, "Rhetoric and Reality in the American Revolution," *William and Mary Quarterly,* 23 (Jan. 1966): 7–24; Jack P. Greene, ed., *The Reinterpretation of the American Revolution, 1763–1789* (New York, 1968), pp. 8–45.

10. Jack P. Greene, "The Social Origins of the American Revolution: An Evaluation and Interpretation," *Political Science Quarterly,* 88 (March 1973): 20. Cf. Joseph Ernst, "Ideology and the Political Economy of Revolution," *Canadian Review of American Studies,* 4 (Fall 1973): 146; J. E. Crowley, *This Sheba, Self: The Conceptualization of Economic Life in Eighteenth-Century America* (Baltimore, 1974), p. 9.

11. Donald Bryant, "Rhetoric: Its Function and Its Scope," *Quarterly*

*Journal of Speech,* 39 (Dec. 1953): 413; Kenneth Burke, *A Rhetoric of Motives* (New York, 1950), p. 41. The many useful treatments of traditional conceptions of rhetoric include Charles Sears Baldwin, *Ancient Rhetoric and Poetic* (New York, 1924); Charles Sears Baldwin, *Medieval Rhetoric and Poetic* (New York, 1928); Burke, *Rhetoric of Motives,* pp. 49–180; Edward P. J. Corbett, *Classical Rhetoric for the Modern Student* (New York, 1971), pp. 594–630; Wilbur S. Howell, *Eighteenth–Century British Logic and Rhetoric* (Princeton, 1971); George P. Kennedy, *The Art of Persuasion in Greece* (Princeton, 1963); George P. Kennedy, *The Art of Rhetoric in the Roman World* (Princeton, 1972); James J. Murphy, *Rhetoric in the Middle Ages: A History of Rhetorical Theory from St. Augustine to the Renaissance* (Berkeley, 1974). On the theory and practice of rhetoric in colonial America see Warren Guthrie, "Rhetorical Theory in Colonial America," in Karl R. Wallace, ed., *History of Speech Education in America* (New York, 1954), pp. 48–59; George V. Bohman, "The Colonial Period," and Ota Thomas, "The Teaching of Rhetoric in the United States during the Classical Period of Education," in William N. Brigance and Marie K. Hochmuth, eds., *A History and Criticism of American Public Address* (New York, 1943–55), 1: 3–54, 193–210.

12. This aspect of the Revolution has been stressed most persistently and most succinctly by Merrill Jensen. See his *Articles of Confederation: An Interpretation of the Social–Constitutional History of the American Revolution, 1774–1781* (Madison, 1940); *The Founding of a Nation: A History of the American Revolution, 1763–1776* (New York, 1968); "The American People and the American Revolution," *Journal of American History,* 57 (June 1970): 5–35; "The Articles of Confederation," in *Fundamental Testaments of the American Revolution* (Washington, D.C., 1973), pp. 75–106.

13. Carl Bridenbaugh, *Cities in Revolt: Urban Life in America, 1743–1776* (New York, 1955), p. 425; Benjamin Rush to Noah Webster, 13 Feb. 1788, in L. H. Butterfield, ed., *Letters of Benjamin Rush* (Princeton, 1951), 1: 450; Carl Bridenbaugh and Jessica Bridenbaugh, *Rebels and Gentlemen: Philadelphia in the Age of Franklin* (London, 1942), p. 367. Also see Marc Egnal and Joseph A. Ernst, "An Economic Interpretation of the American Revolution," *William and Mary Quarterly,* 29 (Jan. 1972): 30; J. Paul Selsam, *The Pennsylvania Constitution of 1776: A Study in Revolutionary Democracy* (Philadelphia, 1936), p. 256; Lawrence H. Gipson, *The British Empire before the American Revolution* (New York, 1936–70), 13: 195.

14. Bridenbaugh and Bridenbaugh, *Rebels and Gentlemen,* p. x.

15. Lloyd F. Bitzer, "The Rhetorical Situation," *Philosophy and Rhetoric,* 1 (Jan. 1968): 3–4.

16. For full discussion of the issues broached in this and the preceding paragraph see Chapter 3.

17. Charles W. Lomas, ed., *The Agitator in American Society* (Englewood Cliffs, 1968), p. 8; letter from a gentleman of Philadelphia to a member of the British Parliament, 26 Dec. 1774, in Peter Force, ed., *American Archives,* 4th ser. (Washington, D.C., 1837–46), 1: 1067; [John Adams], "Novanglus," in *Novanglus and Massachusettensis,* pp. 11–12.

18. Crane Brinton, *Anatomy of Revolution* (New York, 1938); Harry Eckstein, "On the Etiology of Internal War," *History and Theory,* 4 (1965): 133–63; Lyford P. Edwards, *The Natural History of Revolution* (Chicago, 1927); Louis Gottschalk, "Causes of Revolution," *American Journal of Sociology,* 50 (July 1944): 1–8; Ted R. Gurr, *Why Men Rebel* (Princeton, 1970); Mark N. Hagopian, *The Phenomenon of Revolution* (New York, 1974); Rex D. Hopper, "The Revolutionary Process," *Social Forces,* 28 (March 1950): 270–79; Chalmers Johnson, *Revolutionary Change* (Boston, 1966); George S. Pettee, *The Process of Revolution* (New York, 1938).

19. It is worth noting in this connection that although I emphasize the role of ideology in the coming of the Revolution, and although my treatment of the political ideas of Philadelphia Whigs inevitably retraces some of the ground covered by existing treatments of Whig ideology, it is not my aim to forward strictly a neo-Whig interpretation of the Revolution. There is no doubt that ideology was important to the onset of revolutionary struggle in the 1760s and 1770s; revolutionary movements are invariably integrated and energized by a powerful set of shared beliefs about the way the world is and the way it ought to be. The question is not whether American revolutionaries were motivated by ideology (they were), but why some colonists came to hold and act upon a certain ideology regarding America and its relationship with England. I do not pretend to answer that question in full here, for it can only be answered by comprehensive analysis of the multitude of economic, political, social, religious, personal, environmental, rhetorical, and other forces whose interaction shaped the ideas and actions of those colonists who supported revolution. My goal is to explain how the public discourse of Whig writers and speakers contributed to the development of revolutionary beliefs and behaviors in colonial Philadelphia.

20. The concept of social movement is not a creation of the twentieth century. The English word "movement" derives from the medieval Latin *movimentum,* and from the old French verb *movoir,* which means to move, stir, or impel. There are currently two competing academic uses of the term. One is the use of "movement" by historians to designate broad historical movements, trends, drifts, or currents. The other is the appropriation of the term by social scientists to designate, not vast transformations in thought or social relations, but specific "social movements" which take place "when a fairly large number of people band together in order to alter or supplant some portion of the existing culture or social order." I am using the term in the latter sense, but I would hasten to add that particular social and political movements are usually "artificially deliniated stage[s] in a process" of broad historical movement. See Paul Wilkinson, *Social Movement* (New York, 1971), p. 11; Wm. Bruce Cameron, *Modern Social Movements* (New York, 1966), p. 7; Roger W. Brown, "Mass Phenomena," in Gardner Lindzey, ed., *Handbook of Social Psychology* (Reading, 1959), 2:871. Cf. Herbert Blumer, "Collective Behavior," in Joseph B. Gittler, ed., *Review of Sociology: Analysis of a Decade* (New York, 1957), pp. 145–46; Lewis M. Killian,

"Social Movements," in Robert E. Faris, ed., *Handbook of Modern Sociology* (Chicago, 1964), pp. 430–31; Stanley Milgram and Hans Toch, "Collective Behavior: Crowds and Social Movements," in Gardner Lindzey and Elliot Aronson, eds., *Handbook of Social Psychology*, 2d ed. (Reading, 1968–69), 4:585; Michael C. McGee, "Observations on the Theory of 'Movement' " (paper presented at Speech Communication Association annual convention, Houston, 1975).

21. Cameron, *Modern Social Movements,* p. 8.

22. Leland M. Griffin, "The Rhetoric of Historical Movements," *Quarterly Journal of Speech,* 38 (April 1952): 184–88; John Bowers and Donovan Ochs, *The Rhetoric of Agitation and Control* (Reading, 1971); Bruce E. Gronbeck, "The Rhetoric of Social-Institutional Change: Black Action at Michigan," in G. P. Mohrmann et al., eds., *Explorations in Rhetorical Criticism* (University Park, 1973), pp. 96–123. It should be added, however, that few studies deal exactingly with the temporally emergent nature of movement discourse.

23. Griffin, "Rhetoric of Historical Movements"; Leland M. Griffin, "A Dramatistic Theory of the Rhetoric of Movements," in William H. Rueckert, ed., *Critical Responses to Kenneth Burke* (Minneapolis, 1969), pp. 456–78; Paul D. Brandes, *The Rhetoric of Revolt* (Englewood Cliffs, 1971), pp. 1–14.

24. Thomas R. Adams, *American Independence, the Growth of an Idea: A Bibliographical Study of the American Political Pamphlets Printed between 1764 and 1776 Dealing with the Dispute between Great Britain and Her Colonies* (Providence, 1965).

CHAPTER 1.
## THE CITY AND ITS PEOPLE

1. N. D. Mereness, ed., *Travels in the American Colonies* (New York, 1916), pp. 410–11, quoted in Whitfield J. Bell, Jr., "Some Aspects of the Social History of Pennsylvania, 1760–1790," *Pennsylvania Magazine of History and Biography,* 62 (July 1938): 283. Estimates place Philadelphia's population during the revolutionary era at anywhere from 18,000 to 40,000 residents. I have accepted the calculations of John K. Alexander, "The Philadelphia Numbers Game: An Analysis of Philadelphia's Eighteenth-Century Population," ibid., 98 (July 1974): 314–24.

2. By "politically relevant" I mean to designate those Philadelphians who were able to participate meaningfully in political affairs. This category excludes women, children, slaves, indentured servants, and others who could not meet Pennsylvania's naturalization and property requirements for voting. The number of politically relevant Philadelphians was greater, however, than the number of those who comprised its legal electorate because electoral requirements were often circumvented or ignored. See [Thomas Paine], "A Serious Address to the People of Pennsylvania on the Present Situation of Their Affairs," 5 Dec. 1778, in Philip S. Foner, ed., *The Complete Writings of Thomas Paine* (New York, 1945), 2: 287–88. The major segments of Philadelphia's politically relevant population are discussed later in this chapter.

3. There were two major German-language papers in Philadelphia—Christopher Sauer's *Pennsylvanische Berichte* and Henry Miller's *Pennsylvanischer Staatsbote*. For details see John J. Stoudt, "The German Press in Pennsylvania and the American Revolution," *Pennsylvania Magazine of History and Biography*, 59 (1935): 74–90.

4. Major sources for the profiles of newspapers and publishers presented in this and the following paragraph are Dwight L. Teeter, "A Legacy of Expression: Philadelphia Newspapers and Congress during the War for Independence, 1775–1783" (Ph.D. diss., University of Wisconsin, 1966), chaps. 1–2; John T. Scharf and Thompson Westcott, *History of Philadelphia, 1609–1884* (Philadelphia, 1884), 3: 1958–74; Clarence S. Brigham, *History and Bibliography of American Newspapers, 1690–1820* (Worcester, 1947), 2:929–44, 953; Stephen Botein, " 'Meer Mechanics' and an Open Press: The Business and Political Strategies of Colonial American Printers," *Perspectives in American History*, 9 (1975): 127–225. For more detailed information on David Hall see Robert H. Kany, "David Hall: Printing Partner of Benjamin Franklin" (Ph.D. diss., Pennsylvania State University, 1963); on William Bradford see the discussion in Chapter 3 below; on William Goddard see [William Goddard], *The Partnership: or, The History of the Rise and Progress of the Pennsylvania Chronicle . . .* (Philadelphia, 1770), and Ward L. Miner, *William Goddard: Newspaperman* (Durham, 1962).

5. Lawrence W. Murphy, "John Dunlap's *Packet* and Its Competitors," *Journalism Quarterly*, 28 (Winter 1951): 58–62; Dwight L. Teeter, "Benjamin Towne: The Precarious Career of a Persistent Printer," *Pennsylvania Magazine of History and Biography*, 89 (July 1965): 316–30; Ralph A. Brown, *"The Pennsylvania Ledger:* Tory News Sheet," *Pennsylvania History*, 9 (July 1942): 161–75.

6. Arthur M. Schlesinger, *Prelude to Independence: The Newspaper War on Britain, 1764–1776* (New York, 1957), pp. 54, 58–60, 303–4; Philip Davidson, *Propaganda and the American Revolution, 1763–1783* (Chapel Hill, 1941), pp. 225–26, 235; *Statistical Abstract of the United States, 1974* (Washington, D.C., 1974), p. 509.

7. Moses Coit Tyler, *The Literary History of the American Revolution, 1763–1783* (1897; reprint ed., New York, 1957), 1: 18; Davidson, *Propaganda*, pp. 242–45.

8. Benjamin Franklin to William Strahan, quoted in Vernor W. Crane, *Benjamin Franklin's Letters to the Press, 1758–1775* (Chapel Hill, 1950), p. xxxii.

9. Galloway to Benjamin Franklin, 13 Jan. 1766, in Leonard W. Labaree et al., eds., *The Papers of Benjamin Franklin* (New Haven, 1959–   ), 13: 36; Holt to Adams, 29 Jan. 1776, quoted in Schlesinger, *Prelude to Independence*, p. 284; Franklin to Richard Price, 13 June 1782, in Albert H. Smyth, ed., *The Writings of Benjamin Franklin* (New York, 1907), 8: 457; [William Smith], "The Anatomist," *Journal*, 12 Jan. 1769; [John Witherspoon], "Aristides," *Packet*, 13 May 1776. For Smith's and Witherspoon's pseudonyms see Schlesinger, *Prelude to Independence*, pp. 123, 253.

10. Tyler, *Literary History*, 1: 17; "Conversation between Cato and

Plain Truth," *Packet,* 25 March 1776; Bernard Bailyn, *The Ideological Origins of the American Revolution* (Cambridge, 1967), p. 3.

11. Davidson, *Propaganda,* pp. 209–10. Also see Homer L. Calkin, "Pamphlets and Public Opinion during the American Revolution," *Pennsylvania Magazine of History and Biography,* 64 (Jan. 1940): 22–42.

12. Schlesinger, *Prelude to Independence,* p. 44; Davidson, *Propaganda,* p. 218.

13. Carl Bridenbaugh and Jessica Bridenbaugh, *Rebels and Gentlemen: Philadelphia in the Age of Franklin* (London, 1942), p. 72; Daniel Boorstin, *The Americans: The Colonial Experience* (New York, 1958), p. 308.

14. Librarian's report in Carl Bridenbaugh, *Cities in Revolt: Urban Life in America, 1743–1776* (New York, 1955), p. 383; Duché quoted in Bridenbaugh and Bridenbaugh, *Rebels and Gentlemen,* p. 99. In addition, see H. Trevor Colbourn, *The Lamp of Experience: Whig History and the Intellectual Origins of the American Revolution* (Chapel Hill, 1965), pp. 14–15; Bridenbaugh and Bridenbaugh, *Rebels and Gentlemen,* pp. 86–99; E. V. Lamberton, "Colonial Libraries of Pennsylvania," *Pennsylvania Magazine of History and Biography,* 42 (1918): 192–234. We do not know the exact literacy rate in colonial Philadelphia, but it probably compared favorably with that in New England, where more than 80 percent of the population was literate by 1760. See Kenneth A. Lockridge, *Literacy in Colonial New England: An Enquiry into the Social Context of Literacy in the Early Modern West* (New York, 1974).

15. William Tennent, *An Address Occasioned by the Late Invasion of the Liberties of the American Colonies* . . . (Philadelphia, 1774), p. 6; William Smith to Secretary of the Propagation Society, 10 July 1775, in Horace W. Smith, ed., *Life and Correspondence of the Rev. William Smith* (Philadelphia, 1879), 1: 528; Edgar L. Pennington, "The Anglican Clergy of Pennsylvania in the American Revolution," *Pennsylvania Magazine of History and Biography,* 63 (Oct. 1939): 401–29. For the ways the Philadelphia clergy mixed religion and politics in their rhetoric after the outbreak of war in New England see John Carmichael, *A Self-Defensive War Lawful, Proved in a Sermon* . . . (Philadelphia, 1775); Jacob Duché, *The Duty of Standing Fast in Our Spiritual and Temporal Liberties, a Sermon Preached in Christ Church* . . . (Philadelphia, 1775); William Foster, *True Fortitude Deliniated. A Sermon Preached* . . . *to Captain Taylor's Company* . . . (Philadelphia, 1776); David Jones, *Defensive War in a Just Cause Sinless. A Sermon, Preached on the Day of the Continental Fast* . . . (Philadelphia, 1775); Joseph Montgomery, *A Sermon, Preached at Christiana Bridge and Newcastle* . . . (Philadelphia, 1775); William Smith. *A Sermon on the Present State of American Affairs* . . . (Philadelphia, 1775); William Smith, *An Oration in Memory of General Montgomery* . . . (Philadelphia, 1776).

16. Sam Bass Warner, Jr., *The Private City: Philadelphia in Three Periods of Its Growth* (Philadelphia, 1968), pp. 14–19; Allen F. Davis and Mark H. Haller, eds., *The Peoples of Philadelphia: A History of Ethnic Groups and Lower-Class Life, 1790–1940* (Philadelphia, 1973), p. 6. The frequency and rapidity with which rumors swept through the city is

evident from the letter from an unidentified Philadelphian to a friend
in London, 1 Aug. 1775, in Peter Force, ed., *American Archives*, 4th ser.
(Washington, D.C., 1836–47), 3: 3–4; and from several entries in James
Duane, Jr., ed., *Extracts from the Diary of Christopher Marshall, 1774–1781*
(Albany, 1877).

17. Warner, *Private City*, pp. 19–21; Richard C. Graham, "The
Taverns of Colonial Philadelphia," *Transactions of the American Philosophical Society*, 43 (March 1953): 318–25; Bridenbaugh, *Cities in Revolt*,
p. 358.

18. According to the most authoritative study of colonial electoral
practices, about 75 percent of adult taxable males in Philadelphia could
vote (Chilton Williamson, *American Suffrage: From Property to Democracy,
1760–1800* [Princeton, 1960], pp. 33–34). For an interesting picture of
the manner in which elections were conducted see Joan Leonard, "Elections in Colonial Pennsylvania," *William and Mary Quarterly*, 11 (July
1954): 385–401.

19. William S. Hanna, *Benjamin Franklin and Pennsylvania Politics*
(Stanford, 1964), chap. 1 and *passim;* James H. Hutson, *Pennsylvania
Politics, 1746–1770: The Movement for Royal Government and Its Conse-
quences* (Princeton, 1972), pp. 130–32, 148–51, and *passim;* Theodore
Thayer, "The Quaker Party of Pennsylvania, 1755–1765," *Pennsylvania
Magazine of History and Biography*, 71 (Jan. 1947): 19–43; G. B. Warden,
"The Proprietary Group in Pennsylvania, 1754–1764," *William and
Mary Quarterly*, 21 (July 1964): 367–89. The Quaker and Proprietary
factions were joined after 1765 by what Professor Hutson has identified
as the Presbyterian party, which provided much of the impetus behind
organized opposition to England in the city from 1767 on.

20. J. R. Pole, "Historians and the Problem of Early American
Democracy," *American Historical Review*, 67 (April 1962): 626–46;
Charles S. Sydnor, *Gentlemen Freeholders: Political Practices in Wash-
ington's Virginia* (Chapel Hill, 1952); Richard Buel, Jr., "Democracy and
the American Revolution: A Frame of Reference," *William and Mary
Quarterly*, 21 (April 1964): 165–90; James K. Martin, *Men in Rebellion:
Higher Governmental Leaders and the Coming of the American Revolution*
(New Brunswick, 1973), chap. 1. But cf. Gary B. Nash, "The
Transformation of Urban Politics, 1700–1765," *Journal of American His-
tory*, 60 (Dec. 1973): 605–32; John B. Kirby, "Early American Politics—
The Search for Ideology: An Historiographical Analysis and Critique
of the Concept of 'Deference,' " *Journal of Politics*, 32 (Nov. 1970): 808–
38.

21. Cf. the comment of an unidentified correspondent, in *Evening
Post*, 30 July 1776: "Although it be granted on all hands, that all power
originates from the people; yet it is plain that in those colonies where
the government has, from the beginning, been in the hands of a very
few rich men, the ideas of government, both in the minds of those rich
men and of the common people, are rather aristocratical rather than
popular. The rich, having been used to govern, seem to think it is their
right; and the poorer commonality, having hitherto had little or no

hand in government, seem to think it does not belong to them to have any."

The city of Philadelphia was governed, technically, by its Municipal Corporation. But by the 1760s, the growth of the city and the increasing complexity of urban life had rendered the corporation virtually useless. In fact Philadelphia was run by the Pennsylvania Assembly and by a number of ad hoc commissions. See Judith M. Diamondstone, "Philadelphia's Municipal Corporation, 1701–1776," *Pennsylvania Magazine of History and Biography*, 90 (April 1966): 183–201; Scharf and Westcott, *History of Philadelphia*, 3: 1703–69.

22. Thomson to William Henry Drayton, n.d., in "The Papers of Charles Thomson," *Collections of the New York Historical Society*, 11 (1878): 281; "A Son of Liberty," *Chronicle*, 1 Aug. 1768; Philip Padelford, ed., *Colonial Panorama—1775: Dr. Robert Honyman's Journal for March and April* (San Marino, 1939), p. 29, quoted in David Hawke, *In the Midst of a Revolution* (Philadelphia, 1961), p. 17.

23. To Ebenezer Hazard, 2 Aug. 1764, in L. H. Butterfield, ed., *Letters of Benjamin Rush* (Princeton, 1951), 1:7. As "Salus Populi" explained in the *Journal*, 6 March 1776, "We have no [religious] establishment in this province, and consequently little distinction of sects, all men living in good neighborhoods with one another, however different in religious sentiments." The process of secularization in Philadelphia is discussed with considerable insight by Dietmar Rothermund, *The Layman's Progress: Religious and Political Experience in Colonial Pennsylvania, 1740–1770* (Philadelphia, 1961), pp. 57–68.

24. Cf. R. A. Ryerson, "Political Mobilization and the American Revolution: The Resistance Movement in Philadelphia, 1765 to 1776," *William and Mary Quarterly*, 31 (Oct. 1974): 578–81; Wayne L. Bockelman and Owen S. Ireland, "The Internal Revolution in Pennsylvania: An Ethnic–Religious Interpretation," *Pennsylvania History*, 41 (April 1974): 125–60; Hutson, *Pennsylvania Politics*, pp. 207–15, 238–43; Theodore Thayer, *Pennsylvania Politics and the Growth of Democracy, 1740–1776* (Harrisburg, 1954), pp. 134–37, 184–85. Also consult, in general, Alan Heimert, *Religion and the American Mind, from the Great Awakening to the Revolution* (Cambridge, 1966), chaps. 5–10.

25. Reynell quoted in Richard Bauman, *For the Reputation of Truth: Politics, Religion, and Conflict among the Pennsylvania Quakers, 1750–1800* (Baltimore, 1971), pp. 115–16. Similarly, see Thomas Wharton to Benjamin Franklin, 26 April 1766, in Labaree et al., *Papers of Franklin*, 13: 250–51; Thomas Wharton to Samuel Wharton, 31 Jan. 1775, in *Pennsylvania Magazine of History and Biography*, 34 (1910): 41–42; "Candidus," *Evening Post*, 3 Feb. 1776.

26. Benjamin Rush, *Autobiography*, ed. George W. Corner (Princeton, 1948), p. 79; Alexander Mackraby to Sir Philip Francis, 15 June [1768], in *Pennsylvania Magazine of History and Biography*, 11 (1887): 284.

27. "X.," *Journal*, 7 April 1768; "N," ibid., 31 March 1768; "An American Churchman," ibid., 21 April 1768; [William Smith], "The Anatomist," ibid., 29 Sept. 1768. For Smith's pseudonym see Schle-

singer, *Prelude to Independence,* p. 123; and see Carl Bridenbaugh, *Mitre and Sceptre: Transatlantic Faiths, Ideas, Persons, and Politics, 1689–1775* (New York, 1962), chaps. 7–12, for the standard secondary treatment of the colonial debate over an American bishopric during the pre-revolutionary decade.

28. John R. Young, *Memorial History of the City of Philadelphia* (New York, 1895–98), 1: 305–6; Herman L. Collins, *Philadelphia: A Story of Progress* (New York, 1941), 1: 54; Thayer, *Pennsylvania Politics,* pp. 111–12; Joseph A. Ernst, *Money and Politics in America, 1755–1775: A Study in the Currency Act of 1764 and the Political Economy of Revolution* (Chapel Hill, 1973), pp. 94–95; Charles H. Lincoln, *The Revolutionary Movement in Pennsylvania, 1760–1776* (Philadelphia, 1901), p. 141.

29. Reed to Earl of Dartmouth, 25 Sept. 1774, in William B. Reed, ed., *Life and Correspondence of Joseph Reed* (Philadelphia, 1847), 1: 77; Thomson to Benjamin Franklin, [24 Sept. 1765], in Labaree et al., *Papers of Franklin,* 12: 279. Also see Chapter 5 below. There is not a shred of evidence to indicate that Philadelphia conforms to Bernhard Knollenberg's assertion that by 1765 "the colonists had been brought to the brink of rebellion" (*Origin of the American Revolution* [New York, 1960], p. 11).

30. Jack P. Greene, "An Uneasy Connection: An Analysis of the Preconditions of the American Revolution," in Stephen G. Kurtz and James H. Hutson, eds., *Essays on the American Revolution* (Chapel Hill, 1973), pp. 53–61.

31. Hutson, *Pennsylvania Politics,* chap. 3.

32. Bridenbaugh and Bridenbaugh, *Rebels and Gentlemen,* pp. 16–18; Robert Proud, *The History of Pennsylvania* (Philadelphia, 1797–98), 2: 339. The standard treatment of the reorientation of Quaker values in the eighteenth century is Frederick B. Tolles, *Meeting House and Counting House: The Quaker Merchants of Colonial Pennsylvania, 1682–1763* (Chapel Hill, 1948).

33. See Joseph Reed to Earl of Dartmouth, 27 Dec. 1773 and 10 Dec. 1774, in Reed, *Life and Correspondence,* 1: 55, 88. The Quakers' economic strength is suggested by the fact that although Friends constituted one-seventh of the population in 1769, they comprised more than one-half of those Philadelphians who paid taxes in excess of £100. Of the seventeen wealthiest men in the city, twelve had been raised as Quakers (James A. Henretta, *The Evolution of American Society, 1700–1815: An Interdisciplinary Analysis* [Lexington, 1973], p. 102). Quaker political influence was particularly strong upon Philadelphia's German population, as Charles Thomson explained to William Henry Drayton, n.d., in "Papers of Charles Thomson," p. 281.

34. Bauman, *For the Reputation of Truth,* chap. 4 and *passim.*

35. Allen to Thomas Penn, 12 Oct. 1768, quoted in Arthur L. Jensen, *The Maritime Commerce of Colonial Philadelphia* (Madison, 1963), p. 178; Bauman, *For the Reputation of Truth,* pp. 130–35.

36. "Hendrick," *Journal,* 5 Jan. 1774; Charles Thomson to William Henry Drayton, n.d., in "Papers of Charles Thomson," p. 275; Isaac Sharpless, "The Quakers in the American Revolution," in Rufus Jones,

ed., *The Quakers in the American Colonies* (New York, 1966), p. 565. Also
see the discussion in Chapter 6 below. For useful contrasting views of
Quaker attitudes and their historical antecedents in Pennsylvania cf.
Ralph L. Ketcham, "Conscience, War, and Politics in Pennsylvania,
1755–1757," *William and Mary Quarterly*, 20 (July 1963): 416–40; Edwin
B. Bronner, "The Quakers and Non–Violence in Pennsylvania,"
*Pennsylvania History*, 35 (Jan. 1968): 1–22.

37. British visitor quoted in Bell, "Some Aspects of the Social History
of Pennsylvania," p. 285; shipping data in Jensen, *Maritime Commerce*, p.
5.

38. Jensen, *Maritime Commerce*, pp. 11, 89, 104–6, 218; Jackson
Turner Main, *The Social Structure of Revolutionary America* (Princeton,
1965), pp. 85–90, 137–39, 192–93. For enlightening discussions of the
business world of late colonial America, which was quite different from
the business world of today, see Jensen, *Maritime Commerce*, chaps. 1–8;
Robert A. East, *Business Enterprise in the American Revolutionary Era* (New
York, 1938), chap. 1; Harry D. Berg, "The Organization of Business in
Colonial Philadelphia," *Pennsylvania History*, 10 (July 1943): 157–77;
William S. Sachs, "The Business Outlook in the Northern Colonies,
1750–1775" (Ph.D. diss., Columbia University, 1957), pp. 22–27.

39. These episodes will be treated fully in Chapter 2. The point to
note here is that there was no monolithic unity among merchants on the
boycott and allied issues.

40. Charles Thomson to William Henry Drayton, n.d., in "Papers of
Charles Thomson," p. 279; Ryerson, "Political Mobilization," pp. 575–
77; Robert Gough, "Notes on the Pennsylvania Revolutionaries of
1776," *Pennsylvania Magazine of History and Biography*, 96 (Jan. 1972):
97; Robert F. Oaks, "Philadelphia Merchants and the American Revolution, 1765–1776" (Ph.D. diss., University of Southern California, 1970),
pp. 205–12. But cf. the argument of Warner, *Private City*, p. 28, that
both camps of merchants possessed nearly equal amounts of wealth and
that any economic differentiation was generally one separating "new"
(revolutionary) from "old" (anti-revolutionary) wealth.

41. Alexander Graydon, *Memoirs of His Own Time. With Reminiscences
of the Men and Events of the Revolution* (Philadelphia, 1846), p. 122.

42. Charles S. Olton, "Philadelphia Artisans and the American Revo-
lution" (Ph.D. diss., University of California, Berkeley, 1967), chap. 1;
Main, *Social Structure*, pp. 74–83, 133, 174–75; Carl Bridenbaugh, *The
Colonial Craftsman* (Chicago, 1961); Staughton Lynd and Alfred Young,
"After Carl Becker: The Mechanics and New York City Politics, 1774–
1801," *Labor History*, 5 (Fall 1964): 215–24; Martha G. Fales, *Joseph
Richardson and Family, Philadelphia Silversmiths* (Middletown, 1974).
Bridenbaugh, *Cities in Revolt*, p. 283, states that artisans, shopkeepers,
tradesmen, and their families may have comprised up to two-thirds of
the population of northern cities in colonial America. My analysis of occupational data supplied in Jacob Price's "Economic Function and the
Growth of American Port Towns in the Eighteenth Century," *Perspectives in American History*, 8 (1974): 177–83, indicates that mechanics
made up almost exactly 50 percent of the tax-assessed males in

Philadelphia in 1774 (although the proportion of mechanics increases to almost 56 percent if one includes within the classification such occupations as innkeeper, tavernkeeper, milkman, and barber). The question of classification is not an idle one. Olton, for example, devotes considerable effort to distinguishing among "mechanics," "artisans," and "tradesmen," but he concludes that distinctions among the three were "probably not general" in colonial Philadelphia ("Philadelphia Artisans," p. 10).

43. Gottlieb Mittelberger, *Journey to Pennsylvania,* ed. and trans. Oscar Handlin and John Clive (1756; Cambridge, 1960), p. 48. The general prosperity of Philadelphia mechanics should not be taken to reflect an even distribution of wealth in the city. According to the published tax list for 1774, the uppermost 10 percent of the taxpayers owned 89 percent of the taxable property. In the same year, 10 percent of Philadelphia's free adult inhabitants controlled 54 percent of the city's wealth, while the lower 50 percent controlled only 7 percent of the wealth. See Warner, *Private City,* p. 9; Alice Hanson Jones, "Wealth Distribution in the American Middle Colonies . . . ," (paper presented at Organization of American Historians annual conference, New Orleans, 1971), cited in Henretta, *Evolution of American Society,* p. 106.

44. Inferior mechanics are also to be differentiated from indentured and hired servants, unskilled laborers, journeymen, sailors, and other propertyless groups who made up Philadelphia's lower class. Although lower-class citizens would become involved in revolutionary activities in 1775–76, before then they were generally of minor political consequence in Philadelphia. See Main, *Social Structure,* pp. 112–13, 235–36, 271–73; Henretta, *Evolution of American Society,* pp. 96–97; Bridenbaugh, *Cities in Revolt,* pp. 86–87; Charles S. Olton, "Philadelphia's Mechanics in the First Decade of Revolution, 1765–1775," *Journal of American History,* 59 (Sept. 1972): 314–15; Chessman A. Herrick, *White Servitude in Pennsylvania* (Philadelphia, 1926).

45. See the breakdown of Philadelphia churches provided by John F. Watson, *Annals of Philadelphia and Pennsylvania in the Olden Time* (Philadelphia, 1857), 2: 406.

46. Bridenbaugh, *Colonial Craftsman,* p. 165; Bridenbaugh, *Cities in Revolt,* pp. 147–48; Hutson, *Pennsylvania Politics,* pp. 130–31; James H. Hutson, "An Investigation of the Inarticulate: Philadelphia's White Oaks," *William and Mary Quarterly,* 28 (Jan. 1971): 24–25. But also see the critique of Hutson's essay by Jesse Lemisch and John K. Alexander, "The White Oaks, Jack Tar, and the Concept of the 'Inarticulate,' " *William and Mary Quarterly,* 29 (Jan. 1972): 109–34.

47. Olton, "Philadelphia's Mechanics," pp. 312, 316–17. On the degree to which the Pennsylvania Assembly regulated economic affairs see Jensen, *Maritime Commerce,* pp. 26–40.

48. "A Brother Chip," *Gazette,* 27 Sept. 1770.

49. Hutson, "White Oaks," pp. 18–21; Benjamin H. Newcomb, *Franklin and Galloway: A Political Partnership* (New Haven, 1972), pp. 117–19. It should be observed, however, that some members of the mob opposed by the White Oaks were likely mechanics themselves.

50. For other analyses of the election of 1765 see Benjamin H. Newcomb, "Effects of the Stamp Act on Colonial Pennsylvania Politics," *William and Mary Quarterly,* 23 (April 1966): 257–72; Hutson, *Pennsylvania Politics,* p. 203; Charles S. Olton, *Artisans for Independence: Philadelphia Mechanics and the American Revolution* (Syracuse, 1975), pp. 37–40. Also see the discussion in Chapter 3 below.

51. See Chapter 2 for full treatment of this point.

52. Olton, "Philadelphia Artisans," pp. 188–90.

53. See Chapter 8.

## PROLEGOMENON TO PART II

1. [John Dickinson], *Letters from a Farmer in Pennsylvania . . .* (Philadelphia, 1768), p. 16.

2. Benjamin Rush, *Autobiography,* ed. George W. Corner (Princeton, 1948), p. 119.

3. Ibid., pp. 109–10.

4. Background information on all these figures is provided in Allen Johnson and Dumas Malone, eds., *The Dictionary of American Biography* (New York, 1928–36), but only Carl Becker's essay on Franklin treats its subject in any depth. For more detail consult Carl Van Doren, *Benjamin Franklin* (New York, 1938); Vernor W. Crane, *Benjamin Franklin and a Rising People* (Boston, 1954); Paul W. Connor, *Poor Richard's Politics: Benjamin Franklin and His New American Order* (New York, 1965); John W. Wallace, *An Old Philadelphian, Colonel William Bradford* (Philadelphia, 1884); Charles P. Smith, *James Wilson, Founding Father: 1742–1798* (Chapel Hill, 1956); William B. Reed, ed., *Life and Correspondence of Joseph Reed* (Philadelphia, 1847); John F. Roche, *Joseph Reed: A Moderate in the American Revolution* (New York, 1957); Kenneth Rossman, *Thomas Mifflin and the Politics of the American Revolution* (Chapel Hill, 1952); G. S. Rowe, "Thomas McKean and the Coming of the Revolution," *Pennsylvania Magazine of History and Biography,* 96 (Jan. 1972): 3–47.

5. The best book-length study of Dickinson is David L. Jacobson, *John Dickinson and his political ideas* are H. Trevor Colbourn, *The Lamp of* from which the opening phrases of this paragraph are quoted. Charles J. Stillé, *The Life and Times of John Dickinson, 1732–1808* (Philadelphia, 1891), is a complete biography, but is marred by Stillé's tendency to overpraise his subject. Two especially perceptive short discussions of Dickinson and his political ideas are H. Trevour Colbourn, *The Lamp of Experience: Whig History and the Intellectual Origins of the American Revolution* (Chapel Hill, 1965), pp. 107–19; and Bernard Bailyn, ed., *Pamphlets of the American Revolution* (Cambridge, 1965– ), 1: 660–67. Many of Dickinson's important writings are collected in Paul L. Ford, ed., *The Writings of John Dickinson* (Philadelphia, 1895).

6. Edmund C. Burnett, "Charles Thomson," in Johnson and Malone, *Dictionary of American Biography,* 18: 481–82; Pauline Maier, *From Resistance to Revolution: Colonial Radicals and the Development of American Opposition to Britain, 1765–1776* (New York, 1972), pp. 221–22n.; John Zimmerman, "Charles Thomson: 'The Sam Adams of Philadelphia,' "

*Mississippi Valley Historical Review*, 45 (Dec. 1958): 464–80; John F. Watson, *Annals of Philadelphia and Pennsylvania in the Olden Time* (Philadelphia, 1857), 1: 567–73. Most of Thomson's identifiable writings are in "The Papers of Charles Thomson," *Collections of the New York Historical Society*, 11 (1878).

7. Joseph Reed to Earl of Dartmouth, 10 June 1774, in Reed, *Life and Correspondence*, 1: 69; Alexander Graydon, *Memoirs of His Own Time. With Reminiscences of the Men and Events of the Revolution* (Philadelphia, 1846), pp. 117, 135.

8. "A Whig," *Chronicle*, 2 April 1770; "Hendrick," *Journal*, 5 Jan. 1774; "Old Gabriel," ibid., 3 Jan. 1776; *Four Letters on Interesting Subjects* (Philadelphia, 1776), p. 3. There were also some Philadelphians who found the terms Whig and Tory confusing and loosely applied. "A Reasonable Whigess," in the *Evening Post* of 16 November 1775, declared herself "a warm friend to America" and added, with some consternation, "but my misfortune is that some times, whilst I am contending for what I think is true liberty, I am told that I am a Tory; and perhaps the next day, expressing the same sentiments, that I am an outrageous Whig."

9. Gordon S. Wood, "The Democratization of Mind in the American Revolution," in *Leadership in the American Revolution* (Washington, D.C., 1974), p. 67. For more extensive discussion of this aspect of Whig rhetoric see the Afterword, below.

## CHAPTER 2.
## THE ECONOMIC BASIS OF PROTEST

1. Cf. Lawrence H. Gipson, *The Coming of the Revolution, 1763–1775* (New York, 1954), p. 85; James C. Davies, "Toward a Theory of Revolution," *American Sociological Review*, 28 (Feb. 1962): 5–19; Ted R. Gurr, "Sources of Rebellion in Western Societies: Some Quantitative Evidence," *Annals of the American Academy of Political and Social Science*, 393 (Sept. 1970): 128–44, esp. 129; Lawrence Stone, "Theories of Revolution," *World Politics*, 18 (Jan. 1966): 159–76, esp. 173. On the importance of bringing psychological perspectives to bear upon economic activity see George Katona, *Psychological Analysis of Economic Behavior* (New York, 1951).

2. [John Dickinson], *The Late Regulations Respecting the British Colonies on the Continent of America . . .* (Philadelphia, 1765), pp. 19–22. For similar, though less extended, protests against the Stamp Act in Philadelphia see in *Journal*: "N.," 5 Sept. 1765; "A True American," 19 Sept. 1765; "B.W.," 24 Oct. 1765; "L.," 20 March 1766.

3. For economic conditions and attitudes in Philadelphia at the time of the Stamp Act see Pennsylvania Assembly resolves, in *Gazette*, 26 Sept. 1765; Charles Thomson to Cook, Lawrence, and Co., 9 Nov. 1765, in "The Papers of Charles Thomson," *Collections of the New York Historical Society*, 11 (1878): 7–12; Henry D. Biddle, ed., "Extracts from the Letter-Book of Samuel Rhoads, Jr., of Philadelphia," *Pennsylvania Magazine of History and Biography*, 14 (1890): 422–25; Benjamin Rush to

Ebenezer Hazard, 8 Nov. 1765, in L. H. Butterfield, ed., *Letters of Benjamin Rush* (Princeton, 1951), 1: 18; Joseph Galloway to Benjamin Franklin, 13 Jan. 1766, in Leonard W. Labaree et al., eds., *The Papers of Benjamin Franklin* (New Haven, 1959– ), 13: 36–37; David Hall to Benjamin Franklin, 14 Oct. 1765, in ibid., 12:321. The most detailed guides to economic conditions in Philadelphia during the revolutionary era are Anne Bezanson et al., *Prices in Colonial Pennsylvania* (Philadelphia, 1935); Anne Bezanson, *Prices and Inflation during the American Revolution: Pennsylvania, 1770–1790* (Philadelphia, 1951).

4. "Americanus," *Journal,* 29 Aug. 1765. For Galloway's authorship see Arthur M. Schlesinger, *Prelude to Independence: The Newspaper War on Britain, 1764–1776* (New York, 1958), p. 74.

5. [Charles Thomson], "Letter of a Merchant in Philadelphia to a Friend in London," *Journal,* 10 May 1770; "Letter from the Committee of the City of Philadelphia to the Committee of Boston," *Packet,* 6 June 1774. For Thomson's authorship see "Papers of Charles Thomson," pp. 21–25. In fact, the Townshend duties were not especially burdensome in and of themselves. Of the dutied items, only tea was an important article of trade in Philadelphia, and Townshend's legislation actually reduced the total tax on tea, though the remaining tax was now more visible. See Lawrence H. Gipson, *The British Empire before the American Revolution* (New York, 1936–70), 11: 111–12; John C. Miller, *Origins of the American Revolution,* rev. ed. (Stanford, 1952), p. 264; Benjamin W. Labaree, *The Boston Tea Party* (New York, 1964), pp. 20–21, 43.

6. "A Friend to Amity," *Ledger,* 25 Feb. 1775.

7. Newport letter, in *Journal,* 31 March 1768. For a full discussion of the *Letters from a Farmer* see Chapter 3 below.

8. "To the Merchants and Traders of the City of Philadelphia," 26 March 1768, in *Gazette,* 31 March 1768; [John Dickinson], "An Address Read at a Meeting of Merchants to Consider Non-Importation," April 1768, in Paul L. Ford, ed., *The Writings of John Dickinson* (Philadelphia, 1895), pp. 411–17. John J. Zimmerman, "Charles Thomson, 'The Sam Adams of Philadelphia,'" *Mississippi Valley Historical Review,* 45 (Dec. 1959): 472, attributes the speech of 26 March to Thomson. Arthur Jensen, *The Maritime Commerce of Colonial Philadelphia* (Madison, 1963), p. 173, attributes the same speech to Dickinson. Unfortunately, neither author presents evidence to support his conclusion. Internal evidence from the speech itself does not provide significant clues to assign it to either Dickinson or Thomson.

9. The best recent study of Galloway is Benjamin H. Newcomb, *Franklin and Galloway: A Political Partnership* (New Haven, 1972). For political alignments and party strategies in 1768 see James H. Hutson, *Pennsylvania Politics, 1746–1770: The Movement for Royal Government and Its Consequences* (Princeton, 1972), pp. 210–15, 219–33.

10. Major Whig essayists were [John Dickinson], "Letter from a Gentleman in Virginia to a Merchant in Philadelphia," in Ford, *Writings of Dickinson,* pp. 439–45; "A Freeborn American," *Gazette,* 12 May 1768; "Martinus Scriblerius," ibid., 21 July 1768; "C.," ibid., 4 Aug. 1768; "A.L.," *Chronicle,* 30 May 1768; "Cato," ibid., 12 Sept. 1768. Ford, *Writ-*

*ings of Dickinson,* p. 435, attributes "A Freeborn American" and "Martinus Scriblerius" to Thomson. The merchants were defended by "Pacificus" and "A.B.," *Chronicle,* 25 July 1768; "A Chester County Farmer," *Gazette,* 16 June. The pieces by "A.B." and "A Chester County Farmer" have generally been attributed to Galloway; but see Newcomb, *Franklin and Galloway,* pp. 193–94n.

11. Election results in *Chronicle,* 10 Oct. 1768; support of White Oaks in [William Goddard], *The Partnership: or, The History of the Rise and Progress of the Pennsylvania Chronicle . . .* (Philadelphia, 1770), p. 18; Galloway to Franklin, 17 Oct. 1768, in Labaree et al., *Papers of Franklin,* 15: 231. Newcomb, *Franklin and Galloway,* pp. 196–97, is the only previous writer to perceive the significance of the 1768 election to the nonimportation movement; our ultimate interpretations, however, differ widely.

12. "A Tradesman," *Chronicle,* 7 Dec. 1767; "Another Farmer," ibid., 28 Dec. 1767. Also see in ibid.: "A Citizen," 16 Nov. 1767; "Philo-Patriae," 2 Dec. 1767; "Pennsylvaniensis," 21 Dec. 1767; "Oeconomicus," 4 Jan. 1768; "A Lover of Pennsylvania," 11 Jan. 1768; "A Ploughman," 18 Jan. 1768; "O.," *Journal,* 3 Dec. 1767; untitled essay, in *Gazette,* 26 Nov. 1767. The Currency Act prohibited further issues of legal tender paper money in the colonies. Although the act had aroused a fair degree of resentment in Philadelphia in 1764, public complaints against it were subsumed in 1765 and early 1766 by the protest against the Stamp Act. After repeal of the stamp tax, criticisms of the restrictions on paper money reappeared and reached a crescendo early in 1768. For a comprehensive account of the Currency Act, its effects upon colonial economic affairs, and the movements for its repeal see Joseph A. Ernst, *Money and Politics in America, 1755–1775: A Study in the Currency Act of 1764 and the Political Economy of Revolution* (Chapel Hill, 1973).

13. David L. Jacobson, *John Dickinson and the Revolution in Pennsylvania, 1764–1776* (Berkeley, 1965), p. 45. For an analysis of economic conditions in Pennsylvania during 1767–69 see Ernst, *Money and Politics,* pp. 207–10; Bezanson, *Prices and Inflation,* p. 12; William S. Sachs, "The Business Outlook in the Northern Colonies, 1750–1775" (Ph.D. diss., Columbia University, 1957), pp. 199–208.

14. The only published effort I am aware of to unite the economic and political themes came in the speech delivered at the merchants' meeting of 26 March 1768 in which the speaker argued that a boycott would aid the economy by "inclining us to be more frugal, and affording our merchants time to collect their debts, and enabling them to discharge those they owe to the mother country" (*Gazette,* 31 March 1768). It is essential to note, however, that this appeal was directed to the merchants and not to the general citizenry.

15. Exempted from the boycott were twenty-two items used for local manufacturing, ship-ballast, and educational and medicinal purposes. Nonimportation was to continue until the Townshend duties were repealed or until a majority of the subscribers to the agreement voted to alter it. See Arthur M. Schlesinger, *The Colonial Merchants and the American Revolution, 1763–1776* (New York, 1919), pp. 129–30.

16. At the same time, many merchants, for reasons of their own, were coming to look more favorably upon the prospect of nonimportation. Whether they would actually have instituted a boycott if not pressured by the Whigs and their followers is problematic. Theodore Thayer, *Pennsylvania Politics and the Growth of Democracy, 1740–1776* (Harrisburg, 1953), pp. 141–45; Schlesinger, *Colonial Merchants,* pp. 125–30; Jensen, *Maritime Commerce,* pp. 171–80, all provide useful accounts of the 1768–69 debates over nonimportation, though their interpretations differ from that offered here.

17. "A Tradesman," *Chronicle,* 10 Oct. 1768. Similarly, see "Agricola," ibid., 28 Nov. 1768; "The Citizen," *Journal,* 26 Jan. 1769.

18. Carl Bridenbaugh, *Cities in Revolt: Urban Life in America, 1743–1776* (New York, 1955), p. 268; Thayer, *Pennsylvania Politics,* p. 149; James H. Hutson, "An Investigation of the Inarticulate: Philadelphia's White Oaks," *William and Mary Quarterly,* 28 (Jan. 1971): 22–23.

19. John Dickinson to Arthur Lee, 26 June 1769, in Richard Henry Lee, ed., *Life of Arthur Lee* (Boston, 1829): 2: 296.

20. "Amor Patriae," *Journal,* 26 July 1770; "A Pennsylvanian," *Gazette,* 23 Aug. 1770; "A Tradesman," broadside, 24 Sept. 1770 (Evans no. 11892); "A Lover of Liberty and a Mechanics' Friend," broadside, 31 May 1770 (Evans no. 11882).

21. On the extent to which Philadelphia mechanics supported continued nonimportation see Henry Drinker to Abel James, 26 May 1770, in *Pennsylvania Magazine of History and Biography,* 14 (1890): 45; Joseph Galloway to Benjamin Franklin, 21 June 1770, in Labaree et al., *Papers of Franklin,* 17: 177–78; Humphry Marshall to Benjamin Franklin, 28 May 1770, in ibid., p. 151; Thomas Gilpin to Benjamin Franklin, 8 June 1770, in ibid., p. 166.

22. For details see Jensen, *Maritime Commerce,* pp. 193–95.

23. Thayer, *Pennsylvania Politics,* p. 149; Hutson, "White Oaks," p. 23; Hutson, *Pennsylvania Politics,* pp. 235–36; Newcomb, *Franklin and Galloway,* pp. 216–19.

24. "A Brother Chip," *Gazette,* 27 Sept. 1770, complained that mechanics were never consulted by Quaker party leaders or elected to the Assembly, despite the fact that mechanics were the largest single interest group in Philadelphia and owned one-half of the property in the city.

25. According to Edward Burd, Galloway's downfall in the election "was principally owing" to Goddard's pamphlet: Edward Burd to Col. Burd, 4 Oct. 1770, in Thomas Balch, ed., *Letters and Papers Relating Chiefly to the Provincial History of Pennsylvania* (Philadelphia, 1855), p. 225. A clue to the impact of Goddard's pamphlet is that it went through three editions in less than four months.

26. This point is argued most convincingly by Charles S. Olton, "Philadelphia's Mechanics in the First Decade of Revolution, 1765–1775," *Journal of American History,* 59 (Sept. 1972): 320–23. Olton also suggests (pp. 319–20) that the desire of mechanics to promote the sale of home manufactures lay behind their support of nonimportation during the Stamp Act crisis. But since merchants too stood firmly behind

the boycott of 1765–66, there was no need for mechanics to break from the Quaker party at that time.

27. On the Whigs' cultivation of Philadelphia mechanics after 1770 see Hutson, *Pennsylvania Politics,* pp. 241–43. On the role of mechanics in the resistance movement from 1770 see Charles S. Olton, "Philadelphia Artisans and the American Revolution" (Ph.D. diss., University of California, Berkeley, 1967), pp. 167–204.

28. Schlesinger, *Colonial Merchants,* pp. 263–64; Labaree, *Boston Tea Party,* pp. 76–77.

29. On the extent of tea smuggling in Philadelphia see Joseph Reed to Earl of Dartmouth, 22 and 27 Dec. 1773, in William B. Reed, ed., *Life and Correspondence of Joseph Reed* (Philadelphia, 1847), 1: 52, 55–56; [John Drinker], *Observations on the Late Popular Measures . . .* (Philadelphia, 1774), pp. 8–11. Since many merchants were Quakers, whose religious scruples did not countenance smuggling, the contraband traffic in tea, while large and profitable, was confined to a small number of Philadelphia traders. See Jensen, *Maritime Commerce,* pp. 130–45, 196–99; Sachs, "Business Outlook," pp. 223–24.

30. "A Mechanic," *Gazette,* 8 Dec. 1773; "Cassius" and [Thomas Mifflin], "Scaevola," *Journal,* 13 Oct. 1773. For Mifflin's authorship see Benjamin Rush to William Gordon, 10 Oct. 1773, in Butterfield, *Letters of Rush,* 1: 82.

31. "A Mechanic," broadside, 4 Dec. 1773 (Evans no. 13041), reprinted in *Gazette,* 8 Dec. 1773.

32. "Rusticus," broadside, Nov. 1773, in Ford, *Writings of Dickinson,* pp. 459–60.

33. As Jensen, *Maritime Commerce,* p. 205, points out, Philadelphia merchants did not express strong apprehensions about monopoly in their private correspondence but stressed instead the unconstitutionality of taxing Americans without their consent. If merchants were highly distressed over the possible economic consequences of the Tea Act, it was likely because they resented the attempt of yet another British exporting house to increase its business by trading outside established channels, as is suggested by Marc Egnal and Joseph A. Ernst, "An Economic Interpretation of the American Revolution," *William and Mary Quarterly,* 29 (Jan. 1972): 24. For the importance of oriental goods to trade in Philadelphia see Joseph Reed to Earl of Dartmouth, 22 Dec. 1773, in Reed, *Life and Correspondence,* 1: 53.

34. Jensen, *Maritime Commerce,* p. 204.

35. Memorial presented to the Merchants' Committee, and "A.B.," *Chronicle,* 29 Jan. 1770; "A Mechanic," ibid., 16 April 1770. This animus was generally directed toward Philadelphia merchants who sought to corner the market on valued commodities, evidence that the fear of monopoly was general and not restricted to implications of the Tea Act.

36. *Journal,* 20 Oct. 1773.

37. "A Mechanic," *Gazette,* 8 Dec. 1773.

38. Alexander Mackraby to Sir Philip Francis, 2 Jan. 1770, in *Pennsylvania Magazine of History and Biography,* 11 (1887): 492; Henry Drinker

to Abel James, 29 April 1770, in ibid., 14 (1890): 42–43; Martha G. Fales, *Joseph Richardson and Family, Philadelphia Silversmiths* (Middletown, 1974), p. 43.

39. Philip Davidson, *Propaganda and the American Revolution, 1763–1783* (Chapel Hill, 1941), p. 103.

40. On the relative importance of what I have called first-order and second-order economic issues to the development of revolutionary movements in general see Gurr, "Sources of Rebellion," p. 133.

41. For example, Schlesinger, *Colonial Merchants;* Davidson, *Propaganda;* Charles A. Beard and Mary Beard, *The Rise of American Civilization* (New York, 1927); Louis Hacker, "The First American Revolution," *Columbia University Quarterly,* 27 (1935): 259–95.

42. Bernard Bailyn, *The Ideological Origins of the American Revolution* (Cambridge, 1967); Edmund S. Morgan, "The American Revolution Considered as an Intellectual Movement," in Arthur M. Schlesinger, Jr., and Morton White, eds., *Paths of American Thought* (Boston, 1963), pp. 11–33; Thad W. Tate, "The Coming of the Revolution in Virginia: Britain's Challenge to Virginia's Ruling Class, 1763–1776," *William and Mary Quarterly,* 19 (July 1962): 323–43; Clinton W. Rossiter, *The Political Thought of the American Revolution* (New York, 1963). For a succinct recent defense of this view of the Revolution see Bailyn's "The Central Themes of the American Revolution: An Interpretation," in Stephen G. Kurtz and James H. Hutson, eds., *Essays on the American Revolution* (Chapel Hill, 1973), pp. 3–31. Of course, these two schools of thought do not exhaust the manners in which historians have interpreted the Revolution. See Jack P. Greene, ed., *The Reinterpretation of the American Revolution, 1763–1789* (New York, 1968), pp. 2–74, for a useful review of varying scholarly perspectives on the Revolution.

43. "Americanus," *Journal,* 29 Aug. 1765.

44. *The Middle Line: or, An Attempt to Furnish Some Hints for Ending the Differences Subsisting between Great Britain and the Colonies* (Philadelphia, 1775), pp. 15–25; Isaac Hunt, *The Political Family: or, A Discourse Pointing out the Reciprocal Advantages Which Flow from an Uninterrupted Union between Great Britain and Her American Colonies . . .* (Philadelphia, 1775), pp. 10–14, 30–31; [Joseph Galloway], *A Candid Examination of the Mutual Claims of Great Britain and the Colonies . . .* (New York, 1775), p. 45.

45. Gipson, *Coming of the Revolution,* p. 75. But cf. Merrill Jensen, *The Founding of a Nation: A History of the American Revolution, 1763–1776* (New York, 1968), pp. 52–53.

46. [William Hicks], *The Nature and Extent of Parliamentary Power Considered . . .* (Philadelphia, 1768), p. 18; "A.B.," *Gazette,* 9 Jan. 1766.

47. [John Dickinson], *Letters from a Farmer in Pennsylvania . . .* (Philadelphia, 1768), pp. 40–42.

48. This point is discussed in Chapter 5.

49. "Colonus," *Journal,* 12 Sept. 1765; [James Wilson], *Considerations on the Nature and the Extent of the Legislative Authority of the British Parliament* (Philadelphia, 1774), p. 26; "John Hampden," *Gazette,* 23 Jan. 1766.

50. "N.," *Journal,* 5 Sept. 1765; John Carmichael, *A Self-Defensive War Lawful* . . . (Philadelphia, 1775), p. 32; Dickinson, *Late Regulations,* p. 29; "Eugenio," *Journal,* 15 Dec. 1773; "Colonus," ibid., 12 Sept. 1765.

51. [Richard Wells], *A Few Political Reflections, Submitted to the Consideration of the British Colonies* . . . (Philadelphia, 1774), p. 27. Or as another writer stated: "We should doubtless be liable to expedient impositions; but when and by whom they should be laid upon us, and what they should occasionally be, both in nature and degree, are the grand matters in debate" (*Some Observations of Consequence in Three Parts. Occasioned by the Stamp-Tax* . . . [Philadelphia, 1768], p. 18).

52. Dickinson, "An Address Read at a Meeting of Merchants to Consider Non-Importation," April 1768, in Ford, *Writings of Dickinson,* pp. 411–17. In light of what was said earlier about the lack of protest against the first-order economic consequences of the Townshend duties, it is instructive to note that the duties were not mentioned in this address as one of the merchants' principal economic grievances, though they were condemned as unconstitutional.

53. Hicks, *Nature and Extent,* p. 15; Dickinson, *Late Regulations,* pp. 12–13.

54. "L.," *Gazette,* 6 July 1769.

55. Liverpoole letter, in *Journal,* 24 May 1770; "Expositor," *Gazette,* 19 Jan. 1769. Vernor W. Crane, ed., *Benjamin Franklin's Letters to the Press, 1758–1775* (Chapel Hill, 1950), pp. 132–34, attributes the essay by "Expositor" to Franklin.

56. "A Mechanic," *Gazette,* 8 Dec. 1773; "The Citizen," *Journal,* 26 Jan. 1768; "A Countryman," *Packet,* 18 Oct. 1773; "Fillus Americani," *Gazette,* 1 Feb. 1770.

57. "Colonus," *Journal,* 12 Sept. 1765; London letter, in *Packet,* 3 Oct. 1774; "A Tradesman," *Chronicle,* 10 Oct. 1768. The Whigs' depictions of British luxury and corruption are discussed further in Chapter 5 below.

58. "John Hampden," *Gazette,* 23 Jan. 1766.

59. [John Dickinson], "To Friends and Countrymen," broadside, Nov. 1765, in Ford, *Writings of Dickinson,* p. 203; Dickinson, *Letters From a Farmer,* p. 55; Mifflin, "Scaevola," *Journal,* 13 Oct. 1773; untitled essay, in *Packet,* 13 June 1774.

60. London letter, in *Journal,* 5 July 1775. The Whigs' allegations of British conspiracy against America are discussed in Chapter 4 below.

61. Hicks, *Nature and Extent,* p. 27; "Observations on the Act of Parliament Commonly Called the Boston Port Bill," *Journal,* 6 July 1774. Also see Bailyn, *Ideological Origins,* pp. 55–62; Gordon S. Wood, *The Creation of the American Republic, 1776–1787* (Chapel Hill, 1969), pp. 18–28.

62. Dickinson, "Friends and Countrymen," broadside, Nov. 1765, in Ford, *Writings of Dickinson,* p. 203; Hicks, *Nature and Extent,* pp. 21, 27.

63. Edmund S. Morgan, "The American Revolution: Revisions in Need of Revising," *William and Mary Quarterly,* 14 (Jan. 1957): 11–12; Edmund S. Morgan, *Birth of the Republic, 1763–1789* (Chicago, 1956), pp. 16–17, 52–53, 95; J. E. Crowley, *This Shebā, Self: The Conceptualization of Economic Life in Eighteenth-Century America* (Baltimore, 1974), p.

156; Jack P. Greene, "An Uneasy Connection: An Analysis of the Pre-conditions of the American Revolution," in Kurtz and Hutson, *Essays,* pp. 56–61; Rossiter, *Political Thought,* pp. 111–13.

64. *An Essay upon Government, Adopted by the Americans . . .* (Philadelphia, 1775), p. 21.

65. See William Moore Smith, "On the Fall of Empires," *Packet,* 29 May 1775; letter from a committee of merchants in Philadelphia to merchants in London, in *Gazette,* 31 Aug. 1769; "To the Printer," ibid., 20 Feb. 1766; Dickinson, "An Address Read at a Meeting of Merchants to Consider Non-Importation," April 1768, in Ford, *Writings of Dickinson,* pp. 416–17; Dickinson, "To Friends and Countrymen," broadside, Nov. 1765, in ibid., p. 202; "Oeconomicus," *Chronicle,* 4 Jan. 1768.

66. "Philoleutherus," broadside, 21 Sept. 1765 (Evans no. 9942); "Free Swiss," *Evening Post,* 28 Oct. 1775; "A Friend to This Town and the Colony," *Journal,* 10 Dec. 1767.

67. Dickinson, "To Friends and Countrymen," broadside, Nov. 1765, in Ford, *Writings of Dickinson,* p. 202; "To the Printer," *Gazette,* 13 Feb. 1766; *Some Observations of Consequence,* p. 27.

68. Thomson, "Letter from a Merchant in Philadelphia to a Friend in London," *Journal,* 10 May 1770; [Benjamin Rush], "Hamden," *Packet,* 11 Oct. 1773; account of meeting at the State House, 20 July 1768, in *Chronicle,* 8 Aug. 1768. For Rush's pseudonym see his letter to William Gordon, 10 Oct. 1773, in Butterfield, *Letters of Rush,* 1: 82.

69. Dickinson, "An Address Read at a Meeting of Merchants to Consider Non-Importation," April 1768, in Ford, *Writings of Dickinson,* p. 416; Dickinson, *Letters from a Farmer,* p. 68.

70. Henry Drinker to Abel James, 9 Dec. 1769, in *Pennsylvania Magazine of History and Biography,* 14 (1890): 41.

71. "A Son of Liberty," *Journal,* 10 April 1766; [Benjamin Franklin], "F + S," *Chronicle,* 25 April 1768; speech at the State House, 30 July 1768, in *Chronicle,* 1 Aug. 1768. For Franklin's pseudonym see Crane, *Franklin's Letters to the Press,* pp. 106–7.

CHAPTER 3.

## THE CASE FOR AMERICAN RIGHTS

1. "American rights," and various other phrases connoting the same concept, served throughout 1765–75 as what Richard Weaver has called a "god term"—"that expression about which all other expressions are ranked as subordinate" and which, "if one can 'make it stick,' . . . will validate almost anything" (*The Ethics of Rhetoric* [Chicago, 1953], p. 212).

2. Pennsylvania Assembly resolves, 21 Sept. 1765, in *Gazette,* 26 Sept. 1765; Joseph Reed to Earl of Dartmouth, 4 April 1774, in William B. Reed, ed., *The Life and Correspondence of Joseph Reed* (Philadelphia, 1847), 1:57. The journalistic agitation over the vice-admiralty courts in 1774 can be followed in the essays by "Mentor," "Mercator," "Russel," and "Civis," *Journal,* January–April. Also see, in general, Carl Ub-belholde, *The Vice-Admiralty Courts and the American Revolution* (Chapel

Hill, 1960); David S. Lovejoy, " 'Rights Imply Equality': The Case Against Admiralty Jurisdiction in America, 1764–1776," *William and Mary Quarterly*, 16 (Oct. 1959): 459–84.

3. John Shy, *Toward Lexington: The Role of the British Army in the Coming of the American Revolution* (Princeton, 1965), pp. 250, 252–53, 391; John R. Young, *Memorial History of the City of Philadelphia* (New York, 1895–98), 1:341–42.

4. John Zubly, *The Law of Liberty, A Sermon on American Affairs* . . . (Philadelphia, 1775), p. v.

5. See James Tilghman to Henry Wilmot, 2 Oct. 1774, in *Pennsylvania Magazine of History and Biography*, 31 (1907):458–59; Thomas Wharton to Thomas Walpole, 2 May 1774, in ibid., 33 (1909): 329; and the numerous letters from Joseph Reed to Earl of Dartmouth, 1773–75, in Reed, *Life and Correspondence*, 1:51–98.

6. *Gazette*, 26 Sept. 1765.

7. The reliance upon virtual representation by apologists for the Stamp Act is well summarized by Edmund S. Morgan and Helen M. Morgan, *The Stamp Act Crisis: Prologue to Revolution*, rev. ed. (New York, 1962), pp. 105–9.

8. Daniel Dulany's *Considerations on the Propriety of Imposing Taxes in the British Colonies* . . . (Annapolis, 1765), the best known and most influential American response to the doctrine of virtual representation, was at best incidental to the growth of protest against the Stamp Act in Philadelphia. Although Dulany's pamphlet was printed in New York and Boston, it was not published in Philadelphia. Copies of the *Considerations* were available in the city by December 1765, but this was well after opposition to the Stamp Act had solidified. Bibliographic information on the *Considerations* is in Thomas R. Adams, *American Independence, the Growth of an Idea: A Bibliographical Study of the American Political Pamphlets Printed between 1764 and 1776 Dealing with the Dispute between Great Britain and Her Colonies* (Providence, 1965), pp. 8–11. For the availability of Dulany's tract in Philadelphia see the advertisements in *Gazette*, 5 Dec. 1765; and the letter of Edward Shippen to Colonel Shippen, Christmas 1765, in Thomas Balch, ed., *Letters and Papers Relating to the Provincial History of Pennsylvania* (Philadelphia, 1855), p. 212.

9. [James Wilson], *Considerations on the Nature and the Extent of the Legislative Authority of the British Parliament* (Philadelphia, 1774), p. 9. Also see "Instructions of Philadelphia City and County to Their Representatives in Assembly," *Journal*, 21 Oct. 1772; statement of the Patriotic Society, in *Gazette*, 19 Aug. 1772; "A.P.," ibid., 23 Sept. 1772; "A Citizen of Philadelphia," ibid., 22 Sept. 1773; "Publicus," *Chronicle*, 5 Sept. 1772; "Philadelphus" and "A Countryman," ibid., 26 Sept. 1772; "A Mechanic," ibid., 27 Sept. 1773.

10. Charles Thomson to Benjamin Franklin, 19 June 1765, in Leonard W. Larabee et al., eds., *The Papers of Benjamin Franklin* (New Haven, 1959– ), 12:184; "Colonus," *Journal*, 12 Sept. 1765; *The Case of Great Britain and America, Addressed to the King and Both Houses of Parliament* (Philadelphia, 1769), p. 5.

11. "F.L.," *Journal*, 13 March 1766. Also see "G.," *Gazette*, 30 Jan.

1766. Randolph G. Adams, *Political Ideas of the American Revolution*, 3d ed. (New York, 1958), pp. 55–64, reviews plans for American representation in Parliament.

12. "A Friend to the Colony," *Journal*, 13 Feb. 1766. Placing great stress upon Benjamin Franklin's testimony before the House of Commons in February 1766, historians held for many years that in their protests against the Stamp Act, Whigs denied the right of Parliament to impose internal taxes and granted its authority to levy external taxes. In his study of official documents issued by colonial legislatures and the Stamp Act Congress, Edmund Morgan, "Colonial Ideas of Parliamentary Power," *William and Mary Quarterly*, 7 (July 1950): 353–92, demonstrated that these bodies did not discriminate between internal and external taxation but denied the right of Parliament to tax Americans in any fashion whatever. On the other hand, in his authoritative study of colonial pamphlet literature, Bernard Bailyn, *Ideological Origins of the American Revolution* (Cambridge, 1967), pp. 209–21, observed that the internal-external distinction was adhered to by some writers.

Both Morgan and Bailyn are correct. Discriminations between internal and external taxes were not developed in official legislative protests against the Stamp Act; but some pamphleteers made the distinction. The internal-external dichotomy was not commonly made in Philadelphia, as was noted retrospectively by "The Beacon," *Packet*, 11 July 1774. No extant pamphlet published in the city during the dispute over the Stamp Act made an issue of the internal-external distinction. Only one newspaper essay made the differentiation. The only pamphlet published in Philadelphia during 1765–66 which stressed the distinction was that which contained transcripts of Franklin's testimony, *The Examination of Doctor Benjamin Franklin, before an August Assembly, Relating to the Repeal of the Stamp Act*, but it did not appear until September 1766, six months after the Stamp Act was repealed.

13. "Americanus," *Journal*, 29 Aug. 1765; "A True American," ibid., 19 Sept. 1765. [John Dickinson], "To Friends and Countrymen," broadside, Nov. 1765, in Paul L. Ford, ed., *The Writings of John Dickinson* (Philadelphia, 1895), pp. 201–5; [John Dickinson], *The Late Regulations Respecting the British Colonies on the Continent of America . . .* (Philadelphia, 1765).

14. The best sample of the Proprietary faction's rhetoric during this period is [James Biddle], "To the Freeholders and Electors of the Province of Pennsylvania," broadside, 1765 (Evans no. 9915). Good secondary treatments of political alignments and strategies in Philadelphia during the Stamp Act crisis can be found in James H. Hutson, *Pennsylvania Politics, 1746–1770: The Movement for Royal Government and Its Consequences* (Princeton, 1972), pp. 191–94; Benjamin H. Newcomb, "Effects of the Stamp Act on Colonial Pennsylvania Politics," *William and Mary Quarterly*, 23 (April 1966): 257–72; Theodore Thayer, *Pennsylvania Politics and the Growth of Democracy, 1740–1776* (Harrisburg, 1953), pp. 116–20.

15. "B.L.," *Gazette*, 8 March 1775. An excellent account of Bradford's political and journalistic activities is John W. Wallace, *An Old*

*Philadelphian, Colonel William Bradford* (Philadelphia, 1884). Unfortunately, only one hundred copies of this work were printed. A new biography of Bradford is much needed.

16. Joseph Galloway to Benjamin Franklin, 18 July 1765, in Labaree et al., *Papers of Franklin,* 12: 219; John Hughes to Commissioner of Stamps in London, 12 Oct. 1765, in *Journal,* 4 Sept. 1766. In contrast to Bradford, David Hall, publisher of the *Pennsylvania Gazette,* then Philadelphia's only other English-language newspaper, played a passive role in the Stamp Act controversy. Although he clearly opposed the act, Hall did not commit his paper to Whig views before 1766. Not a single notable essay opposing the Stamp Act appeared in the *Gazette* before late December 1765, despite the fact that as early as September the paper was losing subscribers because of its failure to adopt a hard line against Grenville's legislation. The reasons for Hall's behavior are not entirely clear, but he was likely following the wishes of his printing partner, Benjamin Franklin, and giving in to pressure from Franklin's political partner, Joseph Galloway. See Hall to Benjamin Franklin, 20 June and 6 Sept. 1765, in Labaree et al., *Papers of Franklin,* 12: 188–89, 255–59.

17. Carl Becker, *The Declaration of Independence: A Study in the History of Political Ideas* (New York, 1922), p. 93.

18. [John Dickinson], *Letters from a Farmer in Pennsylvania . . .* (Philadelphia, 1768), p. 13.

19. Much the same argument was developed by Daniel Dulany in his *Considerations on the Propriety of Imposing Taxes in the British Colonies,* and was affirmed by William Pitt in his famous reply to Grenville during Parliament's debates on repealing the Stamp Act. Pitt's speech was reprinted in both the *Gazette* and the *Journal;* Dulany's pamphlet was circulating in Philadelphia by December 1765, as discussed in note 8 above.

20. Jefferson quoted in Adams, *Political Ideas,* p. 79; Franklin to William Franklin, 13 March 1768, in Labaree et al., *Papers of Franklin,* 15: 75–76.

21. Cf. David L. Jacobson, *John Dickinson and the Revolution in Pennsylvania, 1764–1776* (Berkeley, 1965), pp. 43–55; Carl F. Kaestle, "The Public Reaction to John Dickinson's *Farmer's Letters,*" *Proceedings of the American Antiquarian Society,* 78 (Oct. 1968): 331–33.

22. Tribute from the Society of Fort St. David's, 12 May 1768, quoted in Charles J. Stillé, *The Life and Times of John Dickinson, 1732–1808* (Philadelphia, 1891), p. 92. Some other of the many tributes paid to Dickinson by fellow colonists are in the *Chronicle,* 18 May, 20 June, and 4 July 1768; *Gazette,* 7 and 28 April, 12 May, and 9 June 1768.

23. "The Citizen" appeared in the *Chronicle* from 21 January to 25 February 1768, and was reprinted, with additions, as [William Hicks], *The Nature and Extent of Parliamentary Power Considered . . .* (Philadelphia, 1768). Merrill Jensen, ed., *Tracts of the American Revolution, 1763–1776* (Indianapolis, 1967), p. xli, identifies Hicks as a supporter of the Proprietary faction. In *The Partnership: or, The History of the Rise and Progress of the Pennsylvania Chronicle . . .* (Philadelphia, 1770),

p. 17, William Goddard referred to Hicks, Dickinson, and Thomson as "the *first* magistrates of this province" during the protests against the Townshend Acts. Goddard's statement intimates that Hicks played a more central role from 1767 to 1770 than has heretofore been recognized.

24. "Machiavel," *Chronicle,* 29 Aug. 1768. Also see "Frank Meanwell," "Little John," "A Barbadian," and "Country Farmer," ibid., 25 July–29 Aug. In part 1 of *The Partnership,* Goddard exposed Galloway's efforts to discredit Dickinson and the *Letters from a Farmer.* For additional discussion of the debates over nonimportation and the Assembly election of 1768 see Chapter 2 above; and for another treatment of Galloway's efforts to defame Dickinson see Benjamin H. Newcomb, *Franklin and Galloway: A Political Partnership* (New Haven, 1972), pp. 189–91, 194–97.

25. William Franklin to Benjamin Franklin, 10 May 1768, quoted in Albert H. Smyth, ed., *The Writings of Benjamin Franklin* (New York, 1907), 5: 78n.; Benjamin Franklin to Jean-Baptiste LeRoy, 21 Sept. 1768, in Labaree et al., *Papers of Franklin,* 15: 206; "A Countryman," *Packet,* 18 Oct. 1773.

26. See, for example, Bailyn, *Ideological Origins,* pp. 204–5; Clinton Rossiter, *The Political Thought of the American Revolution* (New York, 1963), pp. 229–30.

27. [Joseph Galloway], *A Candid Examination of the Mutual Claims of Great Britain and the Colonies . . .* (New York, 1775), pp. 26, 42, 2. Galloway, of course, was not alone in claiming that the Whigs' rejection of the sovereignty of Parliament brought them a great distance toward revolution. Strikingly similar claims were voiced by the opponents of Whigs throughout America.

28. "An Anxious By–Stander," *Gazette,* 4 Jan. 1775; [Richard Wells], *A Few Political Reflections, Submitted to the Consideration of the British Colonies . . .* (Philadelphia, 1774), p. 17.

29. British attitudes are well characterized by Eric Robson, *The American Revolution in Its Political and Military Aspects , 1763–1783* (New York, 1966), chap. 3; Jack P. Greene, "The Plunge of Lemmings: A Consideration of Recent Writings on British Politics and the American Revolution," *South Atlantic Quarterly,* 67 (Winter 1968): 141–75.

30. Bailyn, *Ideological Origins,* pp. 66–77, 176–93, 230–32, 285–301; Adams, *Political Ideas,* pp. 135–49; Gordon S. Wood, *The Creation of the American Republic, 1776–1787* (Chapel Hill, 1969), pp. 259–68.

31. Charles McIlwain, *The American Revolution: A Constitutional Interpretation* (Ithaca, 1923), p. 5.

32. [John Dickinson], *An Address to the Committee of Correspondence in Barbados . . .* (Philadelphia, 1766), p. 4.

33. William Blackstone, *Commentaries on the Laws of England* (London, 1765–69), 1: 251, quoted in Wood, *Creation,* p. 67.

34. "The Beacon," *Packet,* 11 July 1774. By 1776 most Philadelphia Whigs had rejected the British constitution as a proper guide to political conduct. See [Thomas Paine], *Common Sense . . .* (Philadelphia, 1776), pp. 1–29; "Salus Populi," *Journal,* 14 Feb. 1776; "Candidus," *Evening Post,* 3 Feb. 1776.

35. Wilson, *Considerations,* p. iii. The Whigs' use of natural law as rhetorical strategy was not unique. In his *Rhetoric,* Aristotle gave this advice
to advocates: "If the written law tells against our case, clearly we must
appeal to the universal law, and insist on its greater equity and justice"
(1375a 25–35). For a brief summary of those classes of situations in
which natural law has historically assumed rhetorical dominance see
Kathleen M. Jamieson, "Natural Law as Warrant," *Philosophy and Rhetoric,* 6 (Fall 1973): 235–46. The standard introductions to the colonists'
understanding and use of natural law are Charles F. Mullett, *Fundamental Law and the American Revolution, 1760–1776* (New York, 1933); B.
F. Wright, *American Interpretations of Natural Law* (Cambridge, 1931),
chap. 4. A useful recent treatment is Paul K. Conkin, *Self–Evident
Truths: Being a Discourse on the Origins and Development of the First Principles of American Government—Popular Sovereignty, Natural Rights and
Balance and Separation of Powers* (Bloomington, 1974), chap. 5.

36. Benjamin Rush, *Autobiography,* ed. George W. Corner (Princeton,
1948), p. 150. The best biography of Wilson is Charles P. Smith, *James
Wilson, Founding Father: 1742–1798* (Chapel Hill, 1956). A useful short
analysis of Wilson's political and judicial doctrines is the editor's introduction to Robert G. McCloskey, ed., *The Works of James Wilson*
(Cambridge, 1967), 1: 1–48.

37. Wilson, *Considerations,* pp. 2–3.

38. Wells, *Political Reflections,* p. 30; Zubly, *The Law of Liberty,* p. 4;
Hicks, *Nature and Extent,* p. xv; *An Essay upon Government, Adopted by the
Americans* . . . (Philadelphia, 1775), pp. 11–13; *The Middle Line: or, An
Attempt To Furnish Some Hints for Ending the Differences Subsisting between
Great Britain and the Colonies* (Philadelphia, 1775), p. 39.

39. Wilson, *Considerations,* p. 3; *An Essay upon Government,* p. 13.

40. See *The Middle Line,* p. 13; Paine, *Common Sense,* p. 58. The role
and meaning of "happiness" in colonial thought is explored by Howard
Mumford Jones, *The Pursuit of Happiness* (Cambridge, 1953), chap. 3.

41. "Philoleutherus," *Journal,* 2 Jan. 1766; "A Friend to the Colony,"
ibid., 13 Feb. 1766; "Philoleutherus," broadside, 21 Sept. 1765 (Evans
no. 9942). Also see "Freeman," *Gazette,* 26 Dec. 1765; "A Freeborn
American," ibid., 12 May 1768.

42. This belief was graphically illustrated by Benjamin Rush during a
visit to London in 1768. After a tour of Parliament, Rush recorded
these thoughts: "I went a few days ago in company with a Danish phy-
sician to visit the House of Lords and the House of Commons. When I
went into the first, I felt as if I walked on sacred ground. I gazed for
some time at the throne with emotions I cannot describe. . . . From
this I went into the House of Commons. I cannot say I felt as if I walked
on 'sacred ground' here. This, thought I, is the place where the infernal
scheme for enslaving America was first broached. Here the usurping
Commons first endeavored to rob the King of his supremacy over the
colonies and to divide it among themselves. O! cursed haunt of venality,
bribery, and corruption!" (to Ebenezer Hazard, 22 Oct. 1768, in L. H.
Butterfield, ed., *Letters of Benjamin Rush* [Princeton, 1951], 1: 68).

43. Galloway, *Candid Examination,* p. 31; "An English Patriot's Creed,"
*Packet,* 25 Dec. 1775; "Pacificus," *Gazette,* 14 Sept. 1774.

44. "A Constitutional Catechism," *Packet,* 13 Dec. 1773.

45. Joseph Montgomery, *A Sermon Preached at Christiana Bridge and Newcastle* . . . (Philadelphia, 1775), p. 29; William Smith, *A Sermon on the Present Situation of American Affairs* . . . (Philadelphia, 1775), pp. 21, 26; William Smith, *An Oration in Memory of General Montgomery* . . . (Philadelphia, 1776), pp. 25–26. A fortnight after this second speech Smith launched a concerted personal campaign against independence. But though he denied that separating from England was expedient, he never denied that it was lawful. Nor did most Philadelphia Tories: see, for example, Galloway, *Candid Examination,* p. 13.

46. John Adams quoted in Lawrence H. Gipson, *The Coming of the Revolution, 1763–1775* (New York, 1954), p. 38, and in Adams, *Political Ideas,* p. 116; the quotation regarding navigational rights on the Schuylkill is from "Publicus," *Chronicle,* 5 Feb. 1770. The rhetoric surrounding the revolution in Pennsylvania's government in 1776 is treated in Chapter 8 below.

47. Rossiter, *Political Thought,* p. 93. Also see David Ramsay, *The History of the American Revolution* (London, 1793), 1: 31.

48. Granville Sharp, *A Declaration of the People's Natural Right to a Share in the Legislature* . . . (Philadelphia 1774), p. 3; [Thomas Jefferson], *A Summary View of the Rights of British America* . . . (Philadelphia, 1774), p. 22; letter from a woman in Philadelphia to a British officer in Boston, 1775, in Hezekiah Niles, ed., *Acts and Principles of the American Revolution* (Chicago, 1876), pp. 116–17.

49. [John Drinker], *Observations on the Late Popular Measures* . . . (Philadelphia, 1774), pp. 13, 19, 23; "To the Printers," *Journal,* 28 Nov. 1765; "A Friend to the Colony," ibid., 13 Feb. 1766.

50. Edwin Black, *Rhetorical Criticism: A Study in Method* (New York, 1965), p. 56. The benefits of attending to argumentative method are nicely illustrated by Weaver, *Ethics of Rhetoric,* chaps. 3–4.

51. "A Son of Liberty," *Gazette,* 31 May 1770; "Cassius," *Journal,* 13 Oct. 1773.

52. Daniel Boorstin, *The Genius of American Politics* (Chicago, 1953), chap. 3.

53. Jefferson, *Summary View,* pp. 5, 8, 22.

54. Hicks, *Nature and Extent,* pp. 30, 22, 26–27.

55. *Journal,* 3 May 1770.

56. See "A Spectator," *Gazette,* 14 June 1770; "Philo-Veritas," ibid., 19 July and 2 Aug. 1770; "A Philadelphian" ibid., 16 Aug. 1770; "Talonis," *Chronicle,* 6 Aug. 1770; "Philadelphus," ibid., 8 Oct. 1770.

57. "Nestor," *Journal,* 9 Aug. 1770; "A Son of Liberty," *Gazette,* 31 May 1770; "A Pennsylvanian," broadside, 14 July 1770 (Evans no. 11885). As we saw in the previous chapter, Whig writers did not ignore considerations of expediency altogether in the campaign for continued nonimportation, for they appealed directly to Philadelphia mechanics to support the boycott for economic reasons. But telling as the economic appeals proved to be, it was the argument from principle that dominated the Whigs' imprecations against resuming importation.

58. *Journal,* 31 Oct. 1765; ibid., 28 July 1768; *Packet,* 14 Nov. 1774. These and other colonial slogans, as one Englishman noted, "by being

short could be most easily circulated and retained, at the same time that, by being extremely expressive, they carried with them the weight of a great many arguments" (quoted in Arthur M. Schlesinger, *Prelude to Independence: The Newspaper War on Britain, 1764–1776* [New York, 1957], p. 33).

59. "Anglus Americanus," *Journal,* 29 June 1774; "A Plain Dealer," ibid., 13 July 1774. Similarly, "C. M. Scaevola," ibid., 20 July 1774; "Sidney," ibid., 31 Aug. 1774.

60. Resolves of the Philadelphia Committee of Inspection and Observation, 19 Sept. 1775, in Peter Force, ed., *American Archives,* 4th ser. (Washington, D.C., 1837–46), 3: 731.

61. Speech at the State House, 30 July 1768, in *Chronicle,* 1 Aug. 1768; *Some Observations of Consequence in Three Parts. Occasioned by the Stamp-Tax* . . . (Philadelphia, 1768), p. iv; Hicks, *Nature and Extent,* pp. iii, 21.

62. See "A Loyal American" and "To the Inhabitants of the British Colonies in America," *Journal,* 8 June 1774; instructions from the Pennsylvania Convention to the Pennsylvania Assembly, ibid., 23 July 1774.

63. "A Tradesman," *Chronicle,* 21 May 1770.

64. Galloway, "Americanus," *Journal,* 29 Aug. 1765; Galloway, *Candid Examination,* pp. 49–50; [Benjamin Franklin], "An American," *Evening Post,* 28 Jan. 1775. For Franklin's authorship see Vernor W. Crane, ed., *Benjamin Franklin's Letters to the Press, 1758–1775* (Chapel Hill, 1950), pp. 268–76.

65. Thomas Hutchinson, *The History of the Province of Massachusetts Bay* (London, 1828), p. 241.

66. Edmund Burke, speech on American taxation, 9 April 1774, in Chauncey A. Goodrich, ed., *Select British Eloquence* (1852; reprint ed., Indianapolis, 1963), p. 262.

CHAPTER 4.
## THE SPECTER OF CONSPIRACY

1. William Duane, Jr., ed., *Extracts from the Diary of Christopher Marshall, 1774–1781* (Albany, 1877), p. 83; John Adams to Samuel Chase, 9 July 1776, in Edmund C. Burnett, ed., *Letters of Members of the Continental Congress* (Washington, D.C., 1921), 2: 7–8.

2. Bernard Bailyn, *The Ideological Origins of the American Revolution* (Cambridge, 1967), p. ix; Richard Morris, *The American Revolution Reconsidered* (New York, 1967), p. 38.

3. "Freeman," *Gazette,* 26 Dec. 1765; untitled essay, in *Journal,* 5 Sept. 1765; "Philoleutherus," ibid., 2 Jan. 1766; [John Dickinson], *Letters from a Farmer in Pennsylvania* . . . (Philadelphia, 1768) p. 55. The Whigs' concern with the economic consequences of British conspiracy is discussed in Chapter 2 above.

4. For a full discussion of the Whigs' attacks upon British political corruption see Chapters 2 and 5.

5. London letters, in *Journal*, 3 May 1770 and 7 July 1768; *Four Letters on Interesting Subjects* (Philadelphia, 1776), pp. 4–5.

6. London letter, in *Gazette*, 6 July 1769.

7. "Letter of a Merchant in Philadelphia to a Friend in London," *Journal* and *Gazette*, 10 May 1770. Originally written in November 1769 as a private communiqué to Benjamin Franklin, Thomson's letter was subsequently republished for its rhetorical value. For Thomson's authorship see "The Papers of Charles Thomson," *Collections of the New York Historical Society*, 11 (1878): 21–25. For similar allegations of British conspiracy at the time of the Townshend Acts see "Monitor," *Gazette*, 14 April 1768, 22 and 29 June 1769; "The Citizen," *Journal*, 19 Jan. 1769; speech at the State House, 30 July 1768, in *Chronicle*, 1 Aug. 1768.

8. "A Bostonian," *Gazette*, 13 July 1774; "A Mechanic," *Gazette*, 8 Dec. 1773; [John Dickinson], "To the Inhabitants of the British Colonies in America," *Journal*, 1 June 1774. Dickinson's authorship is discussed later in this chapter.

9. [Thomas Jefferson], *A Summary View of the Rights of British America . . .* (Philadelphia, 1774), pp. 5, 11. Jefferson suggested a relatively precise date for the origin of the conspiracy, a subject which was touched upon but seldom discussed explicitly by Philadelphia Whigs. Most felt, as "A.Z." stated in the *Journal* of 20 October 1773, that the plot against American property and liberty was first formulated in 1763 "at a time when the colonies were dandled into the security and slumber which succeeded the tumults of a tedious war" and was first manifested in the Stamp Act.

10. "Mucius," *Packet*, 1 Nov. 1773; "Agricola," *Journal*, 23 Jan. 1766; Dickinson, *Letters from a Farmer*, p. 38; [Benjamin Rush], "Hamden," *Packet*, 11 Oct. 1773. For Rush's pseudonym see his letter to William Gordon, 10 Oct. 1773, in L. H. Butterfield, ed., *Letters of Benjamin Rush* (Princeton, 1951), 1: 82.

11. [Richard Wells], *A Few Political Reflections, Submitted to the Consideration of the British Colonies . . .* (Philadelphia, 1774), p. 58; London letter, in *Journal*, 18 May 1774.

12. The most reliable estimate of Philadelphia's slave population during the 1760s and 1770s is in Gary B. Nash, "Slaves and Slaveowners in Colonial Philadelphia," *William and Mary Quarterly*, 30 (April 1973): 223–56.

13. "A Philadelphian," *Gazette*, 17 Aug. 1774; Wells, *Political Reflections*, pp. 79–80. Also see "A Friend to Liberty," *Journal*, 21 Sept. 1774; "Justice and Humanity," ibid., 8 March 1775; "Humanus," ibid., 18 Oct. 1775; "Anti-Slavetrader," *Chronicle*, 28 Nov. 1768; "A Friend to Liberty," ibid., 4 June 1770; "Amintor," *Packet*, 7 Feb. 1774; untitled essay, in ibid., 9 Jan. 1775; [Benjamin Rush], *An Address to the Inhabitants of the British Settlements in America, Upon Slave-Keeping . . .* (Philadelphia, 1773).

14. Quoted in John Hope Franklin, *From Slavery to Freedom: A History of American Negroes*, 3d ed. (New York, 1967), p. 141.

15. "Russel," *Journal*, 2 March 1774. Indeed, it may have been that the Americans' concern with slavery came readily to mind and

294

possessed emotional resonance because they knew at first-hand the consequences of bondage, as Edmund Burke hypothesized in his 1775 speech in favor of reconciliation. See Paul K. Conkin, *Self-Evident Truths: Being a Discourse on the Origins and Development of the First Principles of American Government—Popular Sovereignty, Natural Rights and Balance and Separation of Powers* (Bloomington, 1974), p. 110.

16. Thus James Chalmers, in closing his anti-revolutionary pamphlet, *Plain Truth . . .* (Philadelphia, 1776), sought to stamp this equation upon the minds of his readers: "INDEPENDENCE AND SLAVERY ARE SYNONYMOUS TERMS." On the general importance of "slavery" in colonial protest rhetoric see Bailyn, *Ideological Origins*, pp. 232–34.

17. Speech at the State House, 30 July 1768, in *Chronicle*, 1 Aug. 1768; *The Case of Great Britain and America, Addressed to the King and to Both Houses of Parliament . . .* (Philadelphia, 1769), p. 8; [John Dickinson], "An Address Read at a Meeting of Merchants to Consider Non-Importation," April 1768, in Paul L. Ford, ed., *The Writings of John Dickinson* (Philadelphia, 1895), p. 415; "A Friend to the Colony," *Journal*, 13 Feb. 1766; Dickinson, "To the Inhabitants of the British Colonies in America," ibid., 25 May 1774.

18. Eric Robson, *The American Revolution in Its Political and Military Aspects, 1763–1783* (New York, 1966), p. 34. Indicative of British confusion was Lord Barrington's comment to Francis Bernard in 1767: "There is the most urgent reason to do what is right, and immediately; but what is right, and who is to do it?"

19. [John Adams], "Novanglus," in *Novanglus and Massachusettensis; or, Political Essays Published in the Years 1774 and 1775 . . .* (Boston, 1819), pp. 11–12. As Charles Lomas observes, "Neither rhetorical nor activist agitations can hope to succeed even partially unless social and political conditions are favorable to the initiation and growth of the movement. There must be clear evidence of *injustice or apparent injustice* deeply affecting the well being of those who compose the audience" (*The Agitator in American Society* [Englewood Cliffs, 1968], p. 8).

20. See J. H. Plumb, *England in the Eighteenth Century* (London, 1950), pp. 116–40, esp. 124–25, from which the final sentence of this paragraph is paraphrased.

21. Among the pamphlets by British authors published in the city were [John Cartwright], *American Independence: The Interest and Glory of Great Britain . . .* (Philadelphia, 1774); Richard Price, *Observations on the Nature of Civil Liberty, the Principles of Government, and the Justice and Policy of the War with America . . .* (Philadelphia, 1776); [Matthew Rokeby], *Considerations on the Measures Carrying on with Respect to the British Colonies in North America . . .* (Philadelphia, 1774); Granville Sharp, *A Declaration of the People's Natural Right to a Share in the Legislature . . .* (Philadelphia, 1774); Jonathan Shipley, *A Sermon Preached before the Incorporated Society for the Propagation of the Gospel in Foreign Parts* (Philadelphia, 1773); [Jonathan Shipley], *A Speech Intended to Have Been Spoken on the Bill for Altering the Charter of the Colony of Massachusetts Bay* (Philadelphia, 1774). The pamphlets by Shipley, Rokeby, and Cartwright are included, with useful introductory notes, in Paul H.

Smith, ed., *English Defenders of American Freedom, 1774–1778: Six Pamphlets Attacking British Policy* (Washington, D.C., 1972).

22. "The Crisis," *Evening Post,* 18 April 1775. This series, after which Thomas Paine later named his collection of wartime essays, originated in London, where its ninety-two installments ran in the press from 4 January 1775 to 8 June 1776. It contained extremely severe assaults upon the king and ministry that echoed above all else the idea that governmental leaders were engaged in a plot to augment their fortunes and power at the expense of public funds and liberties. The third issue assailed George III so vehemently that Parliament declared it a "false, malicious, seditious, and treasonable libel" and ordered that it be publicly burned by the common hangman on two successive days. Several of the installments were published in one or more Philadelphia newspapers, and John Dunlap printed the first fifteen as broadsides.

23. "Junius Americanus," *Journal,* 6 Oct. 1773; "A Son of Liberty," *Gazette,* 31 May 1770. Some further consequences of the belief that the liberties of the whole empire were at stake in the imperial controversy are discussed in the next chapter. Within the context of the present discussion, I would suggest that while some Whiggish Philadelphians were truly concerned about a plot to snuff out constitutional privileges in England, indications of such a scheme primarily reinforced fears of conspiracy against American rights and interests.

24. London letters, in *Gazette,* 13 April, 6 July, and 18 May 1769; London letter, in *Packet,* 19 Sept. 1774.

25. At no time during the decade of protest did Philadelphia newspapers present significantly favorable reports or interpretations of what was happening in England. The degree to which this resulted from deliberate editorial decisions by the city's publishers is not determinable, though it certainly was not utterly accidental. Of all the "personal" letters from London printed in Philadelphia during the years 1765–75, only one of which I am aware forthrightly denied the notion of a conspiracy against America (in *Gazette,* 26 Jan. 1769). When pro-British articles were printed in Philadelphia newspapers they were generally accompanied by several pro-American pieces refuting the pro-British claims. In the *Journal* of 27 February 1766, for example, the Bradfords ran a virulently anti-American essay by "Pacificus." Not only was it followed by three refutative pieces, but it was introduced in this fashion: "A new writer has started up in London, who signs PACIFICUS, and seems to be full freighted against the AMERICANS. The following, for curiosity sake, we have extracted to give the reader a judgment of all his other pieces; and we hope it will serve for part of this day's ENTERTAINMENT."

26. *Journal,* 11 May 1769. Also see David Ramsay, *The History of the American Revolution* (London, 1793), 1: 115–16.

27. Bernard Bailyn, *The Origins of American Politics* (New York, 1967), pp. 11–12, 31–58, 104–5, 136–61; Bailyn, *Ideological Origins,* pp. 34–54, 144. Caroline Robbins, *The Eighteenth–Century Commonwealthman: Studies in the Transmission, Development, and Circumstance of English Liberal Thought from the Restoration of Charles II until the War with the Thirteen*

*Colonies* (Cambridge, 1961), provides the standard exposition of the Commonwealth ideology as expressed in England.

28. Bailyn, *Origins of American Politics*, p. 53.

29. We are most familiar, of course, with the charges of conspiracy which make up a central aspect of the rhetoric of the Radical Right. Yet similar kinds of claims can be found in the literature of black power advocates, new left spokesmen, women's liberationists, pre-Civil War abolitionists, Southern "Fire-Eaters," late nineteenth-century Populists, labor reform agitators, and others. Some reasons for the recurrence of allegations of conspiracy in the language of social movements are suggested by Hans Toch, *The Social Psychology of Social Movements* (Indianapolis, 1965), chap. 5; and can be discerned from Neil J. Smelser, *Theory of Collective Behavior* (New York, 1962).

30. *Four Letters on Interesting Subjects*, p. 5. As Seymour Lipset and Earl Raab explain, "a plot theory will presumably gain popular support only when there is some salient social strain which that theory will serve the purpose of 'explaining'; and the plot theory is most cogent when the social strain can itself be personified through that theory" (*The Politics of Unreason: Right-Wing Extremism in America, 1790–1970* [New York, 1970], p. 38).

31. Herbert W. Simons, "Requirements, Problems, and Strategies: A Theory of Persuasion for Social Movements," *Quarterly Journal of Speech,* 56 (Feb. 1970): 6.

32. Eric Hoffer, *The True Believer* (New York, 1951), p. 86.

33. Arthur L. Smith, *Rhetoric of Black Revolution* (Boston, 1969), pp. 26–27.

34. "Veritas," *Journal,* 14 Dec. 1774; "A Briton," *Gazette,* 12 Oct. 1769; "Junius Americanus," *Journal,* 17 Aug. 1774.

35. Smith, *Rhetoric of Black Revolution,* pp. 29–30.

36. Jefferson, *Summary View,* p. 13; *Some Observations of Consequence in Three Parts. Occasioned by the Stamp–Tax . . .* (Philadelphia, 1768), pp. 20, 47, 61, 48.

37. Richard Hofstadter, *The Paranoid Style in American Politics, and Other Essays* (New York, 1952), p. 31.

38. "Monitor," *Gazette,* 29 June 1769.

39. Dickinson, "To the Inhabitants of the British Colonies in America," *Journal,* 15 June 1774.

40. *Some Observations of Consequence,* p. 14; Dickinson to Arthur Lee, 27 Oct. 1774, in Richard Henry Lee, ed., *Life of Arthur Lee* (Boston, 1829), 2: 307; Wilson, speech of Jan. 1775, in Robert G. McCloskey, ed., *The Works of James Wilson* (Cambridge, 1967), 2: 758.

41. "Phocion's Letter to the K———," *Packet,* 29 Aug. 1774.

42. "Scipio," *Journal,* 5 Oct. 1774. Other attacks upon George III published in Philadelphia in 1774 came mostly from London and condemned the king for assenting to the Quebec Act. See "Shippen," *Packet,* 8 Aug.; "A Scotchman," ibid., 26 Sept.; "Tribunus," *Gazette,* 14 Sept. An important exception was "Political Observations without Order: Addressed to the People of America," *Packet,* 14 Nov. 1774.

43. Bristol letter, in *Packet,* 3 Oct. 1774; "Casca," *Journal,* 27 Oct. 1773.

44. London letters, in *Journal,* 24 May 1770; in *Gazette,* 13 April 1769; in *Journal,* 23 Aug. 1770; in *Chronicle,* 27 Nov. 1769. Also see John Dickinson to Arthur Lee, 21 Sept. 1771, in Lee, *Life of Arthur Lee,* 2: 304; "Monitor," *Chronicle,* 27 Nov. 1769.

45. Adams to Hezekiah Niles, 13 Feb. 1818, in Charles F. Adams, ed., *The Works of John Adams* (Boston, 1856), 10: 283. The only Philadelphia writer who devoted more than a few comments to writs of assistance was Dickinson, *Letters from a Farmer,* pp. 45–46. On civilian-military relations in the city see John Shy, *Toward Lexington: The Role of the British Army in the Coming of the American Revolution* (Princeton, 1965), p. 391; and the discussion in Chapter 3 above.

46. Quoted in Richard D. Brown, *Revolutionary Politics in Massachusetts: The Boston Committee of Correspondence and the Towns, 1772–1774* (Cambridge, 1970), p. 186.

47. David L. Jacobson, *John Dickinson and the Revolution in Pennsylvania, 1764–1776* (Berkeley, 1965), p. 71.

48. Thomas Wharton to Thomas Walpole, 31 May 1774, in *Pennsylvania Magazine of History and Biography,* 33 (1909): 337; Charles Thomson to William Henry Drayton, n.d., in "Papers of Charles Thomson," p. 279. The terms "moderate," "radical" and "conservative" are used here and later in the chapter merely to differentiate groups with conflicting points of view regarding the Coercive Acts and the proper response to them.

49. The political battles in Philadelphia during the summer of 1774 have received considerable attention in almost all accounts of the coming of the Revolution in Pennsylvania. Especially informative and perceptive discussions are those of Charles H. Lincoln, *The Revolutionary Movement in Pennsylvania, 1760–1776* (Philadelphia, 1901), pp. 159–84; Richard A. Ryerson, "Leadership in Crisis: The Revolutionary Committees of Philadelphia and the Coming of the Revolution in Pennsylvania, 1765–1776" (Ph.D. diss., Johns Hopkins University, 1973), chap. 4.

50. Charles Thomson to William Henry Drayton, n.d., and to David Ramsay, 4 Nov. 1786, in "Papers of Charles Thomson," pp. 275, 221.

51. Inexplicably, Dickinson's essays have been virtually ignored by historians and critics, despite Thomson's testimony to their importance. Indicative of this neglect is the fact that Jacobson, *John Dickinson and the Revolution in Pennsylvania,* does not even mention the essays in his treatment of Dickinson's activities against the Coercive Acts. Like other students of the Revolution in Pennsylvania, Jacobson attends closely to the political intrigues of Whig leaders during the spring and summer of 1774, but overlooks the important role of rhetoric—and especially of Dickinson's letters—in shaping a climate of opinion amenable to the radicals' aims.

52. The entire series of letters is reprinted in Ford, *Writings of Dickinson,* pp. 469–501. The quoted passages are from pp. 471, 473, 469, 491, 487, 474, 492–93.

53. "A Philadelphian," *Journal*, 18 May 1774; "A Younger Brother," ibid., 1 June 1774; "Philanthropos," ibid., 22 June 1774; "Civis," ibid., 6 July 1774; "Yet a Free Citizen," ibid., 20 July 1774; "An Old Man," *Gazette*, 22 June 1774; "A Bostonian," ibid., 13 July 1774; "An American," *Packet*, 30 May 1774; "Marcus Brutus," ibid., 27 June 1774.

54. To Lady Juliana Penn, 24 June 1774, in *Pennsylvania Magazine of History and Biography*, 31 (1907): 236. Similarly, see Thomas Wharton to [Thomas Walpole?], 2 Aug. 1774, in ibid., 33 (1909): 438; Joseph Reed to Earl of Dartmouth, 18 July 1774, in William B. Reed, ed., *The Life and Correspondence of Joseph Reed* (Philadelphia, 1847), 1: xv.

55. "A Younger Brother," *Journal*, 1 June 1774; London letter, in ibid., 18 May 1774.

56. Galloway to Benjamin Franklin, 13 Jan. 1766, in Leonard W. Labaree et al., eds., *The Papers of Benjamin Franklin* (New Haven, 1959– ), 13:37; Galloway to William Franklin, 26 March 1775, *New Jersey Archives*, 1st ser. (Newark and Trenton, 1880–1949), 10: 585; letter from Philadelphia to New York, 15 March 1775, in Peter Force, ed., *American Archives*, 4th ser. (Washington, D.C., 1837–46), 2: 133-34; letter from Philadelphia to London, 1 Aug. 1775, in ibid., 3: 3.

57. "Machiavel," *Chronicle*, 29 Aug. 1768; "Country Farmer," ibid., 22 Aug. 1768; "Frank Meanwell," ibid., 25 July 1768. Goddard's comment is from his pamphlet *The Partnership: or, The History of the Rise and Progress of the Pennsylvania Chronicle . . .* (Philadelphia, 1770), p. 14.

58. "Machiavel," *Chronicle*, 15 Aug. 1768. His other essays appeared on 22 and 29 August.

59. "A Freeman," broadside, 21 July 1774 (Evans no. 13096). Galloway was most likely the author of this address.

60. [John Drinker], *Observations on the Late Popular Measures . . .* (Philadelphia, 1774), pp. 20, 8, 13, 18–19. Like Dickinson's "To the Inhabitants of the British Colonies in America," Drinker's pamphlet has not heretofore received the attention it deserves.

61. For a discussion of one such episode see Edmund S. Morgan and Helen M. Morgan, *The Stamp Act Crisis: Prologue to Revolution*, rev. ed. (New York, 1963), chap. 14. On the nature and scope of mob activity in colonial America see Richard M. Brown, "Violence and the American Revolution," in Stephen G. Kurtz and James H. Hutson, eds., *Essays on the American Revolution* (Chapel Hill, 1973), pp. 81–120; Pauline Maier, "Popular Uprisings and Civil Authority in Eighteenth-Century America," *William and Mary Quarterly*, 27 (Jan. 1970): 1–22; Gordon S. Wood, "A Note on Mobs in the American Revolution," ibid., 26 (Oct. 1969): 235–46; Hiller B. Zobel, *The Boston Massacre* (New York, 1970); Dirk Hoerder, *People and Mobs: Crowd Action in Massachusetts during the American Revolution, 1765–1780* (Berlin, 1971).

62. Also see the discussions of this campaign in Chapters 2 and 3.

63. Although some Tory literature was published in the city by the *Pennsylvania Mercury* during its short-lived operation, the major outlet for Philadelphia Tories from the time of the Tea Act was James Rivington's *New York Gazetteer*. Rivington also published Joseph Galloway's important pamphlet, *A Candid Examination of the Mutual Claims of Great*

*Britain and the Colonies* . . . (New York, 1775), for want of a willing publisher in Philadelphia.

64. Gordon S. Wood, "Rhetoric and Reality in the American Revolution," *William and Mary Quarterly,* 23 (Jan. 1966): 31.

CHAPTER 5.
## THE APOTHEOSIS OF AMERICAN DESTINY

1. "Philoleutherus,"*Journal,* 2 Jan. 1766.

2. The degree to which colonists were dependent upon England for normative social and political standards is explicated by Jack P. Greene in three essays: "Search for Identity: An Interpretation of the Meaning of Selected Patterns of Social Response in Eighteenth-Century America," *Journal of Social History,* 3 (Spring 1970): 189–220, esp. 205–18; "The Preconditions of American Republicanism: A Comment," in *The Development of a Revolutionary Mentality* (Washington, D.C., 1972), pp. 119–24, esp. pp. 122–23; and "An Uneasy Connection: An Analysis of the Preconditions of the American Revolution," in Stephen G. Kurtz and James H. Hutson, eds., *Essays on the American Revolution* (Chapel Hill, 1973), pp. 32–80, esp. pp. 50–52.

3. *The Examination of Doctor Benjamin Franklin, before an August Assembly Relating to the Repeal of the Stamp Act,* in Leonard W. Labaree et al., eds., *The Papers of Benjamin Franklin* (New Haven, 1959–   ), 13: 135. For strikingly similar statements by other Philadelphians see Charles Thomson to Benjamin Franklin, [24 Sept. 1765], in ibid., 12: 279; Joseph Reed to Earl of Dartmouth, 25 Sept. 1774, in William B. Reed, ed., *Life and Correspondence of Joseph Reed* (Philadelphia, 1847), 1: 77.

4. Cf. Arthur L. Smith, *Rhetoric of Black Revolution* (Boston, 1969); Robert L. Scott and Donald K. Smith, "The Rhetoric of Confrontation," *Quarterly Journal of Speech,* 55 (Feb. 1969): 1–8; Richard B. Gregg, "The Ego-Function of the Rhetoric of Protest," *Philosophy and Rhetoric,* 4 (Spring 1971): 71–91.

5. London letter, in *Journal,* 3 May 1770; "Colonus," ibid., 12 Jan. 1769; "Monitor," *Gazette,* 22 June 1769.

6. London letters, in *Chronicle,* 27 Nov. 1769, and in *Gazette,* 29 Dec. 1768; William Tennent, *An Address, Occasioned by the Late Invasion of the Liberties of the American Colonies* . . . (Philadelphia, 1774), p. 16.

7. London letter, in *Journal,* 3 May 1770; "Atticus," *Chronicle,* 6 Feb. 1769; [Richard Wells], *A Few Political Reflections, Submitted to the Consideration of the British Colonies* . . . (Philadelphia, 1774), p. 35.

8. See the portraits of British life in Louis Kronenberger, *Kings and Desperate Men: Life in Eighteenth-Century England* (New York, 1942); J. H. Whitely, *Wesley's England: A Survey of Eighteenth-Century Social and Cultural Conditions* (London, 1938).

9. As Kenneth Boulding explains, "An often repeated message which comes with unusual force or authority is able to penetrate the resistance and will be able to alter the image" (*The Image: Knowledge and Life in Society* [Ann Arbor, 1956], p. 12).

10. "Brutus," *Gazette,* 22 June 1769.

11. [John Dickinson], *Letters from a Farmer in Pennsylvania . . .* (Philadelphia, 1768), p. 47; "Atticus," *Chronicle,* 14 Dec. 1767; William Moore Smith, "On the Fall of Empires,"*Evening Post,* 23 May 1775.

12. Dickinson, *Letters from a Farmer,* p. 47; "Brutus," *Gazette,* 22 June 1769; "An Old Mechanic,"*Journal,* 20 Oct. 1773.

13. "The Citizen," *Journal,* 26 Jan. 1769; speech at Carpenters' Hall, 16 March 1775, in *Evening Post,* 13 April 1775; "Eugenio," *Ledger,* 28 Jan. 1775.

14. [John Dickinson], *The Late Regulations Respecting the British Colonies on the Continent of America . . .* (Philadelphia, 1765), p. 29; Thomson to Benjamin Franklin, 26 Nov. 1769, in "The Papers of Charles Thomson," *Collections of the New York Historical Society,* 11 (1878): 23–24.

15. "Sidney," *Journal,* 31 Aug. 1774; "John Hamilton," ibid., 5 Sept. 1765; "Philoleutherus," ibid., 2 Jan. 1766.

16. "A Briton," *Gazette,* 9 Feb. 1769; "An American," ibid., 19 Jan. 1769. These and other of Franklin's essays against the Townshend duties are identified by Vernor W. Crane, *Benjamin Franklin's Letters to the Press, 1758–1775* (Chapel Hill, 1950). See esp. documents 52, 55–56, 60–62, 66–67, 69–72, 76, 80.

17. London letter, in *Gazette,* 10 March 1768; "An Independent Whig," *Journal,* 27 Feb. 1766; *The Power and Grandeur of Great Britain, Founded on the Liberty of the Colonies . . .* (Philadelphia, 1768), p. 22.

18. David Ramsay, *The History of the American Revolution* (London, 1793), 1: 74–75. Also see Edward Burd to E. Shippen, 4 July 1774, in Lewis B. Walker, ed., *The Burd Papers: Selections from Letters Written by Edward Burd, 1763–1828* (privately printed, 1899), pp. 67–68; letter from a gentleman in Philadelphia to a member of the British Parliament, 26 Dec. 1774, in Margaret W. Willard, ed., *Letters on the American Revolution, 1774–1776* (Boston, 1925), p. 42.

19. James Cassedy, *Demography in Early America* (Cambridge, 1969), p. 180. Franklin's *Observations,* with useful introductory notes, is in Labaree et al., *Papers of Franklin,* 4: 225–34.

20. John Zubly, *The Law of Liberty, A Sermon on American Affairs . . .* (Philadelphia, 1775), p. xvi; *Some Observations of Consequence in Three Parts. Occasioned by the Stamp-Tax . . .* (Philadelphia, 1768), p. 41.

21. Richard A. Ryerson, "Leadership in Crisis: The Radical Committees of Philadelphia and the Coming of the Revolution in Pennsylvania, 1765–1776" (Ph.D. diss., Johns Hopkins University, 1973), identifies a Richard Wells—a merchant, possibly a Quaker—as a candidate on the moderate slate for the Philadelphia Committee of Forty-three in June 1774, as a moderate member of the Committee of Sixty-six in November 1774, and as an officer of the United Company of Philadelphia for Promoting American Manufactures in 1775. Although the American Manufactory served as an entry-way into politics for several Philadelphians who became prominent Radical Whigs in 1776, there is no indication whether Wells later joined ranks with the Radicals.

22. Wells, *Political Reflections,* pp. 38–40.

23. Ibid., pp. 52–54, 40.

24. Dickinson, *Late Regulations,* p. 31. Such visions of American power and potential were described most often by Whig publicists, but they were also expressed by many Philadelphia Tories: see, for example, Isaac Hunt, *The Political Family: or, A Discourse Pointing Out the Reciprocal Advantages, Which Flow from an Uninterrupted Union between Great Britain and Her American Colonies* . . . (Philadelphia, 1775), pp. 18–29.

25. Wells, *Political Reflections,* p. 49.

26. "Rationalis," *Journal,* 23 Jan. 1766; Wells, *Political Reflections,* pp. 37, 17–18.

27. Extract from "The Royal American Magazine," in *Packet,* 28 March 1774; "Observation," *Chronicle,* 11 Oct. 1773.

28. Wells, *Political Reflections,* pp. 41, 36; *Some Observations of Consequence,* p. 42.

29. Wells, *Political Reflections,* p. 43; "Observation," *Chronicle,* 11 Oct. 1773; "Look-Out," ibid., 8 Nov. 1773.

30. "Rationalis," *Journal,* 20 Feb. 1766.

31. Cf. Edmund S. Morgan, "The Puritan Ethic and the American Revolution," *William and Mary Quarterly,* 24 (Jan. 1967): 3–43.

32. Here I am emphasizing a point about rhetoric explicated by Edwin Black, "The Second Persona," *Quarterly Journal of Speech,* 56 (April 1970): 109–19, esp. 119.

33. "Eugenio," *Ledger,* 28 Jan. 1775; [Daniel Dulany], *Considerations on the Propriety of Imposing Taxes in the British Colonies* . . . (Annapolis, 1765), p. 46; "Journal of Occurrences," *Journal,* 27 April 1769; Wells, *Political Reflections,* p. 52. On the availability of Dulany's pamphlet in Philadelphia see Chapter 3, note 8, above.

34. Neil J. Smelser, *Theory of Collective Behavior* (New York, 1962).

35. "A Son of Liberty," *Gazette,* 31 May 1770; Franklin to Joseph Galloway, 25 Feb. 1775, in Albert H. Smyth, ed., *The Writings of Benjamin Franklin* (New York, 1907), 6: 312; "Caractacus," *Packet,* 21 Aug. 1775.

36. "N.," *Journal,* 5 Sept. 1765.

37. [Thomas Blacklock], *Remarks on the Nature and Extent of Liberty* (Edinburgh, 1776), p. 43; *The Rights of Great Britain Asserted against the Claims of America* (London, 1776), pp. 85–88; William Pitt, parliamentary address, 1770, all quoted in Edwin G. Burrows and Michael Wallace, "The American Revolution: The Ideology and Psychology of National Liberation," *Perspectives in American History,* 6 (1972): 230, 232–33, 241.

38. [Joseph Galloway], *A Candid Examination of the Mutual Claims of Great Britain and the Colonies* . . . (New York, 1775), p. 50; Hunt, *Political Family,* pp. 29–30.

39. *Power and Grandeur of Great Britain,* p. 20; *Some Observations of Consequence,* p. 66; Dickinson, *Late Regulations,* p. 36; [John Dickinson], "To the Inhabitants of the British Colonies in America," *Journal,* 1 June 1774; "Justice and Humanity," ibid., 10 Nov. 1768. For Dickinson's authorship of "To the Inhabitants of the British Colonies in America" see Chapter 4 above.

40. Wells, *Political Reflections,* pp. 12–13; John Carmichael, *A Self-De-*

*fensive War Lawful* . . . (Philadelphia, 1775), p. 32; [Thomas Paine], "Thoughts on Defensive War," *Pennsylvania Magazine,* July 1775. For Paine's authorship see Philip S. Foner, ed., *The Complete Writings of Thomas Paine* (New York, 1945), 2: 52.

41. Wells, *Political Reflections,* pp. 33–34.

42. [Thomas Jefferson], *A Summary View of the Rights of British America* . . . (Philadelphia, 1774), pp. 6–7; "John Hampden," *Gazette,* 23 Jan. 1766. Consult Chapter 2 above for further discussion of this aspect of Whig rhetoric.

43. Untitled essay, in *Journal,* 28 Nov. 1765; "A.B.," ibid., 17 Oct. 1765; "A Friend to the Colony," ibid., 13 Feb. 1766.

44. Benjamin Rush, *Autobiography,* ed. George W. Corner (Princeton, 1948), p. 161.

45. Dietmar Rothermund, *The Layman's Progress: Religious and Political Experience in Colonial Pennsylvania, 1740–1770* (Philadelphia, 1961), pp. 1–3; John R. Young, *Memorial History of the City of Philadelphia* (New York, 1895), 1: 36.

46. Dickinson, *Letters from a Farmer,* p. 70; "A Plain Dealer," *Journal,* 13 July 1774; William Smith, *A Sermon on the Present Situation of American Affairs* . . . (Philadelphia, 1775), p. 28.

47. Instructions from the Pennsylvania Convention to the Pennsylvania Assembly, in *Journal,* 23 July 1774; Dickinson, "To the Inhabitants of the British Colonies in America," ibid., 15 June 1774.

48. Smith, "On the Fall of Empires," *Evening Post,* 23 May 1775; "A Plain Dealer," *Journal,* 13 July 1774; speech at Carpenters' Hall, 16 March 1775, in *Evening Post,* 13 April 1775.

49. [Charles Lee], *Strictures on a Pamphlet Entitled, "A Friendly Address to All Reasonable Americans, on the Subject of Our Political Confusions"* . . . (Philadelphia, 1774), p. 15; Dickinson, "To the Inhabitants of the British Colonies in America," *Journal,* 15 June 1774.

## PROLEGOMENON TO PART III

1. [Thomas Paine], *Common Sense* . . . (Philadelphia, 1776), p. 31; "A Friend to Posterity and Mankind," *Packet,* 12 Feb. 1776.

2. At least some treatment of the debate over independence in Philadelphia is provided in most general histories of the coming of the Revolution, as well as in virtually every study of Pennsylvania politics during this period. Particularly notable accounts are Arthur M. Schlesinger, *Prelude to Independence: The Newspaper War on Britain, 1764–1776* (New York, 1957), chap. 12; Moses Coit Tyler, *The Literary History of the American Revolution, 1763–1783* (1897; reprint ed., New York, 1957), vol. 1, chaps. 21–22; Charles H. Lincoln, *The Revolutionary Movement in Pennsylvania, 1760–1776* (Philadelphia, 1901), pp. 235–48.

3. For example, Schlesinger, *Prelude to Independence,* p. 280.

4. To Charles Pettit, 30 March 1776, in William B. Reed, ed., *Life and Correspondence of Joseph Reed* (Philadelphia, 1847), 1: 182.

5. Benjamin H. Newcomb, *Franklin and Galloway: A Political Partnership* (New Haven, 1972), pp. 275–85.

6. [Joseph Galloway], *A Candid Examination of the Mutual Claims of Great Britain and the Colonies* . . . (New York, 1775), p. 31.

7. Dickinson defended his opposition to independence in his speech to the Continental Congress, 1 July 1776 (in Hezekiah Niles, ed., *Principles and Acts of the American Revolution* [Chicago, 1876], pp. 400–402) and in his "Vindication" of 1 Jan. 1783 (in Charles J. Stillé, *The Life and Times of John Dickinson, 1732–1808* [Philadelphia, 1891], pp. 364–75). Although it would seem likely that Dickinson wrote at least a few essays for the press during the first months of 1776, there is not a single piece clearly identifiable as having been authored by him. David L. Jacobson, *John Dickinson and the Revolution in Pennsylvania, 1764–1776* (Berkeley, 1965), pp. 104–17, provides a useful survey of Dickinson's activities during the debate over independence. Jacobson, however, attributes *Remarks on a Late Pamphlet Entitled "Plain Truth"* . . . (Philadelphia, 1776) to Dickinson, an attribution that is surely erroneous. See Thomas R. Adams, *American Independence, the Growth of an Idea: A Bibliographical Study of the American Political Pamphlets Printed between 1764 and 1776 Dealing with the Dispute between Great Britain and Her Colonies* (Providence, 1965), p. 178.

8. Smith's abilities as a pulpit orator are noted by Lawrence H. Gipson, in his foreword to Albert F. Gegenheimer, *William Smith: Educator and Churchman, 1727–1803* (Philadelphia, 1943), p. v. For Smith's private attitudes on the increasing possibility of independence see his correspondence of late 1775 in Horace W. Smith, ed., *Life and Correspondence of the Reverend William Smith* (Philadelphia, 1879–80), 1: 524–39. The complete set of "Cato" essays is available in Peter Force, ed., *American Archives*, 4th ser. (Washington, D.C., 1837–46), 5: 125–27, 188–90, 443–46, 514–17, 542–46, 839–43, 850–53, 1049–51. A full study of Smith's career as a rhetorician is much needed.

9. [John Witherspoon], "Aristides," *Packet*, 13 May 1776; [Thomas Paine], "The Forester," ibid., 15 April 1776; John Adams, "Autobiography," in Charles F. Adams, ed., *The Works of John Adams* (Boston, 1856), 2: 509. For representative historical and critical judgments of *Plain Truth* see David Hawke, *In the Midst of a Revolution* (Philadelphia, 1961), p. 24n.; Tyler, *Literary History*, 1: 479–80. Bibliographic information on Chalmers's pamphlet is in Adams, *American Independence*, pp. 152–53. Merrill Jensen, *The Founding of a Nation: A History of the American Revolution, 1763–1776* (New York, 1968), p. 668, identifies Chalmers as a resident of Maryland.

10. Benjamin Rush, *Autobiography*, ed. George W. Corner (Princeton, 1948), p. 85. Hawke, *Midst of a Revolution*, pp. 102–6 and *passim*, writes of a Radical junto that seized control of the Philadelphia Committee of Inspection and Observation in February 1776 and subsequently guided the city into independence and the province into a new frame of government. Hawke identifies the six members of this junto—Rush, Cannon, Paine, Young, Marshall, and Matlack—as the prime movers of Radical politics during the first half of 1776. In a careful and detailed study, Richard A. Ryerson, "Leadership in Crisis: The Radical Committees of Philadelphia and the Coming of the Revolution in Pennsylvania,

1765–1776" (Ph.D. diss., Johns Hopkins University, 1973), chaps. 7–8, argues persuasively that the Radical leadership was far broader in composition and less conspiratorially motivated than Hawke portrays it. Ryerson demonstrates that the leadership of the resistance movement was being radically transformed as early as 1774 and that the rise to prominence and power of "new men" in 1776 was the natural culmination of a process set in motion much earlier. Ryerson's study, like Hawke's, is invaluable to anyone who seeks to understand the political situation in Philadelphia during the debate over independence. For further commentary upon these two works see Chapter 8, note 20, below.

11. James Duane, Jr., ed., *Extracts from the Diary of Chistopher Marshall, 1774–1781* (Albany, 1877), records almost daily meetings among members of the Radical hierarchy to discuss and work out common problems, to formulate political plans, and to consider questions of rhetorical strategy.

12. Adams, "Autobiography," in Adams, *Works*, 2: 509; Rush, *Autobiography*, p. 323. The best biography of Paine is David Freeman Hawke, *Paine* (New York, 1974); the best short account is Crane Brinton's sketch in Allen Johnson and Dumas Malone, eds., *The Dictionary of American Biography* (New York, 1928–36), 14: 159–66. An excellent treatment of Paine's discourse is Harry Hayden Clark, "Thomas Paine's Theories of Rhetoric," *Transactions of the Wisconsin Academy of Sciences, Arts, and Letters*, 28 (1933): 307–39.

13. On Cannon's identity as "Cassandra" see Schlesinger, *Prelude to Independence*, p. 262. Hawke, *Midst of a Revolution*, pp. 105–7, 149–50, 169–71, 186–92, provides a useful introduction to Cannon's persuasive activities, but he seriously overestimates Cannon's abilities as a rhetorician vis-à-vis those of Thomas Paine.

14. Rush, *Autobiography*, p. 110; Samuel Ward to [?], 1 March 1776, quoted in David Freeman Hawke, "Dr. Thomas Young—'Eternal Fisher in Troubled Waters': Notes for a Biography," *New York Historical Society Quarterly*, 54 (Jan. 1970): 24. For bibiliographical information on Green's pamphlet see Adams, *American Independence*, p. 156. The only essay published in Philadelphia during the debate over independence that has been positively identified as having been written by Young is "An Elector," *Packet*, 29 April 1776. I strongly suspect, however, that he also wrote the series of essays published over the signature of "A Watchman" (*Ledger*, 30 April 1776; *Evening Post*, 10 and 13 June 1776; *Packet*, 24 June 1776). For discussion of Young's "Elector" essay see Chapter 7 below.

15. Samuel Adams and his cousin John were deeply involved in Philadelphia politics during the first half of 1776 and played crucial roles in the transactions of May and June that helped topple the Pennsylvania Assembly and bring the province into the independence column in Congress. See Hawke, *Midst of a Revolution, passim;* and the discussion in Chapter 8 below. Samuel Adams's pseudonyms in 1776 are revealed by Schlesinger, *Prelude to Independence*, p. 263.

16. "To the Electors and Freeholders of the City of Philadelphia," broadside, 30 April 1776 (Evans no. 15104).

17. This estimate is based primarily upon Joseph Galloway's judgment of 1 April 1775 that those Philadelphians "determined to bring about a total separation of the two countries at all events" totaled "but one-fourth part of our people" (to Samuel Verplanck, *Pennsylvania Magazine of History and Biography,* 21 [1897]: 482). Galloway's estimate was unquestionably much too high at the time he made it, for only a very few of the most ardent Whigs favored independence before the outbreak of war in New England, but it does give us an idea of the proportion of Philadelphians who were "hard-core" supporters of the resistance movement on the eve of the battles of Lexington and Concord. Since these hard-core Whig partisans probably provided most of the public support for independence at the beginning of 1776, Galloway's calculation provides useful, indeed the best extant, quantitative evidence by which to gauge the degree to which revolutionary ideas had taken hold in the city by the beginning of 1776.

18. "Extracts from the Diary of Dr. James Clitherall, 1776," *Pennsylvania Magazine of History and Biography,* 22 (1898): 469; John Adams, "Diary," in Adams, *Works,* 2: 407–8; Charles Thomson to William Henry Drayton, n.d., in "The Papers of Charles Thomson," *Collections of the New York Historical Society,* 11 (1878): 280–81; Benjamin Rush to John Adams, 8 Feb. 1813, in L. H. Butterfield, ed., *Letters of Benjamin Rush* (Princeton, 1951), 2: 1181–82. Although some younger, less conservative Quakers left the Society and organized "Free Quakers" to support the revolutionary cause, the vast majority of Philadelphia Quakers refused to support either side actively. See Isaac Sharpless, "The Quakers in the American Revolution," in Rufus Jones, ed., *The Quakers in the American Colonies* (New York, 1966), p. 565.

19. I may be overestimating somewhat the upper boundary of this group since many Philadelphians who would remain loyal to England after the Declaration of Independence were still uncommitted in January 1776. Most of the city's Quakers, however, who comprised roughly one-seventh, or 14 percent, of Philadelphia's population, were in the anti-revolutionary camp by the beginning of the year. See note 18 above; Chapter 1 above; and Chapter 6 below. Also see the calculations of Paul H. Smith, "The American Loyalists: Notes on Their Organization and Numerical Strength," *William and Mary Quarterly,* 25 (April 1968): 259–77.

My estimates of the size of the pro- and anti-independence portions of the Philadelphia audience are admittedly inexact. But they are defensible and allow one to discuss political divisions in the city in language more precise than "many," "some," "a great proportion," and the like. They provide a quantitative point of departure for assessing the influence of Radical and Moderate rhetoric.

20. Christopher Schultz quoted in John J. Stoudt, "The German Press in Pennsylvania and the American Revolution," *Pennsylvania Magazine of History and Biography,* 59 (1935): 88; troop information in *Journal,* 14 June 1775.

21. Adams to Abigail Adams, 10 June 1775, in Charles F. Adams, ed., *Letters of John Adams, Addressed to His Wife* (Boston, 1841), 1: 42; Duane, *Diary of Christopher Marshall,* p. 23; unidentified Philadelphian quoted in

John C. Miller, *Origins of the American Revolution,* rev. ed. (Stanford, 1959), p. 416.

22. Sherman to Joseph Trumbull, 6 July 1775, in Edmund C. Burnett, ed., *Letters of Members of the Continental Congress* (Washington, D.C., 1921), 1: 154; Church to Major Kane, 23 July 1775, in Force, *American Archives,* 2: 1714.

23. Reed to George Washington, 3 March 1776, in Reed, *Life and Correspondence,* 1: 163; Adams to Moses Gill, 10 June 1775, in Burnett, *Letters of Members,* 2: 118.

24. Henry quoted in Rush, *Autobiography,* p. 111; Adams to Benjamin Hichborn, 29 May 1776, in Burnett, *Letters of Members,* 1: 467–68.

25. To Abigail Adams, 17 June 1775, and to Moses Gill, 10 June 1775, in Burnett, *Letters of Members,* 1: 132, 118; to Abigail Adams, 11 Feb. 1776, in Adams, *Letters of Adams,* 1: 82.

26. To Joseph Hawley, 15 April 1776, in Harry A. Cushing, ed., *The Writings of Samuel Adams* (New York, 1907), 3: 280. For the extent of the powers of Congress by the end of 1775 see Lawrence H. Gipson, *The British Empire before the American Revolution* (New York, 1936–70), 12: 325ff.

27. To [David Hartley?], 3 Oct. 1775, and to Charles Dumas, 9 Dec. 1775, in Albert H. Smyth, ed., *The Writings of Benjamin Franklin* (New York, 1907), 6: 430–31, 432–36.

28. See John Penn to Thomas Parson, 14 Feb. 1776; Oliver Wolcott to Samuel Lyman, 19 Feb. 1776; Robert Alexander to Maryland Council of Safety, 27 Feb. 1776; Joseph Hewes to Samuel Johnson, 20 March 1776; John Adams to Horatio Gates, 23 March 1776; Elbridge Gerry to James Warren, 26 March 1776; Thomas Stone to Daniel of St. Thomas Jenifer, 24 April 1776, in Burnett, *Letters of Members,* 1: 349, 356, 366, 401, 405–6, 409–10, 431–32.

29. 26 March 1776, in ibid., p. 410.

30. Quoted in Arthur M. Schlesinger, *The Birth of the Nation: A Portrait of the American People on the Eve of Independence* (New York, 1968), p. 242. The extreme personal anxiety caused by the unsettled state of British-American relations after 1774 warrants attention. The extent and intensity of that anxiety in Philadelphia was suggested by Benjamin Rush. Many years after the Revolution he recalled the uncommon number of apoplectic fits in Philadelphia during the years 1774–76. The frequency of these fits increased dramatically after the outbreak of war in 1775, and Rush attributed the death of one man in October 1775 to "the pressure of the uncertainty of those great events upon his mind" (*Medical Inquiries and Observations* [Philadelphia, 1794–98], 1: 271–72, quoted in David Hawke, *Benjamin Rush: Revolutionary Gadfly* [Indianapolis, 1971], p. 125).

CHAPTER 6.
## RHETORIC OF SEPARATION

1. For exceptions see "Moderator," *Packet,* 25 July 1774; "Political Observations without Order: Addressed to the People of America,"

ibid., 14 Nov. 1774. The second of these essays is especially noteworthy in that it presaged many of the ideas developed by Thomas Paine in *Common Sense*. Also consult, in general, J. M. Bumstead, "Things in the Womb of Time: Ideas of American Independence, 1633 to 1763," *William and Mary Quarterly*, 31 (Oct. 1974): 533–64.

2. Assembly instructions, 9 Nov. 1775, in Peter Force, ed., *American Archives*, 4th ser. (Washington, D.C., 1837–46), 3: 1408; "Independent Whig," *Journal*, 29 Nov. 1775. Other participants in the newspaper debate were "A Lover of Order," ibid., 22 Nov. 1775; "A Continental Farmer," ibid., 6 Dec. 1775; "A Pennsylvania Associator," *Ledger*, 25 Nov. 1775; "A Man of Candor," ibid., 9 Dec. 1775. Other Philadelphia writers who openly championed independence during the fall of 1775 were "Antoninus," *Journal*, 11 Oct.; "Salus Populi," ibid., 27 Dec.

3. Thus Benjamin Rush, when prompting Paine to compose an essay to relieve the public's "prejudice and error" regarding divorce from England, warned him "that there were two words which he should avoid by every means as necessary to his own safety and that of the public—*independence* and *republicanism*" (quoted in David Hawke, *Benjamin Rush: Revolutionary Gadfly* [Indianapolis, 1971], p. 137).

4. Writing as "Cato," *Packet*, 11 March 1776, William Smith called *Common Sense* the "first open proposition for independence" in Philadelphia. "A Common Man," *Ledger*, 30 March 1776, observed that public debate on "the question of independency has been lately started, in a pamphlet entitled *Common Sense*." Unless otherwise noted, all subsequent newspaper and broadside citations are from 1776.

5. [Thomas Paine], "The Forester," *Journal*, 10 April. Although at times contradictory and overly self-serving, the most detailed accounts of the writing and publication of *Common Sense* are those provided by Benjamin Rush in his *Autobiography*, ed. George W. Corner (Princeton, 1948), pp. 113–15, and in his letter to James Cheetham, 17 July 1809, in L. H. Butterfield, ed., *Letters of Benjamin Rush* (Princeton, 1951), 2: 1007–9. Whether *Common Sense* was published on 9 or 10 January is not entirely clear. My acceptance of the latter date is based upon Paine's letter to Henry Laurens, 14 Jan. 1779, in Philip S. Foner, ed., *The Complete Writings of Thomas Paine* (New York, 1945), 2: 1162–63.

6. Edward Burd to J. Burd, 15 March 1776, in Lewis B. Walker, ed., *The Burd Papers: Selections from Letters Written by Edward Burd, 1763–1828* (privately printed, 1899), p. 84; Rush to James Cheetham, 17 July 1809, in Butterfield, *Letters of Rush*, 2: 1008. Information on the publication and circulation of *Common Sense* taken from Thomas R. Adams, *American Independence, the Growth of an Idea: A Bibliographical Study of the American Political Pamphlets Printed between 1764 and 1776 Dealing with the Dispute between Great Britain and Her Colonies* (Providence, 1965), pp. 164–71.

7. [Thomas Paine], *Common Sense* . . . (Philadelphia, 1776), pp. 43, 30, 44, 50, 44–45, 30, iii, 38.

8. John Adams, "Autobiography," in Charles F. Adams, ed., *The Works of John Adams* (Boston, 1856), 2: 507.

9. See Chapter 4.

10. For example, after exhorting his listeners to support New England patriots in their battles against "the galling yoke of *perpetual slavery*," John Carmichael reminded them: "You must still continue to revere loyalty, and observe your allegiance to the King, on the true principles of the constitution. Your drawing the sword now must not be against the person of his majesty; but the maladministration of his government by designing, mischief-making ministers" (*A Self-Defensive War Lawful* . . . [Philadelphia, 1775], pp. 6, 10).

11. Paine, *Common Sense,* pp. 10, 57, 47, 20, 14, 28, 29.

12. Ibid., pp. 48–49.

13. Paine to Henry Laurens, 14 Jan. 1779, in Foner, *Writings of Paine,* 2: 1162. Although Paine recalled in his letter to Laurens that *Common Sense* was published the same day George III's speech arrived in Philadelphia, it was likely released one or two days after the king's address reached the city on 8 January. See Richard Smith, "Diary," in Edmund C. Burnett, ed., *Letters of Members of the Continental Congress* (Washington, D.C., 1921), 1: 302; William Duane, Jr., ed., *Extracts from the Diary of Christopher Marshall, 1774–1781* (Albany, 1877), p. 55. The reception in Philadelphia of King George's speech of 26 October 1775 is discussed later in this chapter.

14. Paine, *Common Sense,* p. 60.

15. [Charles Inglis], *The True Interest of America Impartially Stated* . . . (Philadelphia, 1776), p. 34.

16. Much more could be said about the subliminal meanings and functions of Paine's pamphlet, but such is not vital to our purposes here. For an example of the rich critical perspectives that can fruitfully be applied to *Common Sense* see Winthrop Jordan, "Familial Politics: Thomas Paine and the Killing of the King, 1776," *Journal of American History,* 60 (Sept. 1973): 294–308. David Freeman Hawke, *Paine* (New York, 1974), makes noteworthy though at times overly facile attempts to probe the psychological dimensions of Paine's public rhetoric.

17. Harry Hayden Clark, "Thomas Paine's Theories of Rhetoric," *Transactions of the Wisconsin Academy of Sciences, Arts, and Letters,* 38 (1933): 323.

18. Paine quoted in ibid., p. 324; Jefferson quoted in Arnold King, "Thomas Paine in America, 1774–1787" (Ph.D. diss., University of Chicago, 1951), p. 72; Adams to Abigail Adams, 19 March 1776, in Adams, *Works of Adams,* 1: 240n; Adams, "Autobiography," in ibid., 2: 509.

19. Paine, *Common Sense,* pp. 29, 2, 22–23, 28–29, 60, 45, 30. The style of *Common Sense* is discussed further in the Afterword, below.

20. Most recently by Bernard Bailyn, "Common Sense," in *Fundamental Testaments of the American Revolution* (Washington, D.C., 1973), pp. 11–13.

21. Although remarkably adapted to the political and psychological needs of the Philadelphia audience, *Common Sense* could probably not have been written by other than an Englishman. Paine himself often expressed this very thought, as in his letter to Nathanael Greene, 9 Sept. 1780, in Foner, *Writings of Paine,* 2: 1189.

22. "Demophilus," *Packet*, 12 Feb.; William Franklin to Lord George Germain, 28 March 1776, in *New Jersey Archives*, 1st ser. (Newark and Trenton, 1880–1949), 10: 708; letter from Philadelphia to London, 12 March 1776, in Force, *American Archives*, 5: 187.

23. This subject is discussed in Chapter 8.

24. "Salus Populi," *Journal*, 14 Feb.

25. [Thomas Paine], "A Dialogue between the Ghost of General Montgomery . . . and an American Delegate," *Packet*, 19 Feb.; "A Watchman," *Evening Post*, 13 June; London report, in *Journal*, 31 Jan.

26. *Packet*, 19 Feb.

27. John Dickinson to Josiah Quincy, Jr., 28 Oct. 1774, in Eliza S. Quincy, ed., *Memoir of the Life of Josiah Quincy, Junior* (Boston, 1875), p. 169.

28. Olive Branch petition, in Force, *American Archives*, 2: 1870–72; Proclamation of Rebellion, in ibid., 3: 240–41; Charles Thomson to William Henry Drayton, n.d., in "The Papers of Charles Thomson," *Collections of the New York Historical Society*, 11 (1878): 285. On the arrival of the Proclamation of Rebellion in Philadelphia see Duane, *Diary of Christopher Marshall*, p. 50.

29. London letter, in *Evening Post*, 16 Nov. 1775. George's speech of 26 October is in Force, *American Archives*, 6: 1–3.

30. Pauline Maier, *From Resistance to Revolution: Colonial Radicals and the Development of American Opposition to Britain, 1765–1776* (New York, 1972), pp. 211, 269. While the great majority of Philadelphians were not versed in the fine points of Whiggish revolutionary theory, neither were they completely unacquainted with them, as evidenced by James Wilson's speech to the Pennsylvania Provincial Convention, Jan. 1775, in Robert G. McCloskey, ed., *The Works of James Wilson* (Cambridge, 1967), 2: 747–58.

31. "An American," *Journal*, 17 Jan.

32. "Cassandra," *Packet*, 8 April; "An American," *Journal*, 17 Jan.

33. William H. Nelson, "The Revolutionary Character of the American Revolution," *American Historical Review*, 70 (July 1965): 1008; Cecelia Kenyon, "Republicanism and Radicalism in the American Revolution: An Old Fashioned Interpretation," in Jack P. Greene, ed., *The Reinterpretation of the American Revolution, 1763–1789* (New York, 1968), p. 304; James H. Hutson, *Pennsylvania Politics, 1746–1770: The Movement for Royal Government and Its Consequences* (Princeton, 1972), p. 248.

34. Paine, *Common Sense*, p. 5. This is not to say that most Philadelphians were avowed republicans, as we shall see in the next chapter.

35. To Horatio Gates, 10 June 1776, in Harry A. Cushing, ed., *The Writings of Samuel Adams* (New York, 1907), 3: 292.

36. John C. Miller, *Origins of the American Revolution*, rev. ed. (Stanford, 1959), p. 475. For details see Lawrence H. Gipson, *The British Empire before the American Revolution* (New York, 1936–70), 12: 337ff. Word of the commissioners' departure from London was first reported in the *Ledger*, 17 Feb.

37. Extract of a letter from John Adams, 14 April 1776, in Force,

*American Archives,* 5: 931; Reed to George Washington, 15 March 1776, in ibid., p. 235; "Cassandra," *Evening Post,* 2 March.

38. "Cassandra," *Evening Post,* 2 March; untitled essay, in ibid., 26 March; "To All Parents in the Thirteen Colonies," *Packet,* 12 Feb. For other Radical attacks on the commissioners see "Sincerus," *Evening Post,* 13 Feb.; "A Watchman," ibid., 13 June; "Dialogus," ibid., 9 March; "Independent," *Packet,* 18 March; "The Forester," ibid., 1 April; "Candidus," *Gazette,* 6 March.

39. See Chapter 8.

40. "The Forester," *Journal,* 24 April; "Cassandra," *Ledger,* 27 April.

41. According to "Cato," *Ledger,* 23 March, the question at issue was "whether the liberty or happiness of *America* can best be secured by a constitutional reconciliation with *Great Britain,* or by a total separation from it."

42. "Cassandra," *Packet,* 8 April.

43. "A Watchman," *Evening Post,* 13 June; "Salus Populi," *Journal,* 24 Jan.

44. "Cassandra," *Ledger,* 27 April.

45. *Remarks on a Late Pamphlet Entitled "Plain Truth"* . . . (Philadelphia, 1776), p. 22.

46. Paine, *Common Sense,* p. 59; "A Religious Politician," *Journal,* 7 Feb.; "A Watchman," *Evening Post,* 13 June.

47. Paine, *Common Sense,* p. 40; "A Watchman," *Evening Post,* 13 June.

48. "A Common Man," *Ledger,* 30 March. In his second "Forester" essay (*Packet,* 15 April), Paine responded to "A Common Man" by arguing that men's political characters, dependencies, and connections were so integrally tied up with the political measures they advocated that "to prevent our being deceived by the last, we must be acquainted with the first. A total ignorance of men lays us under the danger of mistaking plausibility for principle. Could the wolf bleat like the lamb, the stock would soon be enticed into ruin; wherefore, to prevent the mischief, he ought to be seen as well as heard. There never was, nor ever will be, nor ever ought to be, any important political debate carried on in which a total separation, in all cases, between men and measures could be admitted with sufficient safety. When hypocrisy shall be banished from the earth, the knowledge of men will be unnecessary, because their measures cannot then be fraudulent; but until that time comes (which never will come), they ought, under proper limitations, to go together. We have already too much secrecy in some things, and too little in others. Were men more known, and measures more concealed, we should have fewer hypocrites and more security."

49. "R.," *Packet,* 8 April. John Dickinson, who fell from public favor in 1776 because of his failure to support independence, foresaw in 1768 what would occur if a movement ever developed for separation from England. "Wise and good men," he wrote in his *Letters from a Farmer in Pennsylvania,* "in vain [will] oppose the storm, and may think themselves fortunate if, in attempting to preserve their ungrateful fellow citizens, they do not ruin themselves. Their *prudence* will be called *baseness;* their *moderation* will be called *guilt.*"

50. "Cassandra," *Ledger*, 13 April.

51. This is not to say that all ad hominem arguments lacked substantive import for Philadelphia centrists, as we shall see in the next chapter.

52. "Salus Populi," *Journal*, 14 Feb.; "Reasons for a Declaration of Independence of the American Colonies," *Evening Post*, 20 April; [Jacob Green], *Observations on the Reconciliation of Great Britain and the Colonies* . . . (Philadelphia, 1776), p. 22.

53. David Hawke, *In the Midst of a Revolution* (Philadelphia, 1961), pp. 45–49; Anne Bezanson, *Prices and Inflation during the American Revolution: Pennsylvania, 1770–1790* (Philadelphia, 1951), pp. 321–22; Force, *American Archives*, 5: 764–65.

54. "A.B.," *Journal*, 28 Feb; "A Dialogue between the Ghost of General Montgomery . . . and An American Delegate," *Packet*, 19 Feb.

55. "A.B.," *Journal*, 28 Feb.

56. Cf. Marc Egnal and Joseph Ernst, "An Economic Interpretation of the American Revolution," *William and Mary Quarterly*, 29 (Jan. 1972): 3–32; Charles S. Olton, "Philadelphia's Mechanics in the First Decade of Revolution, 1765–1775," *Journal of American History*, 59 (Sept. 1972): 311–26.

57. Green, *Observations*, p. 29; Paine, *Common Sense*, pp. ii, 60.

58. See Chapter 7.

59. "Salus Populi," *Journal*, 6 March.

60. Ibid.; "Questions and Answers," *Evening Post*, 17 Feb.

61. "Salus Populi," *Journal*, 13 March. Cf. Merrill Jensen, "The American People and the American Revolution," *Journal of American History*, 57 (June 1970): 7.

62. W. Paul Adams, "Republicanism in Political Rhetoric before 1776," *Political Science Quarterly*, 85 (Sept. 1970): 394–421; Roy N. Lokken, "The Concept of Democracy in Colonial Political Thought," *William and Mary Quarterly*, 16 (Oct. 1959): 568–80.

63. [James Wilson], *Considerations on the Nature and the Extent of the Legislative Authority of the British Parliament* (Philadelphia, 1774), p. 14; Rush quoted in Hawke, *Benjamin Rush*, p. 137.

64. *Packet*, 19 Feb.

65. Adams, "Republicanism in Political Rhetoric," p. 420.

66. *Remarks on a Pamphlet Entitled "Plain Truth,"* p. 8; Paine, *Common Sense*, pp. 53, 26, 52; "Salus Populi," *Journal*, 6 March. In an interesting switch, probably designed to secure moderate and conservative support, one Radical writer went so far as to claim that independence would deliver Philadelphians from the direful effects of government by committees and conventions ("Reasons for a Declaration of Independence of the American Colonies," *Evening Post*, 20 April).

67. Cf. Kenyon, "Republicanism and Radicalism in the American Revolution," *passim;* Pauline Maier, "The Beginnings of American Republicanism, 1765–1776," in *The Development of a Revolutionary Mentality* (Washington, D.C., 1972), pp. 99–117; Jack P. Greene, "The Preconditions for American Republicanism: A Comment," in ibid., pp. 119–24.

68. "The Forester," *Packet*, 22 April; Paine, *Common Sense*, p. 78. Also

see "To the Friends of the American Army," *Journal,* 17 April; "Candidus," *Evening Post,* 3 Feb.; "Reasons for a Declaration of Independence of the American Colonies," ibid., 20 April; "Republicus," ibid., 29 June.

69. See Chapter 7.

70. Green, *Observations,* p. 16; Paine, *Common Sense,* p. 32; "Salus Populi,"*Journal,* 14 Feb.

71. Paine, *Common Sense,* pp. 64–68; untitled essay, in *Evening Post,* 30 March; "Questions and Answers," ibid., 17 Feb.

72. Green, *Observations,* p. 16; Paine, *Common Sense,* pp. 61–69; "Questions and Answers," *Evening Post,* 17 Feb.

73. "Questons and Answers," *Evening Post,* 17 Feb.; *Four Letters on Interesting Subjects* (Philadelphia, 1776), p. 9.

74. John Shy, *Toward Lexington: The Role of the British Army in the Coming of the American Revolution* (Princeton, 1965), chap. 8.

75. Radicals naturally sought to downplay these setbacks. Writing in the *Journal* of 17 January, for instance, "An American" hoped his fellow Philadelphians would not despair over the loss of Norfolk "but rather rejoice that half the mischief our enemies may do us is done already." To be sure, Norfolk was the principal trading city in Virginia, but "we are only sharing part of the sufferings of our American brethren, and can now glory in having received one of the keenest strokes of the enemy without flinching."

76. For example, "N.N.," *Chronicle,* 5 Dec. 1768; "Caius," *Journal,* 5 Oct. 1774; [Charles Lee], *Strictures on a Pamphlet Entitled, "A Friendly Address to All Reasonable Americans, on the subject of Our Political Confusions"* . . . (Philadelphia, 1774), pp. 10–12.

77. See Chapter 8.

78. *Remarks on a Pamphlet Entitled "Plain Truth,"* p. 29; Green, *Observations,* p. 19.

79. Richard A. Ryerson, "Leadership in Crisis: The Radical Committees of Philadelphia and the Coming of the Revolution in Pennsylvania, 1765–1776" (Ph.D. diss., Johns Hopkins University, 1973), p. 304. The epistle of January 1775 is in Force, *American Archives,* 1: 1093–94.

80. Force, *American Archives,* 2: 1590–91.

81. Ibid., 3: 1777–79.

82. Duane, *Diary of Christopher Marshall,* pp. 49–50. The committee's "Petition and Remonstrance" was printed in all Philadelphia papers and is readily available in Force, *American Archives,* 3: 1781–83.

83. Both documents are in Force, *American Archives,* 3: 1783–87.

84. Ibid., pp. 1808–10.

85. "Candidus," *Evening Post,* 3 Feb.

86. Force, *American Archives,* 4: 785–87.

87. Richard Bauman, *For the Reputation of Truth: Politics, Religion, and Conflict among the Pennsylvania Quakers, 1750–1800* (Baltimore, 1971), pp. 145–46.

88. Charles Thomson to William Henry Drayton, n.d., in "Papers of Charles Thomson," p. 281.

89. Bauman, *For the Reputation of Truth,* p. 152; Isaac Sharpless, "The

Quakers in the American Revolution," in Rufus Jones, ed., *The Quakers in the American Colonies* (New York, 1966), p. 565; Charles Thomson to William Henry Drayton, n.d., in "Papers of Charles Thomson," pp. 285–86.

90. "Salus Populi," *Journal*, 14 Feb.

91. [Thomas Paine], "Epistle to Quakers," in Foner, *Writings of Paine*, 2: 55–60.

92. Charles Thomson to William Henry Drayton, n.d., in "Papers of Charles Thomson," p. 286.

93. See Carmichael, *A Self-Defensive War Lawful.*

CHAPTER 7.
## RHETORIC OF RECONCILIATION

1. "Moderator," *Ledger,* 27 April 1776. Unless otherwise noted, all subsequent newspaper and broadside citations are from 1776.

2. Smith's series began in the *Ledger,* 9 March; Chalmers's pamphlet was first advertised in the *Journal,* 13 March.

3. According to Arnold King, "Thomas Paine in America, 1774–1787" (Ph.D. diss., University of Chicago, 1951), pp. 59, 65, Paine began composing *Common Sense* in September 1775; David Hawke, *Paine* (New York, 1974), p. 41, states that Paine began writing his famous essay in November.

4. The Radicals' proposal for a provincial convention is treated in Chapter 8. As William Franklin informed Lord George Germain on 28 March 1776, many people "of sense and property" did not comprehend "that there were any persons of consequence, either in or out of the Congress, who harbored such intentions [of independence]." Fortunately, Franklin added, the friends of reconciliation "are now alarmed—see their danger—and begin to venture to express their fears and apprehensions" (*New Jersey Archives,* 1st ser. [Newark and Trenton, 1880–1949], 10: 708).

5. "Cato," *Packet,* 11 March.

6. "Cato," *Ledger,* 27 April. Similarly, "Rationalis," *Gazette,* 28 Feb.; "Moderator," *Ledger,* 27 April.

7. [Charles Inglis], *The True Interest of America Impartially Stated . . .* (Philadelphia, 1776), p. vi. Inglis, of course, was not a Philadelphian. Nor was he directly involved in the city's political affairs in 1776. His pamphlet was well received in the city—at least by anti-independence residents—and went through two local editions in less than two months. Bibliographical information from Thomas R. Adams, *American Independence, the Growth of an Idea: A Bibliographical Study of the American Political Pamphlets Printed between 1764 and 1776 Dealing with the Dispute between Great Britain and Her Colonies* (Providence, 1965), pp. 157–58.

8. "To the Electors and Freeholders of the City of Philadelphia," broadside, 30 April (Evans no. 15104).

9. "Cato," *Packet,* 11 March.

10. See Chapter 6, note 37.

11. "Cato," *Ledger,* 30 March; Inglis, *True Interest,* pp. 48–49.

12. "Cato," *Ledger,* 30 March.

13. [James Chalmers], *Plain Truth . . .* (Philadelphia, 1776), p. 14; Franklin to Charles-Guilluame-Frédéric Dumas, 25 July 1768, in Leonard W. Labaree et al., eds., *The Papers of Benjamin Franklin* (New Haven, 1959–   ), 15: 179–80.

14. Petition of the Stamp Act Congress to the House of Commons, in Edmund S. Morgan, ed., *Prologue to Revolution: Sources and Documents on the Stamp Act Crisis, 1764–1766* (Chapel Hill, 1959), p. 68; "Declaration of Causes of Taking up Arms," 6 July 1775, in Samuel Eliot Morison, ed., *Sources and Documents Illustrating the American Revolution, 1764–1788* (London, 1923), p. 145; Assembly instructions, 9 Nov. 1775, in Peter Force, ed., *American Archives,* 4th ser. (Washington, D.C., 1837–46), 3: 1408.

15. "To the Electors and Freeholders of the City of Philadelphia," broadside, 30 April (Evans no. 15104); "Seek Truth," *Packet,* 22 April; "Cato," *Ledger,* 23 March and 27 April. Also see "Civis," *Gazette,* 1 May; "Cato," *Packet,* 11 March; Chalmers, *Plain Truth,* pp. 60–61.

16. "Civis," *Gazette,* 1 May; "Cato," *Packet,* 11 March; "Cato," *Ledger,* 23 March.

17. To Arthur Lee, 29 April 1775, in Richard Henry Lee, ed., *Life of Arthur Lee* (Boston, 1829), 2: 311. As Thomas Paine perceptively wrote in the first of his "Forester" essays (*Packet,* 1 April), Moderate publicists were unable to write of specific terms for a settlement: "If they be calculated to please the Cabinet, they will not go down with the colonies; and if they be suited to the colonies, they will be rejected by the Cabinet."

18. "T.L.," *Evening Post,* 26 March; Inglis, *True Interest,* p. 51. Also see "Cato," *Packet* 25 March; "Moderator," *Ledger,* 27 April.

19. Chalmers, *Plain Truth,* pp. 17–21, 25–28, 38–41.

20. "Cato," *Packet,* 25 March; Chalmers, *Plain Truth,* p. 22; Inglis, *True Interest,* p. 66.

21. Inglis, *True Interest,* p. 64; "Hamden," *Ledger,* 11 May; "Cato," *Packet,* 25 March and 1 April.

22. "Extracts from 'The Sentiments of a Foreigner on the Disputes of Great Britain and America,'" *Ledger,* 20 Jan.; Inglis, *True Interest,* p. 50; "Hamden," *Ledger,* 18 May.

23. Lawrence H. Gipson, *The British Empire before the American Revolution* (New York, 1936–70), 11: 361–416; David Hawke, *In the Midst of a Revolution* (Philadelphia, 1961), pp. 50–54.

24. Polly Frazer to Persifor Frazer, 27 Aug. 1776, in "Some Extracts from the Papers of General Persifor Frazer," *Pennsylvania Magazine of History and Biography,* 31 (1907): 136; Chalmers, *Plain Truth,* pp. 63–64; "Cato," *Ledger,* 27 April.

25. John Adams to Joseph Hawley, 25 Nov. 1775, in Edmund C. Burnett, ed., *Letters of Members of the Continental Congress* (Washington, D.C., 1921), 1: 260; W. Paul Adams, "Republicanism in Political Rhetoric before 1776," *Political Science Quarterly,* 85 (Sept. 1970): 420–21; "Salus Populi," *Journal,* 13 March. Also see the discussion in the preceding chapter.

26. "Civis," *Ledger,* 6 April; Inglis, *True Interest,* p. 10.

27. "Civis," *Ledger,* 6 April; "Rationalis," *Gazette,* 28 Feb.; Inglis, *True Interest,* p. 53; Chalmers, *Plain Truth,* pp. 9–10; "Cato," *Ledger,* 27 April.

28. "Cato," *Ledger,* 30 March and 13 April; "Rationalis," *Gazette,* 28 Feb.; Chalmers, *Plain Truth,* pp. 5–6.

29. "Cato," *Packet,* 15 April; Inglis, *True Interest,* p. 21.

30. "Cato," *Packet,* 15 April; "Civis," *Ledger,* 6 April. The most extended attack upon republicanism to appear in Philadelphia was [Carter Braxton], *An Address to the Convention of the Colony and Ancient Dominion of Virginia . . .* (Philadelphia, 1776). Braxton's pamphlet reflected the deep divisions over republicanism that existed throughout America, but it was published too late (likely mid-June) to have any real impact on the outcome of the debate over independence in Philadelphia.

31. "Cato," *Ledger,* 27 April and 13 April; "Seek Truth," *Packet,* 22 April.

32. "Cato," *Ledger,* 9 March, 23 March, 27 April; "Cato," *Packet,* 11 March.

33. Charles S. Olton, "Philadelphia Artisans and the American Revolution" (Ph.D. diss., University of California, Berkeley, 1967), pp. 199–200; Alexander Graydon, *Memoirs of His Own Time. With Reminiscences of the Men and Events of the Revolution* (Philadelphia, 1846), p. 122.

34. Philip Davidson, *Propaganda and the American Revolution, 1763–1783* (Chapel Hill, 1941), p. 292; Chalmers, *Plain Truth,* p. 8.

35. See Chapter 1.

36. Resolves of the Philadelphia Committee of Inspection and Observation, 19 Sept. 1775, in *Journal,* 20 Sept. 1775.

37. Graydon, *Memoirs,* pp. 126–27, 284; Benjamin Rush, *Autobiography,* ed. George W. Corner (Princeton, 1948), p. 117.

38. Hawke, *Midst of a Revolution,* pp. 28, 104–5. Also see David Freeman Hawke, "Dr. Thomas Young—'Eternal Fisher in Troubled Waters': Notes for a Biography," *New York Historical Society Quarterly,* 54 (Jan. 1970): 7–29; Henry H. Edes, "Memoir of Dr. Thomas Young, 1731–1777," *Publications of the Colonial Society of Massachusetts,* 11 (1906–7): 2–54.

39. "To the Electors and Freeholders of the City of Philadelphia," broadside, 30 April (Evans no. 15104).

40. "Cato," *Ledger,* 13 April.

41. "To the Electors and Freeholders of the City of Philadelphia," broadside, 30 April (Evans no. 15104).

42. "Civis," *Gazette,* 1 May; "Civis," *Ledger,* 6 April.

43. Charles Thomson to William Henry Drayton, n.d., in "The Papers of Charles Thomson," *Collections of the New York Historical Society,* 11 (1878): 281.

44. "Cato," *Ledger,* 13 April, 30 March, 27 April, 20 April.

## Chapter 8. DENOUEMENT

1. Peter Force, ed., *American Archives,* 4th ser. (Washington, D.C., 1837–46), 3: 1793.

2. The results of the election in Philadelphia, as printed in the *Packet*, 6 May, were as follows: *Moderates*—Samuel Howell (941), Andrew Allen (923), Alexander Wilcox (921), Thomas Willing (911); *Radicals*— George Clymer (923), Frederick Kuhl (904), Owen Biddle (903), Daniel Roberdeau (890).

3. Richard A. Ryerson, "Leadership in Crisis: The Radical Committees of Philadelphia and the Coming of the Revolution in Pennsylvania, 1765–1776" (Ph.D. diss., Johns Hopkins University, 1973), chaps. 2–7, is especially instructive on the conflicts between Philadelphia's Whig leadership and the Assembly during the years 1765–76.

4. "A Lover of Order," *Journal,* 22 Nov. 1775; [Thomas Paine], *Common Sense* . . . (Philadelphia, 1776), p. 74; "The Censor," *Evening Post,* 5 March 1776.

5. See "A Pennsylvania Associator," *Ledger,* 25 Nov. 1775; "Cato," ibid., 23 March 1776.

6. Charles H. Lincoln, *The Revolutionary Movement in Pennsylvania, 1760–1776* (Philadelphia, 1901), pp. 40–52.

7. *Evening Post,* 2 March 1776. All subsequent newspaper and broadside citations are from 1776 unless otherwise noted.

8. Joseph Reed to George Washington, 15 March 1776, in William B. Reed., ed., *Life and Correspondence of Joseph Reed* (Philadelphia, 1847), 1: 173.

9. *Evening Post,* 9 March.

10. The committee was selected on 8 March; the bill adding seventeen new seats was passed on 14 March by a vote of 21–9 (Force, *American Archives,* 5: 679, 683–84).

11. "Cato," *Ledger,* 9 March.

12. Ibid., 23 March.

13. "The Forester," *Packet,* 1 April.

14. "An Elector," ibid., 29 April. Young was answered on 30 April by a broadside entitled "To the Electors and Freeholders of the City of Philadelphia" (Evans no. 15104), and by "Civis," *Gazette,* 1 May.

15. Lincoln, *Revolutionary Movement,* first interpreted the Revolution in Pennsylvania as a dispute centering as much upon who would rule at home as upon home rule. Until recent years the "Lincoln thesis" dominated the thinking of historians about the nature of the Revolutionary experience in Pennsylvania: see J. Paul Selsam, *The Pennsylvania Constitution of 1776: A Study in Revolutionary Democracy* (Philadelphia, 1936); Robert L. Brunhouse, *The Counter-Revolution in Pennsylvania, 1776–1790* (Harrisburg, 1942); Elisha P. Douglass, *Rebels and Democrats: The Struggle for Equal Political Rights and Majority Rule during the American Revolution* (Chapel Hill, 1955), chaps. 12–14. Theodore Thayer, *Pennsylvania Politics and the Growth of Democracy, 1740–1776* (Harrisburg, 1953), revised several features of the traditional interpretation while seconding its view that the revolutionary movement culminated in 1776 in a self-consciously "democratic" triumph for Philadelphia mechanics and backcountry settlers. More substantial challenges to the Lincoln thesis have come from David Hawke, *In the Midst of a Revolution* (Philadelphia, 1961); Charles S. Olton, *Artisans for Independence: Philadelphia Mechanics and the American Revolution* (Syracuse, 1975);

James H. Hutson, *Pennsylvania Politics, 1746–1770: The Movement for Royal Government and Its Consequences* (Princeton, 1972); Ryerson, "Leadership in Crisis."

16. "A Common Man," *Ledger*, 30 March.

17. James Duane, Jr., ed., *Extracts from the Diary of Christopher Marshall, 1774–1781* (Albany, 1877), p. 68.

18. Elbridge Gerry to James Warren, 20 May 1776, in Force, *American Archives*, 6: 517.

19. My interpretation of this period has been influenced by David Hawke's *Midst of a Revolution* (see note 15 above), the most detailed examination of trends and events in Philadelphia during May–July 1776. In his outstanding doctoral disseration, "Leadership in Crisis" (cited in note 3 above), Richard A. Ryerson criticizes Hawke's thesis that Radical leaders conspired after the May election to overthrow the Assembly in order to ensure the success of the revolutionary movement in Pennsylvania. But though Ryerson correctly argues that the Radical leadership was far broader in composition and much more level-headed than Hawke portrayed it, he ultimately agrees that after failing to capture control of the Assembly on 1 May, Radical leaders determined to destroy the authority of the Assembly and establish a new government under which independence could be realized. What might be called the "conspiratorial" interpretation of the Revolution in Pennsylvania is firmly supported by the available evidence and has been espoused by a wide range of historians, among them Selsam, *Pennsylvania Constitution*, pp. 109–29; Douglass, *Rebels and Democrats*, p. 256; Reed, *Life and Correspondence*, 1: 154, 185–88; John T. Scharf and Thompson Westcott, *History of Philadelphia, 1609–1884* (Philadelphia, 1884), 1: 311–16; Charles J. Stillé, *The Life and Times of John Dickinson, 1732–1808* (Philadelphia, 1891), pp. 178–83; Merrill Jensen, *The Founding of a Nation: A History of the American Revolution, 1763–1776* (New York, 1968), pp. 683–87.

20. To William Henry Drayton, n.d., in "The Papers of Charles Thomson," *Collections of the New York Historical Society,* 11 (1878): 282–83.

21. Adams's resolution was approved on 10 May, the preamble on 15 May. Hereafter I shall refer to the resolution and preamble together as the resolve of 15 May. The full text of the resolution was first published in the *Evening Post,* 16 May, and was subsequently printed in all the other Philadelphia papers.

22. Adams to James Warren, 17 May 1776, in *Warren-Adams Letters* (Boston, 1917), p. 245; Adams to Abigail Adams, 17 May 1776, in Force, *American Archives,* 6: 448; "Diary of James Allen, 1770–1778," *Pennsylvania Magazine of History and Biography,* 9 (1885): 187.

23. Caesar Rodney to Thomas Rodney, 29 May 1776, in George H. Ryden, ed., *Letters to and from Caesar Rodney, 1756–1784* (Philadelphia, 1933), p. 85. Also see James Wilson to Horatio Gates, [June 1776?], in *Pennsylvania Magazine of History and Biography,* 36 (1912): 474–75.

24. *Journal,* 22 May; Bradford quoted in Thayer, *Pennsylvania Politics,* p. 181.

25. *Gazette,* 22 May.

26. Ibid., 29 May.

27. Cf. Hawke, *Midst of a Revolution,* pp. 142–43.

28. Charles Thomson to William Henry Drayton, n.d., in "Papers of Charles Thomson," p. 282.

29. Memorial of the Philadelphia Committee of Inspection and Observation, 24 May, in *Journal,* 29 May.

30. "Diary of James Allen," p. 188; statement of James Rankin, in Force, *American Archives,* 6: 621–22.

31. Force, *American Archives,* 6: 755.

32. Protest of the Committee of Privates, in *Ledger,* 22 June. The author of "To the People" was likely David Rittenhouse, George Clymer—both of Philadelphia—or Robert Whitehall of Cumberland County. See Ryerson, "Leadership in Crisis," p. 586n.

33. "To the People," *Gazette,* 26 June.

34. Quotation from "Extracts from the Diary of Dr. James Clitherall, 1776," *Pennsylvania Magazine of History and Biography,* 22 (1898): 471. Also see Hawke, *Midst of a Revolution,* pp. 149–50, 169–70; Olton, "Philadelphia Artisans," pp. 190–91.

35. *Ledger,* 22 June.

36. Hawke, *Midst of a Revolution,* p. 61. See Scharf and Wescott, *History of Philadelphia,* 1: 298–302, for a concise explanation of the origins, duties, and powers of the Committee of Safety. Tension between the Committee of Safety and the Radicals had existed for some time before the row-galley dispute, as is evident from Duane, *Diary of Christopher Marshall,* pp. 45–46.

37. Memorial of the Committee of Privates, 11 May, in Force, *American Archives,* 6: 422; "To the People," *Gazette,* 26 June.

38. "To the People," *Gazette,* 26 June; Force, *American Archives,* 6: 857–66. Ryerson, "Leadership in Crisis," pp. 590–94, assigns partial responsibility for the lack of a quorum to Moderate and conservative legislators who despaired of the Assembly's fate and went home.

39. Statement of the Patriotic Society, in *Evening Post,* 22 June; "To the People," *Gazette,* 26 June.

40. William Whipple to John Langdon, 22 June 1776, in Force, *American Archives,* 6: 1031; "Joseph Reed's Narrative," in "Papers of Charles Thomson," p. 273. For details on the Provincial Conference and Constitutional Convention consult Selsam, *Pennsylvania Constitution,* chap. 4; Lincoln, *Revolutionary Movement,* chap. 14; Thayer, *Pennsylvania Politics,* pp. 183–97; Hawke, *Midst of a Revolution,* pp. 171–95; Ryerson, "Leadership in Crisis," pp. 601–33.

41. *Evening Post,* 11 and 25 June. Lieutenant Colonel Lambert Cadwalader, commander of the Third Battalion, refused to poll his troops.

42. Alexander Graydon, *Memoirs of His Own Time. With Reminiscences of the Men and Events of the Revolution* (Philadelphia, 1846), p. 284.

43. "To the Public in All Parts of the Province," broadside, 21 May, in Force, *American Archives,* 6: 521; Duane, *Diary of Christopher Marshall,* pp. 76–77. The most extensive rationale for coercion was that presented by the Continental Congress in a series of resolutions approved on 2 January 1776. Realizing that many people opposed its ac-

tions, the Congress urged that they be treated kindly, since their errors probably proceeded more from "want of information" than from lack of "virtue or public spirit." For these misinformed individuals Congress suggested an extensive educational program on the "origin, nature, and extent of the present controversy." But it also lamented that there were more truculent individuals who, "regardless of their duty to their Creator, their country, and their posterity, have taken part with our oppressors, and influenced by the hope or possession of ignominious rewards, strive to recommend themselves to the bounty of administration by misrepresenting and traducing the conduct and principles of the friends of American liberty." For such intransigent souls Congress recommended that local conventions, councils of safety, and committees of inspection take the "most speedy and effectual" measures to "restrain" their "wicked practices." These resolutions were printed in all the Philadelphia papers and lent official sanction to the Radicals' activities.

44. "Diary of Dr. James Clitherall," pp. 470–71; "Republicus," *Evening Post,* 29 June.

45. Force, *American Archives,* 6: 954.

46. Oath quoted in Selsam, *Pennsylvania Constitution,* p. 164; "Diary of James Allen," p. 189.

47. Marshall quoted in Hawke, *Midst of a Revolution,* p. 193; Benjamin Rush to Anthony Wayne, 24 Sept. 1776, in L. H. Butterfield, ed., *Letters of Benjamin Rush* (Princeton, 1951), 1: 115. For the saga of politics in Pennsylvania and Philadelphia from September 1776 through the opening months of 1777 consult Selsam, *Pennsylvania Constitution,* chap. 6; Brunhouse, *Counter-Revolution,* chap. 2; Roland M. Baumann, "The Democratic-Republicans of Philadelphia: The Origins, 1776–1797" (Ph.D. diss., Pennsylvania State University, 1970), pp. 16–33.

48. "Joseph Reed's Narrative," in "Papers of Charles Thomson," p. 273; Thomson to Dickinson, 16 Aug. 1776, in *Pennsylvania Magazine of History and Biography,* 35 (1911): 500. "A Watchman," *Evening Post,* 10 June, addressed these remarks to Moderate Whigs: "Had you concurred in the present virtuous and necessary measure of instituting a new government, you would have probably continued to occupy your posts and offices, with that additional luster which they would have received from being the unbiased gifts of freemen; but you have now forfeited the confidence of the people by despising their authority; and you have furnished them with a suspicion that in taking up arms you yielded only to the violence of the times, or that you meant to fight for your offices, and not for your country."

49. To William Henry Drayton, n.d., in "Papers of Charles Thomson," pp. 281–84.

50. Hawke, *Midst of a Revolution,* pp. 34–35. Cf. Ryerson, "Leadership in Crisis," p. 531. The situation was still one of considerable confusion and indecision in June, as James Wilson explained to Horatio Gates: "Our affairs have been in such a fluctuating and disordered situation that it has been almost impossible to make any accurate judgment concerning the transactions as they were passing, and still more nearly im-

possible to make any probable conjectures concerning the turn that things would take" (*Pennsylvania Magazine of History and Biography,* 36 [1912]: 474).

51. To Samuel Cooper, 30 April 1776, in Harry A. Cushing, ed., *The Writings of Samuel Adams* (New York, 1907), 3: 284–85. Hawke, *Midst of a Revolution,* p. 198, indicates that a majority of Philadelphians supported independence by July 1776. On the other hand, Sam Bass Warner, Jr., *The Private City: Philadelphia in Three Periods of Its Growth* (Philadelphia, 1968), p. 25, states that Quakers, Tories, apathetic and neutral citizens probably outnumbered the revolutionaries in Philadelphia. Unfortunately, it is not possible to determine how many Philadelphians actually backed the drive for independence in the spring and summer of 1776. The most important fact, however, is that enough did to allow the Radicals to carry through their reorganization of Pennsylvania government.

52. *Journal,* 22 May. Any doubt about the veracity of these reports was erased on 24 May, when both the *Journal* and *Gazette* published the British treaty with the German princes for supplying troops.

53. St. Clair to William Allen, 1 Sept. 1776, in William H. Smith, ed., *The St. Clair Papers: The Life and Public Services of Arthur St. Clair* (Cincinnati, 1882), 1: 375–76; Shippen to Edward Shippen, 11 May 1776, quoted in Selsam, *Pennsylvania Constitution,* p. 105.

54. British war plans in *Journal,* 22 May; the congressional resolution of 2 Jan. 1776 was printed in all Philadelphia papers; report of battle in *Evening Post,* 22 June. For "evidence" of a slave conspiracy see the statement of William Barry in ibid., 20 June.

55. *Evening Post,* 9 and 11 May; *Journal* and *Gazette,* 15 May; George Read to Caesar Rodney, 10 May 1776, in Ryden, *Caesar Rodney Letters,* p. 76; Adams to Abigail Adams, 12 May 1776, in Charles F. Adams, ed., *Letters of John Adams, Addressed to His Wife* (Boston, 1841), 1: 107.

56. To Abigail Adams, 3 July 1776, in Adams, *Letters of Adams,* 1: 127.

57. Adams to Samuel Cooper, 30 April 1776, in Cushing, *Writings of Samuel Adams,* 3: 284; New York letter, in *Evening Post* 2 March.

58. To Samuel Cooper, 30 April 1776, in Cushing, *Writings of Samuel Adams,* 3: 284.

## AFTERWORD

1. I say "irrevocably undermined" because, although deferential attitudes and practices did not die in Philadelphia during the Revolution, they were so weakened that they never again possessed the authority they had possessed before the 1770s. See Chapter 1 for a discussion of deferential politics in colonial Philadelphia.

2. Participants in this debate include Charles H. Lincoln, *The Revolutionary Movement in Pennsylvania, 1760–1776* (Philadelphia, 1901); Carl L. Becker, *The History of Political Parties in the Province of New York, 1760–1776* (Madison, 1909); J. Franklin Jameson, *The American Revolution Considered as a Social Movement* (Princeton, 1926); Merrill Jensen, *The Articles of Confederation: An Interpretation of the Social-Constitutional History*

*of the American Revolution, 1774–1781* (Madison, 1940); Merrill Jensen, "Democracy and the American Revolution," *Huntington Library Quarterly,* 20 (Aug. 1957): 321–41; Robert E. Brown, *Middle-Class Democracy and the Revolution in Massachusetts, 1691–1780* (Ithaca, 1955); Elisha P. Douglass, *Rebels and Democrats: The Struggle for Equal Political Rights and Majority Rule during the American Revolution* (Chapel Hill, 1961); J. R. Pole, "Historians and the Problem of Early American Democracy," *American Historical Review,* 67 (April 1962): 626–46; Richard Buel, Jr., "Democracy and the American Revolution: A Frame of Reference," *William and Mary Quarterly,* 21 (April 1964): 165–90; Gordon S. Wood, "The Democratization of Mind in the American Revolution," in *Leadership in the American Revolution* (Washington, D.C., 1974), pp. 63–88. For a succinct review of the literature regarding the Revolution as a democratic movement consult Jack P. Greene, ed., *The Reinterpretation of the American Revolution, 1763–1789* (New York, 1968), pp. 8–17, 27–31, 50–59.

3. In 1772, for instance, Jacob Duché stated that "the poorest laborer upon the shore of the *Delaware* thinks himself entitled to deliver his sentiments in matters of religion or politics with as much freedom as the gentleman or scholar" (quoted in Carl Bridenbaugh and Jessica Bridenbaugh, *Rebels and Gentlemen: Philadelphia in the Age of Franklin* [London, 1942], p. 99). Also see "A Brother Chip," *Gazette,* 27 Sept. 1770; "A Citizen of Philadelphia," ibid., 22 Sept. 1773; "Pacificus," *Chronicle,* 20 Sept. 1773; "A Mechanic," ibid., 27 Sept. 1773.

4. Charles S. Olton, *Artisans for Independence: Philadelphia Mechanics and the American Revolution* (Syracuse, 1975), chaps. 5–6; R. A. Ryerson, "Political Mobilization and American Revolution: The Resistance Movement in Philadelphia, 1765–1776," *William and Mary Quarterly,* 31 (Oct. 1974): 565–88.

5. William Shippen to Edward Shippen, 22 July 1776, in *Pennsylvania Magazine of History and Biography,* 44 (1920): 286; Olton, *Artisans for Independence,* p. 80. According to James K. Martin, *Men in Rebellion: Higher Governmental Leaders and the Coming of the American Revolution* (New Brunswick, 1973), p. 44, not a single higher official in Pennsylvania government at the beginning of 1776 was still in office at the end of the year. As Merrill Jensen has written, the Pennsylvania Constitution of 1776 was "the most democratic constitution any American state has ever had" (*Articles of Confederation,* p. 19). The most detailed examination of the constitution is in J. Paul Selsam, *The Pennsylvania Constitution of 1776: A Study in Revolutionary Democracy* (Philadelphia, 1936).

According to the traditional interpretation of Pennsylvania politics after independence, the years 1776–90 witnessed a bitter struggle between the Constitutionalists, who sought to preserve and extend the democratic reforms of 1776, and the Anti-Constitutionalists, Republicans, or Federalists, as they were called at various times, who unceasingly fought to destroy "the frame of '76" and restore rule by the elite. This struggle was finally won by the Federalists, who regained control of Pennsylvania politics in the late 1780s and capped their "counterrevolution" in 1790 by instituting a new state constitution which nullified many of the progressive features of the constitution of 1776. In recent years, however, this interpretation has been seriously questioned. Most important for present purposes, it is now clear that the "counter-revolution" of 1790 was in reality a complex mixture of old and new, democratic and aristocratic, and was supported by the great majority of Philadelphians, including most of those who had backed the internal revolution in 1776. Although the constitution of 1790 dispensed with the all-powerful unicameral legislature created in 1776, it did not restore prewar restrictions on the franchise or the right to hold office. The massive politicization of ordinary citizens that occurred during the Revolution could not have been undone even had the Federalists tried to do so. By 1790 the people had become an integral part of Philadelphia politics. The traditional view of post-Revolution politics in Pennsylvania received its most influential statement in Robert L. Brunhouse, *The Counter-Revolution in Pennsylvania, 1776–1790* (Harrisburg, 1942), and has been restated in most general studies of American politics from 1776 to 1800. It has been modified by Roland M. Baumann, "The Democratic-Republicans of Philadelphia: The Origins, 1776–1797" (Ph.D. diss., Pennsylvania State University, 1970), and substantially weakened by Olton, *Artisans for Independence,* chaps. 7–9.

6. See the Prolegomenon to Part II.

7. "To the Electors and Freeholders of the City of Philadelphia," broadside, 30 April 1776 (Evans no. 15014).

8. See Chapters 3 and 6.

9. Cf. Carl F. Kaestle, "The Public Reaction to John Dickinson's *Farmer's Letters," Proceedings of the American Antiquarian Society,* 78 (Oct. 1968): 333–38. Apropos here is William Reed's statement several years after the Revolution that John Dickinson "lives in my memory as a realization of my beau-ideal of a gentleman" (quoted in John T. Scharf and Thompson Westcott, *History of Philadelphia, 1609–1884* [Philadelphia, 1884], I: 275).

10. Cf. the discussions of Paine's rhetoric in James T. Boulton, *The Language of Politics in the Age of Wilkes and Burke* (London, 1963), chap. 8; Harry Hayden Clark, "Thomas Paine's Theories of Rhetoric," *Transactions of the Wisconsin Academy of Sciences, Arts, and Letters,* 28 (1933): 307–39; Bernard Bailyn, "Common Sense," in *Fundamental Testaments of the American Revolution* (Washington, D.C., 1973), pp. 9–22; Thomas Clark, "Rhetorical Image-Making: A Case Study of the Thomas Paine–William Smith Propaganda Debates," *Southern Speech Communication Journal,* 40 (Spring 1975): 248–61. Eric Foner, *Tom Paine and Revolutionary America* (New York, 1976), which treats Paine as the herald of a "new political language," was published too late for me to use in this connection.

11. Wood, "Democratization of Mind," p. 70. Professor Wood's stunning essay came to my attention after this section of the book had been drafted, but I profited greatly from it in refining the ideas presented here.

12. Thomas Paine, quoted in Clark, "Paine's Theories of Rhetoric," p. 317.

13. The uncommon fury of *Common Sense* did not escape the attention of eighteenth-century readers, as is discussed in Chapter 6. In the first of his "Forester" essays (*Packet*, 1 April 1776), Paine responded to his critics' charges of excessive emotionality by retorting: "Cato's partisans may call me furious; I regard it not. There are men, too, who have not virtue enough to be angry and that crime perhaps is Cato's ."

14. In later years Paine contended that his "leading principle" in writing *Common Sense* had been "to bring forward and establish the representative system of government" ("To the Honorable Senate of the United States," 21 Jan. 1808, in Philip S. Foner, ed., *The Complete Writings of Thomas Paine* [New York, 1945], 2: 1491).

15. To be sure, political writers in Philadelphia did, on occasion, direct their rhetoric to ordinary citizens before 1765. Most notably, during the heated election campaign of 1764, Quaker and Proprietary publicists accused one another of the most scurrilous malefactions, assailed one another in exceedingly vituperative language, and appealed directly to the public for support. The election, however, was unusual in a number of respects. The "popular" nature of much electioneering rhetoric in 1764 can be accounted for by the fact that 1764 was one of the few years during the colonial period that the Proprietary faction actively challenged the Quaker party for the votes of middle-class Philadelphians. Had such electoral confrontations been more common before 1765, it is likely that the tenor of political rhetoric in the city would have been significantly altered as a result. There is no question but that changes in political discourse and practice were underway in Philadelphia before the Stamp Act crisis. The speed and intensity of change, however, were dramatically accelerated during the British-American controversy. Good accounts of the 1764 election can be found in James H. Hutson, *Pennsylvania Politics, 1746–1770: The Movement for Royal Government and Its Consequences* (Princeton, 1972), chap. 3; Benjamin H. Newcomb, *Franklin and Galloway: A Political Partnership* (New Haven, 1972), pp. 82–100; William S. Hannah, *Benjamin Franklin and Pennsylvania Politics* (Stanford, 1964), chap. 10; J. Philip Gleason, "A Scurrilous Colonial Election and Franklin's Reputation," *William and Mary Quarterly*, 18 (Jan. 1961): 68–84. Gary B. Nash, "The Transformation of Urban Politics," *Journal of American History*, 60 (Dec. 1973): 616–20, discusses changes in Philadelphia politics and rhetoric before 1765.

16. See Chapter 2.

17. Joseph Reed to Earl of Dartmouth, 27 Dec. 1773, in William B. Reed, ed., *Life and Correspondence of Joseph Reed* (Philadelphia, 1847), 1:54–55.

18. "Libertas et Natale Solum," *Chronicle*, 4 June 1770; "A Tradesman," ibid., 10 Oct. 1768; "Publicus," ibid., 5 Sept. 1772; "A Citizen," *Journal*, 11 Oct. 1770.

19. "Salus Populi," *Journal*, 24 Jan. 1776; [Thomas Paine], "The Forester," ibid., 8 June 1776; [James Cannon], "Cassandra," *Ledger*, 13

April 1776; "A Watchman," *Packet,* 24 June 1776; "To the Several Battalions of Military Associators in the Province of Pennsylvania," broadside, 26 June 1776 (Evans no. 15115); [Thomas Young], "An Elector," *Packet,* 29 April 1776. Also see Chapter 6 above.

20. For example, "Cato," *Ledger,* 30 March 1776; "Cassandra," *Packet,* 8 April 1776; "The Forester," *Packet,* 1 and 15 April 1776.

# INDEX

Adams, John, 219; defines "real American Revolution," ix; on rhetoric and Revolution, x–xi, xviii; on Charles Thomson, 30; on natural rights, 82–83; on diversity of colonies, 115–16; on *Plain Truth,* 159; on Thomas Paine, 160; on public opinion in Philadelphia, 162, 163, 164, 165, 180, 250; on *Common Sense,* 169, 172; helps destroy Assembly, 233–34; on debate over independence, 251

Adams, Samuel ("Candidus," "Religious Politician"), 165, 168, 219, 233, 250; in debate over independence, 161, 194–95, 198, 234; on public opinion in Philadelphia, 179, 248–49; on rhetoric and events, 248–49, 251, 252

Adams, Thomas R., xx–xxi

"Alarm," 235

Allen, Andrew, 157, 316

Allen, James, 97, 234, 245–46

America, images of, in Whig rhetoric, 131–51

Anglicans, 12–13

Anti-Constitutionalists (Federalists), 246, 321–22

Army, standing, as issue in Whig rhetoric, 61–62

Audience: colonial, nature of, xiv, xvii; Philadelphia, 10–23, 161–66. *See also* Centrists; Germans; Mechanics; Merchants; Quakers

Bailyn, Bernard, xiii, 97

Bayard, John, 159, 246

Biddle, Clement, 17

Biddle, Owen, 17, 159, 316

Blackstone, William, 77, 78

Boorstin, Daniel, 88

Bradford, William, 4, 9, 28, 66–67

Bradford, William, Jr., 236

Bridenbaugh, Carl, xv

Broadsides, 8

Bryan, George, 15, 19

Burke, Edmund, 52, 70, 94–95, 105, 106

Burke, Kenneth, xi

Cannon, James ("Cassandra"), 159, 234, 246; sketch of, 160–61; on public opinion in Philadelphia, 180; opposes reconciliation, 181; calumniates Moderate Whigs, 185, 229, 261; and Committee of Privates, 240

Carmichael, John, 50, 146

Centrists: identified, 162; attitudes of, 162–66, 176, 180, 186, 188, 189, 193–94, 212–13, 214–15, 219–20, 248–50, 252–53

Chalmers, James, 158, 207; *Plain Truth,* 158–59, 202; on military weakness of America, 211–12; derides New England, 215; on dangers of republicanism, 216

Charter of Privileges, 247; attacked by Radical Whigs, 220–21, 230–31; defended by Moderate Whigs, 230, 236–37, 246–47

Church, Benjamin, 163

Clergy, role of, in British-American controversy, 9

328                                                       Index

Ideology: allied with economic
    interest in Whig rhetoric, 46–47,
    53–59; "Commonwealth," 108–9;
    role in revolutionary movements of,
    268
Independence: attitudes toward, in
    Philadelphia, ix, 155, 161–66, 168,
    174–75, 199–200, 201, 248–50, 252–
    53, 320; as topic of public debate,
    27, 167–68, 175; disavowed by Whig
    protesters, 27, 75, 112, 138, 167; ad-
    vocated by Radical Whigs, 167–200;
    attacked by Moderate Whigs, 201–
    24

James, Abel, 121, 198
Jefferson, Thomas, 70; on taxation-
    legislation distinction, 68; on
    natural rights, 84; *A Summary View,*
    88–89; on style of Thomas Paine,
    172
"Junius," 106
Jury, trial by, as issue in Whig rhet-
    oric, 61

Kuhl, Frederick, 316

Language, in social change, xi
Law, natural. *See* Rights, natural
Leonard, Daniel, ix–x
*Letters from a Farmer* (John Dickinson),
    7, 34; initiates campaign for nonim-
    portation, 35; arguments against
    Townshend duties in, 67–68; im-
    pact of, 68–70, 72–73; style of, 70,
    256–58; opposition to, 70–72; com-
    pared with *Common Sense,* 175, 256–
    59; and gentlemanly mode of public
    address, 256–58
Liberty: as theme in Whig rhetoric,
    46; and property, 56–57; ambiguity
    of, fosters unity, 84–86
Lincoln, Charles, 316
Localism, in colonies, xiv, 115–16
Locke, John, 83
Loyalists. *See* Tories
Luxury, British, attacked by Whigs,
    53, 128–31

"Machiavel," 72, 121
Marshall, Christopher, 17, 159, 162,
    233, 244, 246
Matlack, Timothy, 17, 159, 233
McKean, Thomas, 28, 159, 233, 246
Mechanics: term defined, 20; occu-
    pational distinctions among, 20;
    religious diversity of, 20–21; aspira-
    tions of, 21; economic dissatisfac-
    tions of, 21, 187, 207–8; political
    grievances of, 21–22; in Stamp Act
    crisis, 22, 281; and nonimportation,
    23, 37, 39–42, 46, 281; recruited by
    Whigs, 23, 39–43, 259; political role
    of (1773–76), 23, 42–43, 254
Merchants: influence of, 17–18; eco-
    nomic status of, 18; and nonim-
    portation, 18–19, 35–36, 39–42, 46;
    divisions among, 18–19; and Tea
    Act, 44–45; and debate over inde-
    pendence, 187, 207–8
Mifflin, Thomas, 17, 19, 28, 54, 117
Militia (Association): supports inde-
    pendence, 161, 243; formation of,
    162, 196; disputes with Assembly,
    227. *See also* Committee of Privates
Moderate Whigs (1776): identified,
    157–59; rhetorical problems of,
    166, 201–3, 203–4, 206, 210, 223–
    24; calumniated by Radical Whigs,
    184–85; situation in 1776 favors,
    201; delay in responding to *Common
    Sense,* 202; premises of, 202–3;
    defend reconciliation, 203–10; urge
    acceptance of peace commissioners,
    205–6; economic arguments of,
    206–8; identify with Congress, 208–
    10; deny charges of Toryism, 208–
    9; argue from authority, 209–10; at-
    tack independence, 210–23; on
    military weakness of colonies, 210–
    13; predict turmoil as result of inde-
    pendence, 213–15; oppose republi-
    canism, 215–17; denounce Radical
    Whigs, 217–22; and Assembly elec-
    tion of 1 May 1776, 221, 225–26,
    232; appeal to caution, 222–23;
    campaign of, assessed, 223–24;

attitudes of, toward ordinary
citizens, 31, 255, 259–61; first-order
economic arguments of, 32–46, 57,
58; second-order economic arguments of, 33, 49–59; on economic
consequences of Stamp Act, 33–34;
admit Townshend Acts not economically burdensome, 34–35; campaign for nonimportation, 35–43,
90–91; rhetorical errors of, in 1768,
37–39; shift strategy after 1768
Assembly election, 39–40; concede
tax on tea is not burdensome, 43; attack Tea Act for creating East Indian monopoly, 43–45; do not decry
Coercive Acts on economic
grounds, 45; reluctance of, to stress
first-order economic issues,
explained, 45–46, 57, 58; deny
colonies fiscally obligated to England, 48–51; argue colonies are exploited by England, 51–54;
condemn British luxury and corruption, 52–53, 99, 128–31; portray
British-American dispute in moral
terms, 53–54, 58–59, 76, 111, 124–
25, 141, 142, 150; allege British
conspiracy, 54, 98–104, 117–19,
123–24, 131; on power, 54–55; on
liberty and property, 55–57; on
power of purse, 56–57; on vice-admiralty courts, 61; on standing
armies, 61–62; condemn parliamentary taxation as unconstitutional, 62–64, 67–68; reject virtual
representation, 63–64; oppose
American seats in Parliament, 64;
activities of, summer 1765, 65–66;
argue from natural rights, 76–84;
justify resistance to Parliament, 79–
82; use argument from principle,
86–95; oppose compromise with
England, 89–91; deplore British
leaders for acting from expediency,
91–92; use strategies of vilification
and objectification, 110–11; criticize
George III, 113–14; campaign
against Port Act, 116–20; accused of
conspiracy by Tories, 120–23;
redefine image of England, 127–31;
redefine image of America, 131–51;
stress economic strength of colonies,
132–35; glorify American
resources, 135–39; portray colonies
as spiritually superior to England,
139–42; portray England and
America as separate, 142; on
parent-child analogy, 142–47;
venerate original colonists, 147–48;
see American cause as divinely sanctioned, 148–49; portray America as
world's last hope, 149–50; write in
gentlemanly mode of public address, 255; address ordinary
citizens, 259–61. *See also* Coercive
Acts; Presbyterian party; Rhetoric,
of Whigs; Stamp Act; Tea Act;
Townshend Acts
Wilcox, Alexander, 157, 316
Wilkes, John, 113
Willing, Thomas, 157, 316
Wilson, James, 28, 157, 251; on settlement of colonies, 50; on representation, 64; sketch of, 78; denies authority of Parliament, 78–79;
praises British constitution, 189
Witherspoon, John: on influence of
newspapers, 7; denigrates *Plain
Truth,* 159
Wood, Gordon, 258
Writs of assistance, 116, 297

Young, Thomas ("Elector"), 159, 219,
233, 246; in debate over independence, 161, 304; attacks Charter
of Privileges, 220–21; proposes
reform of Assembly, 230–31; de-
fends republicanism, 262